HANDBOOK
OF COMMONLY USED
AMERICAN
IDIOMS

★

Fourth Edition

Adam Makkai, Ph.D.
Maxine T. Boatner, Ph.D.
John E. Gates, Ph.D.

Revised and Updated
by Adam Makkai
Professor of Linguistics
University of Illinois at Chicago

BARRON'S

This book is based on A *Dictionary of American Idioms* (Barron's © 1975) by Maxine Tull Boatner, Ph.D., John Edward Gates, Ph.D., Professor of English, Indiana State University, and Adam Makkai, Ph.D., Professor of Linguistics, University of Ilinois at Chcago.

All inquiries should be addressed to:
Barron's Educational Series, Inc.
250 Wireless Boulevard
Hauppauge, New York 11788

International Standard Book Number 0-7641-2776-4

Library of Congress Catalog Card No. 2004047787

Library of Congress Cataloging-in-Publication Data
Handbook of commonly used American idioms / [edited by] Adam Makkai, Maxine T.
  Boatner, John E. Gates; revised and updated by Adam Makkai.—4th ed.
    p. cm.
  "Based on A dictionary of American idioms"—T.p. verso.
  ISBN 0-7641-2776-4 (alk. paper)
    1. English language—United States—Idioms—Dictionaries. 2.
Americanisms—Dictionaries. I. Mikkai, Adam. II. Boatner, Maxine Tull. III. Gates,
John Edward. IV. Dictionary of American idioms.

PE2839.H36 2004
423'.13—dc22   2004047787

PRINTED IN CHINA
9 8 7 6 5 4 3 2

Table of Contents

Amanda Gamble
Nov. 2005

iii

Acknowledgments

This handbook is the result of the work of many hands. It is based on *A Dictionary of American Idioms,* first published by Barron's Educational Series 1975, which, in turn, had its source in *A Dictionary of Idioms for the Deaf,* edited by Maxine Tull Boatner, project director, aided by chief linguistic advisor, J. Edward Gates, published in 1969 and copyrighted by the American School for the Deaf. The consulting committee consisted of Dr. Edmund E. Boatner, Dr. William J. McClure, Dr. Clarence D. O'Connor, Dr. George T. Pratt, Jack Brady, M.A., Richard K. Lane, and Professor H. A. Gleason, Jr., of the Hartford Seminary Foundation. Special editors for various subcategories, such as usage, sport terms, etc., were Elizabeth Meltzer and E. Ward Gilman; Loy E. Golladay helped as language consultant with reviewing and editing. Definers were Edmund Casetti, Philip H. Cummings, Anne M. Driscoll, Harold J. Flavin, Dr. Frank Fletcher, E. Ward Gilman, Loy E. Golladay, Dr. Philip H. Goepp, Dr. Beatrice Hart, Dr. Benjamin Keen, Kendall Litchfield, Harold E. Niergarth, Ruth Gill Price, Thomas H. B. Robertson, Jess Smith, Rhea Talley Stewart, Harriet Smith, Elizabeth D. Spellman, John F. Spellman, George M. Swanson, Barbara Ann Kipfer, and Justyn Moulds. The following have cooperated as simplifiers: Linda Braun, Dr. G. C. Farquhar, Carey S. Lane, Wesley Lauritsen, Nellie MacDonald, Ruth S. McQueen, and Donald Moores.

For the second edition, Dr. Adam Makkai of the University of Illinois at Chicago, a well-known expert on idioms, added several hundred contemporary idiomatic phrases to the collection and edited the entire text for ease and convenience of reference. Many of the new entries were of the slang character, originating within recent cultural movements, while others reflected the popular usage of terms coined in various technological fields.

Preparing the subsequent editions, Dr. Makkai eliminated dated idioms and added a large number of modern idiomatic phrases. This new edition capitalizes on its astounding past success and brings brand-new idioms from all areas of human endeavor.

Introduction

WHAT IS AN IDIOM?

If you understand every word in a text and still fail to grasp what the text is all about, chances are you are having trouble with the idioms. For example, suppose you read (or hear) the following:

> Sam is a real cool cat. He never blows his stack and hardly ever flies off the handle. What's more, he knows how to get away with things . . . Well, of course, he is getting on, too. His hair is pepper and salt, but he knows how to make up for lost time by taking it easy. He gets up early, works out, and turns in early. He takes care of the hot dog stand like a breeze until he gets time off. Sam's got it made; this is it for him.

Needless to say, this is not great literary style, but most Americans, especially when they converse among themselves, will use expressions of this sort. Now if you are a foreigner in this country and have learned the words *cool* 'not very warm,' *cat* 'the familiar domestic animal,' *blow* 'exhale air with force,' *stack* 'a pile of something, or material heaped up,' *fly* 'propel oneself in the air by means of wings,' *handle* 'the part of an object designed to hold by hand'—and so forth you will still not understand the above sample of conversational American English, because this basic dictionary information alone will not give you the meaning of the forms involved. An idiom—as it follows from these observations—is the assigning of a new meaning to a group of words which already have their own meaning. Below you will find a 'translation' of this highly idiomatic, colloquial American English text, into a more formal, and relatively idiom free variety of English:

> Sam is really a calm person. He never loses control of himself and hardly ever becomes too angry. Furthermore, he knows how to manage his business financially by using a few tricks . . . Needless to say, he, too, is getting older. His hair is beginning to turn gray, but he knows how to compensate for wasted time by relaxing. He rises early, exercises, and goes to bed early. He

manages his frankfurter stand without visible effort, until it is
someone else's turn to work there. Sam is successful; he has
reached his life's goal.

Now if you were to explain how the units are organized in this text, you would have to make a little idiom dictionary. It would look like this:

to be a (real) cool cat	to be a really calm person
to blow one's stack	to lose control over oneself, to become mad
to fly off the handle	to become excessively angry
what's more	furthermore, besides, additionally
to get away with something	to perpetrate an illegitimate or tricky act without repercussion or harm
of course	naturally
to be getting on	to age, to get older
pepper and salt	black or dark hair mixed with streaks of gray
to make up for something	to compensate for something
lost time	time wasted, time spent at fruitless labor
to take it easy	to relax, to rest, not to worry
to get up	to rise from bed in the morning or at other times
to work out	to exercise, to do gymnastics
to turn in	to go to bed at night
like a breeze	without effort, elegantly, easily
time off	period in one's job or place of employment during which one is not performing one's services

| *to have got it made* | to be successful, to have arrived |
| *this is it* | to be in a position or in a place, or to have possession of an object, beyond which more of the same is unnecessary |

Many of the idioms in this little sample list can be found in this dictionary itself. The interesting fact about most of these idioms is that they can easily be identified with the familiar parts of speech. Thus some idioms are clearly verbal in nature, such as *get away with, get up, work out,* and *turn in.* An equally large number are nominal in nature. Thus *hot dog* and *cool cat* are nouns. Many are adjectives, as in our example *pepper* and *salt* meaning *'black hair mixed with gray.'* Many are adverbial, as the examples *like the breeze* 'easily, without effort,' *hammer and tongs* 'violently' (as in *she ran after him hammer and tongs*), and so forth. These idioms, which correlate with the familiar parts of speech, can be called *lexemic idioms.*

The other most important group of idioms are of larger size. Often they are an entire clause in length, as our examples to *fly off the handle,* 'lose control over oneself,' and to *blow one's stack,* 'to become very angry.' There are a great many of these in American English. Some of the most famous ones are: to *kick the bucket* 'die,' to *be up the creek* 'to be in a predicament or a dangerous position,' to *be caught between the devil and deep blue sea* 'to have to choose between two equally unpleasant alternatives,' to *seize the bull by the horns* 'to face a problem and deal with it squarely,' and so on. Idioms of this sort have been called *tournures* (from the French), meaning 'turns of phrase,' or simply *phraseological idioms.* What they have in common is that they do not readily correlate with a given grammatical part of speech and require a paraphrase longer than a word.

Their form is set and only a limited number of them can be said or written in any other way without destroying the meaning of the idiom. Many of them are completely rigid and cannot show up in any other form whatever. Consider the idiom *kick the bucket,* for example. In the passive voice, you get an unacceptable form such as *the bucket has been kicked by the cowboy*, which no longer means that the 'cowboy died.' Rather it means that he struck a pail with his foot. Idioms of this type are regarded as *completely frozen forms.* Notice, however, that even this idiom can be inflected for tense, e.g., it is all right to say *the cowboy kicked the bucket, the cowboy will kick the bucket, he has kicked the bucket,* etc. Speakers disagree as much as do grammarians whether or not, for example, it is all right to use this idiom in the gerund form (a gerund being a noun derived from a verb by adding *–ing* to it, e.g., *singing* from *sing, eating* from *eat,* etc.) in *His kicking the bucket surprised us all.* It is best to avoid this form.

The next largest class of idioms is that of well established sayings and proverbs. These include the famous types of *don't count your chickens before they're hatched* (meaning 'do not celebrate the outcome of an undertaking prematurely because it is possible that you will fail in which case you will look ridiculous'); *don't wash your dirty linen in public* (meaning 'do not complain of your domestic affairs before strangers as it is none of their business'), and so forth. Many of these originate from some well-known literary source or come to us from the earliest English speakers of the North American Continent.

Lack of predictability of meaning (or precise meaning) is not the only criterion of idiomaticity. Set phrases or phraseological units are also idiomatic, even though their meanings may be transparent. What is idiomatic (unpredictable) about them is their construction. Examples include *How about a drink? What do you say, Joe?* (as a greeting); *as a matter of fact, just in case; just to be on the safe side,* and many more.

Another important case of idiomaticity is the one-word idiom that occurs when a word is used in a surprisingly different meaning from the original one. Examples include *lemon,* said of bad watches, cars, or machines in general; and *dog,* said of a bad date or a bad exam. *(My car is a lemon, my math exam was a dog.)*

Why is English, and especially American English, so heavily idiomatic? The most probable reason is that as we develop new concepts, we need new expressions for them, but instead of creating a brand-new word from the sounds of the language, we use some already existent words and put them together in a new sense. This, however, appears to be true of all known languages. There are, in fact, no known languages that do not have some idioms. Consider the Chinese expression for 'quickly,' for example. It is *mǎ shāng*, and translated literally it means 'horseback.' Why should the concept of 'quick' be associated with the back of a horse? The answer reveals itself upon a moment's speculation. In the old days, before the train, the automobile, and the airplane, the fastest way of getting from one place to the other was by riding a horse, i.e., on horseback. Thus Chinese *mǎshāng* is as if we said in English *hurry up! We must go 'on horseback,'* i.e., 'Hurry up! We must go quickly.' Such a form would not be unintelligible in English at all, though the speaker would have to realize that it is an idiom, and the foreigner would have to learn it. However, in learning idioms a person may make an incorrect guess. Consider the English idiom *Oh well, the die is cast!* What would you guess this means—in case you don't know it? Perhaps you may guess that the speaker you heard is acquiescing in something because of the *Oh well* part. The expression means 'I made an irreversible decision and must live with it.' You can now try to reconstruct how this idiom came into being: the image of the die that was cast in gambling cannot be thrown again; that would be illegal; whether you have a one, a three, or a six, you must face the consequences of your throw, that is, win or lose, as the case may be. (Some people may know that the phrase was used by Caesar when he crossed the Rubicon, an event that led to war.)

How, then, having just learned it, will you use this idiom correctly? First of all, wait until you hear it from a native speaker in a natural context; do not experiment yourself with using an idiom until you have mastered the basics of English grammar. Once you have heard the idiom being used more than once, and fully understand its meaning, you can try using it yourself. Imagine that you have two job offers, one sure, but lower paying, and one that pays more, but is only tentative. Because of nervousness and fear of having no job at all, you accept the lower paying job, at which moment

ix

the better offer comes through and naturally you feel frustrated. You can then say *Oh well, the die is cast* . . . If you try this on a native speaker and he looks at you with sympathy and does not ask 'what do you mean?'—you have achieved your first successful placement of a newly learned idiom in an appropriate context. This can be a rewarding experience. Americans usually react to foreigners more politely than do people of other nations, but they can definitely tell how fluent you are. If a person always uses a bookish, stilted expression and never uses an idiom in the right place, he might develop the reputation of being a dry, unimaginative speaker, or one who is trying to be too serious and too official. *The use of idioms is, therefore, extremely important. It can strike a chord of solidarity with the listener.* The more idioms you use in the right context, the more at ease Americans will feel with you and the more they will think to themselves 'this is a nice and friendly person—look at how well he expresses himself!'

We will now take a look at some practical considerations regarding the use of the *Handbook of Commonly Used American Idioms*.

HOW TO USE THIS DICTIONARY

This dictionary can be used successfully by nonnative speakers of English, students, workers, immigrants—in short, anybody who wants to make his English more fluent, more idiomatic. It contains phrases of the types mentioned above, lexemic idioms, phrase idioms, and proverbial idioms, that have a special meaning. When a phrase has a special meaning that you cannot decode properly by looking up and understanding the individual words of which it is composed, then you know you are dealing with an idiom. You may already know some of these idioms or may be able to imagine what they mean. Look in the book for any of the following idioms that you may already know well; this will help you to understand how you should use this book: *boyfriend, girlfriend, outer space, piggy bank, get even, give up, going to, keep on, keep your mouth shut, lead somebody by the nose, look after, show off, throw away, all over, in love, mixed-up, out of this world, throw away, I'll say, both X and Y.*

A dictionary is like any other tool: You must familiarize yourself with it and learn how to use it before it begins to work well for you. Study the directions carefully several times, and practice looking up idioms. That way, searching for an idiom and finding it will become second nature to you. If you hear an idiomatic expression that is not in this book, after using it for a while, you will develop the ability to track down its meaning and write it down for yourself. Keep your own idiom list at home, right beside your regular dictionary. If you read a technical text, or a novel or a newspaper article and do not understand an expression, look it up in your regular school dictionary first; if you do not find it, try this one.

How do you find out if this dictionary can help you understand a hard sentence? Sometimes you can easily see what the phrase is, as with *puppy love, fun house, dog-eat-dog, mixed-up*. If not, pick out an important word from the most difficult part and look for that. If it is the first word in the idiom, you will find the whole phrase, followed by an explanation. Thus the expression *bats in the belfry* is listed in this dictionary under *b*, the word *bats*. If the word you picked is not the first word, you will find a list of idioms that contain that word. For example the word *toe* will be found in entries such as *curl one's hair OR curl one's toes, on one's toes, step on the toes (of somebody)*. You may, of course, find that the reason why you do not understand a particular sentence is not because of any idioms in it; in that case your regular dictionary will be of help to you. Also, there are more idioms than listed in this book; only the most frequently occurring in *American English* are included. British English, for example, or the English spoken in Australia, certainly has many idiomatic expressions that are not a part of American English.

TYPES OF ENTRY

This dictionary contains four kinds of entry: *main entries, run-on entries, and index entries*. A main entry includes a full explanation of the idiom. A run-on entry is a phrase which is derived from another idiom but would be separated from it if it entered at its own alphabetical place. These derived idioms have been run on at the end of the main entry (e.g., *fence-sitter* at *sit on the fence*) with an illustration and a paraphrase; an extra explanation has been added when understanding the derivative from the main explanation seemed difficult. When an idiom has come to be used as more than one part of speech, a separate entry has been made for each usage.

An index entry directs you to all other entries containing the index word. Thus the word *chin* is followed by the phrases of which it is a part, e.g., *keep one's chin up, stick one's chin (or neck) out, take it on the chin, up to the chin in.*

PARTS OF SPEECH LABELS

Those idioms that correlate with a well-defined grammatical form class carry a part of speech label. Sometimes, as with many prepositional phrases, a double label had to be assigned because the given phrase has two grammatical uses, e.g., *in commission* can be either adverbial or adjectival. Many prepositional phrases are adverbial in their literal sense, but adjectival in their nonpredictable, idiomatic sense. *v.* stands for verb; it was assigned to phrases containing a verb and an adverb; verb and preposition; or verb, preposition, and adverb. *v. phr.* stands for 'verbal phrase'; these include verbs with an object, verbs with subject complement, and verbs with a prepositional phrase.

RESTRICTIVE USAGE LABELS

You must pay particular attention to whether it is appropriate for you to use a certain idiom in a certain setting. The label *slang* shows that the idiom is used only among very close friends who are quite familiar with one another. *Informal* indicates that the form is used in conversation but should be avoided in formal composition. *Formal* indicates the opposite; this is a form that people usually do not say, but they will write it in an essay or will state it in a speech or a university lecture. *Literary* alerts you to the fact that people are usually aware that the form is a quotation; it would be inappropriate for you to use these too often. *Vulgar* indicates that you should

xii

altogether avoid the form; recognizing it may, of course, be important to you as you can judge a person by the language he uses. *Substandard* labels a form as chiefly used by less educated people; *nonstandard* means that a phrase is felt to be awkward. *Archaic* (rarely used in this book) means that the form is heavily restricted to Biblical or Shakespearean English. *Dialect* means that the form is restricted to its geographical source; e.g., *chiefly British* means that Americans seldom use it, *Southern* means that the form is of much higher currency in the South of the United States than in the North.

Adam Makkai, Ph.D.
Professor of Linguistics
University of Illinois at Chicago
Executive Director and Director of
Publications Emeritus, Linguistic Association of
Canada and the United States (LACUS), Inc.
Executive Director, Atlantis-Centaur, Inc.

A Handbook of
Commonly Used
American Idioms

abide by *v.* To accept and obey; be willing to follow. ◆*A basketball player may know he did not foul, but he must abide by the referee's decision.* ◆*The members agree to abide by the rules of the club.*

about-face *n.* A sudden change of course or a decision opposite to what was decided earlier. ◆*Her decision to become an actress instead of a dentist was an about-face from her original plans.*

about time *n. phr.* Finally, but later than it should have been; at last. ◆*Mother said, "It's about time you got up, Mary."* ◆*The basketball team won last night. About time.*

about to 1. Close to; ready to.— Used with an infinitive. ◆*We were about to leave when the snow began.* ◆*I haven't gone yet, but I'm about to.* Compare GOING TO, ON THE POINT OF. **2.** *informal* Having a wish or plan to.—Used with an infinitive in negative sentences. ◆*"Will she come with us?" asked Bill. "She's not about to," answered Mary.*

a breath of fresh air *n. phr.* Something new, pleasant, or invigorating. ◆*Sue's arrival at our law firm was a breath of fresh air.*

abscond from *v. phr.* To go away suddenly and furtively, usually having been part of some shady business. ◆*Joe absconded from our shop when we discovered that the books had been tampered with.*

abscond with *v. phr.* To steal or embezzle something. ◆*Al absconded with the uncounted extra cash after we closed for the evening.*

absence makes the heart grow fonder When we don't see someone or something for a long while, we rejoice all the more when we meet again.—A proverb. ◆*"How long will you be gone?" Sue asked, when her husband joined the marines. "Just six months," Joe answered. "It will be over soon; besides, absence makes the heart grow fonder!"*

absent-minded *adj.* Lost in thought; forgetful; unable to concentrate on the task at hand. ◆*"What's the matter with Joe? Why is he so absent-minded?" Pete asked. "I think it's because he is about to get married," I answered, "and he's thinking about the wedding plans."*

absent without leave (AWOL) *adj.* Absent without permission; used mostly in the military. ◆*Jack left Fort Sheridan without asking his commanding officer, and was punished for going AWOL.*

absolve from *v. phr.* To forgive; to allow not to repay a debt. ◆*Joe is very religious; he goes to confession every Saturday. He hopes he will be absolved from his sins that way.* ◆*"How much do I owe you?" Pete asked. "Nothing," I replied, "you are absolved from your debt."*

ace up one's sleeve *or* **have something up one's sleeve** *n., or v. phr.* To have a hidden asset or trick unknown by the opposition, like someone who cheats at cards and has winning cards hidden in his shirtsleeve. ◆*We all hope that the government* *has something up its sleeve in the war against terrorism.*

ache for *or* **be itching to** *v. phr.* To long for something or someone powerfully. ♦ *"I am aching for a piece of chocolate cake," the pregnant woman said.*

acid test *n. phr.* A powerful way of determining if something is genuine or false, going back to the days when gold was differentiated from brass by dipping an object into hydrochloric acid. ♦ *The acid test of a good marriage is fidelity and truthfulness.*

according to *prep.* **1.** So as to match or agree with; so as to be alike in. ♦ *Many words are pronounced according to the spelling but some are not.* ♦ *The boys were placed in three groups according to height.* **2.** On the word or authority of. ♦ *According to the Bible, Adam was the first man.*

account for *v. phr.* **1.** To rationally or scientifically explain the reason for something. ♦ *The view that the earth revolves around its axis and circles the sun in a year accounts much better for the changing of the seasons than the old geocentric view.* **2.** To render accurate inventory of cash, personnel, objects, etc. ♦ *Joe was fired because he failed to account for the missing $50,000.* ♦ *A good platoon commander accounts for every enlisted man under his command.*

ace in the hole *n. phr.* **1.** An ace given to a player face down so that other players in a card game cannot see it. ♦ *When the cowboy bet all his money in the poker game he did not know*

that the gambler had an ace in the hole and would win it from him. **2.** *informal* Someone or something important that is kept as a surprise until the right time so as to bring victory or success. ♦ *The lawyer's ace in the hole was a secret witness who saw the accident.* Compare CARD UP ONE'S SLEEVE.

Achilles' heel *n. phr., literary* A physical or psychological weakness named after the Greek hero Achilles who was invulnerable except for a spot on his heel. ♦ *John's Achilles' heel is his lack of talent with numbers and math.*

across the board *adv. phr.* **1.** So that equal amounts of money are bet on the same horse to win a race, to place second, or third. ♦ *I bet $6 on the white horse across the board.*—Often used with hyphens as an adjective. ♦ *I made an across-the-board bet on the white horse.* **2.** *informal* Including everyone or all, so that all are included. ♦ *The president wanted taxes lowered across the board.*—Often used with hyphens as an adjective. ♦ *The workers at the store got an across-the-board pay raise.*

act of faith *n. phr.* An act or a deed that shows unquestioning belief in someone or something. ♦ *It was a real act of faith on Mary's part to entrust her jewelry to her younger sister's care.*

act of God *n.* An occurrence (usually some sort of catastrophe) for which the people affected are not responsible; said of earthquakes, floods, etc. ♦ *Hurricane Andrew destroyed many houses in Florida, but some* *types of insurance did not compensate the victims, claiming that the hurricane was an act of God.*

act up *v., informal* **1.** To behave badly; act rudely or impolitely. ♦*The dog acted up as the postman came to the door.* **2.** To work or run poorly (as a machine); skip; miss. ♦*The car acted up because the spark plugs were dirty.*

add fuel to the flame *v. phr.* To make a bad matter worse by adding to its cause; spread trouble, increase anger or other strong feelings by talk or action. ♦*Bob was angry with Ted and Ted added fuel to the flame by laughing at him.*

add insult to injury *v. phr.* **1.** To hurt someone's feelings after doing him harm. ♦*He added insult to injury when he called the man a rat after he had already beaten him up.* **2.** To make bad trouble worse. ♦*We started on a picnic, and first it rained, then to add insult to injury, the car broke down.*

add up *v.* **1.** To come to the correct amount. ♦*The numbers wouldn't add up.* **2.** *informal* To make sense; be understandable. ♦*His story didn't add up.*

add up to *v.* **1.** To make a total of; amount to. ♦*The bill added up to $12.95.* **2.** *informal* To mean; result in. ♦*The rain, the mosquitoes, and the heat added up to a spoiled vacation.*

afraid of one's shadow *adj. phr., informal* Scared of small or imaginary things; very easily frightened; jumpy; nervous. ♦*Mrs. Smith won't stay alone in her house at night; she is afraid of her own shadow.*

after all *adv. phr.* **1.** As a change in plans; anyway.—Used with emphasis on *after*. ♦*Bob thought he couldn't go to the party because he had too much homework, but he went after all.* **2.** For a good reason that you should remember.—Used with emphasis on *all*. ♦*Why shouldn't Betsy eat the cake? After all, she baked it.*

ahead of the game *adv. or adj. phr., informal* **1.** In a position of advantage; winning (as in a game or contest); ahead (as by making money or profit); making it easier to win or succeed. ♦*The time you spend studying when you are in school will put you ahead of the game in college.* **2.** Early; too soon; beforehand. ♦*When Ralph came to school an hour early, the janitor said, "You're ahead of the game."*

ahead of time *adv. phr.* Before the expected time; early. ♦*The new building was finished ahead of time.* Contrast BEHIND THE TIMES.

a hell of a *or* **one hell of a** *adj., or adv. phr. informal* Extraordinary; very. ♦*He made a hell of a shot during the basketball game.* ♦*Max said seven months was a hell of a time to have to wait for a simple visa.*

aim high *v. phr.* (given as advice) To set your goals high; to be ambitious. ♦*If you want to achieve a comfortable position by the time you're fifty, you must aim high!*

air one's dirty linen in public *or* **wash one's dirty linen in public** *v. phr.* To talk about your private quarrels or disgraces where others can hear; make public something embarrassing that should be kept secret. ♦*No one knew that the boys' mother was a drug addict, because the family did not wash its dirty linen in public.*

albatross around one's neck *n. phr., literary* Guilt, the haunting past, an unforgettable problem. ♦*Even though it was an accident, John's father's death has been an albatross around John's neck.*

a little bird told me To have learned something from a mysterious, unknown, or secret source. ♦*"Who told you that Dean Smith was resigning?" Peter asked. "A little bird told me," Jim answered.*

a little knowledge is a dangerous thing *literary* A person who knows a little about something may think he knows it all and make bad mistakes.—A proverb. ♦*John has read a book on driving a car and now he thinks he can drive. A little knowledge is a dangerous thing.*

alive and kicking *adj. phr.* Very active; vigorous; full of energy. ♦*Grandpa was taken to the hospital with pneumonia, but he was discharged yesterday and is alive and kicking.*

all along *or (informal)* **right along** *adv. phr.* All the time; during the whole time. ♦*I knew all along that we would win.* ♦*I knew right along that Jane would come.*

all at once *adv. phr.* **1.** At the same time; together. ♦*The teacher told the children to talk one at a time; if they all talked at one time, she could not understand them.* ♦*Bill can play the piano, sing, and lead his orchestra all at once.* **2.** *or* **all of a sudden**

Without warning; abruptly; suddenly; unexpectedly. ♦*All at once we heard a shot and the soldier fell to the ground.*

all better *adj. phr.* Fully recovered; all well again; no longer painful.—Usually used to or by children. ♦*"All better now," he kept repeating to the little girl.*

all but *adv. phr.* Very nearly; almost. ♦*Crows all but destroyed a farmer's field of corn.*

all ears *adj. phr., informal* Very eager to hear; very attentive.—Used in the predicate. ♦*Go ahead with your story; we are all ears.*

alley cat *n., slang* **1.** A stray cat. **2.** A person (usually a female) of rather easygoing, or actually loose, sexual morals; a promiscuous person. ♦*You'll have no problem dating her; she's a regular alley cat.*

all eyes *adj. phr., informal* Wide-eyed with surprise or curiosity; watching very closely.—Used in the predicate. ♦*At the circus the children were all eyes.*

all over *adv. phr.* **1.** In every part; everywhere. ♦*He has a fever and aches all over.* ♦*I have looked all over for my glasses.* **2.** *informal* In every way; completely. ♦*She is her mother all over.* **3.** *informal* Coming into very close physical contact, as during a violent fight; wrestling. ♦*Before I noticed what happened, he was all over me.*

all right[1] *adv. phr.* **1.** Well enough. *The new machine is running all right.* **2.** *informal* I am willing; yes. ♦*"Shall we watch television?" "All right."* **3.** *informal* Beyond question, certainly.—Used for emphasis and placed after the word it modifies. ♦*It's* *time to leave, all right, but the bus hasn't come.*

all right² *adj. phr.* **1.** Good enough; correct; suitable. ◆*His work is always all right.* **2.** In good health or spirits; well. ◆*"How are you?" "I'm all right."* **3.** *slang* Good. ◆*He's an all right guy.*

all right for you *interj.* I'm finished with you! That ends it between you and me!—Used by children. ◆*All right for you! I'm not playing with you any more!*

all set *adj. phr.* Ready to start. ◆*"Is the plane ready for takeoff?" the bank president asked. "Yes, Sir," the pilot answered. "We're all set."*

all shook up *also* **shook up** *adj., slang* In a state of great emotional upheaval; disturbed; agitated. ◆*What are you so shook up about?*

all systems go *Originally from space English, now general colloquial usage.* Everything is complete and ready for action; it is now all right to proceed. ◆*After they wrote out the invitations, it was all systems go for the wedding.*

all the¹ *adj. phr., dial.* The only. ◆*A hut was all the home he ever had.*

all the² *adv. phr.* Than otherwise; even.—Used to emphasize comparative adjectives, adverbs, and nouns. ◆*Opening the windows made it all the hotter.*

all the way *or* **the whole way** *adv. phr.* **1.** From start to finish during the whole distance or time. ◆*Jack climbed all the way to the top of the tree.* ◆*Joe has played the whole way in the football game and it's almost over.* **2.** In

complete agreement; with complete willingness to satisfy.— Often used in the phrase *go all the way with.* ◆*I go all the way with what George says about Bill.* ◆*Mary said she was willing to kiss Bill, but that did not mean she was willing to go all the way with him.*

all wet *adj., slang* Entirely confused or wrong; mistaken. ◆*When the Wright brothers said they could build a flying machine, people thought they were all wet.*

along for the ride *adv. phr., informal* Being in a group for the fun or the credit without doing any of the work. ◆*He wants no members in his political party who are just along for the ride.*

along in years *or* **on in years** *adj. phr.* Elderly; growing old. ◆*As Grandfather got on in years, he became quiet and thoughtful.*

alongside of *prep.* **1.** At or along the side of. ◆*We walked alongside of the river.* **2.** Together with. ◆*I played alongside of Tom on the same team.* **3.** *informal* Compared with or to; measured next to. ◆*His money doesn't look like much alongside of a millionaire's.*

a lot *n., informal* A large number or amount; very many or very much; lots. ◆*I learned a lot in Mr. Smith's class.* ◆*A lot of our friends are going to the beach this summer.*—Often used like an adverb. ◆*Ella is a jolly girl; she laughs a lot.*—Also used as an adjective with *more, less,* and *fewer.* ◆*There was a good crowd at the game today, but a lot more will come next week.*— Often used with *whole* for emphasis. ♦*Jerry is a whole lot taller than he was a year ago.*

ambulance chaser *n.* An attorney who specializes in representing victims of traffic accidents. By extension, a lawyer of inferior rank or talent. ♦*Don't hire Jones; he's just another ambulance chaser.*

American plan *n.* A system of hotel management in which meals are included with the room, as opposed to the European plan that does not include meals. ♦*American tourists in Europe sometimes expect that their meals will be included, because they are used to the American plan.*

amount to *v.* Signify; add up to. ♦*John's total income didn't amount to more than a few hundred dollars.*

and how! *interj. informal* Yes, that is certainly right!—Used for emphatic agreement. ♦*"Did you see the game?" "And how!"* ♦*"Isn't Mary pretty?" "And how she is!"*

and then some And a lot more; and more too. ♦*It would cost all the money he had and then some.*

answer for *v.* **1.** To take responsibility for; assume charge or supervision of. ♦*The secret service has to answer for the safety of the president and his family.* **2.** To say you are sure that (someone) has good character or ability; guarantee; sponsor. ♦*When people thought Ray had stolen the money, the principal said, "Ray is no thief. I'll answer for him."* **3.** Take the blame or punishment for. ♦*When Mother found out who*

ate the cake, Tom had to answer for his mischief.

ante up *v., informal* To produce the required amount of money in order to close a transaction; to pay what one owes. ♦*"I guess I'd better ante up if I want to stay an active member of the Association," Max said.*

ants in one's pants *n. phr., slang* Nervous overactivity; restlessness. ♦*You have ants in your pants today. Is something wrong?*

apple of discord *n. phr.* The reason for a prolonged quarrel (from the story of Venus and Paris in Homer's *Iliad*). ♦*The unfair distribution of wealth will always remain the apple of discord in society.*

apple of one's eye *n. phr.* Something or someone that is adored; a cherished person or object. ♦*Charles is the apple of his mother's eye.*

apple-pie order *n. phr., informal* Exact orderly arrangement, neatness; tidy arrangement. ♦*Like a good secretary, she kept the boss's desk in apple-pie order.*

arm and a leg *n., slang* An exorbitantly high price that must be paid for something that isn't really worth it. ♦*It's true that to get a decent apartment these days in New York you have to pay an arm and a leg.*

arm in arm *adv. phr.* With your arm under or around another person's arm, especially in close comradeship or friendship. ♦*Sally and Joan were laughing and joking together as they walked arm in arm down the street.* ♦*When they arrived at the party, the partners* *walked arm in arm to meet the hosts.* Compare HAND IN HAND.

around Robin Hood's barn *adv. phr.* In a roundabout, tricky, indirect sort of way. ♦*They weren't at all straight with me; they were leading me around Robin Hood's barn.*

around the clock *also* **the clock around** *adv. phr.* For 24 hours a day continuously all day and all night. ♦*The factory operated around the clock until the order was filled.* ♦*He studied around the clock for his history exam.*—**round-the-clock** *adj.* ♦*That filling station has round-the-clock service.*

as hard as nails *adj. phr.* Very unfeeling; cruel, and unsympathetic. ♦*Uncle Joe is as hard as nails; although he is a millionaire, he doesn't help his less fortunate relatives.*

as it were *adv. phr.* As it might be said to be; as if it really were; seemingly.—Used with a statement that might seem silly or unreasonable, to show that it is just a way of saying it. ♦*In many ways children live, as it were, in a different world from adults.*

ask for *v., informal* To make (something bad) likely to happen to you; bring (something bad) upon yourself. ♦*Charles drives fast on worn-out tires; he is asking for trouble.* ♦*The workman lost his job, but he asked for it by coming to work drunk several times.*

ask for one's hand *v. phr.* To ask permission to marry someone. ♦*"Sir," John said timidly to Mary's father, "I came to ask for your daughter's hand."*

ask for the moon *or* **cry for the moon** *v. phr.* To want something that you cannot reach or have; try for the impossible. ♦*John asked his mother for a hundred dollars today. He's always asking for the moon.*

asleep at the switch *adj. phr.* **1.** Asleep when it is one's duty to move a railroad switch for cars to go on the right track. ♦*The new man was asleep at the switch and the two trains crashed.* **2.** *informal* Failing to act promptly as expected; not alert to an opportunity. ♦*When the ducks flew over, the hunter was asleep at the switch and missed his shot.*

as luck would have it *adv. clause* As it happened; by chance; luckily or unluckily. ♦*As luck would have it, no one was in the building when the explosion occurred.* ♦*As luck would have it, there was rain on the day of the picnic.*

as much *n.* The same; exactly that. ♦*Don't thank me, I would do as much for anyone.* ♦*Did you lose your way? I thought as much when you were late in coming.*

as soon as *conj.* Just after; when; immediately after. ♦*As soon as the temperature falls to 70, the furnace is turned on.* ♦*As soon as you finish your job let me know.* ♦*He will see you as soon as he can.*

as the crow flies *adv. clause* By the most direct way; along a straight line between two places. ♦*It is seven miles to the next town as the crow flies, but it is ten miles by the road, which goes around the mountain.*

as the story goes *adv. phr.* As the story is told; as one has heard through rumor. ◆*As the story goes, Jonathan disappeared when he heard the police were after him.*

as well as *conj.* In addition to; and also; besides. ◆*Hiking is good exercise as well as fun.* ◆*He was my friend as well as my doctor.* ◆*The book tells about the author's life as well as about his writings.*

as yet *adv. phr.* Up to the present time; so far; yet. ◆*We know little as yet about the moon's surface.* ◆*She has not come as yet.*

at all *adv. phr.* At any time or place, for any reason, or in any degree or manner.—Used for emphasis with certain kinds of words or sentences. **1.** Negative ◆*It's not at all likely he will come.* **2.** Limited ◆*I can hardly hear you at all.* **3.** Interrogative ◆*Can it be done at all?* **4.** Conditional ◆*She will walk with a limp, if she walks at all.*

at all costs *adv. phr.* At any expense of time, effort, or money. Regardless of the results. ◆*Mr. Jackson intended to save his son's eyesight at all costs.*

at all hours *adv. phr.* Any time; all the time; at almost any time. ◆*The baby cried so much that we were up at all hours trying to calm her down.*

at a loss *adj. phr.* In a state of uncertainty; without any idea; puzzled. ◆*A good salesman is never at a loss for words.* ◆*When Don missed the last bus, he was at a loss to know what to do.*

at any rate *adv. phr.* In any case; anyhow. ◆*It isn't much of a car, but at any rate it was not expensive.*

at bay *adv. or adj. phr.* In a place where you can no longer run away; unable to go back farther; forced to stand and fight, or face an enemy; cornered. ◆*The police chased the thief to a roof, where they held him at bay until more policemen came to help.*

at best *or* **at the best** *adv. phr.* **1.** Under the best conditions; as the best possibility. ◆*A coal miner's job is dirty and dangerous at best.* ◆*We can't get to New York before ten o'clock at best.* **2.** In the most favorable way of looking at something; even saying the best about the thing. ◆*The treasurer had at best been careless with the club's money, but most people thought he had been dishonest.*

at cross purposes *adv. phr.* With opposing meanings or aims; with opposing effect or result; with aims which hinder or get in each other's way. ◆*Tom's parents acted at cross purposes in advising him; his father wanted him to become a doctor, but his mother wanted him to become a minister.*

at death's door *adj. or adv. phr.* Very near death; dying. ◆*He seemed to be at death's door from his illness.*

at each other's throats *prep. phr.* Always arguing and quarreling. ◆*Joan and Harry have been at each other's throats so long that they have forgotten how much they used to love one another.*

at face value *prep. phr.* What one can actually hear, read, or see; literally. ◆*John is so honest that you can take his words at face value.* ◆*This store's advertise-*

ments are honest; take them at face value.

at fault *adj. phr.* Responsible for an error or failure; to blame. ◆*The driver who didn't stop at the red light was at fault in the accident.*

at first *adv. phr.* In the beginning; at the start. ◆*The driver didn't see the danger a first.* ◆*At first the job looked good to Bob, but later it became tiresome.*

at first blush *adv. phr.* When first seen; without careful study. ◆*At first blush the offer looked good, but when we studied it, we found things we could not accept.*

at first glance *or* **at first sight** *adv. or adj. phr.* After a first quick look. ◆*At first sight, his guess was that the whole trouble between the two men resulted from personalities that did not agree.* ◆*Tom met Mary at a party, and it was love at first sight.*

at hand *also* **at close hand** *or* **near at hand** *adv. phr.* **1.** Easy to reach; nearby. ◆*When he writes, he always keeps a dictionary at hand.* **2.** *formal* Coming soon; almost here. ◆*Examinations are past and Commencement Day is at hand.*

at heart *adv. phr.* **1.** In spite of appearances; at bottom; in reality. ◆*His manners are rough but he is a kind man at heart.* **2.** As a serious interest or concern; as an important aim or goal. ◆*He has the welfare of the poor at heart.*

at large *adv. or adj. phr.* **1.** Not kept within walls, fences, or boundaries; free. ◆*The killer remained at large for weeks.* Compare AT LIBERTY. ◆*Cattle*

and sheep roamed at large on the big ranch. **2.** In a broad, general way; at length; fully. ◆*The superintendent talked at large for an hour about his hopes for a new school building.* **3.** As a group rather than as individuals; as a whole; taken together. ◆*The junior class at large was not interested in a senior yearbook.* **4.** As a representative of a whole political unit or area rather than one of its parts; from a city rather than one of its wards, or a state rather than one of its districts. ◆*He was elected congressman at large.*

at last *also* **at long last** *adv. phr.* After a long time; finally. ◆*The war had been long and hard, but now there was peace at last.* ◆*The boy saved his money until at last he had enough for a bicycle.*

at least *adv. phr.* **1.** *or* **at the least** At the smallest guess; no fewer than; no less than. ◆*You should brush your teeth at least twice a day.* ◆*At least three students are failing in mathematics.* **2.** Whatever else you may say; anyhow; anyway. ◆*She broke her arm, but at least it wasn't the arm she writes with.* ◆*He's not coming— at least that's what he said.*

at leisure *adj. or adv. phr.* **1.** Not at work; not busy; with free time; at rest. ◆*Come and visit us some evening when you're at leisure.* **2.** *or* **at** one's **leisure** When and how you wish to at your convenience; without hurry. ◆*You may read the book at your leisure.*

at length *adv. phr.* **1.** In detail; fully. ◆*You must study the subject at length to understand it.*

♦*The teacher explained the new lesson at length to the students.* **2.** In the end; at last; finally. ♦*The movie became more and more exciting, until at length people were sitting on the edge of their chairs.*

at liberty *adv. or adj. phr.* Free to go somewhere or do something; not shut in or stopped. ♦*The police promised to set the man at liberty if he told the names of the other robbers.*

at loggerheads *adj. or adv. phr.* In a quarrel; in a fight; opposing each other. ♦*The two senators had long been at loggerheads on foreign aid.* ♦*Because of their barking dog, the Morrises lived at loggerheads with their neighbors.*

at odds *adj. phr.* In conflict or disagreement; opposed. ♦*The boy and girl were married a week after they met and soon found themselves at odds about religion.*

at once *adv. phr.* Without delay; right now or right then; immediately. ♦*Put a burning match next to a piece of paper and it will begin burning at once.*

at one's beck and call *or* **at the beck and call of** *adj. phr.* Ready and willing to do whatever someone asks; ready to serve at a moment's notice. ♦*A good parent isn't necessarily always at the child's beck and call.*

at one's best *prep. phr.* In best form; displaying one's best qualities. ♦*Tim is at his best when he has had a long swim before a ballgame.*

at one's door *or* **at one's doorstep** *adv. phr.* Very close; very near where you live or work. ♦*John-*

ny is very lucky because there's a swimming pool right at his doorstep.

at one's wit's end *or* **at wit's end** *adj. phr.* Having no ideas as to how to meet a difficulty or solve a problem; feeling puzzled after having used up all of your ideas or resources; not knowing what to do; puzzled. ♦*The designer was at his wit's end: he had tried out wings of many different kinds but none would fly.*

at pains *adj. phr.* Making a special effort. ♦*At pains to make a good impression, she was prompt for her appointment.*

at sea[1] *adv. or adj. phr.* **1.** On an ocean voyage; on a journey by ship. ♦*They had first met at sea.* **2.** Out on the ocean; away from land. ♦*By the second day the ship was well out at sea.* ♦*Charles had visited a ship in dock, but he had never been on a ship at sea.*

at sea[2] *adj. phr.* Not knowing what to do; bewildered; confused; lost. ♦*The job was new to him, and for a few days he was at sea.*

at the drop of a hat *adv. phr., informal* **1.** Without waiting; immediately; promptly. ♦*If you need a baby-sitter quickly, call Mary, because she can come at the drop of a hat.* **2.** Whenever you have a chance; with very little cause or urging. ♦*He was quarrelsome and ready to fight at the drop of a hat.*

at the eleventh hour *prep. phr.* At the last possible time. ♦*Aunt Mathilda got married at the eleventh hour; after all, she was already 49 years old.*

at the end of the day *adv. phr.* After all previous arrangements have been completed; finally; at last. *At the end of the day, the hostile foreign government will have to realize that it is better to cooperate with the U.N.*

at the mercy of *or* **at one's mercy** *adj. phr.* In the power of; subject to the will and wishes of; without defense against. *The small grocer was at the mercy of people he owed money to.*

at the ready *adj. phr.* Ready for use. *The sailor stood at the bow, harpoon at the ready, as the boat neared the whale.*

at the tip of one's tongue *or* **on the tip of one's tongue** *adv. phr. informal* **1.** Almost spoken; at the point of being said. *It was at the tip of my tongue to tell him, when the phone rang.* **2.** Almost remembered; at the point where one can almost say it but cannot because it is forgotten. *I have his name on the tip of my tongue.*

at the top of one's voice *or* **at the top of one's lungs** *adv. phr.* As loud as one can; with the greatest possible sound; very loudly. *He was singing at the top of his voice. *He shouted at the top of his lungs.*

at this juncture *adv. phr.* Now; at this critical point; at this conjuncture of affairs. *At this juncture it is wiser to retire than to fight a bankrupt company.*

at this rate *or* **at that rate** *adv. phr.* At a speed like this or that; with progress like this or that. *"Three 100's in the last four tests! At this rate you'll soon be teaching the subject," Tom said to Mary.*

at will *adv. phr.* As you like; as you please or choose freely. *With an air conditioner you can enjoy comfortable temperatures at will.*

average out *v. phr.* To reach a certain average after proper calculation. *"My monthly salary averages out to no more than $1,500," the young teaching assistant sadly remarked.*

AWOL See ABSENT WITHOUT LEAVE.

ax to grind *n. phr., informal* Something to gain for yourself: a selfish reason. *In praising movies for classroom use he has an ax to grind; he sells motion picture equipment.*

babe in the woods n. phr. A person who is inexperienced or innocent in certain things. ◆He is a good driver, but as a mechanic he is just a babe in the woods.

baby boom n. A sudden increase in the birth rate. ◆The universities were filled to capacity due to the baby boom that followed World War II.

baby grand n. A small grand piano no longer than three feet, maximally four feet. ◆This apartment can't take a regular grand piano, so we'll have to buy a baby grand.

back and forth adv. Backwards and forwards. ◆The tiger is pacing back and forth in his cage. Compare TO AND FRO.

back away v. To act to avoid or lessen one's involvement in something; draw or turn back; retreat. ◆The townspeople backed away from the building plan when they found out how much it would cost.

back down or **back off** v., informal To give up a claim; not follow up a threat. ◆Bill said he could beat Ted, but when Ted put up his fists Bill backed down. ◆Harry claimed Joe had taken his book, but backed down when the teacher talked with him.

backhanded compliment n. phr. A remark that sounds like a compliment but is said sarcastically. ◆"Not bad for a girl" the coach said, offering a backhanded compliment.

back out v. phr. **1.** To move backwards out of a place or enclosure. ◆Bob slowly backed his car out of the garage. **2.** To withdraw from an activity one has promised to carry out. ◆Jim tried to back out of the engagement with Jane, but she insisted that they get married.

backseat driver n., informal A bossy person in a car who always tells the driver what to do. ◆The man who drove the car became angry with the backseat driver.

back talk n. A sassy, impudent reply. ◆Such back talk will get you nowhere, young man!

back the wrong horse v. phr. To support a loser. ◆In voting for George Bush, voters in 1992 were backing the wrong horse.

back-to-back adv. **1.** Immediately following. ◆The health clinic had back-to-back appointments for the new students during the first week of school. **2.** Very close to, as if touching. ◆Sardines are always packed in the can back-to-back.

back to square one or **back to the basics** or **back to the drawing board** adv. phr. To start at the beginning again in an attempt to correct whatever mistakes were made initially. ◆After the first American rockets misfired, NASA decided to go back to square one.

back to the salt mines informal Back to the job; back to work; back to work that is as hard or as unpleasant as working in a salt mine would be.—An overworked phrase, used humorously. ◆The lunch hour is over, boys. Back to the salt mines!

back to the wall or **back against the wall** adv. phr. In a trap, with no way to escape; in bad trouble. ◆The soldiers had their *backs to the wall.* ♦*He was in debt and could not get any help; his back was against the wall.* ♦*The team had their backs to the wall in the second half.*

back up *v.* **1.** To move backwards. ♦*The train was backing up.* **2.** To help or be ready to help; stay behind to help; agree with and speak in support of. ♦*Jim has joined the Boy Scouts and his father is backing him up.* **3.** To move behind (another fielder) in order to catch the ball if he misses it. ♦*The shortstop backed up the second baseman on the throw.*

back-up *adj.* Supplementary; auxiliary; kept in need for safety. ♦*When at war, it is essential to keep the lines open for back-up troops and supplies.* ♦*When the policeman saw what happened, he called in for back-up support.*

bad blood *n., informal* Anger or misgivings due to bad relations in the past between individuals or groups. ♦*There's a lot of bad blood between Max and Jack; I bet they'll never talk to each other again.* Compare BAD SHIT.

bad egg *n., slang* A ne'er-do-well; good-for nothing; a habitual offender. ♦*The judge sent the bad egg to prison at last.*

bad mouth (someone) *v., slang* To say uncomplimentary or libelous things about someone; deliberately to damage another's reputation. ♦*It's not nice to bad mouth people.*

bad news *n., slang* An event, thing, or person which is disagreeable, or an unpleasant surprise. ♦*What's the new professor like?—He's all bad news to me.*

bad paper *n., slang* **1.** A check for which there are no funds in the bank. **2.** Counterfeit paper money. ♦*Why are you so mad? —I was paid with some bad paper.*

bad seed *n. phr.* A person who never does anything well; a person who veers from the straight and narrow and acts like a criminal. ♦*Jim is a bad seed; he doesn't belong in our family.*

bad shit *n., vulgar, avoidable* An unpleasant event or situation, such as a long-lasting and unsettled quarrel or recurring acts of vengeance preventing two people or two groups from reaching any kind of reconciliation. ♦*There is so much bad shit between the two gangs that I bet there will be more killings this year.*

bad trip *n., slang, also used colloquially* A disturbing or frightening experience, such as terrifying hallucinations, while under the influence of drugs; hence, by colloquial extension any bad experience in general. ♦*Why's John's face so distorted?—He had a bad trip.* ♦*How was your math exam?—Don't mention it; it was a bad trip.*

bag and baggage *adv., informal* With all your clothes and other personal belongings, especially movable possessions; completely. ♦*If they don't pay their hotel bill they will be put out bag and baggage.*

baker's dozen *n., informal* Thirteen. ♦*"How many of the jelly doughnuts, Sir?" the salesclerk asked. "Oh, make it a baker's dozen."*

ball game *n., slang, also informal* The entire matter at hand; the whole situation; the entire contest. ◆*You said we can get a second mortgage for the house? Wow! That's a whole new ball game.*

bang up *adj., informal* Very successful; very good; splendid; excellent. ◆*The football coach has done a bang-up job this season.* ◆*John did a bang-up job painting the house.*

bank on *v.,* To depend on; put one's trust in; rely on. ◆*He knew he could bank on public indignation to change things, if he could once prove the dirty work.* ◆*The students were banking on the team to do its best in the championship game.*

bargain for *or* **bargain on** *v.* To be ready for; expect. ◆*When John started a fight with the smaller boy he got more than he bargained for.* ◆*The final cost of building the house was much more than they had bargained on.*

bargain hunter *n. phr.* A person who likes to shop in inexpensive stores, such as factory outlets and garage sales, and always looks for the lowest possible price. ◆*Having lived in the bargaining environment of the Far East, my wife and I have become regular bargain hunters.*

barge in *v. phr., informal* To appear uninvited at someone's house or apartment, or to interrupt a conversation. ◆*I'm sorry for barging in like that, Sir, but my car died on me and there is no pay phone anywhere.*

bark up the wrong tree *v. phr., informal* To choose the wrong person to deal with or the wrong course of action; mistake an aim. ◆*If he thinks he can fool me, he is barking up the wrong tree.* ◆*He is barking up the wrong tree when he blames his troubles on bad luck.* ◆*The police were looking for a tall thin man, but were barking up the wrong tree; the thief was short and fat.*

bark worse than one's bite *informal* Sound or speech more frightening or worse than your actions. ◆*The small dog barks savagely, but his bark is worse than his bite.* ◆*The boss sometimes talks roughly to the men, but they know that his bark is worse than his bite.* ◆*She was always scolding her children, but they knew her bark was worse than her bite.*

basket case *n., slang, also informal* **1.** A person who has had both arms and both legs cut off as a result of war or other misfortune. **2.** A helpless person who is unable to take care of himself, as if carted around in a basket by others. ◆*Stop drinking, or else you'll wind up a basket case!*

bat an eye *or* **bat an eyelash** *v. phr., informal* To show surprise, fear, or interest; show your feelings.—Used in negative sentences. ◆*Bill told his story without batting an eyelash, although not a word of it was true.*

bats in one's belfry *or* **bats in the belfry** *n. phr., slang* Wild ideas in his mind; disordered senses; great mental confusion. ◆*When he talked about going to the moon he was thought to have bats in his belfry.*

batting average *n. phr.* Degree of accomplishment (originally used as a baseball term). ♦*Dr. Grace has a great batting average with her heart transplant operations.*

battle of nerves *n. phr.* A contest of wills during which the parties do not fight physically but try to wear each other out. ♦*It has been a regular battle of nerves to get the new program accepted at the local state university.*

bawl out *v., informal* To reprove in a loud or rough voice; rebuke sharply; scold. ♦*The teacher bawled us out for not handing in our homework.*

beach bunny *n., slang* An attractive girl seen on beaches— mostly to show off her figure; one who doesn't get into the water and swim. ♦*What kind of a girl is Susie?—She's a beach bunny; she always comes to the Queen's Surf on Waikiki but I've never seen her swim.*

be a drag *v. phr.* Be boring; soporiphic, somniferous ♦*My math teacher is the biggest drag I've ever met.* ♦*People who overexplain obvious things can be a drag.*

be a fly on the wall *v. phr.* To eavesdrop on a secret conversation. ♦*How I wish I could be a fly on the wall to hear what my fiance's parents are saying about me!*

be after someone or something *v. phr.* To hound or pursue someone or something; to chase or keep after a person or a goal. ♦*John is after Mary in a real big way.* ♦*Ted is after his boss' job.*

be all at sea *v. phr.* To find oneself at a loss; to have lost one's way; to be unable to find where one has to go, or what the truth is in a given matter. ♦*When it comes to Chinese grammar, Steven is all at sea.*

bear a grudge *v. phr.* To persist in bearing ill feeling toward someone after a quarrel or period of hostility. ♦*Come on, John, be a good sport and don't bear a grudge because I beat you at golf.*

bear down *v.* 1. To press or push harder; work hard; give full strength and attention. ♦*The sergeant bears down on lazy soldiers.* 2. To move toward in an impressive or threatening way.—Often used with *on.* ♦*While he was crossing the street a big truck bore down on him.* ♦*The little ship tried to escape when the big pirate ship bore down.*

bear the brunt *v. phr.* To shoulder or manage the hardest part of an undertaking, such as work, negotiations, or battle. ♦*The marines bore the brunt of many a battle during the Gulf War.*

bear up *v.* 1. To hold up; carry; support; encourage. ♦*The old bridge can hardly bear up its own weight any more.* 2. To keep up one's courage or strength; last.—Often used with *under.* ♦*This boat will bear up under hurricane winds.* ♦*She bore up well at the funeral.*

bear watching *v. phr.* 1. To be worth watching or paying attention to; have a promising future. ♦*That young ball player will bear watching.* 2. To be dangerous or untrustworthy.

♦*Those tires look badly worn; they will bear watching.*

bear with *v., formal* To have patience with; not get angry with. ♦*Your little sister is sick. Try to bear with her when she cries.* ♦*It is hard to bear with criticism.*

beat about the bush *or* **beat around the bush** *v. phr., slang* To talk about things without giving a clear answer; avoid the question or the point. ♦*He beat about the bush for a half hour without coming to the point.*

beat a retreat *v. phr.* **1.** To give a signal, esp. by beating a drum, to go back. ♦*The Redcoats' drums were beating a retreat.* **2.** To run away. ♦*The cat beat a hasty retreat when he saw the dog coming.*

beat into one's head *v. phr., informal* To teach by telling again and again; repeat often; drill, also, to be cross and punish often. ♦*Tom is lazy and stubborn and his lessons have to be beaten into his head.*

beat it *v., slang* To go away in a hurry; get out quickly. ♦*When he heard the crash he beat it as fast as he could.*—Often used as a command. ♦*The big boy said, "Beat it, kid. We don't want you with us."*

beat one to it *v. phr.* To arrive or get ahead of another person. ♦*I was about to call you, John, but you have beat me to it! Thanks for calling me.*

beat one's brains out *or* **beat one's brains** *v. phr., slang* To try very hard to understand or think out something difficult; tire yourself out by thinking. ♦*It was too hard for him and he beat his brains out trying to get the answer.*

beat one's gums *v. phr., slang* To engage in idle talk, or meaningless chatter; generally to talk too much. ♦*"Stop beating your gums, Jack," Joe cried. "I am falling asleep."*

beat one's head against a wall *v. phr.* To struggle uselessly against something that can't be beaten or helped; not succeed after trying very hard. ♦*Trying to make him change his mind is just beating your head against a wall.*

beat the bushes *also* **beat the brush** *v. phr., informal* To try very hard to find or get something. ♦*The mayor was beating the bushes for funds to build the playground.*

beat the drum *v. phr.* To attract attention in order to advertise something or to promote someone, such as a political candidate. ♦*Mrs. Smith has been beating the drum in her town in order to get her husband elected mayor.*

beat the rap *v. phr.* To escape the legal penalty one ought to receive. ♦*In spite of the strong evidence against him, the prisoner beat the rap and went free.*

beat to *v., informal* To do something before someone else does it. ♦*We were planning to send a rocket into space but the Russians beat us to it.*

beat to the punch *or* **beat to the draw** *v. phr., slang* To do something before another person has a chance to do it. ♦*John was going to apply for the job, but Ted beat him to the draw.* ♦*Lois bought the dress before Mary could beat her to the punch.*

beat up v., informal To give a hard beating to; hit hard and much; thrash; whip. ♦When the new boy first came, he had to beat up several neighborhood bullies before they would leave him alone.—Also used with on. ♦The tough boy said to Bill, "If you come around here again, I'll beat up on you."

beauty sleep n. A nap or rest taken to improve the appearance. ♦She took her beauty sleep before the party. ♦Many famous beauties take a beauty sleep every day.

because of prep. On account of; by reason of; as a result of. ♦The train arrived late because of the snowstorm.

bed of nails n. phr. A difficult or unhappy situation or set of circumstances. ♦"There are days when my job is a regular bed of nails," Jim groaned. Contrast BED OF ROSES.

bed of roses or **bowl of cherries** n. phr. A pleasant easy place, job, or position; an easy life. ♦A coal miner's job is not a bed of roses. ♦After nine months of school, summer camp seemed a bowl of cherries.

bed of thorns n. phr. A thoroughly unhappy time or difficult situation. ♦I'm sorry I changed jobs; my new one turned out to be a bed of thorns.

beef up v., informal To make stronger by adding men or equipment; make more powerful; reinforce. ♦The general beefed up his army with more big guns and tanks.

bee in one's bonnet n. phr., informal A fixed idea that seems fanciful, odd, or crazy. ♦Grandmother has some bee in her bonnet about going to the dance.

be even-Steven v. phr. To be in a position of owing no favors or debt to someone. ♦Yesterday you paid for my lunch, so today I paid for yours; now we're even-Steven.

be far out v. phr. To be so unusual as to defy credibility or likeability. ♦My history teacher is so far out that I have difficulty understanding what she's saying.

before long adv. phr. In a short time; without much delay; in a little while, soon. ♦Class will be over before long. ♦We were tired of waiting and hoped the bus would come before long.

before one can say Jack Robinson adv. cl., informal Very quickly; suddenly.—An overused phrase. ♦Before I could say Jack Robinson, the boy was gone.

beg off v. To ask to be excused. ♦I accepted an invitation to a luncheon, but a headache made me beg off.

beg the question v. phr., literary To accept as true something that is still being argued about, before it is proved true; avoid or not answer a question or problem. ♦Laura told Tom that he must believe her argument because she was right. Father laughed and told Laura she was begging the question.

be hard on v. phr. To be strict or critical with another; be severe. ♦"Don't be so hard on Jimmy," Tom said. "He is bound to rebel as he gets older."

behind bars adv. phr. In jail; in prison. ♦He was a pickpocket and had spent many years *behind bars.* ♦*That boy is always in trouble and will end up behind bars.*

behind one's back *adv. phr.* When one is absent; without one's knowledge or consent; in a dishonest way; secretly; sneakily. ♦*Say it to his face, not behind his back.* ♦*It is not right to criticize a person behind his back.*

behind the eight-ball *adj. phr., slang* In a difficult position; in trouble. ♦*Bill can't dance and has no car, so he is behind the eight-ball with the girls.*

behind the scenes *adv. phr.* Out of sight; unknown to most people; privately. ♦*Much of the committee's work was done behind the scenes.* ♦*John was president of the club, but behind the scenes Lee told him what to do.*

behind the times *adj. phr.* Using things not in style; still following old ways; old-fashioned. ♦*The science books of 30 years ago are behind the times now.*

be-in *n., slang, hippie culture* A gathering or social occasion with or without a discernible purpose, often held in a public place like a park or under a large circus tent. ♦*The youngsters really enjoyed the great springtime jazz be-in at the park.*

be in a stew *v. phr.* To be worried, harassed, upset. ♦*Al has been in a stew ever since he got word that his sister was going to marry her worst enemy.*

be into something *v. phr., informal* To have taken something up partly as a hobby, partly as a serious interest of sorts (basically resulting from the new consciousness and self-realiza-

tion movement that originated in the late Sixties). ♦*Did you know that Syd is seriously into transcendental meditation?* ♦*Jack found out that his teenage son is into pot smoking and gave him a serious scolding.*

believe one's ears *v. phr.* **1.** To believe what one hears; trust one's hearing.—Used with a negative or limiter, or in an interrogative or conditional sentence. ♦*He thought he heard a horn blowing in the distance, but he could not believe his ears.* **2.** To be made sure of (something). ♦*Is he really coming? I can hardly believe my ears.*

believe one's eyes *v. phr.* **1.** To believe what one sees; trust one's eyesight.—Used with a negative or limiter or in an interrogative or conditional sentence. ♦*Is that a plane? Can I believe my eyes?* **2.** To be made sure of seeing something. ♦*She saw him there but she could hardly believe her eyes.*

belly up *adj., informal* Dead, bankrupt, or financially ruined. ♦*Tom and Dick struggled on for months with their tiny computer shop, but last year they went belly up.*

belly up *v., informal* To go bankrupt, become afunctional; to die. ♦*Uncompetitive small businesses must eventually all belly up.*

below the belt *adv. phr.* **1.** In the stomach; lower than is legal in boxing. ♦*He struck the other boy below the belt.* **2.** *informal* In an unfair or cowardly way; against the rules of sportsmanship or justice; unsportingly; wrongly. ♦*Pete told the students* to vote against Harry because he was bound to a wheelchair and would therefore make a poor congressman, but they thought Pete was hitting below the belt.

be my guest! *v. phr.* Said to someone wishing to borrow something not too valuable or worth returning it; also said to someone who wants one to do him or her a small favor such as giving him or her a seat on a bus, etc. *♦"Can I borrow that red tie?" Joe asked his roommate Tim. "But of course! Be my guest!" Tim answered.*

beneath one *adj. phr.* Below one's ideals or dignity. *♦Bob felt it would have been beneath him to work for such low wages.*

bent on *or* **bent upon** Very decided, determined, or set. *♦The sailors were bent on having a good time. ♦The policeman saw some boys near the school after dark and thought they were bent on mischief. ♦The bus was late, and the driver was bent upon reaching the school on time.*

be nuts about *v. phr.* To be enthusiastic or very keen about someone or something; be greatly infatuated with someone. *♦Hermione is nuts about modern music. ♦"I am nuts about you, Helen," Jim said. "Please let's get married!"*

be off *v. phr.* 1. *v.* To be in error; miscalculate. *♦The estimator was off by at least 35% on the value of the house.* 2. *v.* To leave. *♦Jack ate his supper in a hurry and was off without saying good-bye.* 3. *adj.* Cancelled; terminated. *♦The weather was so bad that we were told that*

the trip was off. 4. *adj.* Crazy. *♦I'm sure Aunt Mathilda is a bit off; no one in her right mind would say such things.* 5. *adj.* Free from work; having vacation time. *♦Although we were off for the rest of the day, we couldn't go to the beach because it started to rain.*

be on *v. phr.* 1. To be in operation; be in the process of being presented. *♦The news is on now on Channel 2; it will be off in five minutes.* 2. To be in the process of happening; to take place. *♦We cannot travel now to certain parts of Africa, as there is a civil war on there right now.* 3. To be on duty. *♦"Is the night guard on Saturday and Sunday?" the new tenant asked the landlady. "No, he's off on weekends," she answered.*

be on the verge of *v. phr.* To be about to do something; be very close to. *♦We were on the verge of going bankrupt when, unexpectedly, my wife won the lottery and our business was saved.*

be out of it *v. phr.* 1. To not be aware of what is happening around one. *♦Joe has been studying so hard for his finals that he didn't get any sleep for several days; the poor guy is totally out of it.* 2. To be thoroughly exhausted. *♦Dad has been working so hard finishing the basement that he is out of it for the rest of the evening.*

be out to *v. phr.* To intend to do; to plan to commit. *♦The police felt that the gang may be out to rob another store.*

be over *v. phr.* To be ended; be finished. *♦The show was over by*

11 P.M. ◆*The war will soon be over.*

beside oneself *adj. phr.* Very much excited; somewhat crazy. ◆*She was beside herself with fear.* ◆*He was beside himself, he was so angry.* ◆*When his wife heard of his death, she was beside herself.*

beside the point *or* **beside the question** *adj. or adv. phr.* Off the subject; about something different. ◆*What you meant to do is beside the point; the fact is you didn't do it.*

best man *n.* The groom's aid (usually his best friend or a relative) at a wedding. ◆*When Agnes and I got married, my brother Gordon was my best man.*

best-seller *n.* An item (primarily said of books) that outsells other items of a similar sort. ◆*Catherine Neville's novel* The Eight *has been a national best-seller for months.* ◆*Among imported European cars, the Volkswagen is a best-seller.*

bet one's boots *or* **bet one's bottom dollar** *or* **bet one's shirt** *v. phr., informal* **1.** To bet all you have. ◆*This horse will win. I would bet my bottom dollar on it.* ◆*Jim said he would bet his boots that he would pass the examination.* **2.** *or* **bet one's life.** To feel very sure; have no doubt. ◆*Was I scared when I saw the bull running at me? You bet your life I was!*

bet on the wrong horse *v. phr., informal* To base your plans on a wrong guess about the result of something; misread the future; misjudge a coming event. ◆*To count on the small family farm as an important thing in the American future*

now looks like betting on the wrong horse.

better half *n., informal* One's marriage partner (mostly said by men about their wives.) ◆*"This is my better half, Mary," said Joe.*

better late than never It is better to come or do something late than never.—A proverb. ◆*The firemen didn't arrive at the house until it was half burned, but it was better late than never.*

between the devil and the deep blue sea *or literary* **between two fires** *or* **between a rock and a hard place** *adv. phr.* Between two dangers or difficulties, not knowing what to do. ◆*The pirates had to fight and be killed or give up and be hanged; they were between the devil and the deep blue sea.* ◆*The boy was between a rock and a hard place; he had to go home and be whipped or stay in town all night and be picked up by the police.* ◆*When the man's wife and her mother got together, he was between two fires.*

be up to no good *v. phr., informal* To be plotting and conniving to commit some illegal act or crime. ◆*"Let's hurry!" Susan said to her husband. "It's dark here and those hoodlums obviously are up to no good."*

beyond measure *adj. or adv. phr., formal* So much that it can not be measured or figured without any limits. ◆*With her parents reunited and present at her graduation, she had happiness beyond measure.*

beyond one's depth *adj. or adv. phr.* **1.** Over your head in water; in water too deep to touch bottom. ◆*Jack wasn't a good swim-*

mer and nearly drowned when he drifted out beyond his depth. **2.** In or into something too difficult for you; beyond your understanding or ability. ♦*Bill decided that his big brother's geometry book was beyond his depth.* ♦*Sam's father started to explain the atom bomb to Sam but he soon got beyond his depth.*

beyond one's means *adj. phr.* Too expensive, not affordable. ♦*Unfortunately, a new Mercedes Benz is beyond my means right now.*

beyond the pale *adv. or adj. phr.* In disgrace; with no chance of being accepted or respected by others; not approved by the members of a group. ♦*After the outlaw killed a man he was beyond the pale and not even his old friends would talk to him.* ♦*Tom's swearing is beyond the pale; no one invites him to dinner anymore.*

bide one's time *v. phr.* To await an opportunity; wait patiently until your chance comes. ♦*Refused work as an actor, Tom turned to other work and bided his time.*

big as life *or* **large as life** *adj. phr.* **1.** or **life-size** The same size as the living person or thing. ♦*The statue of Jefferson was big as life.* ♦*The characters on the screen were life-size.*

big cheese *or* **big gun** *or* **big shot** *or* **big wheel** *or* **big wig** *n., slang* An important person; a leader; a high official; a person of high rank. ♦*Bill had been a big shot in high school.* ♦*John wanted to be the big cheese in his club.*

big daddy *n., slang, informal* The most important, largest thing,

person or animal in a congregation of similar persons, animals, or objects. ♦*The whale is the big daddy of everything that swims in the ocean.* ♦*The H-bomb is the big daddy of all modern weapons.* ♦*Al Capone was the big daddy of organized crime in Chicago during Prohibition.*

big deal *interj., slang, informal* (loud stress on the word *deal*) Trifles; an unimportant, unimpressive thing or matter. ♦*So you became college president— big deal!*

big frog in a small pond *n. phr., informal* An important person in a small place or position; someone who is respected and honored in a small company, school, or city; a leader in a small group. ♦*As company president, he had been a big frog in a small pond, but he was not so important as a new congressman in Washington.*

big hand *n.* Loud and enthusiastic applause. ♦*When Pavarotti finished singing the aria from* Rigoletto, *he got a very big hand.*

big head *n., informal* Too high an opinion of your own ability or importance; conceit. ♦*When Jack was elected captain of the team, it gave him a big head.*

big lie, the *n., informal* A major, deliberate misrepresentation of some important issue made on the assumption that a bold, gross lie is psychologically more believable than a timid, minor one. ♦*We all heard the big lie during the Watergate months.* ♦*The pretense of democracy by a totalitarian* *regime is part of the big lie about its government.*

big stink *n., slang* A major scandal; a big upheaval. ♦*I'll raise a big stink if they fire me.*

big time *n., informal* 1. A very enjoyable time at a party or other pleasurable gathering. ♦*I certainly had a big time at the club last night.* 2. The top group; the leading class; the best or most important company. ♦*After his graduation from college, he soon made the big time in baseball.* ♦*Many young actors go to Hollywood, but few of them reach the big time.*

big-time *adj.* Belonging to the top group; of the leading class; important. ♦*Jean won a talent contest in her home town, and only a year later she began dancing on big-time television.* Often used in the phrase *big-time* operator. ♦*Just because Bill has a new football uniform he thinks he is a big-time operator.*

big wheel *n., informal* An influential or important person who has the power to do things and has connections in high places. ♦*Uncle Ferdinand is a big wheel in Washington; maybe he can help you with your problem.*

bird has flown *slang* The prisoner has escaped; the captive has got away. ♦*When the sheriff returned to the jail, he discovered that the bird had flown.*

bird in the hand is worth two in the bush (a) Something we have, or can easily get, is more valuable than something we want that we may not be able to get; we shouldn't risk losing something sure by trying to get

something that is not sure.—A proverb. ♦*Johnny has a job as a paperboy, but he wants a job in a gas station. His father says that a bird in the hand is worth two in the bush.*

bird of a different feather *n. phr.* A person who is free thinking and independent. ♦*Syd won't go along with recent trends in grammar; he created his own. He is a bird of a different feather.*

birds of a feather flock together People who are alike often become friends or are together; if you are often with certain people, you may be their friends or like them.—A proverb. ♦*Don't be friends with bad boys. People think that birds of a feather flock together.*

birds and the bees (the) *n. phr., informal* The facts we should know about our birth. ♦*At various ages, in response to questions, a child can be told about the birds and the bees.*

birthday suit *n.* The skin with no clothes on; complete nakedness. ♦*The little boys were swimming in their birthday suits.*

bite off more than one can chew *v. phr., informal* To try to do more than you can; be too confident of your ability. ♦*He started to repair his car himself, but realized that he had bitten off more than he could chew.*

bite one's head off *v. phr.* To answer someone in great anger; answer furiously. ♦*I'm sorry to tell you that I lost my job, but that's no reason to bite my head off!*

bite one's lips *v. phr.* To force oneself to remain silent and not to reveal one's feelings. ◆*I had to bite my lips when I heard my boss give the wrong orders.*

bite the dust *v. phr., informal* **1.** To be killed in battle. ◆*Captain Jones discharged his gun and another guerrilla bit the dust.* **2.** To fall in defeat; go down before enemies; be overthrown; lose. ◆*Our team bit the dust today.*

bite the hand that feeds one *v. phr.* To turn against or hurt a helper or supporter; repay kindness with wrong. ◆*He bit the hand that fed him when he complained against his employer.*

bitter pill *n.* Something hard to accept; disappointment. ◆*Jack was not invited to the party and it was a bitter pill for him.*

black and blue *adj.* Badly bruised. ◆*Poor Jim was black and blue after he fell off the apple tree.*

black and white *n. phr.* **1.** Print or writing; words on paper, not spoken; exact written or printed form. ◆*He insisted on having the agreement down in black and white.* **2.** The different shades of black and white of a simple picture, rather than other colors. ◆*He showed us snapshots in black and white.*

black-and-white *adj.* Divided into only two sides that are either right or wrong or good or bad, with nothing in between; thinking or judging everything as either good or bad. ◆*The old man's religion shows his black-and-white thinking; everything is either completely good or completely bad.*

black day *n.* A day of great unhappiness; a disaster. ◆*It was a black day when our business venture collapsed.*

black eye *n.* **1.** A dark area around one's eye due to a hard blow during a fight, such as boxing. ◆*Mike Tyson sported a black eye after the big fight.* **2.** Discredit. ◆*Bob's illegal actions will give a black eye to the popular movement he started.*

blackout *n.* (stress on *black*) **1.** The darkening of a city during an air raid by pulling down all curtains and putting out all street lights. ◆*The city of London went through numerous blackouts during World War II.* **2.** A cessation of news by the mass media. ◆*There was a total news blackout about the kidnapping of the prime minister.*

black out *v.* **1.** To darken by putting out or dimming lights. ◆*In some plays the stage is blacked out for a short time and the actors speak in darkness.* ◆*In wartime, cities are blacked out to protect against bombing from planes.* **2.** To prevent or silence information or communication; refuse to give out truthful news. ◆*In wartime, governments often black out all news or give out false news.* ◆*Dictators usually black out all criticism of the government.* **3.** *informal* To lose consciousness; faint. ◆*It had been a hard and tiring day, and she suddenly blacked out.*

black sheep *n.* A person in a family or a community considered unsatisfactory or disgraceful. ◆*My brother Ted is a high school dropout who joined a circus; he is the black sheep in our family.*

blast off *v.* **1.** To begin a rocket flight. ◆*The astronaut will blast* *off into orbit at six o'clock.* **2.** *Also* **blast away** *informal* To scold or protest violently. ♦*The coach blasted off at the team for poor playing.*

blaze a trail *v. phr.* **1.** To cut marks in trees in order to guide other people along a path or trail, especially through a wilderness. ♦*Daniel Boone blazed a trail for other hunters to follow in Kentucky.* **2.** To lead the way; make a discovery; start something new. ♦*Henry Ford blazed a trail in manufacturing automobiles.*

bleeding-heart liberal *n. phr.* A reasonably well-situated member of the bourgeoisie, who for sentimental reasons of left-leaning political views, always espouses the liberal cause, whether sensibly or not. ♦*Many bleeding-heart liberals, who once thought that marijuana should be legalized, change their minds when their own children become addicted to drugs.*

blessing in disguise *n. phr.* Some unexpected good that came about as the result of something bad or undesirable. ♦ *"It was a blessing in disguise that I forgot my car keys and had to go back for them," Joe said. "If I hadn't, I would not have noticed that I left the burner on in the kitchen, and I could have had a fire."*

blind alley *n.* **1.** A narrow street that has only one entrance and no exit. ♦*The blind alley ended in a brick wall.* **2.** A way of acting that leads to no good results. ♦*John did not take the job because it was a blind alley.*

blind as a bat/beetle/mole/owl *adj. phr.* Anyone who is blind

or has difficulty in seeing; a person with very thick glasses. ♦*Without my glasses I am blind as a bat.*

blind date *n.* An engagement or date arranged by friends for people who have not previously known one another. ♦ *A blind date can be a huge success, or a big disappointment.*

blind leading the blind One or more people who do not know or understand something trying to explain it to others who do not know or understand. ♦*Jimmy is trying to show Bill how to skate. The blind are leading the blind.*

blind spot *n.* **1.** A place on the road that a driver cannot see in the rearview mirror. ♦*I couldn't see that truck behind me, Officer, because it was in my blind spot.* **2.** A matter or topic a person refuses to discuss or accept. ♦*My uncle Ted has a real blind spot about religion.*

blood is thicker than water Persons of the same family are closer to one another than to others; relatives are favored or chosen over outsiders. ♦*Mr. Jones hires his relatives to work in his store. Blood is thicker than water.*

blood runs cold *also* **blood freezes** *or* **blood turns to ice** You are chilled or shivering from great fright or horror; you are terrified or horrified.— Usually used with a possessive. ♦*The horror movie made the children's blood run cold.* ♦*Mary's blood froze when she had to walk through the cemetery at night.* ♦*Oscar's blood turned to ice when he saw the* *shadow pass by outside the window.*

blot on the landscape *n. phr.* Something that spoils the scenery, disfigures the landscape. ◆*All that uncollected garbage the city is unable to dispose of is quite a blot on the landscape.*

blot out *v. phr.* **1.** To obstruct; cover; obscure. ◆*The high-rise building in front of our apartment house blots out the view of the ocean.* **2.** To wipe out of one's memory. ◆*Jane can't remember the details when she was attacked in the streets; she blotted it out of her memory.*

blow a fuse *or* **blow a gasket** *or* **blow one's top** *or* **blow one's stack** *v. phr., slang* To become extremely angry; express rage in hot words. ◆*When Mr. McCarthy's son got married against his wishes, he blew a fuse.* ◆*When the umpire called Joe out at first, Joe blew his top and was sent to the showers.*

blow in *v., slang* To arrive unexpectedly or in a carefree way. ◆*The house was already full of guests when Bill blew in.*

blow into *v., slang* To arrive at (a place) unexpectedly or in a carefree way. ◆*Bill blows into college at the last minute after every vacation.* ◆*Why Tom, when did you blow into town?*

blow one's brains out *v. phr.* **1.** To shoot yourself in the head. ◆*Mr. Jones lost all his wealth, so he blew his brains out.* **2.** *slang* To work very hard; overwork yourself. ◆*The boys blew their brains out to get the stage ready for the play.* ◆*Mary is not one to blow her brains out.*

blow one's cool *v. phr., slang, informal* To lose your composure or self-control. ◆*Whatever you say to the judge in court, make sure that you don't blow your cool.*

blow one's lines *or* **fluff one's lines** *v. phr., informal* To forget the words you are supposed to speak while acting in a play. ◆*The noise backstage scared Mary and she blew her lines.*

blow one's mind *v. phr., slang, informal; originally from the drug culture* **1.** To become wildly enthusiastic over something as if understanding it for the first time in an entirely new light. ◆*Read Lyall Watson's book* Supernatura, *it will simply blow your mind!* **2.** To lose one's ability to function, as if due to an overdose of drugs. ◆*Joe is entirely incoherent—he seems to have blown his mind.*

blow one's own horn *or* **toot one's own horn** *v. phr., slang* To praise yourself; call attention to your own skill, intelligence, or successes; boast. ◆*A person who does things well does not have to toot his own horn; his abilities will be noticed by others.*

blow one's top *v. phr.* To become very excited, angry, hysterical, or furious. ◆*"No need to blow your top, Al," his wife said, "just because you lost a few dollars."*

blow out *v. phr.* **1.** To cease to function; fail; explode (said of tires and fuses). ◆*The accident occurred when Jim's tire blew out on the highway.* ◆*The new dishwasher blew out the fuses in the whole house.* **2.** To extinguish. ◆*Jane blew out her birth-*

day cake candles before offering pieces to the guests.

blowout n. 1. An explosion of a tire or a fuse. ◆*Jim's van veered sharply to the right after his car had a blowout.* 2. A big party. ◆*After graduation from college, my son and his friends staged a huge blowout.*

blow over v. To come to an end; pass away with little or no bad effects. ◆*The sky was black, as if a bad storm were coming, but it blew over and the sun came out.* ◆*He was much criticized for the divorce, but it all blew over after a few years.*

blow the lid off v. phr., informal Suddenly to reveal the truth about a matter that has been kept as a secret either by private persons or by some governmental agency. ◆*The clever journalists blew the lid off the Watergate cover-up.*

blow the whistle on v. phr., slang 1. To inform against; betray. ◆*The police caught one of the bank robbers, and he blew the whistle on two more.* 2. To act against, stop, or tell people the secrets of (crime or lawlessness). ◆*The mayor blew the whistle on gambling.* ◆*The police blew the whistle on hot rodding.*

blow up v. 1a. To break or destroy or to be destroyed by explosion. ◆*He blew up the plane by means of a concealed bomb.* 1b. informal To explode with anger or strong feeling; lose control of yourself. ◆*When Father bent the nail for the third time, he blew up.* 1c. To stop playing well in a game or contest, usually because you are in danger of losing or are tired; especial-

ly: To lose skill or control in pitching baseball. ◆*The champion blew up and lost the tennis match.* 2. informal To be ruined as if by explosion; be ended suddenly. ◆*The whole scheme for a big party suddenly blew up.* 3a. To pump full of air; inflate. ◆*He blew his tires up at a filling station.* 3b. To make (something) seem bigger or important. ◆*It was a small thing to happen but the newspapers had blown it up until it seemed important.* 4. To bring on bad weather; also, to come on as bad weather. ◆*The wind had blown up a storm.* 5. To copy in bigger form; enlarge. ◆*He blew up the snapshot to a larger size.*

blow up in one's face v. phr., informal To fail completely and with unexpected results. ◆*The thief's plan to rob the bank blew up in his face when a policeman stopped him.*

blue collar worker n. phr. A manual laborer who is probably a labor union member. ◆*Because Jack's father is a blue collar worker, Jack was so anxious to become an intellectual.*

blue in the face adj. phr., informal Very angry or upset; excited and very emotional. ◆*Tom argued with Bill until he was blue in the face.*

bog down v. phr. To be immobilized in mud, snow, etc.; slow down. ◆*Our research got bogged down for a lack of appropriate funding.* ◆*Don't get bogged down in too much detail when you write an action story.*

bog down, to get bogged down v. phr., mostly intransitive or passive 1. To stop progressing; to slow to a halt. ◆*Work on the* *new building bogged down, because the contractor didn't deliver the needed concrete blocks.* **2.** To become entangled with a variety of obstacles making your efforts unproductive or unsatisfying. ♦*The novelist wrote little last summer because she got bogged down in housework.*

boggle the mind *v. phr., informal* To stop the rational thinking process by virtue of being too fantastic or incredible. ♦*It boggles the mind that John should have been inside a flying saucer!*

boil down *v.* **1.** To boil away some of the water from; make less by boiling. ♦*She boiled down the maple sap to a thick syrup.* **2.** To reduce the length of; cut down; shorten. ♦*The reporter boiled the story down to half the original length.* **3.** To reduce itself to; come down to; be briefly or basically. ♦*The whole discussion boils down to the question of whether the government should fix prices.*

bonehead *n., slang* An unusually dense or stupid person. ♦*John is such a bonehead—small wonder he flunks all of his courses.*

bone of contention *n. phr.* Something to fight over; a reason for quarrels; the subject of a fight. ♦*The use of the car was a bone of contention between Joe and his wife.*

bone to pick *or* **crow to pick** *n. phr., informal* A reason for dispute; something to complain of or argue about.—Often used jokingly. ♦*"I have a bone to pick with you," he said.* ♦*There was always a crow to pick about which one would shave*

first in the morning. Compare
BONE OF CONTENTION.

bone up *v., informal* To fill with information; try to learn a lot about something in a short time; study quickly. ♦*Carl was boning up for an examination.* ♦*Jim had to make a class report the next day on juvenile delinquency, and he was in the library boning up on how the courts handle it.*

bore to tears *v. phr.* To fill with tired dislike; tire by dullness or the same old thing bore. ♦*The party was dull and Roger showed plainly that he was bored to tears.* ♦*Mary loved cooking, but sewing bores her to tears.*

born with a silver spoon in one's mouth *adj. phr.* Born to wealth and comfort; provided from birth with everything wanted; born rich. ♦*The stranger's conduct was that of a man who had been born with a silver spoon in his mouth.*

born yesterday *adj. phr.* Inexperienced and easily fooled; not alert to trickery; easily deceived or cheated. ♦*I won't give you the money till I see the bicycle you want to sell me. Do you think I was born yesterday?*

bosom friend *n. phr.* A very close friend; an old buddy with whom one has a confidential relationship. ♦*Sue and Jane have been bosom friends since their college days.*

boss one around *v. phr.* To keep giving someone orders; to act overbearingly toward someone. ♦*"If you keep bossing me around, darling," Tom said to Jane, "the days of our relationship are surely numbered."*

botch up v. phr. To ruin, spoil, or mess something up. ◆*"I botched up my chemistry exam," Tim said, with a resigned sigh.*

bottleneck n. A heavy traffic congestion. ◆*In Chicago the worst bottleneck is found where the Kennedy and the Eden's expressways separate on the way to the airport.*

bottle up v. 1. To hide or hold back; control. ◆*There was no understanding person to talk to, so Fred bottled up his unhappy feeling.* 2. To hold in a place from which there is no escape; trap. ◆*Our warships bottled up the enemy fleet in the harbor.*

bottom dollar n., v. phr., informal One's last penny, one's last dollar. ◆*He was down to his bottom dollar when he suddenly got the job offer.*

bottom drop out or **bottom fall out** v. phr. informal 1. To fall below an earlier lowest price. ◆*The bottom dropped out of the price of peaches.* 2. To lose all cheerful qualities; become very unhappy, cheerless, or unpleasant. ◆*The bottom dropped out of the day for John when he saw his report card.*

bottom line n., informal (stress on line) 1. The last word on a controversial issue; a final decision. ◆*"Give me the bottom line on the proposed merger," said John.* 2. The naked truth without embellishments. ◆*Look, the bottom line is that poor Max is an alcoholic.* 3. The final dollar amount; for example, the lowest price two parties reach in bargaining about a sale. ◆*"Five-hundred," said the used car dealer, "is the bottom line. Take it or leave it."*

bottom line v., informal (stress on bottom) To finish; to bring to a conclusion. ◆*Okay, you guys, let's bottom line this project and break for coffee.*

bottom out v. phr. To reach the lowest point (said chiefly of economic cycles). ◆*According to the leading economic indicators the recession will bottom out within the next two months.*

bow out v., informal 1. To give up taking part; excuse yourself from doing any more; quit. ◆*Mr. Black often quarreled with his partners, so finally he bowed out of the company.* ◆*While the movie was being filmed, the star got sick and had to bow out.* 2. To stop working after a long service; retire. ◆*He bowed out as train engineer after forty years of railroading.*

box office n., informal 1. The place at movies and theaters where tickets may be purchased just before the performance instead of having ordered them through the telephone or having bought them at a ticket agency. ◆*No need to reserve the seats; we can pick them up at the box office.* 2. adj. A best selling movie, musical, or drama (where the tickets are all always sold out and people line up in front of the box office). ◆*Denzel Washington's last movie was a box office smash.*

boyfriend n., informal 1. A male friend or companion. ◆*"John and his boyfriends have gone to the ball game," said his mother.* 2. A girl's steady date, a woman's favorite man friend; a male lover or sweetheart. ◆*Jane's new boyfriend is a senior in high school.*

boys will be boys Boys are only children and must sometimes get into mischief or trouble or behave too roughly. *Boys will be boys and make a lot of noise, so John's mother told him and his friends to play in the park instead of the back yard.*

brain bucket n., slang A motorcycle helmet. *If you want to share a ride with me, you've got to wear a brain bucket.*

brain drain n., informal 1. The loss of the leading intellectuals and researchers of a country due to excessive emigration to other countries where conditions are better. *Britain suffered a considerable brain drain to the United States after World War II.* 2. An activity requiring great mental concentration resulting in fatigue and exhaustion. *That math exam I took was a regular brain drain.*

brainstorm v. (stress on brain) To have a discussion among fellow researchers or co-workers on a project in order to find the best solution to a given problem. *Dr. Watson and his research assistants are brainstorming in the conference room.*

brainstorm n. A sudden insight; a stroke of comprehension. *Listen to me, I've just had a major brainstorm, and I think I found the solution to our problem.*

brain trust n. A group of specially trained, highly intelligent experts in a given field. *Albert Einstein gathered a brain trust around himself at the Princeton Institute of Advanced Studies.*

brainwash v. phr. To change someone's way of thinking mostly about politics or religion, by constantly bombarding them with the desired information under duress, until the victim "believes" what he or she is being told. *Both the Nazis and the Communists used to brainwash the population with their ideology.*

brainwashing n. The act of submitting someone to unrelenting propaganda. *The Iraqi regime is guilty of brainwashing the population into a personality cult for Saddam Hussein.*

branch off v. To go from something big or important to something smaller or less important; turn aside. *At the bridge a little road branches off from the highway and follows the river. *Martin was trying to study his lesson, but his mind kept branching off onto what girl he should ask to go with him to the dance.*

branch out v. To add new interests or activities; begin doing other things also. *First Jane collected stamps; then she branched out and collected coins, too. *John started a television repair shop; when he did well, he branched out and began selling television sets too.*

brand-new also **bran-new** adj. As new or fresh as when just made and sold by the manufacturer; showing no use or wear. *He had taken a brand-new car from the dealer's floor and wrecked it.*

brazen it out v. phr. To pretend you did nothing wrong; be suspected, accused, or scolded without admitting you did wrong; act as if not guilty. *The teacher found a stolen pen that the girl had in her desk, but the* *girl brazened it out; she said someone else must have put it there.*

bread and butter *n. phr.* The usual needs of life; food, shelter, and clothing. ◆*Ed earned his bread and butter as a bookkeeper, but added a little jam by working with a dance band on weekends.*

bread-and-butter letter *n.* A written acknowledgment of hospitality received. ◆*Jane wrote the Browns a bread-and-butter letter when she returned home from her visit to them.*

break away *or* **break loose** *v. phr.* To liberate oneself from someone or something. ◆*Jane tried to break loose from her attacker, but he was too strong.*

break down *v.* (stress on *down*) **1.** To smash or hit (something) so that it falls; cause to fall by force. ◆*The firemen broke down the door.* **2.** To reduce or destroy the strength or effect of; weaken; win over. ◆*By helpful kindness the teacher broke down the new boy's shyness.* **3.** To separate into elements or parts; decay. ◆*Water is readily broken down into hydrogen and oxygen.* **4.** To become unusable because of breakage or other failure; lose power to work or go. ◆*The car broke down after half an hour's driving.* ◆*His health broke down.*

break even *v. phr., informal* (stress on *even*) To end a series of gains and losses having the same amount you started with; have expenses equal to profits; have equal gain and loss. ◆*If you gamble you are lucky when you break even.*

break-even *n.* The point of equilibrium in a business venture when one has made as much money as one had invested, but not more—that would be "profit." ◆*"We've reached the break-even point at long last!" Max exclaimed with joy.*

break ground *v. phr.* To begin a construction project by digging for the foundation; especially, to turn the formal first spadeful of dirt. ◆*City officials and industrial leaders were there as the company broke ground for its new building.*

break in *v.* (stress on *in*) **1a.** To break from outside. ◆*The firemen broke in the door of the burning house.* **1b.** To enter by force or unlawfully. ◆*Thieves broke in while the family was away.* **2.** To enter suddenly or interrupt. ◆*A stranger broke in on the meeting without knocking.* ◆*The secretary broke in to say that a telegram had arrived.* **3.** To make a start in a line of work or with a company or association; begin a new job. ◆*He broke in as a baseball player with a minor league.* **4.** To teach the skills of a new job or activity to. ◆*An assistant foreman broke in the new man as a machine operator.* **5.** To lessen the stiffness or newness of by use. ◆*Breaking in a new car requires careful driving at moderate speeds.*

break-in *n.* (stress on *break*) A robbery; a burglary. ◆*We lost our jewelry during a break-in.*

break into *v.* **1.** To force an entrance into; make a rough or unlawful entrance into. ◆*Thieves broke into the store at night.* **2.** *informal* To succeed in beginning (a career, business, or a social life) ♦*He broke into television as an actor.* 3. To interrupt. ♦*He broke into the discussion with a shout of warning.* 4. To begin suddenly. ♦*He broke into a sweat.* ♦*She broke into tears.*

break it up! *v. phr. command* Disperse; stop the gathering (or fight), and keep moving away from the scene. ♦*"Come on you guys! Break it up!" the coach shouted, when the two basketball teams started a brawl in mid-court.*

break new ground *v. phr.* 1. To start a new activity previously neglected by others; do pioneering work. ♦*Albert Einstein broke new ground with his theory of relativity.* 2. To begin something never done before. ♦*The school broke new ground with reading lessons that taught students to guess the meaning of new words.*

break off *v.* 1. To stop suddenly. ♦*The speaker was interrupted so often that he broke off and sat down.* ♦*When Bob came in, Jean broke off her talk with Linda and talked to Bob.* 2. *informal* To end a friendship or love. ♦*I hear that Tom and Alice have broken off.*

break one's balls *v. phr., slang, vulgar, avoidable* To do something with maximum effort; to do something very difficult or taxing ♦*I've been breaking my balls to buy you this new color TV set and you aren't the least bit appreciative!*

break one's heart *v. phr.* To discourage greatly; make very sad or hopeless. ♦*His son's disgrace broke his heart.* ♦*When Mr. White lost everything he*

had worked so hard for, it broke his heart.

break one's neck *v. phr., slang* To do all you possibly can; try your hardest.—Usually used with a limiting adverb or negative. ♦*John nearly broke his neck trying not to be late to school.*

break one's word *v. phr.* To renege on a promise. ♦*When Jake broke his word that he would marry Sarah, she became very depressed.*

break out *v.* 1. To begin showing a rash or other skin disorder.—Often used with *with.* ♦*He broke out with scarlet fever.* 2. To speak or act suddenly and violently. ♦*She broke out laughing.* ♦*She broke out, "That is not so!"* 3. To begin and become noticeable. ♦*Fire broke out after the earthquake.* ♦*War broke out in 1812.* 4. *informal* To bring out; open and show. ♦*When Mr. Carson's first son was born, he broke out the cigars he had been saving.*

break the ice *v. phr., informal* 1. To conquer the first difficulties in starting a conversation, getting a party going, or making an acquaintance. ♦*To break the ice Ted spoke of his interest in mountain climbing, and they soon had a conversation going.* 2. To be the first person or team to score in a game. ♦*The Wolves broke the ice with a touchdown.*

break the record *v. phr.* To set or to establish a new mark or record. ♦*Algernon broke the record in both the pentathlon and the decathlon and took home two gold medals from the Olympics.*

break through *v.* (stress on *through*) To be successful after overcoming a difficulty or bar to success. ♦*Dr. Salk failed many times but he finally broke through to find a successful polio vaccine.*

breakthrough n. (stress on *break*) A point of sudden success after a long process of experimentation, trial, and error. ♦*The U.S. Space Program experienced a major breakthrough when Armstrong and Aldrin landed on the moon in June of 1969.*

break up v. phr. (stress on *up*) To end a romantic relationship, a marriage, or a business partnership. ♦*Tom and Jane broke up because Tom played so much golf that he had no time for her.*

break up v. (stress on *up*) **1.** To break into pieces. ♦*The workmen broke up the pavement to dig up the pipes under it.* ♦*River ice breaks up in the spring.* **2.** *informal* To lose or destroy spirit or self-control.—Usually used in the passive. ♦*Mrs. Lawrence was all broken up after her daughter's death, and did not go out of the house for two months.* **3.** To come or to put to an end, especially by separation; separate. ♦*Some men kept interrupting the speakers, and finally broke up the meeting.* ♦*The party broke up at midnight.*—Often used in the informal phrase *break it up.* ♦*The boys were fighting, and a passing policeman ordered them to break it up.* **4.** *informal* To stop being friends. ♦*Mary and June were good friends and did everything together, but then they had a quarrel and broke up.*

break-up n. (stress on *break*) The end of a relationship, personal or commercial. ♦*The break-up finally occurred when Smith and Brown decided to sue each other for embezzlement.*

break with v. To separate yourself from; end membership in; stop friendly association with. ♦*He broke with the Democratic Party on the question of civil rights.*

breathe down one's neck v. phr., *informal* To follow closely; threaten from behind; watch every action. ♦*Too many creditors were breathing down his neck.* ♦*The carpenter didn't like to work for Mr. Jones, who was always breathing down his neck.*

breathe easily *or* **breathe freely** v. To have relief from difficulty or worry; relax; feel that trouble is gone; stop worrying. ♦*Now that the big bills were paid, he breathed more easily.* ♦*His mother didn't breathe easily until he got home that night.*

breathe one's last v. phr. To die. ♦*The wounded soldier fell back on the ground and breathed his last.*

bright and early adj. phr. Prompt and alert; on time and ready; cheerful and on time or before time. ♦*He came down bright and early to breakfast.* ♦*She arrived bright and early for the appointment.*

bring about v. To cause; produce; lead to. ♦*The war had brought about great changes in living.* ♦*Drink brought about his downfall.*

bring around *or* **bring round** v. **1.** *informal* To restore to health or consciousness; cure. ♦*He was quite ill, but good nursing brought him around.* **2.** To cause a change in thinking; persuade; convince; make willing. ♦*After a good deal of discussion he brought her around to his way of thinking.*

bringdown *n., slang, informal* (stress on *bring*) **1.** (from *bring down*, past *brought down*). A critical or cutting remark said sarcastically in order to deflate a braggard's ego. ♦*John always utters the right bringdown when he encounters a braggard.* **2.** A person who depresses and saddens others by being a chronic complainer. ♦*John is a regular bringdown.*

bring down *v. phr., slang, informal* (stress on *down*) **1.** To deflate (someone's ego). ♦*John brought Ted down very cleverly with his remarks.* **2.** To depress (someone). ♦*The funeral brought me down completely.*

bring down the house *v. phr., informal* To start an audience laughing or clapping enthusiastically. ♦*The president made a fine speech which brought down the house.*

bring home *v.* To show clearly; emphasize; make (someone) realize; demonstrate. ♦*The accident caused a death in his family, and it brought home to him the evil of drinking while driving.*

bring home the bacon *v. phr., informal* **1.** To support your family; earn the family living. ♦*He was a steady fellow, who always brought home the bacon.* **2.** To win a game or prize. ♦*The football team brought home the bacon.*

bring in *v.* To tune one's radio so that a station can be heard. ♦ *"Can you bring in the BBC on*

that portable machine of yours?"

bring into line *v. phr.* To make someone conform to the accepted standard. ♦*Sam had to be brought into line when he refused to take his muddy shoes off the cocktail table.*

bring off *v.* To do (something difficult); perform successfully (an act of skill); accomplish (something requiring unusual ability). ♦*He tried several times to break the high jump record, and finally he brought it off.*

bring on *v.* To result in; cause; produce. ♦*The murder of Archduke Franz Ferdinand in the summer of 1914 brought on the First World War.* ♦*Spinal meningitis brought on John's deafness when he was six years old.* ♦*Reading in a poor light may bring on a headache.*

bring to *v.* (stress on *to*) **1.** To restore to consciousness; wake from sleep, anesthesia, hypnosis, or fainting. ♦*Smelling salts will often bring a fainting person to.* **2.** To bring a ship or boat to a stop. ♦*Reaching the pier, he brought the boat smartly to.*

bring to one's knees *v. phr.* To seriously weaken the power or impair the function of. ♦*The fuel shortage brought the automobile industry to its knees.*

bring to pass *v. phr., informal* To make (something) happen; succeed in causing. ♦*The change in the law was slow in coming, and it took a disaster to bring it to pass.*

bring to terms *v. phr.* To make (someone) agree or do; make surrender. ♦*The war won't end until we bring the enemy to terms.*

bring up v. 1. To take care of (a child); raise, train, educate. ◆He gave much attention and thought to bringing up his children. ◆Joe was born in Texas but brought up in Oklahoma. 2. informal To stop; halt.— Usually used with short. ◆He brought the car up short when the light changed to red. ◆Bill started to complain, I brought him up short. 3. To begin a discussion of; speak of; mention. ◆At the class meeting Bob brought up the idea of a picnic.

bring up the rear v. phr. 1. To come last in a march, parade, or procession; end a line. ◆The governor and his staff brought up the rear of the parade. 2. informal To do least well; do the most poorly of a group; be last. ◆In the race, John brought up the rear. ◆In the basketball tournament, our team brought up the rear.

brown-bagger n., slang, informal A person who does not go to the cafeteria or to a restaurant for lunch at work, but who brings his homemade lunch to work in order to save money. ◆John became a brown-bagger not because he can't afford the restaurant, but because he is too busy to go there.

brown-nose v., slang, avoidable, though gaining in acceptance To curry favor in a subservient way, as by obviously exaggerated flattery. ◆Max brown-noses his teachers, that's why he gets all A's in his courses.

brush off or **give the brush off** v. phr. 1. To refuse to hear or believe; quickly and impatiently; not take seriously or think important. ◆John brushed off Bill's warning that he might fall from the tree. 2. informal To be unfriendly to; not talk or pay attention to (someone); get rid of. ◆Mary brushed off Bill at the dance.

brush up or **brush up on** v. To refresh one's memory of or skill at by practice or review; improve; make perfect. ◆She spent the summer brushing up on her American History as she was to teach that in the fall. ◆He brushed up his target shooting.

bubble gum music n., slang The kind of rock'n'roll that appeals to young teenagers. ◆When will you learn to appreciate Mozart instead of that bubble gum music?

buckle down or **knuckle down** v. To give complete attention (to an effort or job); attend. ◆They chatted idly for a few moments then each buckled down to work. ◆Jim was fooling instead of studying; so his father told him to buckle down.

bug-eyed adj., slang Wide-eyed with surprise. ◆He stood there bug-eyed when told that he had won the award.

bug out v. phr. To get out of a place in a great hurry; to escape. ◆"Come on! Lets bug out!" Sergeant O'Leary cried, when the enemy started to shoot at the foxhole where the marines hid.

buggy-whip n., slang An unusually long, thin radio antenna on a car that bends back like a whip when the car moves fast. ◆He's very impressed with himself ever since he got a buggy whip.

bughouse[1] *n., slang* An insane asylum. ◆*They took Joe to the bughouse.*

bughouse[2] *adj., slang* Crazy, insane. ◆*Joe's gone bughouse.*

bug in one's ear *n. phr., informal* A hint; secret information given to someone to make him act; idea. ◆*I saw Mary at the jeweler's admiring the diamond pin; I'll put a bug in Henry's ear.*

build a fire under *v. phr.* To urge or force (a slow or unwilling person) to action; get (someone) moving; arouse. ◆*The health department built a fire under the restaurant owner and got him to clean the place up by threatening to cancel his license.*

build castles in the air *or* **build castles in Spain** *v. phr.* To make impossible or imaginary plans, dream about future successes that are unlikely. ◆*He liked to build castles in the air, but never succeeded in anything.* ◆*To build castles in Spain is natural for young people and they may work hard enough to get part of their wishes.*

build on sand *v. phr.* To lay a weak or insufficient foundation for a building, a business, or a relationship. ◆*"I don't want to build my business on sand," John said, "so please, Dad, give me that loan I requested."*

build up *v.* **1.** To make out of separate pieces or layers; construct from parts. ◆*Johnny built up a fort out of large balls of snow.* **2.** To cover over or fill up with buildings. ◆*A driver should slow down when he comes to an area that is built up.* **3a.** To increase slowly or by small amounts; grow. ◆*John built up*

a bank account by saving regularly. **3b.** To make stronger or better or more effective. ◆*Fred exercised to build up his muscles.* **3c.** *informal* To advertise quickly and publicize so as to make famous. ◆*The press agent built up the young actress.*

build up to *v. phr.* To be in the process of reaching a culmination point. ◆*The clouds were building up to a violent storm.* ◆*Their heated words were building up to a premature divorce.*

bull in a china shop *n. phr.* A rough or clumsy person who says or does something to anger others or upset plans; a tactless person. ◆*We were talking politely and carefully with the teacher about a class party, but John came in like a bull in a china shop and his rough talk made the teacher say no.*

bull session *n., slang* A long informal talk about something by a group of persons. ◆*After the game the boys in the dormitory had a bull session until the lights went out.*

bullshit *n., vulgar, but gaining in acceptance by some* Exaggerated or insincere talk meant to impress others. ◆*"Joe, this is a lot of bullshit!"*

bullshit *v., vulgar to informal, gaining in social acceptance by some* To exaggerate or talk insincerely in an effort to make yourself seem impressive. ◆*"Stop bullshitting me, Joe, I can't believe a word of what you're saying."*

bullshit artist *n., slang, vulgar, but gaining in social acceptance* A person who habitually makes exaggerated or insincerely flattering speeches designed to impress others. ♦*Joe is a regular bullshit artist, small wonder he keeps getting promoted ahead of everyone else.*

bump off *v., slang* To kill in a violent way; murder in gangster fashion. ♦*Hoodlums in a speeding car bumped him off with Tommy guns.*

bum steer *n.* Wrong or misleading directions given naively or on purpose. ♦*Man, you sure gave me a bum steer when you told me to go north on the highway; you should have sent me south!*

bundle of laughs *n. phr.* A very amusing person, thing, or event. ♦*Uncle Lester tells so many jokes that he is a bundle of laughs.*

bundle of nerves *adj. phr.* Extremely nervous, jumpy, fidgety, restless. ♦*Is your son Bobby always such a bundle of nerves? You should have him seen by a doctor for hyperactivity.*

burn one's bridges *also* **burn one's boats** *v. phr.* To make a decision that you cannot change; remove or destroy all the ways you can get back out of a place you have got into on purpose; leave yourself no way to escape a position. ♦*When Dorothy became a nun, she burned her bridges behind her.*

burn one's fingers *v. phr., informal* To get in trouble doing something and fear to do it again; learn caution through an unpleasant experience. ♦*Some people can't be told; they have to burn their fingers to learn.*

burn out *v. phr.* (stress on *out*) **1.** To destroy by fire or by overheating. ♦*Mr. Jones burned out*

the clutch on his car. **2.** To destroy someone's house or business by fire so that they have to move out. ♦*Three racists burned out the black family's home.* **3a.** To go out of order; cease to function because of long use or overheating. ♦*The light bulb in the bathroom burned out, and Father put in a new one.* ♦*The electric motor was too powerful, and it burned out a fuse.* **3b.** To break, tire, or wear out by using up all the power, energy, or strength of. ♦*Bill burned himself out in the first part of the race and could not finish.* ♦*The farmer burned out his field by planting the same crop every year for many years.*

burn-out *n.* (stress on *burn*) A point of physical or emotional exhaustion. ♦*There are so many refugees all over the world that charitable organizations as well as individuals are suffering from donor burn-out.*

burn the candle at both ends *v. phr.* To work or play too hard without enough rest; get too tired. ♦*He worked hard every day as a lawyer and went to parties and dances every night; he was burning the candle at both ends.*

burn the midnight oil *v. phr.* To study late at night. ♦*Exam time was near, and more and more pupils were burning the midnight oil.*

burn up *v.* **1.** To burn completely; destroy or be destroyed by fire. ♦*Mr. Scott was burning up old letters.* ♦*The house burned up before the firemen got there.* **2.** *informal* To irritate, anger, annoy. ♦*The boy's laziness and rudeness burned up his teacher.*

burn up the road *v. phr., informal* To drive a car very fast. ♦*Speed demons burning up the road often cause accidents.*

burst at the seams *v. phr., informal* To be too full or too crowded. ♦*John ate so much he was bursting at the seams.*

burst into *v. phr.* **1.** To enter suddenly. ♦*Stuart burst into the room, screaming angrily.* **2.** To break out. ♦*The crowd burst out cheering when the astronauts paraded along Fifth Avenue.*

burst into flames *v. phr.* To begin to burn suddenly. ♦*The children threw away some burning matches and the barn burst into flames.*

burst into tears *v. phr.* To suddenly start crying. ♦*Mary burst into tears when she heard that her brother was killed in a car accident.*

bury the hatchet *v. phr., informal* To settle a quarrel or end a war; make peace. ♦*The two men had been enemies a long time, but after the flood they buried the hatchet.*

busy work *n.* Work that is done not to do or finish anything important, but just to keep busy. ♦*When the teacher finished all she had to say it was still a half hour before school was over. So she gave the class a test for busy work.*

butterflies in one's stomach *n. phr.* A queer feeling in the stomach caused by nervous fear or uncertainty; a feeling of fear or anxiety in the stomach. ♦*When Bob walked into the factory office to ask for a job, he had butterflies in his stomach.*

butter up *v., informal* To try to get the favor or friendship of (a person) by flattery or pleasantness. ♦*He began to butter up the boss in hope of being given a better job.*

butt in *v., slang* To join in with what other people are doing without asking or being asked; interfere in other people's business; meddle. ♦*Mary was explaining to Jane how to knit a sweater when Barbara butted in.* Often used with *on.* ♦*John butted in on Bill and Tom's fight, and got hurt.*

buy for a song *v. phr.* To buy something very cheaply. ♦*Since the building on the corner was old and neglected, I was able to buy it for a song.*

buy off *v.* To turn from duty or purpose by a gift. ♦*When the police threatened to stop the gambling business, the owner bought them off.*

buy out *v.* **1.** To buy the ownership or a share of; purchase the stock of. ♦*He bought out several small stockholders.* **2.** To buy all the goods of; purchase the merchandise of. ♦*Mr. Harper bought out a nearby hardware store.*

buy up *v. phr.* To purchase the entire stock of something. ♦*The company is trying to buy up all the available shares.*

buzz word *n.* A word that sounds big and important in a sentence but, on closer inspection, means little except the speaker's indication to belong to a certain group. ♦*The politician's speech was nothing but a lot of misleading statements and phony promises hidden in a bunch of buzz words.*

by a long shot *adv. phr., informal* By a big difference; by far.— Used to add emphasis. ◆*Bert was the best swimmer in the race, by a long shot.* ◆*Our team didn't win—not by a long shot.*

by and large *adv. phr.* As it most often happens; more often than not; usually; mostly. ◆*There were bad days, but it was a pleasant summer, by and large.* ◆*By and large, women can bear pain better than men.*

by chance *adv. phr.* Without any cause or reason; by accident; accidentally. ◆*Tom met Bill by chance.* ◆*The apple fell by chance on Bobby's head.*

by choice *adv. phr.* As a result of choosing because of wanting to; freely. ◆*John helped his father by choice.*

by dint of *prep.* By the exertion of; by the use of; through. ◆*His success in college was largely by dint of hard study.*

by ear *adv. phr.* **1.** By sound, without ever reading the printed music of the piece being played. ◆*The church choir sang the hymns by ear.* **2.** Waiting to see what will happen. ◆*I don't want to plan now; let's just play it by ear.*

by far *adv. phr.* By a large difference; much. ◆*His work was better by far than that of any other printer in the city.* ◆*The old road is prettier, but it is by far the longer way.*

by fits and starts *or* **jerks** *adv. phr.* With many stops and starts, a little now and a little more later; not all the time; irregularly. ◆*You will never get anywhere if you study just by fits and starts.*

by heart *adv. phr.* By exact memorizing; so well that you remember it; by memory. ◆*The pupils learned many poems by heart.*

by hook or by crook *adv. phr.* By honest or dishonest ways in any way necessary. ◆*The wolf tried to get the little pigs by hook or by crook.*

by leaps and bounds *adv. phr.* With long steps; very rapidly. ◆*The school enrollment was going up by leaps and bounds.*

by means of *prep.* By the use of; with the help of. ◆*By means of monthly payments, people can buy more than in the past.*

by mistake *adv. phr.* As the result of a mistake; through error. ◆*He picked up the wrong hat by mistake.*

B.Y.O. *(Abbreviation) informal* Bring Your Own. Said of a kind of party where the host or hostess does not provide the drinks or food but people bring their own.

B.Y.O.B. *(Abbreviation) informal* Bring Your Own Bottle. Frequently written on invitations for the kind of party where people bring their own liquor.

by oneself *adv. phr.* **1.** Without any others around; separate from others; alone. ◆*The house stood by itself on a hill.* ◆*Tom liked to go walking by himself.* **2.** Without the help of anyone else; by your own work only. ◆*John built a flying model airplane by himself.*

by the dozen *or* **by the hundred** *or* **by the thousand** *adv. phr.* Very many at one time; in great numbers. ◆*Tommy ate cookies by the dozen.* Often used in the plural, meaning even larger numbers. ◆*The ants arrived at the picnic by the hundreds.* ◆*The enemy attacked the fort by the thousands.*

by the piece *adv. phr.* Counted one piece at a time, separately for each single piece. ◆*John bought boxes full of bags of potato chips and sold them by the piece.*

by the same token *adv. phr.* Apropos of which; this reminds me of another thing; actually this is similar to what was talked about before. ◆*By the same token, let me mention that not only is the entire state budget shot, but the university won't be getting any money either.*

by the skin of one's teeth *adv. phr.* By a narrow margin; with no room to spare; barely. ◆*The drowning man struggled, and I got him to land by the skin of my teeth.* ◆*She passed English by the skin of her teeth.*

by the sweat of one's brow *adv. phr.* By hard work; by tiring effort; laboriously. ◆*Even with modern labor-saving machinery, the farmer makes his living by the sweat of his brow.*

by the way *also* **by the bye** *adv. phr.* Just as some added fact or news; as something else that I

think of.—Used to introduce something related to the general subject, or brought to mind by it. ◆*We shall expect you; by the way, dinner will be at eight.* ◆*I was reading when the earthquake occurred, and, by the way, it was* The Last Days of Pompeii *that I was reading.*

by turns *adv. phr.* First one and then another in a regular way; one substituting for or following another according to a repeated plan. ◆*On the drive to Chicago, the three men took the wheel by turns.*

by virtue of *also* **in virtue of** *prep.* On the strength of; because of; by reason of. ◆*By virtue of his high rank and position, the president takes social leadership over almost everyone else.*

by way of *prep.* **1.** For the sake or purpose of; as. ◆*By way of example, he described his own experience.* **2.** Through; by a route including; via. ◆*He went from New York to San Francisco by way of Chicago.*

by word of mouth *adv. phr.* From person to person by the spoken word; orally. ◆*The news got around by word of mouth.* ◆*The message reached him quietly by word of mouth.*

call a spade a spade *v. phr.* To call a person or thing a name that is true but not polite; speak bluntly; use the plainest language. ◆*A boy took some money from Dick's desk and said he borrowed it, but I told him he stole it; I believe in calling a spade a spade.*

call girl *n., slang* A prostitute catering to wealthy clientele, especially one who is contacted by telephone for an appointment. ◆*Rush Street is full of call girls.*

calling down *also* **dressing down** *n. phr., informal* A scolding; reprimand. ◆*The judge gave the boy a calling down for speeding.*

call in question *or* **call into question** *or* **call in doubt** *v. phr.* To say (something) may be a mistake; express doubt about; question. ◆*Bill called in question Ed's remark that basketball is safer than football.*

call it a day *v. phr.* To declare that a given day's work has been accomplished and go home; to quit for the day. ◆ *"Let's call it a day," the boss said, "and go out for a drink."*

call it a night *v. phr.* To declare that an evening party or other activity conducted late in the day is finished. ◆*I am so tired that I am going to call it a night and go to bed.*

call it quits *v. phr., informal* **1.** To decide to stop what you are doing; quit. ◆*When Tom had painted half the garage, he called it quits.* **2.** To agree that each side in a fight is satisfied; stop fighting because a wrong has been paid back; say things

are even. ◆*Pete called Tom a bad name, and they fought till Tom gave Pete a bloody nose; then they called it quits.* **3.** To cultivate a habit no longer. ◆ *"Yes, I called it quits with cigarettes three years ago."*

call names *v. phr.* To use ugly or unkind words when speaking to someone or when talking about someone.—Usually used by or to children. ◆*Bill got so mad he started calling Frank names.*

call off *v.* To stop (something planned); quit; cancel. ◆*The baseball game was called off because of rain.*

call on *or* **call upon** *v.* **1.** To make a call upon; visit. ◆*Mr. Brown called on an old friend while he was in the city.* **2.** To ask for help. ◆*He called on a friend to give him money for the bus fare to his home.*

call one's bluff *v. phr., informal* To ask someone to prove what he says he can or will do. (Originally from the card game of poker.) ◆*Tom said he could jump twenty feet and so Dick called his bluff and said "Let's see you do it!"*

call one's shot *v. phr.* **1.** To tell before firing where a bullet will hit. ◆*An expert rifleman can call his shot regularly.* ◆*The wind was strong and John couldn't call his shots.* **2.** *or* **call the turn** To tell in advance the result of something before you do it. ◆*Mary won three games in a row, just as she said she would. She called her turns well.*

call on the carpet *v. phr., informal* To call (a person) before an authority (as a boss or teacher) for a scolding or reprimand. ♦*The worker was called on the carpet by the boss for sleeping on the job.*

call the roll *v. phr.* To read out the names on a certain list, usually in alphabetical order. ♦*The sergeant called the roll of the newly enlisted volunteers in the army.*

call the shots *v. phr., informal* To give orders; be in charge; direct; control. ♦*Bob is a first-rate leader who knows how to call the shots.*

call the tune *v. phr., informal* To be in control; give orders or directions; command. ♦*Bill was president of the club but Jim was secretary and called the tune.*

call to account *v. phr.* **1.** To ask (someone) to explain why he did something wrong (as breaking a rule). ♦*The principal called Jim to account after Jim left school early without permission.* **2.** To scold (as for wrong conduct); reprimand. ♦*The father called his son to account for disobeying him.*

call to arms *v. phr.* To summon into the army. ♦*During World War II millions of Americans were called to arms to fight for their country.*

call to mind *v. phr.* To remember; cause to remember. ♦*Your story calls to mind a similar event that happened to us a few years back.*

call to order *v. phr.* **1.** To open (a meeting) formally. ♦*The chairman called the committee to order.* ♦*The president pounded with his gavel to call the convention to order.* **2.** To warn not to break the rules of a meeting.

♦*The judge called the people in the court room to order when they talked too loud.*

call out *v. phr.* **1.** To shout; speak loudly. ♦*My name was called out several times, but I was unable to hear it.* **2.** To summon someone. ♦*If the rioting continues, the governor will have to call out the National Guard.*

call up *v.* (stress on *up*) **1.** To make someone think of; bring to mind; remind. ♦*The picture of the Capitol called up memories of our class trip.* **2.** To tell to come (as before a court). ♦*The district attorney called up three witnesses.* **3.** To bring together for a purpose; bring into action. ♦*Jim called up all his strength, pushed past the players blocking him, and ran for a touchdown.* ♦*The army called up its reserves when war seemed near.* **4.** To call on the telephone. ♦*She called up a friend just for a chat.*

call-up *n. phr.* (stress on *call*) An occasional invitee from another or a junior group to play in another sports club. ♦*"Who is that player?" "He's a call-up from the minor league."*

calm down *v. phr.* To become quiet; relax. ♦*"Calm down, Mr. Smith," the doctor said with a reassuring smile. "You are going to live a long time."*

cancer stick *n., slang* A cigarette. ♦*Throw away that cancer stick! Smoking is bad for you!*

canned laughter *n., informal* The sounds of laughter heard on certain television programs that were obviously not recorded in front of a live audience and are played for the benefit of the audience from a stereo track to

underscore the funny points.
♦ *"How can there be an audience in this show when it is taking place in the jungle?—Why, it's canned laughter you're hearing."*

canned music *n.* Recorded music, as opposed to music played live. ♦ *"Let us go to a real concert, honey," Mike said. "I am tired of all this canned music we've been listening to."*

can of worms *n., slang, informal* 1. A complex problem, or complicated situation. ♦ *Let's not get into big city politics—that's a different can of worms.* 2. A very restless, jittery person. ♦ *Joe can't sit still for a minute—he is a can of worms.*

can't make an omelette without breaking (some) eggs To achieve a certain goal one must sometimes incur damage, experience difficulties, or make sacrifices.—A proverb. ♦ *When we drove across the country, we put a lot of mileage on our car and had a flat tire, but it was a pleasant trip. "Well, you can't make an omelette without breaking some eggs," my wife said with a smile.*

can't make bricks without straw Often heard when one sees someone trying to produce something without the proper ingredients, no matter how insignificant they may seem.—A proverb. ♦ *That fancy new printer of yours won't work without toner. Go and get some—you can't make bricks without straw, you know!*

can't see the wood for the trees *or* **can't see the woods for the trees** *or* **can't see the forest for the trees** *v. phr.* To be unable to

judge or understand the whole because of attention to the parts; criticize small things and not see the value or the aim of the future achievement. ♦ *Teachers sometimes notice language errors and do not see the good ideas in a composition; they cannot see the woods for the trees.*

card up one's sleeve *n. phr., informal* Another help, plan, or argument kept back and produced if needed; another way to do something. ♦ *John knew his mother would lend him money if necessary, but he kept that card up his sleeve.* ♦ *Bill always has a card up his sleeve, so when his first plan failed he tried another.* Compare ACE IN THE HOLE 2.

car pool *n.* A group of people who take turns driving each other to work or on some other regular trip. ♦ *It was John's father's week to drive his own car in the car pool.*

carrot and stick *n. phr.* The promise of reward and threat of punishment, both at the same time. ♦ *John's father used the carrot and stick when he talked about his low grades.*

carry a torch *or* **carry the torch** *v. phr.* 1. To show great and unchanging loyalty to a cause or a person. ♦ *Although the others gave up fighting for their rights, John continued to carry the torch.* 2. *informal* To be in love, usually without success or return. ♦ *He is carrying a torch for Anna, even though she is in love with someone else.*

carry a tune *v. phr.* To sing the right notes without catching any false ones. ♦ *Al is a wonderful fellow, but he sure can't* *carry a tune and his singing is a pain to listen to.*

carry away *v.* To cause very strong feeling; excite or delight to the loss of cool judgment. ♦*The music carried her away.* ♦*He let his anger carry him away.*—Often used in the passive. ♦*She was carried away by the man's charm.*

carry coals to Newcastle *v. phr.* To do something unnecessary; bring or furnish something of which there is plenty. ♦*The man who waters his grass after a good rain is carrying coals to Newcastle.* [Newcastle is an English city near many coal mines, and coal is sent out from there to other places.]

carrying charge *n.* An extra cost added to the price of something bought on weekly or monthly payments. ♦*The price of the bicycle was $50. Jim bought it for $5.00 a month for ten months plus a carrying charge of $1 a month.*

carry off *v.* **1.** To cause death of; kill. ♦*Years ago smallpox carried off hundreds of Indians of the Sioux tribe.* Compare WIPE OUT. **2.** To succeed in winning. ♦*Jim carried off two gold medals in the track meet.* **3.** To succeed somewhat unexpectedly in. ♦*The spy planned to deceive the enemy soldiers and carried it off very well.*

carry on *v.* **1.** To work at; be busy with; manage. ♦*Bill and his father carried on a hardware business.* ♦*Mr. Jones and Mr. Smith carried on a long correspondence with each other.* **2.** To keep doing as before; continue. ♦*After his father died, Bill carried on with the busi-*

ness. **3a.** *informal* To behave in a noisy, foolish, and troublesome manner. ♦*The boys carried on in the swimming pool until the lifeguard ordered them out.* **3b.** *informal* To make too great a show of feeling, such as anger, grief, and pain. ♦*John carried on for ten minutes after he hit his thumb with the hammer.* **4.** *informal* To act in an immoral or scandalous way; act disgracefully. ♦*The neighbors said that he was carrying on with an underage girl.*

carry one's cross *or (literary)* **bear one's cross** *v. phr.* To live with pain or trouble; keep on even though you suffer or have trouble. ♦*Weak ankles are a cross Joe carries while the other boys play basketball.*

carry out *v.* To put into action; follow; execute. ♦*The generals were determined to carry out their plans to defeat the enemy.*

carry over *v.* **1.** To save for another time. ♦*What you learn in school should carry over into adult life.* **2.** To transfer (as a figure) from one column, page, or book to another. ♦*When he added up the figures, he carried over the total into the next year's account book.* **3.** To continue in another place. ♦*The story was carried over to the next page.*

carry the ball *v. phr., informal* To take the most important or difficult part in an action or business. ♦*When the going is rough, Fred can always be depended on to carry the ball.*

carry the day *v. phr., informal* To win completely; to succeed in getting one's aim accomplished. ♦*The defense attor-*

ney's summary before the jury helped him carry the day.

carry through v. **1a.** To put into action. ◆*Mr. Green was not able to carry through his plans for a hike because he broke his leg.* **1b.** To do something you have planned; put a plan into action. ◆*Jean makes good plans but she cannot carry through with any of them.* **2.** To keep (someone) from failing or stopping; bring through; help. ◆*When the tire blew out, the rules Jim had learned in driving class carried him through safely.*

carry weight n. To be influential; have significance and/or clout; impress. ◆*A letter of recommendation from a full professor carries more weight than a letter from an assistant professor.*

cart before the horse (to put) n. phr., informal Things in wrong order; something backwards or mixed up.—An overused expression. Usually used with put but sometimes with get or have. ◆*To get married first and then get a job is getting the cart before the horse.*

case in point n. phr. An example that proves something or helps to make something clearer. ◆*An American can rise from the humblest beginnings to become president. Abraham Lincoln is a case in point.*

case the joint v. phr., slang **1.** To study the layout of a place one wishes to burglarize. ◆*The hooded criminals carefully cased the joint before robbing the neighborhood bank.* **2.** To familiarize oneself with a potential workplace or vacation spot as a matter of preliminary planning. ◆*"Hello Fred,"* he

said. *"Are you working here now?"* *"No, not yet,"* Fred answered. *"I am merely casing the joint."*

cash-and-carry[1] adj. Selling things for cash money only and letting the customer carry them home, not having the store deliver them; *also* sold in this way. ◆*This is a cash-and-carry store only.* ◆*You can save money at a cash-and-carry sale.*

cash-and-carry[2] adv. With no credit, no time payments, and no deliveries. ◆*Some stores sell cash-and-carry only.* ◆*It is cheaper to buy cash-and-carry.*

cash crop n. A crop grown to be sold. ◆*Cotton is a cash crop in the South.* ◆*They raise potatoes to eat, but tobacco is their cash crop.*

cash in v. **1.** To exchange (as poker chips or bonds) for the value in money. ◆*When the card game ended, the players cashed in their chips and went home.* **2.** or **cash in one's chips** slang To die. ◆*When the outlaw cashed in his chips, he was buried with his boots on.*

cash in on v., informal To see (a chance) and profit by it; take advantage of (an opportunity or happening). ◆*Mr. Brown cashed in on people's great interest in camping and sold three hundred tents.*

cash on the barrelhead n. phr., informal Money paid at once; money paid when something is bought. ◆*Father paid cash on the barrelhead for a new car.* ◆*Some lawyers want cash on the barrelhead.*

cast or **shed** or **throw light upon** v. phr. To explain; illuminate; clarify. ◆*The letters that were found* suddenly cast a new light on the circumstances of Tom's disappearance. ◆*Einstein's General Theory of Relativity threw light upon the enigma of our universe.*

cast off *v.* **1a.** *or* **cast loose** To unfasten; untie; let loose (as a rope holding a boat). ◆*The captain of the boat cast off the line and we were soon out in open water.* **1b.** To untie a rope holding a boat or something suggesting a boat. ◆*We cast off and set sail at 6 A.M.* **2.** To knit the last row of stitches. ◆*When she had knitted the twentieth row of stitches she cast off.* **3.** To say that you do not know (someone) any more; not accept as a relative or friend. ◆*Mr. Jones cast off his daughter when she married against his wishes.*

cast pearls before swine *or* **cast one's pearls before swine** *n. phr., literary* To waste good acts or valuable things on someone who won't understand or be thankful for them, just as pigs won't appreciate pearls.— Often used in negative sentences. ◆*I won't waste good advice on John any more because he never listens to it. I won't cast pearls before swine.*

cast the first stone *v. phr., biblical* To be the first to blame someone, lead accusers against a wrongdoer. ◆*Jesus said that a person who was without sin could cast the first stone.*

catch-as-catch-can[1] *adv. phr.* In a free manner; in any way possible; in the best way you can. ◆*On moving day everything is packed and we eat meals catch-as-catch-can.*

catch-as-catch-can[2] *adj. phr.* Using any means or method; unplanned; free. ◆*Politics is rather a catch-as-catch-can business.*

catch cold *v. phr.* **1.** *or* **take cold** To get a common cold-weather sickness that causes a running nose, sneezing, and sometimes sore throat and fever or other symptoms. ◆*Don't get your feet wet or you'll catch cold.* **2.** *informal* To catch unprepared or not ready for a question or unexpected happening. ◆*I had not studied my lesson carefully, and the teacher's question caught me cold.*

catch (someone) dead *v. phr., informal* To see or hear (someone) in an embarrassing act or place at any time. Used in the negative usually in the passive. ◆*John wouldn't be caught dead in the necktie he got for Christmas.*

catch fire *v. phr.* **1.** To begin to burn. ◆*When he dropped a match in the leaves, they caught fire.* **2.** To become excited. ◆*The audience caught fire at the speaker's words and began to cheer.*

catch hold of *v. phr.* To grasp a person or a thing. ◆*"I've been trying to catch hold of you all week," John said, "but you were out of town."* ◆*The mountain climber successfully caught hold of his friend's hand and thereby saved his life.*

catch it *or* **get it** *v. phr., informal* To be scolded or punished.— Usually used of children. ◆*John knew he would catch it when he came home late for supper.* ◆*Wow, Johnny! When your mother sees those torn pants, you're going to get it.*

catch off balance *v. phr.* To confront someone with physical force or with a statement or question he or she is not prepared to answer or deal with; to exploit the disadvantage of another. ♦*Your question has caught me off balance; please give me some time to think about your problem.*

catch off guard *v. phr.* To challenge or confront a person at a time of lack of preparedness or sufficient care. ♦*The suspect was caught off guard by the detective and confessed where he had hidden the stolen car.*

catch on *v., informal* **1.** To understand; learn about.—Often used with *to.* ♦*You'll catch on to the job after you've been here awhile.* ♦*Don't play any tricks on Joe. When he catches on, he will beat you.* **2.** To become popular; be done or used by many people. ♦*The song caught on and was sung and played everywhere.* **3.** To be hired; get a job. ♦*The ball player caught on with a big league team last year.*

catch one's breath *v. phr.* **1.** To breathe in suddenly with fear or surprise. ♦*The beauty of the scene made him catch his breath.* **2a.** To rest and get back your normal breathing, as after running. ♦*After running to the bus stop, we sat down to catch our breath.* **2b.** To relax for a moment after any work. ♦*After the day's work we sat down over coffee to catch our breath.*

catch one's death of *or* **take one's death of** *v. phr., informal* To become very ill with (a cold, pneumonia, flu). ♦*Johnny fell in the icy water and almost took*

his death of cold. Sometimes used in the short form *"catch your death."* ♦*"Johnny! Come right in here and put your coat and hat on. You'll catch your death!"*

catch one's eye *v. phr.* To attract your attention. ♦*I caught his eye as he moved through the crowd, and waved at him to come over.* ♦*The dress in the window caught her eye when she passed the store.*

catch red-handed *v. phr.* To apprehend a person during the act of committing an illicit or criminal act. ♦*Al was caught red-handed at the local store when he was trying to walk out with a new camera he had not paid for.*

catch sight of *v. phr.* To see suddenly or unexpectedly. ♦*Allan caught sight of a kingbird in a maple tree.*

catch some rays *v. phr., slang, informal* To get tanned while sunbathing. ♦*Tomorrow I'll go to the beach and try to catch some rays.*

catch some Z's *v. phr., slang, informal* To take a nap, to go to sleep. (Because of the *z* sound resembling snoring.) ♦*I want to hit the sack and catch some Z's.*

catch-22 *n., informal* From Joseph Heller's novel *Catch-22,* set in World War II. **1.** A regulation or situation that is self-contradictory or that conflicts with another regulation. In Heller's book it referred to the regulation that flight crews must report for duty unless excused for reasons of insanity, but that any one claiming such an excuse must, by definition, be sane. ♦*Government rules* *require workers to expose any wrongdoing in their office, but the Catch-22 prevents them from doing so, because they are not allowed to disclose any information about their work.* 2. A paradoxical situation. *The Catch-22 of job-hunting was that the factory wanted to hire only workers who had experience making computers but the only way to get the experience was by working at the computer factory.*

catch up *v.* 1. To take or pick up suddenly; grab (something). *She caught up the book from the table and ran out of the room.* 2. To capture or trap (someone) in a situation; concern or interest very much.— Usually used in the passive with *in*. *We were so caught up in the movie we forgot what time it was.* 3. To go fast enough or do enough so as not to be behind; overtake; come even.—Often used with *to* or *with*. *Johnny ran hard and tried to catch up to his friends.* *Mary missed two weeks of school; she must work hard to catch up with her class.* Compare UP TO. 4. To find out about or get proof to punish or arrest.—Usually used with *with*. *A man told the police where the robbers were hiding, so the police finally caught up with them.* 5. To result in something bad; bring punishment.— Usually used with *with*. *The boy's fighting caught up with him and he was expelled from school.* 6. To finish; not lose or be behind.—Used with *on* and often in the phrase *get caught up on.* *Frank stayed up late to get caught up on his homework.*

catch with one's pants down *v. phr., slang* To surprise someone in an embarrassing position or guilty act. *They thought they could succeed in the robbery, but they got caught with their pants down.*

cat got one's tongue *v. phr.* You are not able or willing to talk because of shyness. Usually used about children or as a question to children. *The little girl had a poem to recite, but the cat got her tongue.*

cathouse *n., slang* A house of ill repute, a house of prostitution. *Massage parlors are frequently cathouses in disguise.*

caught short *adj. phr., informal* Not having enough of something when you need it. *Mrs. Ford was caught short when the newspaper boy came for his money a day early.* *The man was caught short of clothes when he had to go on a trip.*

cave in *v.* 1. To fall or collapse inward. *The mine caved in and crushed three miners.* *Don't climb on that old roof. It might cave in.* 2. *informal* To weaken and be forced to give up. *The children begged their father to take them to the circus until he caved in.* *After the atomic bomb, Japan caved in and the war ceased.*

cease fire *v.* To give a military command ordering soldiers to stop shooting. *"Cease fire!" the captain cried, and the shooting stopped.*

cease-fire *n.* A period of negotiated nonaggression, when the warring parties involved promise not to attack. *Unfortunately, the cease-fire in Bosnia was broken many times by all parties concerned.*

chain letter *n.* A letter which each person receiving it is asked to copy and send to several others. ♦*Most chain letters die out quickly.*

chain-smoke *v.* To smoke cigarettes or cigars one after another without stopping. ♦*Mr. Jones is very nervous. He chain-smokes cigars.* **chain smoker** *n.* ♦*Mr. Jones is a chain smoker.* **chain-smoking** *adj. or n.* ♦*Chain smoking is very dangerous to health.*

chain stores *n.* A series of stores in different locations, joined together under one ownership and general management. ♦*The goods in chain stores tend to be more uniform than in independent ones.*

chalk up *v., informal* **1.** To write down as part of a score; record. ♦*The scorekeeper chalked up one more point for the home team.* **2.** To make (a score or part of a score); score. ♦*The team chalked up another victory.* ♦*Bob chalked up a home run and two base hits in the game.* ♦*Mary chalked up good grades this term.*

champ at the bit *v. phr.* To be eager to begin; be tired of being held back; want to start. ♦*The horses were champing at the bit, anxious to start racing.*

chance it *v. phr.* To be willing to risk an action whose outcome is uncertain. ♦*"Should we take the boat out in such stormy weather?" Jim asked. "We can chance it," Tony replied. "We have enough experience."*

chance of a snowball in hell *or* **chance of a fart in a windstorm** *slang; the second version is vulgar, hence avoidable* To have practically no chance at all of accomplishing what one has set out to do.—*A proverb.* ♦*If we continue to move as slowly as we do, we'll have the chance of a snowball in hell to arrive at the Olympics in time.*

chance on *also* **chance upon** *v.* To happen to find or meet; find or meet by accident. ♦*On our vacation we chanced upon an interesting antique store.* ♦*Mary dropped her ring in the yard, and Mother chanced on it as she was raking.*

change hands *v. phr.* To change or transfer ownership. ♦*Ever since our apartment building changed hands, things are working a lot better.*

change horses in the middle of a stream *or* **change horses in midstream** *v. phr.* To make new plans or choose a new leader in the middle of an important activity. ♦*When a new president is to be elected during a war, the people may decide not to change horses in the middle of a stream.*

change off *v., informal* To take turns doing something; alternate. ♦*John and Bill changed off at riding the bicycle.*

change of heart *n. phr.* A change in the way one feels or thinks about a given task, idea or problem to be solved. ♦*Joan had a change of heart and suddenly broke off her engagement to Tim.*

change of life *n. phr.* The menopause (primarily in women). ♦*Women usually under-*

go a change of life in their for-ties or fifties.

change of pace *n. phr.* A quick change in what you are doing. ♦*John studied for three hours and then read a comic book for a change of pace.*

change one's mind *v. phr.* To alter one's opinion or judgment on a given issue. ♦*I used to hate Chicago, but as the years passed I gradually changed my mind and now I actually love living here.*

change one's tune *v. phr.*, *informal* To make a change in your story, statement, or claim; change your way of acting. ♦*The man said he was innocent, but when they found the stolen money in his pocket he changed his tune.*

charge account *n.* An agreement with a store through which you can buy things and pay for them later. ♦*Mother bought a new dress on her charge account.*

charge something to something *v.* **1.** To place the blame on; make responsible for. ♦*John failed to win a prize, but he charged it to his lack of experi-ence.* **2.** To buy something on the credit of. ♦*Mrs. Smith bought a new pocketbook and charged it to her husband.*

charge up *v. phr.* **1.** To submit to a flow of electricity in order to make functional. ♦*I mustn't for-get to charge up my razor before we go on our trip.* **2.** To use up all the available credit one has on one's credit card(s). ♦*"Let's charge dinner on the Master Card,"* Jane said. *"Unfortunately I can't,"* Jim replied. *"All of my credit cards are completely charged up."*

charge with *v. phr.* To accuse someone in a court of law. ♦*The criminal was charged with aggravated kidnapping across a state line.*

charmed life *n.* A life often saved from danger; a life full of lucky escapes. ♦*He was in two air-plane accidents, but he had a charmed life.*

cheapskate *n.*, *informal* A selfish or stingy person; a person who will not spend much.—An insulting term. ♦*None of the girls like to go out on a date with him because he is a cheap-skate.*

cheat on someone or **something** *v. phr.* **1.** To be unfaithful to one's husband, wife, or "signif-icant other." ♦*"Do you think Albert cheats on Vanessa?" "Well, in fact, she cheats on him as well."* **2.** To use crib notes during a final examina-tion, a cause for dismissal from most colleges and universities. ♦*Oliver was thrown out of West Point Military Academy because he cheated on his final math exam.*

check in *v.* **1a.** To sign your name (as at a hotel or convention). ♦*The last guests to reach the hotel checked in at 12 o'clock.* **1b.** *informal* To arrive. ♦*The friends we had invited did not check in until Saturday.* **2.** To receive (something) back and make a record of it. ♦*The coach checked in the football uniforms at the end of the school year.* ♦*The students put their books on the library desk, and the librarian checked them in.*

check off *v.* To put a mark beside (the name of a person or thing on a list) to show that it has been counted. ◆*The teacher checked off each pupil as he got on the bus.*

check on someone/thing *or* **check up on someone/thing** *v.* To try to find out the truth or rightness of; make sure of; examine; inspect; investigate. ◆*We checked on Dan's age by getting his birth record.*

check out *v.* **1a.** To pay your hotel bill and leave. ◆*The last guests checked out of their rooms in the morning.* **1b.** *informal* To go away; leave. ◆*I hoped our guest would stay but he had to leave, check out before Monday.* **2a.** To make a list or record of. ◆*They checked out all the goods in the store.* **2b.** To give or lend (something) and make a record of it. ◆*The boss checked out the tools to the workmen as they came to work.* **2c.** To get (something) after a record has been made of it. ◆*I checked out a book from the library.* **3.** *informal* To test (something, like a part of a motor). ◆*The mechanic checked out the car battery.* ◆*"He checked out from the motel at nine," said the detective, "then he checked out the air in the car tires and his list of local clients."* **4.** *slang* To die. ◆*He seemed too young to check out.*

check up *v.* (stress on *up*) To find out or try to find out the truth or correctness of something; make sure of something; investigate. ◆*Mrs. Brown thought she had heard a burglar in the house, so Mr. Brown checked up, but found nobody.* ◆*Bill thought he had a date with Janie, but phoned her to check up.*

checkup *n.* (stress on *check*) A periodic examination by a physician or of some equipment by a mechanic. ◆*I am overdue for my annual physical checkup.* ◆*I need to take my car in for a checkup.*

check with *v. phr.* **1.** To consult. ◆*I want to check with my lawyer before I sign the papers.* **2.** To agree with. ◆*Does my reconciliation of our account check with the bank statement?*

cheer up *v.* **1.** To feel happy; stop being sad or discouraged; become hopeful, joyous, or glad. ◆*Jones was sad at losing the business, but he cheered up at the sight of his daughter.* ◆*Cheer up! The worst is over.* **2.** To make cheerful or happy. ◆*The support of the students cheered up the losing team and they played harder and won.* ◆*We went to the hospital to cheer up a sick friend.* ◆*Flowers cheer up a room.*

cheesecake *n., slang, informal* A showing of the legs of an attractive woman or a display of her breasts as in certain magazines known as cheesecake magazines. ◆*Photographer to model: "Give us some cheesecake in that pose!"*

chew out *v., slang* To scold roughly. ◆*The boy's father chewed him out for staying up late.* ◆*The coach chews out lazy players.*

chew the fat *or* **chew the rag** *v. phr., slang* To talk together in an idle, friendly fashion; chat. ◆*We used to meet after work, and chew the fat over coffee and doughnuts.* ◆*The old man would chew the rag for hours* *with anyone who would join him.*

chew the scenery *v. phr., slang* To act overemotionally in a situation where it is inappropriate; to engage in histrionics. ♦*I don't know if Joe was sincere about our house, but he sure chewed up the scenery!*

chicken-brained *adj.* Stupid; narrow-minded; unimaginative. ♦*I can't understand how a bright woman like Helen can date such a chicken-brained guy as Oliver.*

chicken feed *n., slang* A very small sum of money. ♦*John and Bill worked very hard, but they were only paid chicken feed.* ♦*Mr. Jones is so rich he thinks a thousand dollars is chicken feed.*

chicken-hearted *adj.* Cowardly; excessively timid. ♦*"Come on, let's get on that roller coaster,"* she cried. *"Don't be so chicken-hearted."*

chicken-livered *adj., slang, colloquial* Easily scared; cowardly. ♦*Joe sure is a chicken-livered guy.*

chicken out *v. phr., informal* To stop doing something because of fear; to decide not to do something after all even though previously having decided to try it. ♦*I used to ride a motorcycle on the highway, but I've chickened out.*

chickens come home to roost *informal* Words or acts come back to cause trouble for a person; something bad you said or did receives punishment; you get the punishment that you deserve. ♦*Fred's chickens finally came home to roost today. He was late so often that the*

teacher made him go to the principal.—Often used in a short form. ♦*Mary's selfishness will come home to roost some day.*

chicken switch *n., slang, Space English* **1.** The emergency eject button used by test pilots in fast and high flying aircraft by means of which they can parachute to safety if the engine fails; later adopted by astronauts in space capsules. ♦*Don't pull the chicken switch, unless absolutely necessary.* **2.** The panic button; a panicky reaction to an unforeseen situation, such as unreasonable or hysterical telephone calls to friends for help. ♦*Joe pulled the chicken switch on his neighbor when the grease started burning in the kitchen.*

child's play *adj.* Easy; requiring no effort. ♦*Mary's work as a volunteer social worker is so agreeable to her that she thinks of it as child's play.*

chime in *v.* **1.** *informal* To join in. ♦*The whole group chimed in on the chorus.* ♦*When the argument got hot, John chimed in.* **2.** To agree; go well together.— Usually used with *with.* ♦*Dick was happy, and the holiday music chimed in with his feelings.*

chip in *or* **kick in** *v., informal* To give together with others, contribute. ♦*The pupils chipped in a dime apiece for the teacher's Christmas present.* ♦*All the neighbors kicked in to help after the fire.*

chip off the old block *n. phr.* A person whose character traits closely resemble those of his parents. ♦*I hear that Tom plays* the violin in the orchestra his father conducts; he sure is a chip off the old block.

chip on one's shoulder *n. phr., informal* A quarrelsome nature; readiness to be angered. ◆He went through life with a chip on his shoulder. ◆Jim often gets into fights because he goes around with a chip on his shoulder.

choke off *v.* To put a sudden end to; stop abruptly or forcefully. ◆The war choked off diamond shipments from overseas.

choke up *v.* **1a.** To come near losing calmness or self-control from strong feeling; be upset by your feelings. ◆When one speaker after another praised John, he choked up and couldn't thank them. **1b.** *informal* To be unable to do well because of excitement or nervousness. ◆Bill was a good batter, but in the championship game he choked up and did poorly. **2.** To fill up; become clogged or blocked; become hard to pass through. ◆The channel had choked up with sand so that boats couldn't use it.

claim check *n.* A ticket needed to get back something. ◆The man at the parking lot gave Mrs. Collins a claim check.

clamp down *v., informal* To put on strict controls; enforce rules or laws. ◆After the explosion, police clamped down and let no more visitors inside the monument. ◆The school clamped down on smoking.

clam up *v., slang* To refuse to say anything more; stop talking. ◆The suspect clammed up, and the police could get no more information out of him.

clean bill of health *n. phr.* **1.** A certificate that a person or animal has no infectious disease. ◆The government doctor gave Jones a clean bill of health when he entered the country. **2.** *informal* A report that a person is free of guilt or fault. ◆The stranger was suspected in the bank robbery, but the police gave him a clean bill of health.

clean break *n. phr.* A complete separation. ◆Tom made a clean break with his former girlfriends before marrying Pamela.

clean out *v.* **1.** *slang* To take everything from; empty; strip. ◆George's friends cleaned him out when they were playing cards last night. ◆The sudden demand for paper plates soon cleaned out the stores. **2.** *informal* To get rid of; remove; dismiss. ◆The new mayor promised to clean the crooks out of the city government.

clean slate *n. phr.* A record of nothing but good conduct, without any errors or bad deeds; past acts that are all good without any bad ones. ◆Johnny was sent to the principal for whispering. He had a clean slate so the principal did not punish him.

clean up *v. phr.* **1.** To wash and make oneself presentable. ◆After quitting for the day in the garage, Tim decided to clean up and put on a clean shirt. **2.** To finish; terminate. ◆The secretary promised her boss to clean up all the unfinished work before leaving on her Florida vacation. **3.** *informal* To make a large profit. ◆The clever investors cleaned up on the stock market last week.

clean-up n. **1.** An act of removing all the dirt from a given set of objects. ♦What this filthy room needs is an honest clean-up. **2.** The elimination of pockets of resistance during warfare or a police raid. ♦The FBI conducted a clean-up against the drug pushers in our district.

clear up v. **1.** To make plain or clear; explain; solve. ♦The teacher cleared up the harder parts of the story. ♦Maybe we can clear up your problem. **2.** To become clear. ♦The weather cleared up after the storm. **3.** To cure. ♦The pills cleared up his stomach trouble. **4.** To put back into a normal, proper, or healthy state. ♦The doctor can give you something to clear up your skin. ♦Susan cleared up the room. **5.** To become cured. ♦This skin trouble will clear up in a day or two.

cliff dweller n., slang, informal A city person who lives on a very high floor in an apartment building. ♦Joe and Nancy have become cliff dwellers—they moved up to the 30th floor.

cliff-hanger n., informal A sports event or a movie in which the outcome is uncertain to the very end, keeping the spectators in great suspense and excitement. ♦Did you see The Fugitive? It's a regular cliff-hanger.

clip joint n. slang A low-class night club or other business where people are cheated. ♦The man got drunk and lost all his money in a clip joint.

clip one's wings v. phr. To limit or hold you back, bring you under control; prevent your success. ♦When the new president tried to become dictator, the generals soon clipped his wings.

cloak-and-dagger adj. Of or about spies and secret agents. ♦It was a cloak-and-dagger story about some spies who tried to steal atomic secrets.

close call or **shave** n. phr. A narrow escape. ♦That sure was a close call when that truck came near us from the right! ♦When Tim fell off his bicycle in front of a bus, it was a very close shave.

closed book n. A secret; something not known or understood. ♦The man's early life is a closed book. ♦For Mary, science is a closed book. ♦The history of the town is a closed book.

closed-door adj. Away from the public; in private or in secret; limited to a few. ♦The officers of the club held a closed-door meeting. ♦The committee decided on a closed-door rule for the investigation.

close down or **shut down** v. To stop all working, as in a factory; stop work entirely; also: to stop operations in. ♦The factory closed down for Christmas. ♦The company shut down the condom plant for Easter.

closed shop n. phr. **1.** A plant or factory that employs only union workers. ♦Our firm has been fighting the closed shop policy for many years now. **2.** A profession or line of work dominated by followers of a certain mode of thinking and behaving that does not tolerate differing views or ideas. ♦Certain groups of psychologists, historians, and linguists often behave with a closed-shop mentality.

close finish *n. phr.* An exciting race or contest during which it is difficult to tell who will be the winner. ♦*The presidential election of 2000 between Republican George W. Bush and Democrat Al Gore was a very close finish.*

close in *v.* To come in nearer from all sides. ♦*We wanted the boat to reach shore before the fog closed in.*—Often used with *on*. ♦*The troops were closing in on the enemy.*

close its doors *v. phr.* 1. To keep someone or something from entering or joining; become closed. ♦*The club has closed its doors to new members.* 2. To fail as a business; go bankrupt. ♦*The fire was so damaging that the store had to close its doors.* ♦*Business was so poor that we had to close our doors after six months.*

close-knit *adj.* Closely joined together by ties of love, friendship, or common interest; close. ♦*The Joneses are a close-knit family.* ♦*The three boys are always together. They form a very close-knit group.*

close ranks *v. phr.* 1. To come close together in a line especially for fighting. ♦*The soldiers closed ranks and kept the enemy away from the bridge.* 2. To stop quarreling and work together; unite and fight together. ♦*The Democrats and Republicans closed ranks to win the war.* ♦*The leader asked the people to close ranks and plan a new school.*

close the books *v. phr.* To stop taking orders; end a bookkeeping period. ♦*The tickets were all sold, so the manager said to close the books. ♦*The department store closes its books on the 25th of each month.*

close the door *or* **bar the door** *or* **shut the door** *v. phr.* To prevent any more action or talk about a subject. ♦*The president's veto closed the door to any new attempt to pass the bill.* ♦*Joan was much hurt by what Mary said, and she closed the door on Mary's attempt to apologize.*

close to home *adv. phr.* Too near to someone's personal feelings, wishes, or interests. ♦*When John made fun of Bob's way of walking, he struck close to home.*

close-up *n.* A photograph, motion picture, or video camera shot taken at very close range. ♦*Directors of movies frequently show close-ups of the main characters.*

close up shop *v. phr.* 1. To shut a store at the end of a day's business, *also,* to end a business. ♦*The grocer closes up shop at 5 o'clock.* ♦*After 15 years in business at the same spot, the garage closed up shop.* 2. *informal* To stop some activity; finish what you are doing. ♦*After camping out for two weeks, the scouts took down their tents and closed up shop.* ♦*The committee finished its business and closed up shop.*

coast is clear No enemy or danger is in sight; there is no one to see you. ♦*When the teacher had disappeared around the corner, John said, "Come on, the coast is clear."* ♦*The men knew when the night watchman would pass. When he had gone, and the coast was clear, they robbed the safe.*

cock-and-bull story n. phr. An exaggerated or unbelievable story. ♦ "Stop feeding me such cock-and-bull stories," the detective said to the suspect.

cockeyed adj. Drunk; intoxicated. ♦ Frank has been drinking all day and, when we met, he was so cockeyed he forgot his own address.

cocksure adj. Overconfident; very sure. ♦ Paul was cocksure that it wasn't going to snow, but it snowed so much that we had to dig our way out of the house.

C.O.D. n. phr. Abbreviation of "cash on delivery." ♦ If you want to receive a piece of merchandise by mail and pay when you receive it, you place a C.O.D. order.

coffee break n. A short recess or time out from work in which to rest and drink coffee. ♦ The girls in the office take a coffee break in the middle of the morning and the afternoon.

coffin nail n., slang A cigarette. ♦ "I stopped smoking," Algernon said. "In fact, I haven't had a coffin nail in well over a year."

cold cash or **hard cash** n. Money that is paid at the time of purchase; real money; silver and bills. ♦ Mr. Jones bought a new car and paid cold cash for it. ♦ Some stores sell things only for cold cash.

cold feet n. phr., informal A loss of courage or nerve; a failure or loss of confidence in yourself. ♦ Ralph was going to ask Mary to dance with him but he got cold feet and didn't.

cold fish n., informal A queer person; a person who is unfriendly or does not mix with others. ♦ No one knows the new doctor, he is a cold fish. ♦ Nobody invites Eric to parties because he is a cold fish.

cold-shoulder v., informal To act towards a person; with dislike or scorn; be unfriendly to. ♦ It is impolite and unkind to cold-shoulder people.

cold shoulder n., informal Unfriendly treatment of a person, a showing of dislike for a person or of looking down on a person.—Used in the clichés give the cold shoulder or turn a cold shoulder to or get the cold shoulder. ♦ When Bob asked Mary for a date she gave him the cold shoulder.

cold snap n. A short time of quick change from warm weather to cold. ♦ The cold snap killed everything in the garden.

cold turkey adv., slang, informal 1. Abruptly and without medical aid to withdraw from the use of an addictive drug or from a serious drinking problem. ♦ Joe is a very brave guy; he kicked the habit cold turkey. 2. n. An instance of withdrawal from drugs, alcohol, or cigarette smoking. ♦ Joe did a cold turkey.

cold war n. A struggle that is carried on by other means and not by actual fighting; a war without shooting or bombing. ♦ After World War II, a cold war began between Russia and the United States.

collect dust v. phr. To sit in storage and remain unused. ♦ "What happened to your twenty-speed racing bike?" John asked. "It's just sitting in our old garage, collecting dust."

come about v. 1. To take place; happen; occur. ♦ Sometimes it is *hard to tell how a quarrel comes about.* ♦*When John woke up he was in the hospital, but he didn't know how that had come about.* 2. *nautical use* To change direction; to turn around. ♦*When you want to bring the sailing boat home, you first have to come about.*

come a cropper 1. To fall off your horse. ♦*John's horse stumbled, and John came a cropper.* 2. To fail. ♦*Mr. Brown did not have enough money to put into his business and it soon came a cropper.*

come across *v.* 1. *or* **run across** To find or meet by chance. ♦*He came across a dollar bill in the suit he was sending to the cleaner.* ♦*The other day I ran across a book that you might like.* ♦*I came across George at a party last week; it was the first time I had seen him in months.* 2. To give or do what is asked. ♦*The robber told the woman to come across with her purse.* ♦*For hours the police questioned the man suspected of kidnapping the child, and finally he came across with the story.*

come again *v., informal* Please repeat; please say that again.— Usually used as a command. ♦*"Harry has just come into a fortune," my wife said. "Come again?" I asked her, not believing it.* ♦*"Come again," said the hard-of-hearing man.*

come alive *or* **come to life** *v.* 1. *informal* To become alert or attentive; wake up and look alive; become active. ♦*When Mr. Simmons mentioned money, the boys came alive.* ♦*Bob pushed the starter button, and*

the engine came alive with a roar. 2. To look real; take on a bright, natural look. ♦*Under skillful lighting, the scene came alive.* ♦*The president came alive in the picture as the artist worked.*

come along *v.* To make progress; improve; succeed. ♦*He was coming along well after the operation.* ♦*Rose is coming right along on the piano.*

come a long way *v. phr.* To show much improvement; make great progress. ♦*The school has come a long way since its beginnings.* ♦*Little Jane has come a long way since she broke her leg.*

come apart at the seams *v. phr., slang, informal* To become upset to the point where one loses self-control and composure as if having suffered a sudden nervous breakdown. ♦*After his divorce Joe seemed to be coming apart at the seams.*

come at *v.* 1. To approach; come to or against; advance toward. ♦*The young boxer came at the champion cautiously.* 2. To understand (a word or idea) or master (a skill); succeed with. ♦*The sense of an unfamiliar word is hard to come at.*

come back *v., informal* (stress on *back*) 1. To reply; answer. ♦*The lawyer came back sharply in defense of his client.* ♦*No matter how the audience heckled him, the comedian always had an answer to come back with.* 2. To get a former place or position back; to reach again a place which you have lost. ♦*After a year off to have her baby, the singer came back to even greater fame.* ♦*It is hard for a* *retired prize fighter to come back and beat a younger man.*

comeback *n., v. phr., slang, citizen's band radio jargon* (stress on *come*) A return call. ♦*Thanks for your comeback.*

come back to earth *or* **come down to earth** *v. phr.* To return to the real world; stop imagining or dreaming; think and behave as usual. ♦*Bill was sitting and daydreaming so his mother told him to come down to earth and to do his homework.*

come between *v.* To part; divide; separate. ♦*John's mother-in-law came to live in his home, and as time passed she came between him and his wife.* ♦*Bill's hot rod came between him and his studies, and his grades went down.*

come by *v.* To get; obtain; acquire. ♦*A good job like that is hard to come by.* ♦*Money easily come by is often easily spent.* ♦*How did she come by that money?*

come clean *v. phr., slang* To tell all; tell the whole story; confess. ♦*The boy suspected of stealing the watch came clean after long questioning.*

comedown *n.* (stress on *come*) Disappointment; embarrassment; failure. ♦*It was quite a comedown for Al when the girl he took for granted refused his marriage proposal.*

come down *v.* (stress on *down*) **1.** To reduce itself; amount to no more than.—Followed by *to*. ♦*The quarrel finally came down to a question of which boy would do the dishes.* **2.** To be handed down or passed along, descend from parent to child; pass from older generation to

younger ones. ♦*Mary's necklace had come down to her from her grandmother.*

come down hard on *v., informal* **1.** To scold or punish strongly. ♦*The principal came down hard on the boys for breaking the window.* **2.** To oppose strongly. ♦*The minister in his sermon came down hard on drinking.*

come down with *v., informal* To become sick with; catch. ♦*We all came down with the mumps.* ♦*After being out in the rain, George came down with a cold.*

come full circle *v. phr., informal* **1.** To become totally opposed to one's own earlier conviction on a given subject. ♦*Today's conservative businessperson has come full circle from former radical student days.* **2.** To change and develop, only to end up where one started. ♦*From modern permissiveness, ideas about child raising have come full circle to the views of our grandparents.*

come hell or high water *adv. phr., informal* No matter what happens; whatever may come. ♦*Grandfather said he would go to the fair, come hell or high water.*

come in *v.* **1.** To finish in a sports contest or other competition. ♦*He came in second in the hundred-yard dash.* **2.** To become the fashion; begin to be used. ♦*Swimming trunks for men came in after World War I; before that men used full swim suits.*

come in for *v.* **1.** To receive. ♦*He came in for a small fortune when his uncle died.* ♦*His conduct came in for much criticism.* **2.** To receive blame or praise. ♦*The mayor of New York City, Rudolph Giuliani, came in for a lot of praise in the wake of 9/11/01.*

come in handy *v. phr., informal* To prove useful. ♦*The French he learned in high school came in handy when Tom was in the army in France.*

come into *v.* To receive, especially after another's death; get possession of. ♦*He came into a lot of money when his father died.*

come off *v.* **1.** To take place; happen. ♦*The picnic came off at last, after being twice postponed.* **2.** *informal* To do well; succeed. ♦*The attempt to bring the quarreling couple together again came off, to people's astonishment.*

come off as *v. phr.* To give the impression of possessing certain qualities. ♦*Wilbur is often disliked because he has a tendency to come off as a vulgar person.*

come off it *also* **get off it** *v. phr., slang* Stop pretending; bragging, or kidding; stop being silly.—Used as a command. ♦*"So I said to the duchess…" Jimmy began. "Oh, come off it," the other boys sneered.* ♦*Fritz said he had a car of his own. "Oh, come off it," said John. "You can't even drive."*

come off *or* **through with flying colors** *v. phr.* To succeed; triumph. ♦*John came off with flying colors in his final exams at college.*

come on *v.* **1.** To begin; appear. ♦*Rain came on toward morning.* ♦*He felt a cold coming on.* **2.** To grow or do well; thrive. ♦*The wheat was coming on.* ♦*His business came on splen-*

didly. **3.** *or* **come upon.** To meet accidentally; encounter; find. ♦*He came on an old friend that day when he visited his club.* ♦*He came upon an interesting idea in reading about the French Revolution.* **4.** *informal* Let's get started; let's get going; don't delay; don't wait.—Used as a command. ♦*"Come on, or we'll be late," said Joe, but Lou still waited.* **5.** *informal* Please do it!—Used in begging someone to do something. ♦*Sing us just one song, Jane, come on!*

come-on *n., slang* An attractive offer made to a naive person under false pretenses in order to gain monetary or other advantage. ♦*Joe uses a highly successful come-on when he sells vacant lots on Grand Bahama Island.*

come on strong *v. phr., slang* To overwhelm a weaker person with excessively strong language, personality, or mannerisms; to insist extremely strongly and claim something with unusual vigor. ♦*Joe came on very strong last night about the War in Indochina; most of us felt embarrassed.*

come on to *v. phr.* To make sexual advances. ♦*"I think my boss is coming on to me; what should I do?" Mary complained to her husband.*

come out *v.* **1.** *Of a girl:* To be formally introduced to polite society at about age eighteen, usually at a party; begin to go to big parties. ♦*In society, girls come out when they reach the age of about eighteen, and usually it is at a big party in their honor; after that they are looked on as adults.* **2.** To be published. *The* book came out two weeks ago. **3.** To become publicly known. ◆*The truth finally came out at his trial.* **4.** To end; result; finish. ◆*How did the story come out?* ◆*The game came out as we had hoped.* ◆*The snapshots came out well.* **5.** To announce support or opposition; declare yourself (for or against a person or thing). ◆*The party leaders came out for an acceptable candidate.* ◆*Many Congressmen came out against the bill.* **6.** See GO OUT FOR.—**coming-out** *adj.* Introducing a girl to polite society. ◆*Mary's parents gave her a coming-out party when she was 17.*

come out for *v. phr.* To support; declare oneself in favor of another, especially during a political election. ◆*Candidates for the presidency of the United States are anxious for the major newspapers to come out for them.*

come out in the open *v. phr.* **1.** To reveal one's true identity or intentions. ◆*Fred finally came out in the open and admitted that he was gay.* **2.** To declare one's position openly. ◆*The conservative Democratic candidate came out in the open and declared that he would join the Republican Party.*

come out of the closet *v. phr.* To expose something about oneself that was previously kept as a secret. Used mostly in connection with homosexuals. ◆*I heard that Al is coming out of the closet, after living with Joe for more than twenty years!*

come out with *v. phr.* **1.** To make a public announcement of; make known. ◆*He came out*

with a clear declaration of his principles. **2.** To say. ◆*He comes out with the funniest remarks you can imagine.*

come over *v.* **1.** To take control of; cause sudden strong feeling in; happen to. ◆*A sudden fit of anger came over him.* ◆*A great tenderness came over her.* ◆*What has come over him?* **2.** To visit someone. ◆*Why don't you come over some time? We would love to have you pay us a visit.*

come round *or* **come around** *v.* **1.** To happen or appear again and again in regular order. ◆*And so Saturday night came around again.* ◆*I will tell him when he comes round again.* **2.** *informal* To get back health or knowledge of things; get well from sickness or a faint. ◆*Jim has come around after having had stomach ulcers.* **3.** To change direction. ◆*The wind has come round to the south.* **4.** *informal* To change your opinion or purpose to agree with another's. ◆*Tom came round when Dick told him the whole story.*

come through *v., informal* To be equal to a demand; meet trouble or a sudden need with success; satisfy a need. ◆*John needed money for college and his father came through.*

come through for *v. phr.* To come to the aid of someone as promised or as expected. ◆*I knew my brother Jack would come through for me; he loaned me the money to survive when I lost my job.*

come to *v.* (stress on *to*) **1.** To wake up after losing consciousness; get the use of your senses back again after fainting or being knocked out. ◆*The boxer who was knocked out did not come to for five minutes.* ◆*The doctor gave her a pill and after she took it she didn't come to for two days.* **2.** (stress on *come*) To get enough familiarity or understanding to; learn to; grow to.—Used with an infinitive. ◆*John was selfish at first, but he came to realize that other people counted, too.* **3.** To result in or change to; reach the point of; arrive at. ◆*Mr. Smith lived to see his invention come to success.* **4.** To have something to do with; be in the field of; be about.—Usually used in the phrase *when it comes to.* ◆*Joe is not good in sports, but when it comes to arithmetic he's the best in the class.*

come to a dead end *v. phr.* To reach a point from which one cannot proceed further, either because of a physical obstacle or because of some forbidding circumstance. ◆*The factory expansion project came to a dead end because of a lack of funds.*

come to a head *v. phr.* To reach a point where immediate and urgent decision is unavoidable. ◆*Discussions have come to a head regarding the enlargement of the European Union. Seven new nations are now scheduled to join.*

come to blows *v. phr.* To begin to fight. ◆*The two countries came to blows because one wanted to be independent from the other.*

come to grief *v. phr.* To have a bad accident or disappointment; meet trouble or ruin; end badly; wreck; fail. ◆*Bill came to grief learning to drive a car.*

come to grips with *v. phr.* **1.** To get hold of (another wrestler) in close fighting. ◆*After circling around for a minute, the two wrestlers came to grips with each other.* **2.** To struggle seriously with (an idea or problem). ◆*Mr. Blake's teaching helps students come to grips with the important ideas in the history lesson.* ◆*Harry cannot be a leader, because he never quite comes to grips with a problem.*

come to light *v. phr.* To be discovered; become known; appear. ◆*New facts about ancient Egypt have recently come to light.*

come to mind *v. phr.* To occur to someone. ◆*A new idea for the advertising campaign came to mind as I was reading your book.*

come to nothing also formal **come to naught** *v. phr.* To end in failure; fail; be in vain. ◆*The dog's attempts to climb the tree after the cat came to nothing.*

come to one's senses *v. phr.* **1.** Become conscious again; wake up. ◆*The boxer was knocked out and did not come to his senses for several minutes.* **2.** To think clearly; behave as usual or as you should; act sensibly. ◆*Don't act so foolishly. Come to your senses!*

come to pass *v. phr., literary* To happen; occur. ◆*Strange things come to pass in troubled times.*

come to rest *v. phr.* To stop. ◆*The runaway truck finally came to rest in a muddy cornfield although all of its brakes were gone.*

come to terms *v. phr.* To reach an agreement. ◆*Management and the labor union came to terms* *about a new arrangement and a strike was prevented.*

come to the point *or* **get to the point** *v. phr.* To talk about the important thing; reach the important facts of the matter; reach the central question or fact. ◆*A good newspaper story must come right to the point and save the details for later.*

come to think of it *v. phr., informal* As I think about it; indeed; really. ◆*Come to think of it, I should write my daughter today.*

come up *v.* **1.** To become a subject for discussion or decision to talk about or decide about. ◆*The question of wage increases came up at the board meeting.* ◆*Mayor Jones comes up for reelection this fall.* **2.** To be equal; match in value.—Used with *to.* ◆*The new model car comes up to last year's.* **3.** To approach; come close. ◆*We saw a big black bear coming up on us from the woods.* ◆*Christmas is coming up soon.* **4.** To provide; supply; furnish.—Used with *with.* ◆*The teacher asked a difficult question, but finally Ted came up with a good answer.*

come up smelling like a rose *v. phr.* To escape from a difficult situation or misdeed unscathed or without punishment. ◆*It is predicted that Congressman Brown, in spite of the current investigation into his financial affairs, will come up smelling like a rose at the end.*

come up with *v. phr.* **1.** To offer. ◆*We can always depend on John Smith to come up with a good solution for any problem we might have.* **2.** To produce

on demand. ◆*I won't be able to buy this car, because I cannot come up with the down payment you require.* **3.** To find. ◆*How on earth did you come up with such a brilliant idea?*

comings and goings *n. pl., informal* **1.** Times of arriving and going away; movements. ◆*I can't keep up with the children's comings and goings.* **2.** Activities; doings; business. ◆*Mary knows all the comings and goings in the neighborhood.*

common ground *n.* Shared beliefs, interests, or ways of understanding; ways in which people are alike. ◆*Bob and Frank don't like each other because they have no common ground.*

common touch *n.* The ability to be a friend of the people; friendly manner with everyone. ◆*Voters like a candidate who has the common touch.*

compare notes *v. phr., informal* To exchange thoughts or ideas about something; discuss together. ◆*Mother and Mrs. Barker like to compare notes about cooking.*

conk out *v. phr., slang, informal* To fall asleep suddenly with great fatigue or after having drunk too much. ◆*We conked out right after the guests had left.*

conversation piece *n.* Something that interests people and makes them talk about it; something that looks unusual, comical, or strange. ◆*Uncle Fred has a glass monkey on top of his piano that he keeps for a conversation piece.*

cook one's goose v. phr., slang To ruin someone hopelessly; destroy one's future expectations or good name. ♦The dishonest official knew his goose was cooked when the newspapers printed the story about him.

cook up v., informal To plan and put together; make up; invent. ♦The boys cooked up an excuse to explain their absence from school.

cool as a cucumber adj. phr., informal Very calm and brave; not nervous, worried, or anxious; not excited; composed. ♦Bill is a good football quarterback, always cool as a cucumber.

cool, calm, and collected adj. phr. Describing a desired quality in people, especially ones in a leadership position, whereby the person is alert, yet not excited and ready to act. ♦Peter Murphy would make a fine commanding officer. I don't know anyone else quite so cool, calm, and collected as he is.

cool customer n. Someone who is calm and in total control of himself; someone showing little emotion. ♦Jim never gets too excited about anything; he is a cool customer.

cool down or **cool off** v. To lose or cause to lose the heat of any deep feeling (as love, enthusiasm, or anger); make or become calm, cooled or indifferent; lose interest. ♦A heated argument can be settled better if both sides cool down first. ♦The neighbor's explanation about his illness cooled the argument down.

cool one's heels v. phr., slang To be kept waiting by another's pride or rudeness; be forced to wait by someone in power or authority; wait. ♦I was left to cool my heels outside while the others went into the office.

coop up v. phr. To hedge in; confine; enclose in a small place. ♦How can poor Jane work in that small office, cooped up all day long?

cop a plea v. phr., slang, colloquial To plead guilty during a trial in the hope of getting a lighter sentence as a result. ♦The murderer of Dr. Martin Luther King, Jr., copped a plea of guilty, and got away with a life sentence instead of the death penalty.

cop out v. phr., slang, informal (stress on out) To avoid committing oneself in a situation where doing so would result in difficulties. ♦Nixon copped out on the American people with Watergate.

cop-out n. phr., slang, informal (stress on cop) An irresponsible excuse made to avoid something one has to do, a flimsy pretext. ♦Come on, Jim, that's a cheap cop-out, and I don't believe a word of it!

copy cat n. Someone who copies another person's work or manner.—Usually used by children or when speaking to children. ♦He called me a copy cat just because my new shoes look like his.

corn ball n., slang, informal 1. A superficially sentimental movie or musical in which the word love is mentioned too often; a theatrical performance that is trivially sentimental. ♦That *movie last night was a corn ball.* **2.** A person who behaves in a superficially sentimental manner or likes performances portraying such behavior. ♦*Suzie can't stand Joe; she thinks he's a corn ball.*

couch case *n., slang, informal* A person judged emotionally so disturbed that people think he ought to see a psychiatrist (who, habitually, make their patients lie down on a couch). ♦*Joe's divorce messed him up so badly that he became a couch case.*

couch doctor *n., slang, colloquial* A psychoanalyst who puts his patients on a couch following the practice established by Sigmund Freud. ♦*I didn't know your husband was a couch doctor, I thought he was a gynecologist!*

couch potato *n.* A person who is addicted to watching television all day. ♦*Poor Ted has become such a couch potato that we can't persuade him to do anything.*

cough up *v., slang* **1.** To give (money) unwillingly; pay with an effort. ♦*Her husband coughed up the money for the party with a good deal of grumbling.* **2.** To tell what was secret; make known. ♦*He coughed up the whole story for the police.*

couldn't care less *v. phr., informal* To be indifferent; not care at all. ♦*The students couldn't care less about the band; they talked all through the concert.* Also heard increasingly as *could care less* (nonstandard in this form.)

countdown *n., Space English, informal* **1.** A step-by-step

process which leads to the launching of a rocket. ♦*Countdown starts at 23:00 hours tomorrow night and continues for 24 hours.* **2.** Process of counting inversely during the acts leading to a launch; liftoff occurs at zero. **3.** The time immediately preceding an important undertaking, borrowed from Space English. ♦*We're leaving for Hawaii tomorrow afternoon; this is countdown time for us.*

count off *v.* **1.** To count aloud from one end of a line of men to the other, each man counting in turn. ♦*The soldiers counted off from right to left.* **2.** To place into a separate group or groups by counting. ♦*The coach counted off three boys to carry in the equipment.* ♦*Tom counted off enough newspapers for his route.*

count on *v.* To depend on; rely on; trust. ♦*The team was counting on Joe to win the race.* ♦*I'll do it; you know you can count on me.*

count one's chickens before they're hatched *v. phr., informal* To depend on getting a profit or gain before you have it; make plans that suppose something will happen; be too sure that something will happen. Usually used in negative sentences. ♦*Maybe some of your customers won't pay, and then where will you be? Don't count your chickens before they're hatched.*

count out *v.* **1.** To leave (someone) out of a plan; not expect (someone) to share in an activity; exclude. ♦ *"Will this party cost anything? If it does, count me* *out, because I'm broke."* **2.** To count out loud to ten to show that (a boxer who has been knocked down in a fight) is beaten or knocked out if he does not get up before ten is counted. ♦*The champion was counted out in the third round.* **3a.** To add up; count again to be sure of the amount. ♦*Mary counted out the number of pennies she had.* **3b.** To count out loud (especially the beats in a measure of music). ♦*The music teacher counted out the beats "one-two-three-four," so the class would sing in time.*

count to ten *v. phr., informal* To count from one to ten so you will have time to calm down or get control of yourself; put off action when angry or excited so as not to do anything wrong. ♦*Father always told us to count to ten before doing anything when we got angry.*

cover girl *n.* A pretty girl or woman whose picture is put on the cover of a magazine. ♦*Ann is not a cover girl, but she is pretty enough to be.*

cover ground *or* **cover the ground** *v. phr.* **1.** To go a distance; travel. ♦*Mr. Rogers likes to travel in planes, because they cover ground so quickly.* **2.** *informal* To move over an area at a speed that is pleasing; move quickly over a lot of ground. ♦*Jack's new car really covers ground!* **3.** To give or receive the important facts and details about a subject. ♦*The class spent two days studying the Revolutionary War, because they couldn't cover that much ground in one day.*

cover one's tracks *or* **cover up one's tracks** *v. phr.* **1.** To hide and not leave anything, especially foot marks, to show where you have been, so that no one can follow you. ♦*The deer covered his tracks by running in a stream.* **2.** *informal* To hide or not say where you have been or what you have done; not tell why you do something or what you plan to do. ♦*The boys covered their tracks when they went swimming by saying that they were going for a walk.*

cover the waterfront *v. phr.* To talk or write all about something; talk about something all possible ways. ♦*The principal pretty well covered the waterfront on student behavior.*

cover up *v., informal* (stress on *up*) **1.** To hide something wrong or bad from attention. ♦*The spy covered up his picture-taking by pretending to be just a tourist.* **2.** *In boxing:* To guard your head and body with your gloves, arms, and shoulders. ♦*Jimmy's father told him to cover up and protect his chin when he boxed.* **3.** To protect someone else from blame or punishment; protect someone with a lie or alibi.—Often used with *for.* ♦*The burglar's friend covered up for him by saying that he was at his home when the robbery occurred.*

cover-up *n.* (stress on *cover*) A plan or excuse to escape blame or punishment; lie, alibi. ♦*When the men robbed the bank, their cover-up was to dress like policemen.*

cowboy *n., slang, informal* A person who drives his car carelessly and at too great a speed in order to show off his courage. ◆*Joe's going to be arrested some day—he is a cowboy on the highway.*

cozy up *v., slang* To try to be close or friendly; try to be liked.—Usually used with *to*. ◆*John is cozying up to Henry so he can join the club.*

crack a book *v. phr., slang* To open a book in order to study.—Usually used with a negative. ◆*Many students think they can pass without cracking a book.*

crack a joke *v. phr., informal* To make a joke; tell a joke. ◆*The men sat around the stove, smoking and cracking jokes.*

crack a smile *v. phr., informal* To let a smile show on one's face; permit a smile to appear. ◆*Bob told the whole silly story without even cracking a smile.*

crack down *v. phr., informal* To enforce laws or rules strictly; require full obedience to a rule. ◆*After a speeding driver hit a child, the police cracked down.*—Often used with *on*. ◆*Police suddenly cracked down on the selling of liquors to minors.*

crack of dawn *n. phr.* The time in the morning when the sun's rays first appear. ◆*The rooster crows at the crack of dawn and wakes up everybody on the farm.*

cracked up *adj. phr., informal* Favorably described or presented; praised.—Usually used in the expression *not what it's cracked up to be*. ◆*The independent writer's life isn't always everything it's cracked up to be.*

crackpot *n., attrib. adj., informal* 1. *n.* An eccentric person with ideas that don't make sense to most other people. ◆*Don't believe what Uncle Noam tells you—he is a crackpot.* 2. *attrib. adj.* Eccentric or lunatic. ◆*That's a crackpot idea.*

crack the whip *v. phr., informal* To get obedience or cooperation by threats of punishment. ◆*If the children won't behave when I reason with them, I have to crack the whip.*

crack up *v.* 1. To wreck or be wrecked; smash up. ◆*The airplane cracked up in landing.* 2. *informal* To become mentally ill under physical or mental overwork or worry. ◆*It seemed to be family problems that made him crack up.* 3. burst into laughter *or* cause to burst into laughter. ◆*That comedian cracks me up.*

cramp one's style *v. phr., informal* To limit your natural freedom; prevent your usual behavior; limit your actions or talk. ◆*It cramped his style a good deal when he lost his money.* ◆*Army rules cramped George's style.*

crash the gate *v. phr., slang* To enter without a ticket or without paying; attend without an invitation or permission. ◆*Three boys tried to crash the gate at our party but we didn't let them in.*

credibility gap *n., hackneyed phrase, politics* An apparent discrepancy between what the government says and what one can observe for oneself. ◆*There was a tremendous credibility gap in the USA during the Watergate years.*

creep up on *v.* 1. To crawl towards; move along near the ground; steal cautiously towards so as not to be seen or noticed. ◆*The mouse did not see the snake creeping up on it over the rocks.* **2.** *or* **sneak up on** To come little by little; arrive slowly and unnoticed. ◆*The woman's hair was turning gray as age crept up on her.*

crew cut *or* **crew haircut** *n.* A boy's or man's hair style, cut so that the hair stands up in short, stiff bristle. ◆*Many boys like to get crew cuts during the summer to keep cooler.*

crocodile tears *n.* Pretended grief; a show of sorrow that is not really felt. ◆*When his rich uncle died, leaving him his money, John shed crocodile tears.*

crop up *v.* To come without warning; appear or happen unexpectedly. ◆*Problems cropped up almost every day when Mr. Reed was building his TV station.*

cross a bridge before one comes to it *v. phr.* To worry about future events or trouble before they happen—Usually used in negative sentences, often as a proverb. ◆*"Can I be a soldier when I grow up, Mother?" asked Johnny. "Don't cross that bridge until you come to it," said his mother.*

cross fire *n.* **1.** Firing in a fight or battle from two or more places at once so that the lines of fire cross. ◆*The soldiers on the bridge were caught in the cross fire coming from both sides of the bridge.* **2.** Fast or angry talking back and forth between two or more people; *also,* a dispute; a quarrel. ◆*There was a cross fire of excited questions and answers between the parents*

and the children who had been lost in the woods.

cross one's fingers *v. phr.* **1a.** To cross two fingers of one hand for good luck. ◆*Mary crossed her fingers during the race so that Tom would win.* **1b.** *or* **keep one's fingers crossed** *informal* To wish for good luck. ◆*Keep your fingers crossed while I take the test.* **2.** To cross two fingers of one hand to excuse an untruth that you are telling. ◆*Johnny crossed his fingers when he told his mother the lie.*

cross one's heart *or* **cross one's heart and hope to die** *v. phr., informal* To say that what you have said is surely true; promise seriously that it is true.— Often used by children in the longer form. Children often make a sign of a cross over the heart as they say it, for emphasis. ◆*"Cross my heart, I didn't steal your bicycle," Harry told Tom.* ◆*"I didn't tell the teacher what you said. Cross my heart and hope to die," Mary said to Lucy.*

cross one's mind *or* **pass through one's mind** *v. phr.* To be a sudden or passing thought; be thought of by someone; come to your mind; occur to you. ◆*When Jane did not come home by midnight, many terrible fears passed through her mother's mind.*

cross one's path *v. phr.* To meet or encounter someone; to come upon someone more by accident than by plan. ◆*Surprisingly, I crossed John's path in Central Park one afternoon.*

cross swords *v. phr., literary* To have an argument with; fight.— Often used with *with*. ◆*Don't argue with the teacher; you're not old enough to cross swords with her.*

cross the wire *v. phr.* To finish a race. ◆*The Russian crossed the wire just behind the American.*

crux of the matter *n. phr.* The basic issue at hand; the core essence that one must face. ◆*The crux of the matter is that he is incompetent and we will have to fire him.*

cry or scream bloody murder *v. phr.* To bitterly and loudly complain against an indignity. ◆*Pete cried bloody murder when he found out that he didn't get the promotion he was hoping for.*

cry for or cry out for *v., informal* To need badly; be lacking in. ◆*It has not rained for two weeks and the garden is crying for it.* ◆*The school is crying out for good teachers.*

cry on one's shoulder *v. phr.* To find a willing listener to whom one can complain all one wants for psychological comfort. ◆*"I am sorry to be crying on your shoulders, Dad," Tim said, "but I lost my job and my wife left me. I have no one else to talk to."*

cry out *v.* 1. To call out loudly; shout; scream. ◆*The woman in the water cried out "Help!"* 2. To complain loudly; protest strongly.—Used with *against*. ◆*Many people are crying out against the new rule.*

cry over spilled milk or cry over spilt milk *v. phr., informal* To cry or complain about something that has already happened; be unhappy about something that cannot be helped. ◆*You have lost the game but don't cry over spilt milk.*

crystal ball *n.* 1. A ball, usually made of quartz crystal (glass) that is used by fortune-tellers. ◆*The fortune-teller at the fair looked into her crystal ball and told me that I would take a long trip next year.* 2. Any means of predicting the future. ◆*My crystal ball tells me you'll be rich.*

cry wolf *v. phr.* To give a false alarm; warn of a danger that you know is not there. ◆*The general said that the candidate was just crying wolf when he said that the army was too weak to fight for the country.*

cue in *v. phr., informal* To add new information to that which is already known. ◆*Let's not forget to cue in Joe on what has been happening.*

culture vulture *n., slang, informal* A person who is an avid cultural sightseer, one who seeks out cultural opportunities ostentatiously, such as going to the opera or seeing every museum in a town visited, and brags about it. ◆*My Aunt Mathilda is a regular culture vulture; she spends every summer in a different European capital going to museums and operas.*

cup of tea *also* **dish of tea** *n. phr., informal* 1. Something you enjoy or do well at; a special interest, or favorite occupation. Used with a possessive. ◆*You could always get him to go for a walk: hiking was just his cup of tea.* 2. Something to think about; thing; matter. ◆*That's another cup of tea.*

curiosity killed the cat *informal* Getting too nosy may lead a person into trouble.—A proverb. ◆"*Curiosity killed the cat*," *Fred's father said, when he found Fred hunting around in closets just before Christmas.*

curl one's hair *v. phr., slang* To shock; frighten; horrify; amaze. ◆*Wait till you read what it says about you—this'll curl your hair.*

curry favor *v.* To flatter or serve someone to get his help or friendship. ◆*Jim tried to curry favor with the new girl by telling her she was the prettiest girl in the class.*

cut a class *v. phr.* To be truant; to deliberately miss a class and do something else instead. ◆"*If you keep cutting classes the way you do, you will almost surely flunk this course*," *John's professor said to him.*

cut a deal *or* **hammer out** *v. phr.* To reach an agreement after long and arduous negotiations. ◆*It took the airline employees four weeks to hammer out an agreement with the management.* ◆*I know you're just as anxious to get down to business as I am, so let us cut a deal here and now.*

cut a figure *v. phr.* To make a favorable impression; carry off an activity with dignity and grace. ◆*With his handsome face and sporty figure, Harry cuts quite a figure with all the ladies.*

cut across *v.* 1. To cross or go through instead of going around; go a short way. ◆*John didn't want to walk to the corner and turn, so he cut across the yard to the next street.* 2. To go beyond to include; stretch over to act on; affect. ◆*The love*

for reading cuts across all classes of people, rich and poor.

cut-and-dried *adj. phr.* Decided or expected beforehand; following the same old line; doing the usual thing. ◆*The decision of the judge was cut-and-dried.*

cut back *v.* 1. To change direction suddenly while going at full speed. ◆*The halfback started to his left, cut back to his right, and ran for a touchdown.* 2. To use fewer or use less. ◆*The school employed forty teachers until a lower budget forced it to cut back.*

cut back *v. phr.* (stress on *back*) To diminish; lessen; decrease (said of budgets). ◆*The state had to cut back on the university budget.*

cutback *n.* (stress on *cut*) An act of decreasing monetary sources. ◆*The cutback in military spending has caused many bases to be closed.*

cut both ways *or* **cut two ways** *v. phr.* To have two effects; cause injury to both sides. ◆*People who gossip find it cuts both ways.*

cut corners *v. phr.* 1. To take a short way; not go to each corner. ◆*He cut corners going home in a hurry.* 2. To save cost or effort; manage in a thrifty way; be saving. ◆*John's father asked him to cut corners all he could in college.* 3. To do less than a very good job; do only what you must do on a job. ◆*He had cut corners in building his house, and it didn't stand up well.*

cut down *v.* To lessen; reduce; limit. ◆*Tom had to cut down expenses.* ◆*The doctor told Mr. Jones to cut down on smoking.*

cut down to size v. phr., informal To prove that someone is not as good as he thinks. ◆The big boy told John he could beat him, but John was a good boxer and soon cut him down to size.

cut ice v. phr., informal To make a difference; make an impression; be accepted as important.—Usually used in negative, interrogative, or conditional sentences. ◆When Frank had found a movie he liked, what others said cut no ice with him.

cut in v. 1. To force your way into a place between others in a line of cars, people, etc.; push in. ◆After passing several cars, Fred cut in too soon and nearly caused an accident.—Often used with on. ◆A car passed Jean and cut in on her too close; she had to brake quickly or she would have hit it. 2. To stop a talk or program for a time; interrupt. ◆While we were watching the late show, an announcer cut in to tell who won the election. 3. informal To tap a dancer on the shoulder and claim the partner. ◆Mary was a good dancer and a boy could seldom finish a dance with her; someone always cut in.—Often used with on. ◆At the leap year dance, Jane cut in on Sally because she wanted to dance with Sally's handsome date. 4. To connect to an electrical circuit or to a machine. ◆Harry threw the switch and cut in the motor. 5. informal To take in; include. ◆When John's friends got a big contract, they cut John in.

cut into v. 1. To make less; reduce. ◆The union made the company pay higher wages, which cut into the profits. ◆At first Smith led in votes, but more votes came in and cut into his lead. 2. To get into by cutting in. ◆While Bill was passing another car, a truck came around a curve heading for him, and Bill cut back into line quickly.

cut loose v. 1. To free from ties or connections, cut the fastenings of. ◆The thief hastily cut the boat loose from its anchor. 2. informal To break away from control; get away and be free. ◆The boy left home and cut loose from his parents' control. 3. informal To behave freely or wildly. ◆The men had come to the convention to have a good time, and they really cut loose.

cut off v. 1. To separate or block. ◆The flood cut the townspeople off from the rest of the world. ◆The woods cut off the view. 2. To interrupt or stop. ◆The television show was cut off by a special news report. ◆We were told to pay the bill or the water would be cut off. 3. To end the life of; cause the death of. ◆Disease cut Smith off in the best part of life. 4. To give nothing to at death; leave out of a will. ◆Jane married a man her father hated, and her father cut her off. 5. To stop from operating; turn a switch to stop. ◆The ship cut off its engines as it neared the dock.

cut off one's nose to spite one's face v. phr. To suffer from an action intended originally to harm another person. ◆In walking out and leaving his employer in the lurch, John really cut off his nose to spite his face, since no business wanted to hire him afterwards.

cut one's throat *v. phr., informal* To spoil one's chances; ruin a person. ◆*He cut his own throat by his carelessness.*

cut out[1] *v., slang* **1.** To stop; quit. ◆*All right, now—let's cut out the talking.* ◆*He was teasing the dog and Joe told him to cut it out.* **2.** To displace in favor. ◆*John cut out two or three other men in trying for a better job.*

cut out[2] *adj.* **1.** Made ready; given for action; facing. ◆*Mary agreed to stay with her teacher's children all day; she did not know what was cut out for her.*—Often used in the phrase *have one's work cut out for one.* ◆*If Mr. Perkins wants to become a senator, he has his work cut out for him.* **2.** Suited to; fitted for. ◆*Warren seemed to be cut out for the law.*

cut rate[1] *n.* A lower price; a price less than usual. ◆*Toys are on sale at the store for cut rates.*

cut-rate[2] *adj.* Sold for a price lower than usual; selling cheap things. ◆*If you buy cut-rate things, be sure they are good quality first.*

cut short *v.* To stop or interrupt suddenly; end suddenly or too soon. ◆*Rain cut short the ball game.* ◆*An auto accident cut short the man's life.*

cut the mustard *v. phr., slang* To do well enough in what needs to be done; to succeed. ◆*His older brothers and sisters helped Max through high school, but he couldn't cut the mustard in college.*

cut-throat *adj.* Severe; intense; unrelenting. ◆*There is cut-throat competition among the various software companies today.*

cut to pieces *v. phr.* **1.** To divide into small parts with something sharp; cut badly or completely. ◆*Baby has cut the newspaper to pieces with scissors.* **2.** To destroy or defeat completely. ◆*When Dick showed his book report to his big sister for correction, she cut it to pieces.*

cut to the bone *v. phr.* To make (something) the least or smallest possible amount; reduce severely; leave out everything extra or unnecessary from. ◆*Father cut Jane's allowance to the bone for disobeying him.* ◆*When father lost his job, our living expenses had to be cut to the bone.*

cut to the quick *v. phr.* To hurt someone's feelings deeply. ◆*The children's teasing cut Mary to the quick.*

cut up *v.* **1.** *informal* To hurt the feelings of; wound.—Usually used in the passive. ◆*John was badly cut up when Susie gave him back his ring.* **2.** *slang* To act funny or rough; clown. ◆*Joe would always cut up if there were any girls watching.*

cybercrime *n. phr.* A new kind of crime that came in with the general availability of the personal computer; such as breaking into a bank or stealing someone's identity together with their credit card numbers, etc. ◆*"My brother Sam, whom I used to envy for his knowledge of computers, is doing fifteen years in jail for committing a major cybercrime."*

damned if one does, damned if one doesn't *adj. phr.* No matter what one does, someone is likely to criticize one. ◆*No matter what decisions I make, there are always some people who will approve them and those who won't. It is a classical case of "damned if I do, damned if I don't."*

damn with faint praise *v. phr.* To express one's dislike or scorn for a piece of writing, music, scholarship, or art, by not saying anything directly against it, but praising it in such general terms that amount to condemnation. ◆*When it comes to Milton scholarship, Stanley Fish is a master of damning the work of his colleagues with faint praise.*

dance to another tune *v. phr.* To talk or act differently, usually better because things have changed; be more polite or obedient because you are forced to do it. ◆*Johnny refused to do his homework but punishment made him dance to another tune.*

dare say *v. phr.* To think; probable; suppose; believe.—Used in first person. ◆*There is no more ice cream on the table, but I dare say we can find some in the kitchen.*

dare one to do something *v. phr.* To challenge someone to do something. ◆*"I dare you to jump off that rock into the sea,"* Fred said to Jack.

dark horse *n., informal* A political candidate little known to the general voting public; a candidate who was not expected to run. ◆*Every once in a while a dark horse candidate gets elected president.*

dash light *n.* A light on the front inside of a car or vehicle. ◆*Henry stopped the car and turned on the dash lights to read the road map.*

dash off *v.* To make, do, or finish quickly; especially, to draw, paint, or write hurriedly. ◆*John can dash off several letters while Mary writes only one.* ◆*Charles had forgotten to write his English report and dashed it off just before class.*

dawn on *v.* To become clear to. ◆*It dawned on Fred that he would fail the course if he did not study harder.*

day and night *or* **night and day** *adv.* **1.** For days without stopping; continually. ◆*Some filling stations on great highways are open day and night 365 days a year.* **2.** Every day and every evening. ◆*The girl knitted day and night to finish the sweater before her mother's birthday.*

day by day *adv.* Gradually. ◆*The patient got better day by day.*

daydream *v.* To spend time in reverie; be absentminded during the day. ◆*John spends so much time daydreaming that he never gets anything done.*

day in and day out *or* **day in, day out** *adv. phr.* Regularly; consistently; all the time; always. ◆*He plays good tennis day in and day out.*—Also used with several other time words in place of *day: week, month, year.* ◆*Every summer, year in, year out, the ice cream man comes back to the park.*

day in court *n. phr.* A chance to be heard; an impartial hearing; a chance to explain what one has done. ♦*The letters from the faculty members to the dean gave Professor Smith his day in court.*

day of reckoning *n. phr.* **1.** A time when one will be made to account for misdeeds. ♦*When the criminal was caught and brought to trial his victims said, "finally, the day of reckoning has come."* **2.** A time when one's will and judgment are severely tested. ♦*"You always wanted to run the department," the dean said to Professor Smith. "Now here is your chance; this is your day of reckoning."*

day off *n.* A day on which one doesn't have to work, not necessarily the weekend. ♦*Monday is his day off in the restaurant, because he prefers to work on Saturdays and Sundays.*

days are numbered (Someone or something) does not have long to live or stay. ♦*When a man becomes ninety years old, his days are numbered.*

dead as a doornail *adj. phr.* Completely dead without the slightest hope of resuscitation. ♦*This battery is dead as a doornail; no wonder your car won't start.*

deadbeat *n., slang* **1.** A person who never pays his debts and who has a way of getting things free that others have to pay for. ♦*You'll never collect from Joe—he's a deadbeat.* **2.** **dead beat** *adj. phr.* Totally exhausted. ♦*I feel dead beat all day after yawning through three boring meetings.*

dead center *n.* The exact middle. ♦*The treasure was buried in the dead center of the island.* Often used like an adverb. ♦*The arrow hit the circle dead center.*

dead duck *n., slang* A person or thing in a hopeless situation or condition; one to whom something bad is sure to happen. ♦*When the pianist broke her arm, she was a dead duck.*

dead end *n. phr.* A hopeless situation, from which one is unable to advance. ♦*That job in Podunk, Missouri, where he works as a short-order cook, is a dead end for my poor cousin Joe.*

deadhead *n., slang* An excessively dull or boring person. ♦*You'll never get John to tell a joke—he's a deadhead.*

dead letter *n. phr.* An undeliverable letter that ends up in a special office holding such letters. ♦*There is a dead letter office in most major cities.*

deadline *n.* A final date by which a project, such as a term paper, is due. ♦*The deadline for the papers on Shakespeare is November 10.*

dead loss *n. phr.* A total waste; a complete loss. ♦*Our investment in Jack's company turned out to be a dead loss.*

dead on one's feet *adv. phr., informal* Very tired but still standing or walking; too tired to do more; exhausted. ♦*After the soldiers march all night, they are dead on their feet.*

deadpan *adj., adv., slang* With an expressionless or emotionless face; without betraying any hint of emotion. ♦*She received* *the news of her husband's death deadpan.*

dead ringer *n. phr.* A person who strongly resembles someone else. ◆*Charlie is a dead ringer for his uncle.*

dead tired *adj. phr., informal* Very tired; exhausted; worn out. ◆*She was dead tired at the end of the day's work.*

dead to the world *adj. phr., informal* 1. Fast asleep. ◆*Tim went to bed very late and was still dead to the world at 10 o'clock this morning.* 2. As if dead; unconscious. ◆*Tom was hit on the head by a baseball and was dead to the world for two hours.*

dead-end *n.* A street closed at one end; a situation that leads nowhere. ◆*Jim drove into a dead-end street and had to back out.* ◆*Mary was in a dead-end job.*

dead-end *v.* To not continue normally but end in a closure (said of streets). ◆*Our street dead-ends on the lake.*

deal in *v. phr.* To sell; do business in a certain commodity. ◆*Herb's firm deals in sporting goods.*

deal with *v. phr.* 1. To conduct negotiations or business dealings with. ◆*John refuses to deal with the firm of Brown and Miller.* 2. To handle a problem. ◆*Ted is a very strong person and dealt with the fact that his wife had left him much better than anyone else I know.*

dear me *interj.* Used to show surprise, fear, or some other strong feeling. ◆*Dear me! My purse is lost, what shall I do now?*

death knell *n. formal* 1. The ringing of a bell at a death or funeral. ◆*The people mourned at the death knell of their friend.* 2. *literary* Something which shows a future failure. ◆*His sudden deafness was the death knell of his hope to become president.*

decked out *adj. phr., informal* Dressed in fancy clothes; specially decorated for some festive occasion. ◆*The school band was decked out in bright red uniforms with brass buttons.* ◆*Main Street was decked with flags for the Fourth of July.*

deep-six *v., slang* To throw away; dispose of. ◆*As the police boat came near, the drug smugglers deep-sixed their cargo.*

deep water *n.* Serious trouble or difficulty. ◆*When Dad tried to take Mom's place for a day, he found himself in deep water.*

deliver the goods *v. phr.* 1. To carry things and give them to the person who wants them. ◆*Lee delivered the goods to the right house.* 2. *slang* To succeed in doing well what is expected. ◆*This personal computer surely delivers the goods.*

Dennis the Menace *n. phr.* After the notorious comic strip character of a young boy who always creates trouble for the grownups. Any hyperactive little boy who needs calming down. ◆*"Your son, Joey, is becoming a regular 'Dennis the Menace,'" Jane said to Elvira.*

devil-may-care *adj.* Not caring what happens; unworried. ◆*Johnny has a devil-may-care feeling about his school work.*

devil-may-care attitude *n. phr.* An attitude of no concern for financial or other loss. ♦*"Easy come, easy go," John said in a devil-may-care attitude when he lost all of his money during a poker game.*

devil of it *or* **heck of it** *n. phr.* **1.** The worst or most unlucky thing about a trouble or accident; the part that is most regrettable. ♦*When I had a flat tire, the devil of it was that my spare tire was flat too.* **2.** Fun from doing mischief.—Used after *for.* ♦*The boys carried away Miss White's front gate just for the devil of it.*

diamond in the rough *n. phr.* A very smart person without a formal education who may have untutored manners. ♦*Jack never went to school but he is extremely talented; he is a veritable diamond in the rough.*

die is cast *v. phr., literary* To make an irrevocable decision. ♦*Everything was ready for the invasion of Europe, the die had been cast, and there was no turning back now.*

die off *v.* To die one at a time. ♦*The flowers are dying off because there has been no rain.*

die on the vine *or* **wither on the vine** *v. phr.* To fail or collapse in the planning stages. ♦*The program for rebuilding the city died on the vine.*

die out *v.* To die or disappear slowly until all gone. ♦*This kind of bird is dying out.*

dig in *v., informal* **1.** To dig ditches for protection against an enemy attack. ♦*The soldiers dug in and waited for the enemy to come.* **2a.** To go seriously to

work; work hard. ♦*John dug in and finished his homework very quickly.* **2b.** To begin eating. ♦*Mother set the food on the table and told the children to dig in.*

dig up *v., informal* To find or get (something) with some effort. ♦*Sue dug up some useful material for her English composition.* ♦*Jim asked each boy to dig up twenty-five cents to pay for the hot dogs and soda.*

dime a dozen *adj. phr., informal* Easy to get and so of little value; being an everyday thing because there are many of them; common. ♦*Mr. Jones gives A's to only one or two students, but in Mr. Smith's class, A's are a dime a dozen.*

dine out *v. phr.* To not eat at home but to go to a restaurant. ♦*"Let's dine out tonight, honey," she said to her husband. "I am tired of cooking dinner every night."*

dirt cheap *adj.* Extremely inexpensive. ♦*The apartment we are renting is dirt cheap compared to other apartments of similar size in this neighborhood.*

dirty look *n., informal* A look that shows dislike. ♦*Miss Parker sent Joe to the principal's office for giving her a dirty look.*

dirty old man *n. phr.* An older man who shows an unhealthy interest in young girls. ♦*"Stay away from Uncle Algernon, Sally," her mother warned. "He is a dirty old man."*

dirty one's hands *or* **soil one's hands** *v. phr.* To lower or hurt one's character or good name; do a bad or shameful thing.

*The teacher warned the children not to dirty their hands by cheating in the examination. *I would not soil my hands by going with bad people and doing bad things.

dirty story n. phr. An improper or obscene story. *Uncle Bill is much too fond of telling dirty stories in order to embarrass his friends.

dirty trick n. phr. A treacherous action; an unfair act. *That was a dirty trick John played on Mary when he ran away with her younger sister.

dish out v. 1. To serve (food) from a large bowl or plate. *Ann's mother asked her to dish out the beans. 2. informal To give in large quantities. *That teacher dished out so much homework that her pupils complained to their parents. 3. slang To scold; treat or criticize roughly. *Jim likes to dish it out, but he hates to take it.

dish the dirt v. phr., slang To gossip, to spread rumors about others. *Stop dishing the dirt, Sally, it's really quite unbecoming!

disk jockey n. An employee at a radio station or in a dance club who puts on the records that will be broadcast. *Jack is working as a disk jockey at the local FM station.

dispose of v. 1. To throw away; give away, or sell; get rid of. *John's father wants to dispose of their old house and buy a new one. *The burglars had difficulty in disposing of the stolen jewelry. 2. To finish with; settle; complete. *The boys were hungry, and quickly disposed of their dinner. *The committee soon disposed of all its business. 3. To destroy or defeat. *The champion disposed of the other fighter by knocking him out in the second round. *Our planes disposed of two enemy planes.

do a double take v. phr., informal To look again in surprise; suddenly understand what is seen or said. *John did a double take when he saw Bill in girls' clothes.

do a job on v. phr., slang To damage badly; do harm to; make ugly or useless. *Jane cut her hair and really did a job on herself.

do a stretch v. phr. To spend time in jail serving one's sentence. *Jake has disappeared from view for a while; he is doing a stretch for dope smuggling.

do away with v. 1. To put an end to; stop. *The teachers want to do away with cheating in their school. *The city has decided to do away with overhead wires. 2. To kill; murder. *The robbers did away with their victims.

doctor up v. phr. To meddle with; adulterate. *You don't have to doctor up this basic salad with a lot of extras as I am trying to lose weight.

do duty for v. phr. To substitute for; act in place of. *The bench often does duty for a table.

doesn't add up to a can of beans v. phr. To be of little or no value. (Said of plans, ideas, etc.) *"That's a fairly interesting concept you got there, Mike, but the competition is bound to say that it doesn't add up to a can of beans."

do for v., *informal* To cause the death or ruin of; cause to fail.—Used usually in the passive form *done for.* ◆*The poor fellow is done for and will die before morning.* ◆*If Jim fails that test, he is done for.*

dog days n. phr. The hottest days of the year in the Northern Hemisphere (July and August). ◆ *"The dog days are upon us,"* John said. *"It's time to go swimming in the lake."*

dog-eat-dog[1] n. A way of living in which every person tries to get what he wants for himself no matter how badly or cruelly he must treat others to get it; readiness to do anything to get what you want. ◆*In some early frontier towns it was dog-eat-dog.*

dog-eat-dog[2] adj. Ready or willing to fight and hurt others to get what you want. ◆*During the California gold rush, men had a dog-eat-dog life.*

doggy bag n. phr. A small Styrofoam, plastic, or paper container in which food left on one's plate in a restaurant may be taken home instead of being thrown away. The food is mostly for oneself and not for a "dog." ◆*"Waiter, may I have a doggy bag, please?" "But of course, Sir," the waiter replied. "Every restaurant has them these days."*

dog in the manger n. phr. A person who is unwilling to let another use what he himself has no use for. ◆*Although Valerie lives alone in that big house, she is like a dog in the manger when it comes to letting someone share it with her.*

dog one's steps v. phr. To follow someone closely. ◆*All the time he was in Havana, Castro's police were dogging his steps.*

dole out v. phr. To measure out sparingly. ◆*Since the water ration was running low in the desert, the camp commandant doled out small cups of water to each soldier.*

doll up v., *slang* **1.** To dress in fine or fancy clothes. ◆*The girls dolled up for the big school dance of the year.* ◆*The girls were all dolled up for the Christmas party.* **2.** To make more pretty or attractive. ◆*The classrooms were all dolled up with Christmas decorations.*

done for adj. phr. Finished; dead. ◆*When the police burst in on the crooks, they knew they were done for.*

done with adj. phr. Finished; completed. ◆*As soon as you're done with your work, give us a call.*

don't shoot the messenger Said when one hears some bad news brought by some innocent person. One has a tendency to get angry or irritated at the message bearer who had nothing to do with the message's contents.— A proverb. ◆ *"Sir, I just saw your wife walk into a motel room with your colleague, but please don't shoot the messenger."*

do one dirt v. phr. **1.** To besmirch one's reputation by spreading false gossip about the person. ◆*Poor Mr. Wong was done dirt by the other restaurant owners in the city who spread the false rumor that he was using dog meat in his dishes.* **2.** To cheat someone in a seemingly honest business transaction. ♦*I am afraid to do business with those guys, because they may do me dirt.*

do one good *v. phr.* To benefit. ♦*The fresh air will do you good after having been inside the house all day.*

do-or-die *adj.* Strongly decided, very eager and determined. ♦*With a real do-or-die spirit the team scored two touchdowns in the last five minutes of the game.* ♦*The other army was larger but our men showed a do-or-die determination and won the battle.*

double check *n.* A careful second check to be sure that something is right; a careful look for errors. ♦*The policeman made a double check on the doors in the shopping area.*

double-check *v.* 1. To do a double check on; look at again very carefully. ♦*When the last typing of his book was finished, the author double-checked it.* 2. To make a double check; look carefully at something. ♦*The proofreader double-checks against errors.*

double-cross *v.* To promise one thing and deliver another; to deceive. ♦*The lawyer double-crossed the inventor by manufacturing the gadget instead of fulfilling his promise to arrange a patent for his client.*

double date *n., informal* A date on which two couples go together. ♦*John and Nancy went with Mary and Bill on a double date.*

double-date *v., informal* To go on a double date; date with another couple. ♦*John and Nancy and Mary and Bill double-date.*

double duty *n.* Two uses or jobs; two purposes or duties. ♦*Our new washer does double duty; it washes the clothes and also dries them.*

double-header *n.* Two games or contests played one right after the other, between the same two teams or two different pairs of teams. ♦*The Yankees and the Dodgers played a double-header Sunday afternoon.*

double-talk *n.* 1. Something said that is worded, either on purpose or by accident, so that it may be understood in two or more different ways. ♦*The politician avoided the question with double-talk.* 2. Something said that does not make sense; mixed up talk or writing; nonsense. ♦*The man's explanation of the new tax bill was just a lot of double-talk.*

double up *v.* 1. To bend far over forward. ♦*Jim was hit by the baseball and doubled up with pain.* 2. To share a room, bed, or home with another. ♦*When relatives came for a visit, Ann had to double up with her sister.*

do up *v.* 1a. To clean and prepare for use or wear; launder. ♦*Ann asked her mother to do up her dress.* 1b. To put in order; straighten up; clean. ♦*At camp the girls have to do up their own cabins.* 2. To tie up or wrap. ♦*Joan asked the clerk to do up her purchases.* 3a. To set and fasten (hair) in place. ♦*Grace helped her sister to do up her hair.* 3b. *informal* To dress or clothe. ♦*Suzie was* *done up in her fine new skirt and blouse.*

do with *v.* **1.** To find enough for one's needs; manage.— Usually follows *can.* ♦*Some children can do with very little spending money.* **2.** To make use of; find useful or helpful.—Follows *can* or *could.* ♦*After a hard day's work, a man can do with a good, hot meal.*

do without *or* **go without** *v.* **1.** To live or work without (something you want); manage without. ♦*We had to go without hot food because the stove was broken.* **2.** To live or work without something you want; manage. ♦*If George cannot earn money for a bicycle, he will have to do without.*

down and out *adj. phr.* Without money; without a job or home; broke. ♦*Poor Sam lost his job after his wife had left him; he is really down and out.*

down in the dumps *or* **down in the mouth** *adj. phr., informal* Sad or discouraged; gloomy; dejected. ♦*The boys were certainly down in the dumps when they heard that their team had lost.*

down on *adj. phr., informal* Having a grudge against; angry at. ♦*John is down on his teacher because she gave him a low grade.*

down the drain *adj. or adv. phr., informal* Wasted; lost. ♦*It is money down the drain if you spend it all on candy.* ♦*Our plans to go swimming went down the drain when it rained.*

down the garden path *or* **down the primrose path** *adv. phr.* In a misleading way. ♦*Professor Bloch created a phony argument to see if anyone would catch on; he was leading the class down the primrose path.*

down the hatch! *v. phr., informal* Let us drink! ♦*When we celebrated Mom's birthday, we all raised our glasses and cried in unison, "Down the hatch!"*

down the line *adv. phr., informal* **1.** Down the road or street; straight ahead. ♦*The church is down the line a few blocks.* **2.** All the way; completely; thoroughly. ♦*Bob always follows the teacher's directions right down the line.*

downtime *n. phr.* Intermittent period during which a computer installation does not work, either because of power failure or some internal problem specific to the given system. ♦*"We can't complete your transaction without our computers, Sir, we're having a downtime. Please come back in half an hour."*

down-to-earth *adj.* Showing good sense; practical. ♦*The committee's first plan for the party was too fancy, but the second was more down-to-earth.*

down to the last detail *adv. phr.* In complete detail from the beginning to the end, no matter how small. ♦*The new employee recounted his past employment history down to the last detail.*

down to the wire *adj., slang* **1.** Running out of time, nearing a deadline. ♦*Bob is down to the wire on his project* **2.** Being financially almost broke, being very low on cash or other funds. ♦*We can't afford going* *to a restaurant tonight—we're really down to the wire!*

drag in *v.* To insist on bringing (another subject) into a discussion; begin talking about (something different.) *No matter what we talk about, Jim drags in politics.*

draw a blank *v. phr., informal* **1.** To obtain nothing in return for an effort made or to get a negative result. *I looked up all the Joneses in the telephone book but I drew a blank every time I asked for Archibald Jones.* **2.** To fail to remember something. *I am trying to think of the name but I keep drawing a blank.* **3.** To be consistently unsuccessful at doing something. *I keep trying to pass that math exam but each time I try it I draw a blank.*

draw back *v.* To move back; back away; step backward; withdraw; move away from. *When the man spotted the rattlesnake, he drew back and aimed his shotgun. *The children drew back from the dog when it barked at them.*

drawback *n.* Disadvantage; obstacle; hindrance. *The biggest drawback of Bill's plan is the cost involved.*

draw blood *v. phr., informal* To make someone feel hurt or angry. *If you want to draw blood, ask Jim about his last money-making scheme. *Her sarcastic comments drew blood.*

draw fire *v. phr.* **1.** To attract or provoke shooting; be a target. *The general's white horse drew the enemy's fire.* **2.** To bring criticism or argument; make people say bad things about you. *Having the newest car in your group is sure to draw fire.*

drawing card *n.* The most important figure in a multi-person event; the top entertainer during a show; the best professor or researcher at a university, etc. *The biggest drawing card at many a university is the resident Nobel Laureate.*

draw up *v.* **1.** To write (something) in its correct form; put in writing. *The rich man had his lawyers draw up his will so that each of his children would receive part of his money when he died.* **2.** To plan or prepare; begin to write out. *The two countries drew up a peace treaty after the war ended.* **3.** To hold yourself straight or stiffly, especially because you are proud or angry. *When we said that Mary was getting fat, she drew herself up angrily and walked out of the room.* **4.** To stop or come to a stop. *A big black car drew up in front of the house.*

dress up *v.* **1a.** To put on best or special clothes. *Billy hated being dressed up and took off his best suit as soon as he got home from church.* **1b.** To put on a costume for fun or clothes for a part in a play. *Mary was dressed up to play Cinderella in her school play.* **2.** To make (something) look different; make (something) seem better or more important. *A fresh coat of paint will dress up the old bicycle very much.*

drift off *v. phr.* **1.** To fall asleep. *He kept nodding and drifting off to sleep while the lecturer was speaking.* **2.** To depart;

leave gradually. ◆*One by one, the sailboats drifted off over the horizon.*

drink down *v. phr.* To drink in one gulp; swallow entirely. ◆*Steve was so thirsty that he drank down six glasses of orange juice in rapid succession.*

drink in *v. phr.* To absorb with great interest. ◆*The tourists stood on the beach drinking in the wonderful Hawaiian sunset.*

drink like a fish *v. phr.* To drink (alcoholic beverages) in great quantities; to be addicted to alcohol. ◆*John is a nice guy but, unfortunately, he drinks like a fish.*

drink up *v. phr.* To finish drinking; empty one's glass. ◆*"Drink up that cough syrup," the nurse said, "and never mind the taste."*

drive a bargain *or* **drive a hard bargain** *v. phr.* **1.** To buy or sell at a good price; succeed in a trade or deal. ◆*Jack drove a hard bargain with the real estate agent when we bought his new house.* **2.** To make an agreement that is better for you than for the other person; make an agreement to your advantage. ◆*The French drove a hard bargain in demanding that Germany pay fully for World War I damages.*

drive at *v.* To try or want to say; mean.—Used in the present participle. ◆*Jack had been talking for half an hour before anyone realized what he was driving at.*

drive home *v. phr.* To argue convincingly; make a strong point. ◆*The doctor's convincing arguments and explanation of his X-ray pictures drove home the point to Max that he needed surgery.*

drive-in *adj./n.* A kind of movie theater, fast food restaurant, or church, where the customers, spectators, or worshippers do not leave their automobiles but are served the food inside their cars, can watch a motion picture from inside their cars, or can participate in a religious service in their cars. ◆*Let's not waste time on the road; let's just eat at the next drive-in restaurant.* ◆*There is a drive-in theater not far from where we live.*

drive off 1. *v. phr.* To stave off an attacker. ◆*The army drove off the attackers with much effort and many casualties.* **2.** To make go away; to get rid of something. ◆*These pills will help you to drive off your headaches.*

drive one ape, bananas, crazy, mad *or* **nuts** *v. phr., informal* To irritate, frustrate, or tickle someone's fancy so badly that they think they are going insane. ◆*"Stop teasing me, Mary," John said. "You are driving me nuts."* ◆*"You are driving me bananas with all your crazy riddles," Steve said.*

drop a bombshell *v. phr.* To announce some sensationally good or shockingly bad news. ◆*Freddy dropped a bombshell when he told his astonished parents that he had just married a widow with seven children.*

drop off *v.* **1.** To take (someone or something) part of the way you are going. ◆*Joe asked Mrs.*

Jones to drop him off at the library on her way downtown. 2. To go to sleep. ◆*Jimmy was thinking of his birthday party as he dropped off to sleep.* 3. To die. ◆*The patient dropped off in his sleep.* 4. *or* fall off To become less. ◆*Business picked up in the stores during December, but dropped off again after Christmas.*

dropout *n.* (stress on *drop*) Someone who did not finish school, high school and college primarily. ◆*Tim is having a hard time getting a better job as he was a high-school dropout.*

drown out *v.* To make so much noise that it is impossible to hear (some other sound). ◆*The actor's words were drowned out by applause.*

drum out of *v. phr.* To make someone in the army, a club, a fraternity, etc. leave in shame as punishment for some offense. ◆*The young lieutenant, who tried to seduce the general's wife, got drummed out of the army.*

drum up *v.* 1. To get by trying or asking again and again; attract or encourage by continued effort. ◆*The car dealer tried to drum up business by advertising low prices.* 2. To invent. ◆*I will drum up an excuse for coming to see you next week.*

duck out *v. phr.* To avoid; escape from something by skillful maneuvering. ◆*Somehow or other Jack always manages to duck out of any hard work.*

duck soup *n., slang* 1. A task easily accomplished or one that does not require much effort. ◆*That history test was duck soup.* 2. A person who offers no resistance; a pushover. ◆*How's the new history teacher?—He's duck soup.*

dust off *v., informal* 1. To get ready to use again. ◆*Four years after he graduated from school, Tom decided to dust off his algebra book.* 2. To throw a baseball pitch close to. ◆*The pitcher dusted off the other team's best hitter.*

dutch treat *n., informal* A meal in a restaurant or an outing at the movies, concert, or theater where each party pays his or her own way. ◆*"I am willing to accept your invitation," Mary said, "but it will have to be Dutch treat."*

dwell on *or* dwell upon *v.* To stay on a subject; not leave something or want to leave; not stop talking or writing about. ◆*Joe dwelt on his mistake long after the test was over.* ◆*Our eyes dwelled on the beautiful sunset.* ◆*The principal dwelled on traffic safety in his talk.*

dyed-in-the-wool *adj. phr.* Thoroughly committed; inveterate; unchanging. ◆*Max is a dyed-in-the-wool Conservative Republican.*

dying to *adj. phr.* Having a great desire to; being extremely eager to. ◆*Seymour is dying to date Mathilda, but she keeps refusing him.*

each and every *adj. phr.* Every.—Used for emphasis. ◆*The captain wants each and every man to be here at eight o'clock.*

early bird *n* An early riser from bed. ◆*Jane and Tom are real early birds; they get up at 6 A.M. every morning.*

early bird catches the worm *or* **early bird gets the worm** A person who gets up early in the morning has the best chance of succeeding; if you arrive early or are quicker, you get ahead of others.—A proverb. ◆*When Billy's father woke him up for school he said, "The early bird catches the worm."*

earn one's keep *v. phr.* To merit one's salary or keep by performing the labor or chores that are expected of one. ◆*John earned his keep at the music conservatory by cleaning all the musical instruments every day.*

ear to the ground *n. phr., informal* Attention directed to the way things are going, or seem likely to go, or to the way people feel and think. ◆*Reporters keep an ear to the ground so as to know as soon as possible what will happen.*

ease off *or* **ease up** *v.* To make or become less nervous; relax; work easier. ◆*When the boss realized that John had been overworking, he eased off his load.*

easier said than done *adj. phr.* This idiom is often heard when one braggingly suggests that he or she can accomplish something difficult, meaning that talking is much less than acting.—A proverb. ◆*"I've decided to swim across Lake Michigan on Christmas day," Johnny said. "That's easier said than done, son," his father replied.*

easygoing *adj.* Amiable in manner; relaxed; not excited. ◆*Because Al has an easygoing personality, everybody loves him.*

easy come, easy go *truncated sent. informal* Something you get quickly and easily may be lost or spent just as easily. ◆*Grandfather thought Billy should have to work for the money Father gave him, saying "Easy come, easy go."*

easy does it *informal* Let's do it carefully, without sudden movements and without forcing too hard or too fast; let's try just hard enough but not too hard. ◆*"Easy does it," said the boss as they moved the piano through the narrow doorway.*

easy mark *n.* A foolishly generous person; one from whom it is easy to get money. ◆*Bill is known to all the neighborhood beggars as an easy mark.*

easy money *n. informal* Money gained without hard work; money that requires little or no effort. ◆*The movie rights to a successful play mean easy money to the writer of the play.*

eat away *v.* **1.** To rot, rust, or destroy. ◆*Rust was eating away the pipe. Cancer ate away the healthy flesh.* **2.** To gradually consume. ◆*The ocean waves were gradually eating the volcanic rocks until they turned into black sand.*

eat crow *v. phr.* To admit you are mistaken or defeated; take back a mistaken statement. ◆*John* had boasted that he would play on the first team; but when the coach did not choose him, he had to eat crow.

eat dirt v. phr., informal To act humble; accept another's insult or bad treatment. ♦Mr. Johnson was so afraid of losing his job that he would eat dirt whenever the boss got mean.

eat humble pie v. phr. To be humbled; to accept insult or shame; admit your error and apologize. ♦Tom told a lie about George, and when he was found out, he had to eat humble pie.

eat like a bird v. phr. To eat very little; have little appetite. ♦Mrs. Benson is on a diet and she eats like a bird.

eat like a horse v. phr. To eat a lot; eat hungrily. ♦The harvesters worked into the evening, and then came in and ate like horses.

eat one out of house and home v. phr. 1. To eat so much as to cause economic hardship. ♦Our teenaged sons are so hungry all the time that they may soon eat us out of house and home. 2. To overstay one's welcome. ♦We love Bob and Jane very much, but after two weeks we started to feel that they were eating us out of house and home.

eat one's cake and have it too v. phr. To use or spend something and still keep it; have both when you must choose one of two things. Often used in negative sentences. ♦Mary wants to buy a beautiful dress she saw at the store, but she also wants to save her birthday money for camp. She wants to eat her cake and have it too.

eat one's heart out v. phr. To grieve long and hopelessly; to become thin and weak from sorrow. ♦For months after her husband's death, Joanne simply ate her heart out.

eat one's words also **swallow one's words** v. phr. To take back something you have said; admit something is not true. ♦John had called Harry a coward, but the boys made him eat his words after Harry bravely fought a big bully.

edge in (on) v. phr. 1. To gradually approach an individual or a group with the intent of taking over or wielding power. ♦Jack was edging in on the firm of Smith and Brown and after half a year actually became its vice president. 2. To approach for capture (said of a group). ♦The hunters were edging in on the wounded leopard.

egg on v. To urge on; excite; lead to action. ♦Joe's wife egged him on to spend money to show off.

eke out v. 1. To fill out or add a little to; increase a little. ♦Mr. Jones eked out a country teacher's small salary by hunting and trapping in the winter. 2. To get (little) by hard work; to earn with difficulty. ♦Fred eked out a bare living by farming on a rocky hillside.

elbow grease n. Exertion; effort; energy. ♦"You'll have to use a little more elbow grease to get these windows clean," Mother said to Ed.

end up v. 1. To come to an end; be ended or finished; stop. ♦How does the story end up? 2. To finally reach or arrive; land. ♦I hope you don't end up in jail. 3. informal To die, be killed. ♦The *gangster ended up in the electric chair.* **4.** or **finish up**. To put an end to; finish; stop. ◆*The politician finally ended up his speech.*

even Steven *adj. phr.* Free of indebtedness toward one another. ◆*"You have paid me back my $100," John said, "so now we're even Steven."*

everybody and his dog *v. phr.* Absolutely everyone; the whole community. ◆*"Don't shout so loud, for heaven's sake!" Valerie complained in a bitter voice. "Do you want everybody and his dog to hear that we're having a fight?"*

every cloud has a silver lining Every trouble has something hopeful that you can see in it, like the bright edge around a dark cloud.—A proverb. ◆*The doctor told Tommy to cheer up when he had measles. "Every cloud has a silver lining," he said.*

every dog has his day Everyone will have his chance or turn; everyone is lucky or popular at some time.—A proverb. ◆*Jack will be able to go to boxing matches like his brother when he grows up. Every dog has his day.*

every now and then *or* **every now and again** *or* **every so often** *or* **every once in a while** *adv. phr.* At fairly regular intervals; fairly often; repeatedly. ◆*John comes to visit me every now and then.* ◆*It was hot work, but every so often Susan would bring us something cold to drink.*

every which way *also* **any which way** In all directions. ◆*Bricks and boards were scattered in confusion on the ground every which way, just as they had fallen after the tornado.*

eye out Careful watch or attention; guard.—Used after *keep, have* or *with*. ◆*Keep an eye out. We're close to Joe's house.* Usually used with *for*. ◆*Mary has her eye out for bargains.*

eyes are bigger than one's stomach *informal* You want more food than you can eat. ◆*Annie took a second big helping of pudding, but her eyes were bigger than her stomach.*

eyes in the back of one's head *n. phr., informal* Ability to know what happens when your back is turned. ◆*Mother must have eyes in the back of her head, because she always knows when I do something wrong.*

eyes open **1.** Careful watch or attention; readiness to see—Usually used with *for*. ◆*Keep your eyes open for a boy in a red cap and sweater.* **2.** Full knowledge; especially of consequences; understanding of what will or might result.—Used with *have* or *with*. ◆*Automobile racing is dangerous. Bob went into it with his eyes open.*

eyes pop out *informal* (You) are very much surprised.—Used with a possessive noun or pronoun. ◆*When Joan found a new computer under the Christmas tree, her eyes popped out.*

eye to **1.** Attention to.—Usually used with *have* or *with*. ◆*Have an eye to spelling in these test papers.* **2.** Plan for, purpose of.—Usually used with *have* or *with*. ◆*Save your money now with an eye to the future.*

face down v. phr. To get the upper hand over someone by behaving forcefully; disconcert someone by the displaying of great self-assurance. ◆*The night guard faced down the burglar by staring him squarely in the face.*

face lift n. phr. 1. A surgical procedure designed to make one's face look younger. ◆*Aunt Jane, who is in her seventies, had an expensive face lift and now she looks as if she were 40.* 2. A renovation, a refurbishing. ◆*Our house needs a major face lift to make it fit in with the rest of the neighborhood.*

face the music v. phr., informal To go through trouble or danger, especially because of something you did; accept your punishment. ◆*The official who had been taking bribes was exposed by a newspaper, and had to face the music.*

face-to-face[1] adv. phr. 1. With your face looking toward the face of another person; each facing the other. ◆*Turning a corner, he found himself face-to-face with a policeman.* 2. In the presence of another or others. ◆*She was thrilled to meet the President face-to-face.* 3. To the point where you must do something.—Used with *with*. ◆*The solution of the first problem brought him face-to-face with a second problem.*

face-to-face[2] adj. Being in the presence of a person; being right with someone. ◆*The British prime minister came to Washington for a face-to-face meeting with the president.*

face up to v. phr. 1. To bravely confront a person or a challenge;

admit. ◆*Jack doesn't want to face up to the fact that Helen doesn't love him anymore.* 2. To confess something to someone; confess to having done something. ◆*Jim had to face up to having stolen a sweater from the department store.*

face value n. 1. The worth or price printed on a stamp, bond, note, piece of paper money, etc. ◆*The savings bond had a face value of $25.* 2. The seeming worth or truth of something. ◆*She took his stories at face value and did not know he was joking.*

faced with adj. phr. Confronted with. ◆*We were all faced with the many wars that broke out in the wake of the collapse of communism.*

facts of life n. phr. 1. The truth which we should know about sex, marriage, and births. ◆*His father told him the facts of life when he was old enough.* 2. The truths one learns about people and their good and bad habits of life, work or play. ◆*As a cub reporter he would learn the facts of life in the newspaper world.*

fair play n. Equal and right action (to another person); justice. ◆*The visiting team did not get fair play in the game.*

fair sex n., informal Women in general; the female sex. ◆ *"Better not use four-letter words in front of a member of the fair sex,"* Joe said.

fair shake n., informal Honest treatment. ◆*Joe has always given me a fair shake.*

fair-weather enemy n. phr. A country that is another country's competitor, short of war. ◆*The Soviet Union was America's fair-*

weather enemy during the Cold War.

fair-weather friend *n. phr.* A person who is a friend only while one is very successful. ◆*John didn't realize how many fair-weather friends he had until his firm had to declare bankruptcy and people turned their backs on him.*

fairy godmother *n.* **1.** A fairy believed to help and take care of a baby as it grows up. **2.** A person who helps and does much for another. ◆*The rich man played fairy godmother to the boys and had a baseball field made for them.*

fall asleep at the switch *v. phr.* To fail to perform an expected task; be remiss in one's duty. ◆*The dean promised our department $250,000 but the foundation never sent the money because someone in the dean's office fell asleep at the switch.*

fall away *v. phr.* To decline; diminish. ◆*I was shocked to see how haggard Alan looked; he seems to be falling away to a shadow.*

fall flat *v., informal* To be a failure; fail. ◆*His joke fell flat because no one understood it.*

fall for *v., slang* **1.** To begin to like very much. ◆*Dick fell for baseball when he was a little boy.* **2.** To begin to love (a boy or a girl.) ◆*Helen was a very pretty girl and people were not surprised that Bill fell for her.* **3.** To believe (something told to fool you.) ◆*Nell did not fall for Joe's story about being a jet pilot.*

fall from grace *v. phr.* To go back to a bad way of behaving; do something bad again. ◆*The boy fell from grace when he lied.*

fall guy *n. slang* The "patsy" in an illegal transaction; a sucker; a dupe; the person who takes the punishment others deserve. ◆*When the Savings and Loan Bank failed, due to embezzlement, the vice president had to be the fall guy, saving the necks of the owners.*

fall in *v.* **1.** To go and stand properly in a row like soldiers. ◆*The captain told his men to fall in.* **2.** To collapse. ◆*The explosion caused the walls of the house to fall in.*

falling-out *n.* Argument; disagreement; quarrel. ◆*The boys had a falling-out when each said that the other had broken the rules.*

fall off the wagon *v. phr., slang alcoholism and drug culture* To return to the consumption of an addictive, such as alcohol or drugs, after a period of abstinence. ◆*Poor Joe has fallen off the wagon again—he is completely incoherent today.*

fallout *n.* **1.** Result of nuclear explosion; harmful radioactive particles. *Some experts consider fallout as dangerous as the bomb itself.* **2.** Undesirable aftereffects in general. ◆*As a fallout of Watergate, many people lost their faith in the government.*

fall out *v.* **1.** To happen. ◆*As it fell out, the Harpers were able to sell their old car.* **2.** To quarrel; fight; fuss; disagree. ◆*The thieves fell out over the division of the loot.* **3.** To leave a military formation. ◆*You men are dismissed. Fall out!* **4.** To leave a building to go and line up. ◆*The soldiers fell out of the barracks for inspection.*

fall over backwards *or* **fall over oneself** *v. phr.* To do everything you can to please someone; try very hard to satisfy someone. ◆*The hotel manager fell over backwards to give the movie star everything she wanted.*

fall short *v.* To fail to reach (some aim); not succeed. ◆*His jump fell three inches short of the world record.*

fall through *v., informal* To fail; be ruined; not happen or be done. ◆*Jim's plans to go to college fell through at the last moment.*

famous last words *n. phr.* Issued as a warning after an optimistic statement indicating that the person with the optimistic outlook could easily be wrong. ◆*"Such a terrible thing as the exploding of a skyscraper with a hijacked airplane could never happen in America!" Joe said. "Famous last words!" Peter answered.*

far cry *n.* Something very different. ◆*His last statement was a far cry from his first story.* ◆*The first automobile could run, but it was a far cry from a modern car.*

farm out *v.* **1.** To have another person do (something) for you; send away to be done. ◆*Our teacher had too many test papers to read, so she farmed out half of them to a friend.* **2.** To send away to be taken care of. ◆*While Mother was sick, the children were farmed out to relatives.* **3.** To send a player to a league where the quality of play is lower. ◆*The player was farmed out to Rochester to gain experience.*

far-out *adj.* **1.** Very far away; distant. ◆*Scientists are planning rocket trips to the moon and far-out planets.* **2.** *informal* Very different from others; queer; odd, unusual. ◆*He enjoyed being with beatniks and other far-out people.* ◆*Susan did not like some of the paintings at the art show because they were too far-out for her.*

feather in one's cap *n. phr.* Something to be proud of; an honor. ◆*It was a feather in his cap to win first prize.*

feather one's nest *v. phr., informal* **1.** To use for yourself money and power, especially from a public office or job in which you are trusted to help other people. ◆*The man feathered his nest in politics by getting money from contractors who built roads.* **2.** To make your home pleasant and comfortable; furnish and decorate your house. ◆*Furniture stores welcome young couples who want to feather their nests.*

fed up *(informal)* ALSO *(slang)* **fed to the gills** *or* **fed to the teeth** *adj. phr.* Having had too much of something; at the end of your patience; disgusted; bored; tired. ◆*People get fed up with anyone who brags all the time.* ◆*John quit football because he was fed to the gills with practice.*

feel a different person *v. phr.* To feel recovered and well again after some illness or draining ordeal. ◆*After she finally managed to get rid of her alcoholic husband, Irene felt like a different person.*

feel down *v. phr.* To feel tired, miserable, exhausted, sad, or depressed. *John doesn't eat right; that's why he feels down so often.* ♦ *"You're feeling down just now, because Suzie left you," the psychologist said, "but you're young, and life is long. Pretty soon you will find someone else."*

feel for someone *v. phr., informal* To be able to sympathize with someone's problems. ♦ *I can really feel for you, John, for losing your job.*

feel like a million *or* **feel like a million dollars** *v. phr., informal* To be in the best of health and spirits. ♦ *I feel like a million this morning.* ♦ *He had a headache yesterday but feels like a million dollars today.*

feel like a new man *v. phr.* To feel healthy, vigorous, and well again after a major physical illness or emotional upheaval. ♦ *Ted felt like a new man after his successful heart bypass operation.*

feel low *v. phr.* To be depressed; be in low spirits. ♦ *I don't know what's the matter with Mary, but she says she has been feeling very low all afternoon.*

feel one's age *v. phr.* To be conscious of one's advancing years and to give signs of one's waning powers and energy. ♦ *"I started to feel my age," Grandpa said. "I'm ninety, you know, and it's getting harder and harder to stay up all night dancing with the girls than when I was only eighty."*

feel one's way *v. phr.* To proceed cautiously by trial and error; probe. ♦ *I won't ask her to marry me directly; I will feel my way first.*

feel ten feet tall *v. phr.* To feel self-confident, happy, optimistic, full of energy. ♦ *Winning the Nobel Prize for medicine, made Dr. McDermott feel ten feet tall.*

feel the pinch *v. phr.* To be short of money; experience monetary difficulties. ♦ *If we are going to have a recession, everybody will feel the pinch.*

feel up *v. phr., vulgar, avoid* To arouse sexually by manual contact. ♦ *You mean to tell me that you've been going out for six months and he hasn't ever tried to feel you up?*

feel up to something *v. phr., informal* To feel adequately knowledgeable, strong, or equipped to handle a given task. ♦ *Do you feel up to jogging a mile a day with me?*

feet of clay *n. phr.* A hidden fault or weakness in a person which is discovered or shown. ♦ *The famous general showed he had feet of clay when he began to drink liquor.*

feet on the ground *n. phr.* An understanding of what can be done; sensible ideas. Used with a possessive. ♦ *John has his feet on the ground; he knows he cannot learn everything at once.*

fence-sitter *n.* A person unable to pick between two sides; a person who does not want to choose. ♦ *Dad says he is a fence-sitter because he doesn't know which man he wants for president.*

fence-sitting *n. or adj.* Choosing neither side. ♦ *You have been fence-sitting for too long. It is time you made up your mind.*

ferret out *literary or* **smell out** *or* **sniff out** *v.* To hunt or drive from hiding; to bring out into the open; search for and find. ◆*John ferreted out the answer to the question in the library.* ◆*Jane smelled out the boys' secret hiding place in the woods.*

few and far between *adj. phr.* Not many; few and scattered; not often met or found; rare.—Used in the predicate. ◆*People who will work as hard as Thomas A. Edison are few and far between.*

fifty-fifty[1] *adv., informal* Equally; evenly. ◆*When Dick and Sam bought an old car, they divided the cost fifty-fifty.*

fifty-fifty[2] *adj., informal* **1.** Divided or shared equally. ◆*It will be a fifty-fifty arrangement; half the money for me and half for you.* **2.** Half for and half against; half good and half bad. ◆*There is only a fifty-fifty chance that we will win the game.*

fight fire with fire *v. phr. slightly formal, of Biblical origin* To fight back in the same way one was attacked; make a defense similar to the attack. ◆*The candidate was determined to fight fire with fire in the debate.*

fight off *v. phr.* **1.** To struggle against someone so as to free oneself; push an attacker back. ◆*Suzy fought off her two attackers in Central Park with a couple of karate chops.* **2.** To strive to overcome something negative. ◆*After twelve hours at the computer terminal, Jane had to fight off her overwhelming desire to go to sleep.*

figure out *v.* **1.** To find an answer by thinking about (some problem or difficulty); solve. ◆*Tom couldn't figure out the last problem on the arithmetic test.* ◆*Sam couldn't figure out how to print a program until the teacher showed him how.* **2.** To learn how to explain; understand. ◆*Laurence is an odd boy; I can't figure him out.*

figure up *v. phr.* To calculate; add up. ◆*If you can figure up how many phone calls I've made from your home, I will pay you right away.*

fill in *v.* **1.** To write words needed in blanks; put in; fill. ◆*You should fill in all the blanks on an application for a job.* **2.** *informal* To tell what you should know. ◆*The teacher filled in Mary about class work done while she was sick.* **3.** To take another's place; substitute. ◆*The teacher was sick and Miss Jones filled in for her.*

fill one's shoes *v. phr.* To take the place of another and do as well; to substitute satisfactorily for. ◆*When Jack got hurt, the coach had nobody to fill his shoes.*

fill out *v.* **1.** To put in what is missing; complete; finish; *especially,* to complete (a printed application blank or other form) by writing the missing facts in the blank spaces; to write down facts which are asked for in (a report or application.) ◆*After Tom passed his driving test he filled out an application for his driver's license.* **2.** To become heavier and fatter; gain weight. ◆*The girl was pale and thin after her sickness, but in a few months she filled out.*

fill the bill *v. phr., informal* To be just what is needed; be good enough for something; be just right. ◆*The boss was worried* *about hiring a deaf boy, but after he tried Tom out for a few weeks, he said that Tom filled the bill.*

filthy rich *adj. phr.* Extremely rich but without cultural refinement; nouveau riche. ♦*"The Murgatroyds are filthy rich," Ted complained. "They are rolling in money but they never learned how to behave properly at a dinner table."*

finders keepers *or* **finders keepers, losers weepers** *informal* Those who find lost things can keep them.—Used usually by children to claim the right to keep something they have found. ♦*I don't have to give it back; it's finders keepers.* ♦*Finders keepers, losers weepers! It's my knife now!*

find out *v.* **1.** To learn or discover (something you did not know before.) ♦*I don't know how this car works, but I'll soon find out.* ♦*He watched the birds to find out where they go.* **2.** To get facts; to get facts about. ♦*He wrote to find out about a job in Alaska.* **3.** To discover (someone) doing wrong; catch. ♦*The boy knew that if he cheated on the test the teacher would find him out.*

fine-tooth comb *n. phr.* Great care; careful attention so as not to miss anything. ♦*The police searched the scene of the crime with a fine-tooth comb for clues.*

finger in the pie *n. phr., informal* Something to do with what happens; part interest or responsibility. ♦*When the girls got up a Christmas party, I felt sure Alice had a finger in the pie.* ♦*The Jones Company was cho-*

sen to build the new hospital and we knew Mr. Smith had a finger in the pie.

firebug *n.* An arsonist; one who willfully sets fire to property. ♦*The police caught the firebug just as he was about to set another barn ablaze in the country.*

firing squad *n.* A group of soldiers chosen to shoot a prisoner to death or to fire shots over a grave as a tribute. ♦*A dictator often sends his enemies before a firing squad.*

first come, first served *truncated sent. informal* If you arrive first, you will be served first; people will be waited on in the order they come; the person who comes first will have his turn first. ♦*Get in line for your ice cream, boys. First còme, first served.* ♦*The rule in the restaurant is first come, first served.* ♦*There are only a few seats left so it's first come, first served.*

first of all *adv. phr.* Chiefly; primarily; as the first thing. ♦*After we get to Chicago, we will, first of all, try to find a reliable used car.*

first-run *adj. phr.* Shown for the first time; new. ♦*The local theater showed only first-run movies.*

fish for a compliment *v. phr.* To try to make someone pay a compliment. ♦*When Jim showed me his new car, I could tell that he was fishing for a compliment.*

fish in muddy *or* **troubled waters** *v. phr.* To take advantage of a troubled or confusing situation; seek personal advantage. ♦*With the police disorganized after the collapse of communism in*

Europe, many criminals started to fish in troubled waters.

fish out of water *n. phr.* A person who is out of his proper place in life; someone who does not fit in. ♦*She was the only girl at the party not in a formal dress and she felt like a fish out of water.*

fit as a fiddle *adj. phr.* In very good health. ♦*The man was almost 90 years old but fit as a fiddle.*

fit for *v. phr.* To be suited for; be prepared for. ♦*"What kind of job is Ted fit for?" the social worker asked.*

fit in with *v. phr.* To fall into agreement or accord with. ♦*His plans to take a vacation in early July fit in perfectly with the university schedule.*

fit like a glove *v. phr.* To fit perfectly. ♦*Her new dress fits her like a glove.*

fit out *or* **fit up** *v.* To give things needed; furnish. ♦*The soldiers were fitted out with guns and clothing.* ♦*The government fitted out warships and got sailors for them.*

fit to be tied[1] *adj. phr., informal* Very angry or upset. ♦*She was fit to be tied when she saw the broken glass.*

fit to be tied[2] *adv. phr., substandard* Very hard.—Used for emphasis. ♦*Uncle Willie was laughing fit to be tied at the surprised look on Mother's face.*

fit to hold a candle to *adj. phr., always in the negative* Much inferior to; worth less; cannot be compared with someone or something. ♦*"I am not fit to hold a candle to Professor Teller when it comes to nuclear physics," Joe said.*

fix someone's wagon *or* **fix someone's little red wagon** *v. phr., informal* 1. (Said to a child as a threat) to administer a spanking. ♦*Stop that right away or I'll fix your (little red) wagon!* 2. (Said of an adult) to thwart or frustrate another, to engineer his failure. ♦*If he sues me for slander, I will counter-sue him for malicious prosecution. That will fix his wagon!*

fix someone up with *v. phr., informal* To help another get a date with a woman or man by arranging a meeting for the two. ♦*Say Joe, can you possibly fix me up with someone this weekend? I am so terribly lonesome!*

fix up *v. phr.* 1. To repair. ♦*The school is having the old gym fixed up.* 2. To arrange. ♦*I think I can fix it up with the company so that John gets the transfer he desires.* 3. To arrange a date that might lead to a romance or even to marriage. ♦*Mary is a great matchmaker; she fixed up Ron and Betty at her recent party.*

fizzle out *v., informal* 1. To stop burning; die out. ♦*The fuse fizzled out before exploding the firecracker.* 2. To fail after a good start; end in failure. ♦*The party fizzled out when everyone went home early.*

flag down *v., informal* To stop by waving a signal flag or as if waving a signal flag. ♦*A policeman flagged down the car with his flashlight.*

flare up *v.* (stress on *up*) 1. To burn brightly for a short time especially after having died down. ♦*The fire flared up again and then died.* 2. To become suddenly angry. ♦*The mayor flared up at the reporter's* remark. **3.** To begin again suddenly, especially for a short time after a quiet time. ♦*Mr. Gray's arthritis flared up sometimes.*

flare-up *n.* (stress on *flare*) The reoccurrence of an infection or an armed conflict. ♦*He had a flare-up of his arthritis. There was a bad flare-up of hostilities in some countries.*

flatfoot *n., slang, derogatory* A policeman. ♦*"What does Joe do for a living?—He's a flatfoot."*

flat-out *adv. phr., informal* **1.** Without hiding anything; plainly; openly. ♦*The student told his teacher flat-out that he was not listening to her.* **2.** At top speed; as fast as possible. ♦*He saw two men running flat-out from the wild rhinoceros.*

flea in one's ear *n. phr., informal* An idea or answer that is not welcome; an annoying or surprisingly sharp reply or hint. ♦*I'll put a flea in his ear if he bothers me once more.*

flea market *n. phr.* A place where antiques, second-hand things, and cheap articles are sold, and especially one in the open air. ♦*There are many outdoor flea markets in Europe.*

flesh and blood *n.* **1.** A close relative (as a father, daughter, brother); close relatives. Used in the phrase *one's own flesh and blood.* ♦*Such an answer from her—and she's my own flesh and blood, too!* **2.** The appearance of being real or alive. ♦*The author doesn't give his characters any flesh and blood.* **3.** The human body. ♦*Before child labor laws, small children often worked 50 or 60 hours a week in factories. It*

was more than flesh and blood could bear.

flip one's lid *also* **flip one's wig** *slang* **1.** To lose one's temper. ♦*When that pushy salesman came back Mom really flipped her lid.* **2.** To lose your mind; become insane. ♦*When he offered me three times the pay I was getting, I thought he had flipped his lid.* **3.** To become unreasonably enthusiastic. ♦*She flipped her lid over a hat she saw in the store window.*

flip out *v. phr., slang, informal* To go insane, to go out of one's mind. ♦*It is impossible to talk to Joe today—he must have flipped out.*

flunk out *v. phr.* To have to withdraw from school or college because of too many failing grades. ♦*Fred flunked out of college during his junior year.*

flush it *v. phr., slang* **1.** To fail (something). ♦*I really flushed it in my math course.* **2.** *interj., used imperatively* Expression registering refusal to believe something considered stupid or false. ♦*"You expect me to buy that story? Flush it!"*

fly blind *v. phr.* **1.** To fly an airplane by instruments alone. ♦*In the heavy fog he had to fly blind.* **2.** *informal* To do something without understanding what you are doing. ♦*I'm glad the car runs now; I was flying blind when I fixed it.*

fly-by-night[1] *adj.* Set up to make a lot of money in a hurry, then disappear so people can't find you to complain about poor work, etc.; not trustworthy; not reliable. ♦*Mrs. Blank bought her vacuum cleaner from a new company; when she tried to* *have it fixed, she found it was a fly-by-night business.*

fly-by-night[2] *n., informal* **1.** A company that sells many cheap things for a big profit and then disappears. ◆*A dependable company honors its guarantees, but a fly-by-night only wants your money.* **2.** A person who does not pay his bills, but sneaks away (as at night.) ◆*Hotels are bothered by fly-by-nights.*

fly by the seat of one's pants *v. phr., slang* To fly an airplane by feel and instinct rather than with the help of the instruments. ◆*Many pilots in World War I had to fly by the seat of their pants.*

flying high *adj., slang* Very happy; joyful. ◆*Jack was flying high after his team won the game.*

fly in the face of *or* **fly in the teeth of** *v. phr.* To ignore; go against; show disrespect or disregard for. ◆*You can't fly in the face of good business rules and expect to be successful.*

fly in the ointment *n. phr., informal* An unpleasant part of a pleasant thing; something small that spoils your fun. ◆*We had a lot of fun at the beach; the only fly in the ointment was George's cutting his foot on a piece of glass.*

fly off the handle *v. phr., informal* To become very angry. ◆*John flew off the handle whenever Mary made a mistake.* ◆*The children's noise made the man next door fly off the handle.*

fly the coop *v. phr., slang* To leave suddenly and secretly; run away. ◆*The robbers flew the coop before the police arrived.*

flying visit *n. phr.* A visit of very short duration. ◆*Tom came to New York for only a flying visit.* ◆*We had hardly eaten lunch when he had to leave.*

foam at the mouth *v. phr., slang* To be very angry, like a mad dog. ◆*By the time Uncle Henry had the third flat tire he was really foaming at the mouth.*

fob off *v., informal* **1.** To get something false accepted as good or real. ◆*The peddler fobbed off pieces of glass as diamonds.* **2.** To put aside; not really answer but get rid of. ◆*Her little brother asked where she was going, but she fobbed him off with an excuse.*

follow one's nose *v. phr., informal* **1.** To go straight ahead; continue in the same direction. ◆*Just follow your nose and you'll get there.* **2.** To go any way you happen to think of. ◆*Oh, I don't know just where I want to go. I'll just follow my nose and see what happens.*

follow suit *v. phr.* **1.** To play a card of the same color and kind that another player has put down. ◆*When diamonds were led, I had to follow suit.* **2.** To do as someone else has done; follow someone's example. ◆*When the others went swimming, I followed suit.*

follow through *v. phr.* To finish an action that you have started. ◆*Bob drew plans for a table for his mother, but he did not follow through by making it.*

follow up *v. phr., informal* **1.** To chase or follow closely and without giving up. ◆*The hunters followed up the wounded buffalo until it fell dead.* **2.** Make (one action) more successful by doing something more. ◆*After Mary sent a letter to apply for a job; she followed it up by going to talk to the personnel manager.* **3a.** To hunt for (more news about something that has already been in the newspapers, radio, or TV news); find more about. ◆*The day after news of the fire at Brown's store, the newspaper sent a reporter to follow up Mr. Brown's future plans.* **3b.** To print or broadcast (more news about some happening that has been in the news before). ◆*The fire story was printed Monday, and Tuesday's paper followed it up by saying that Mr. Brown planned to build a bigger and better store at the same place.*

follow-up *n.* Additional work or research by means of which an earlier undertaking's chances of success are increased. ◆*I hope you'll be willing to do a bit of follow-up.*

fond of Having a liking for; attracted to by strong liking. ◆*Alan is fond of candy.* ◆*Uncle Bill was the children's favorite, and he was fond of them too.*

food for thought *n. phr.* Something to think about or worth thinking about; something that makes you think. ◆*The teacher told John that she wanted to talk to his father, and that gave John food for thought.* ◆*There is much food for thought in this book.*

fool and his money are soon parted A foolish person soon wastes his money.—A proverb. ◆*Jimmy spends all his pennies for candy. A fool and his money are soon parted.*

fool around *or* **mess around** *or* **play around** *or* **monkey around** *v., informal* **1.** To spend time playing, fooling, or joking instead of being serious or working; waste time. ◆*If you go to college, you must work, not fool around.* **2.** To treat or handle carelessly. ◆*Bob cut himself by fooling around with a sharp knife.* ◆*Suzie says she wishes John would quit playing around with the girls and get married.* **3.** *or* **fiddle around** To work or do something in an irregular or unplanned way; tinker. ◆*Jimmy likes to monkey around with automobile engines.*

foot in the door *n. phr., informal* The first step toward getting or doing something; a start toward success; opening. ◆*Don't let Jane get her foot in the door by joining the club or soon she'll want to be president.*

footloose and fancy-free *adj. phr.* Free and free to do what one wants (said of unmarried men). ◆*Ron is a merry bachelor and seems to enjoy greatly being footloose and fancy-free.*

foot the bill *v. phr.* To cover the expenses of; pay for something. ◆*The bride's father footed two-thirds of the bill for his daughter's wedding.*

for all I know *adv. phr.* To the extent that I am familiar with the situation or the circumstances. ◆*For all I know, Suzie may have left town.*

for all that *adv. phr.* In spite of what has been said, alleged, or rumored. ◆*Well, for all that, we think that she is still the most deserving candidate for Congress.*

for all the world *adv. phr.* **1.** Under no circumstances. ◆*Betty said she wouldn't marry Jake for all the world.* **2.** Precisely; exactly. ◆*It began for all the world like a successful baseball season for the UIC Flames, when suddenly they lost to the Blue Demons.*

for a song *adv. phr., informal* At a low price; for a bargain price; cheaply. ◆*They bought the house for a song and sold it a few years later at a good profit.*

for better or worse *or* **for better or for worse** *adv. phr.* **1.** With good or bad effect, depending on how one looks at the matter. ◆*The historian did justice, for better or worse, to the careers of several famous men.* **2.** Under any eventuality; forever; always. ◆*Alex and Masha decided to leave Moscow and come to Chicago, for better or for worse.* **3.** (Marriage vows) Forever, for as long as one may live. ◆*With this ring I thee wed, for richer or poorer, in sickness and in health, for better or worse, til death do us part.*

for crying out loud *informal* Used as an exclamation to show that you feel surprised or cross. ◆*For crying out loud, look who's here!*

for days on end *adv. phr.* For a long time; for many days. ◆*The American tourists tried to get used to Scottish pronunciation for days on end, but still couldn't understand what the Scots were saying.*

for dear life *adv. phr.* As though afraid of losing your life. ◆*When the horse began to run, she held on for dear life.*

forever and a day *adv. phr., informal* For a seemingly endless time; forever; always. Used for emphasis. ◆*We waited forever and a day to find out who won the contest.*

for good *also* **for good and all** Permanently, forever, for always. ◆*He hoped that the repairs would stop the leak for good.* ◆*When John graduated from school, he decided that he was done with study for good and all.*

for good measure *adv. phr.* As something more added to what is expected or needed; as an extra. ◆*He sold me the car at a cheap price and included the radio for good measure.*

for Heaven's sake! *adv. phr.* Please. ◆*"Help me, for Heaven's sake!" the injured man cried.*

for hours on end *adv. phr.* For many hours; for a very long time. ◆*We have been trying to get this computer going for hours on end, but we need serious professional help.*

for keeps *adv. phr.* **1.** For the winner to keep. ◆*They played marbles for keeps.* **2.** *informal* For always; forever. ◆*He left town for keeps.* **3.** Seriously, not just for fun. ◆*This is not a joke, it's for keeps.*

for love or money *adv. phr.* For anything; for any price. Used in negative sentences. ◆*I wouldn't give him my dog for love or money.*

for short *adv. phr.* So as to make shorter; as an abbreviation or nickname. ◆*The National Broadcasting Company is called NBC for short.*

for sure *or* **for certain** *adv. phr.* **1.** Without doubt; certainly; surely. ◆*He couldn't tell for sure* *from a distance whether it was George or Tom.* ♦*He didn't know for certain which bus to take.* ♦*I know for certain that he has a car.* 2. *slang* Certain. ♦ *"That car is smashed so badly it's no good any more." "That's for sure!"*

for that matter *adv. phr.* With regard to that; about that. ♦*I don't know, and for that matter, I don't care.* ♦*Alice didn't come, and for that matter, she didn't even telephone.*

for the asking *adv. phr.* By asking; by asking for it; on request. ♦*John said I could borrow his bike any time. It was mine for the asking.*

for the better *adj. or adv. phr.* With a better result; for something that is better. ♦*The doctor felt that moving Father to a dry climate would be for the better.*

for the birds *adj. phr., slang* Not interesting; dull; silly; foolish; stupid. ♦*I think history is for the birds.* ♦*I saw that movie. It's for the birds.*

for the life of one *adv., informal* No matter how hard you try.— Used for emphasis with negative statements. ♦*I can't for the life of me remember his name.*

foul one's own nest *v. phr.* To denigrate one's own country or family. ♦*Peter sure fouled his own nest when in a drunken stupor he blurted out that the family fortune started during Prohibition when his grandfather used to work for Al Capone.*

foul play *n.* Treachery; a criminal act (such as murder). ♦*After they discovered the dead body, the police suspected foul play.* ♦ *"She must have met with foul*

play," the chief inspector said when they couldn't find the 12-year-old girl who had disappeared.

foul up *v., informal* (stress on *up*) 1. To make dirty. ♦*The birds fouled up his newly washed car.* 2. To tangle up. ♦*He tried to throw a lasso but he got the rope all fouled up.* 3. To ruin or spoil by stupid mistakes; botch. ♦*He fouled the whole play up by forgetting his part.* 4. To make a mistake; to blunder. ♦*Blue suit and brown socks! He had fouled up again.* 5. To go wrong. ♦*Why do some people foul up and become criminals?*

foul-up *n.* (stress on *foul*) 1. *informal* A confused situation; confusion; mistake. ♦*The luncheon was handled with only one or two foul-ups.* 2. *informal* A breakdown. ♦*There was a foul-up in his car's steering mechanism.* 3. *slang* A person who fouls up or mixes things. ♦*He had gotten a reputation as a foul-up.*

fraidy-cat *or* **fraid-cat** *or* **scaredy-cat** *or* **scared cat** *n., informal* A shy person; someone who is easily frightened.— Usually used by or to children. ♦*Tom was a fraidy-cat and wouldn't go in the water.*

frame of mind *n. phr.* One's mental outlook; the state of one's psychological condition. ♦*There is no use trying to talk to him while he is in such a negative frame of mind.*

freak-out[1] *n., slang* An act of losing control; a situation that is bizarre or unusual. ♦*The party last night was a regular freak-out.*

freak out² *v. phr., slang* To lose control over one's conscious self due to the influence of hallucinogenic drugs. *◆Joe freaked out last night.*

free and easy *adj.* Not strict; relaxed or careless. *◆They were free and easy with their money and it was soon gone.*

free enterprise *n. phr.* A system in which private business is controlled by as few government rules as possible. *◆The United States is proud of its free enterprise.*

free hand *n.* Great freedom. *◆The teacher had a free hand in her classroom.*

freeload *v.* To have oneself supported in terms of food and housing at someone else's expense. *◆When are you guys going to stop freeloading and do some work?*

free rein *n.* Freedom to do what you want. *◆Father is strict with the children, but Mother gives them free rein.*

free-for-all *n.* **1.** Unlimited, free access to something everybody wants. *◆The Smith's party was a lavish free-for-all; everybody could eat and drink as much as they wanted.* **2.** A barroom, tavern, or street fight in which everybody participates. *◆The celebration after the soccer game victory turned into an uncontrollable free-for-all.*

freeze out *v., informal* To force out or keep from a share or part in something by unfriendly or dishonest treatment. *◆The other boys froze John out of the club.*

freeze over *v.* To become covered with ice. *◆The children wanted the lake to freeze over so they could ice-skate.*

friend in need *n. phr.* A dependable friend, who is likely to come to one's aid even if one is unable to offer anything in return. *◆As the old saying says, "A friend in need is a friend indeed."*

friendly fire *n. phr., military* An accident during a battle when one is shot not by the enemy but by one's own comrades in arms in error due to faulty reconnaissance. *◆Both during the first and the second Gulf Wars, several American and British soldiers were killed by friendly fire.*

from hand to hand *adv. phr.* From one person to another and another. *◆The box of candy was passed from hand to hand.*

from rags to riches *adv. phr.* Suddenly making a fortune; becoming rich overnight. *◆The Smiths went from rags to riches when they unexpectedly won the lottery.*

from scratch *adv. phr., informal* With no help from anything done before; from the beginning; from nothing. *◆Dick built a radio from scratch.*

from the bottom of one's heart *or* **with all one's heart** *adv. phr.* With great feeling; sincerely. *◆The people welcomed the returning soldiers from the bottom of their hearts.*

from the heart *adv.* Sincerely; honestly. *◆John always speaks from the heart.*

from the sublime to the ridiculous *adv. phr.* Covering an entire range of things or ideas from the extremely lofty and elevated to the negligible and trivial. *◆The couple's prenuptial negotiations covered* *absolutely every detail of their future life together from the sublime to the ridiculous.*

from time to time *adv. phr.* Not often; not regularly; sometimes; occasionally; at one time and then again at another time. ♦*Even though the Smiths have moved, we still see them from time to time.* ♦*Mother tries new recipes from time to time, but the children never like them.*

from way back *adv. phr.* From a previous time; from a long time ago. ♦*They have known one another from way back when they went to the same elementary school.*

fuck around *v. phr., vulgar, avoidable* 1. To be promiscuous. ♦*John fucks around with the secretaries.* 2. To play at something without purpose, to mess around. ♦*He doesn't accomplish anything, because he fucks around so much.*

fuck off *v. phr., vulgar, avoidable* 1. Go away! ♦*Can't you see you're bothering me? Fuck off!* 2. To be lazy. ♦*John said "I don't feel like working, so I'll fuck off today."*

fuck up *v. phr., vulgar, avoidable* To make a mess of something or oneself. ♦*Because he was totally unprepared, he fucked up his exam.* ♦*He is so fucked up he doesn't know whether he is coming or going.*

fuck-up *n. vulgar, avoidable* A mess; a badly botched situation. ♦*What a fuck-up the dissolution of the USSR created!*

fuddy-duddy *n.* A person whose ideas and habits are old-fashioned. ♦*His students think Professor Jones is an old fuddy-duddy.*

full blast *adv.* At full capacity. ♦*With all the research money at their disposal, the new computer firm was going ahead full blast.*

full-bodied *adj.* Mature; of maximum quality. ♦*The wines from that region in California have a rich, full-bodied flavor.*

full-fledged *adj.* Having everything that is needed to be something; complete. ♦*A girl needs three years of training to be a full-fledged nurse.*

full tilt *adv.* At full speed; at high speed. ♦*He ran full tilt into the door and broke his arm.*

fun and games *n., slang, informal* 1. A party or other entertaining event. 2. Something trivially easy. 3. Petting, or sexual intercourse. 4. (Ironically) An extraordinary difficult task. ♦*How was your math exam? (With a dismayed expression):—Yeah, it was all fun and games, man.*

fun house *n.* A place where people see many funny things and have tricks played on them to make them laugh or have a good time. ♦*The boys and girls had a good time looking at themselves in mirrors in the fun house.*

funny bone *n.* 1. The place at the back of the elbow that hurts like electricity when accidentally hit. ♦*He hit his funny bone on the arm of the chair.* 2. *or informal* **crazy bone** Sense of humor; understanding jokes. ♦*Her way of telling the story tickled his funny bone.*

gain ground *v. phr.* **1.** To go forward; move ahead. ◆*The soldiers fought hard and began to gain ground.* **2.** To become stronger; make progress; improve. ◆*Under Lincoln, the Republican Party gained ground.*

gallows' humor *n. phr.* Bitter joke(s) that make fun of a very serious matter, e.g., death, imprisonment, etc. ◆*When the criminal was led to the electric chair on Monday morning, he said, "Nice way to start the week, eh?"*

game is up *or slang* **jig is up** The secret or plan won't work; we are caught or discovered. ◆*The jig's up; the principal knows the boys have been smoking in the basement.*

gang up on *or* **gang up against** *v. phr., informal* To jointly attack someone, either physically or verbally; take sides in a group against an individual. ◆*The class bully was stronger than all the other boys, so they had to gang up on him to put him in his place.*

garbage down *v. phr., slang* To eat eagerly and at great speed without much regard for manners or social convention. ◆*The children garbaged down their food.*

gas up *v., informal* **1.** To fill the gasoline tank. ◆*The mechanics gassed up the planes for their long trip.* **2.** To fill the tank with gasoline. ◆*The big truck stopped at the filling station and gassed up.*

gee whiz *interj., informal* Used as an exclamation to show surprise or other strong feeling. Rare in written English. ◆*Gee whiz! I am late again.*

generation gap *n., informal, hackneyed phrase* The difference in social values, philosophies, and manners between children and their parents, teachers, and relatives which causes a lack of understanding between them and frequently leads to violent confrontations. ◆*My daughter is twenty and I am forty, but we have no generation gap in our family.*

generous to a fault *adj. phr.* Excessively generous. ◆*Generous to a fault, my Aunt Elizabeth gave away all her rare books to her old college.*

get across *v.* **1.** To explain clearly, make (something) clear; to make clear the meaning of. ◆*Mr. Brown is a good coach because he can get across the plays.* **2.** To become clear. ◆*The teacher tried to explain the problem, but the explanation did not get across to the class.*

get a feel for *or* **get the hang of** *v. phr.* To gain an understanding of how something works, to become more skilled at handling something. ◆*I was trying to learn how to play chess, but I can't seem to get a feel for it.* ◆*John practiced surfing long enough, until he got the hang of it.*

get a fix *or* **give a fix** *v. phr., slang, drug culture* To provide (someone) with an injection of narcotics. ◆*The neighborhood pusher gave Joe a fix.* Contrast GET A FIX ON.

get a fix on *v. phr., informal* Receive a reading of a distant object by electronic means, as by radar or sonar. ◆*Can you get*

a fix on the submarine?
Contrast GET A FIX.

get after v., *informal* **1.** To try or try again to make someone do what he is supposed to do. ◆*Ann's mother gets after her to hang up her clothes.* **2.** To scold or make an attack on. ◆*The police are getting after the crooks in the city.*

get a grip on v. phr. To take firm control of something. ◆*If Tim wants to keep his job, he had better get a grip on himself and start working harder.*

get ahead v. **1.** *informal* To become successful. ◆*The person with a good education finds it easier to get ahead.* **2.** To be able to save money; get out of debt. ◆*After Father pays all the doctor bills, maybe we can get a little money ahead and buy a car.*

get a head start on v. phr. To receive preliminary help or instruction in a particular subject so that the recipient is in a favorable position compared to his or her peers. ◆*At our school, children get a head start on their reading ability thanks to a special program.*

get (a) hold of oneself v. phr. To gain composure over oneself, to stop being upset or excited. ◆*"Get hold of yourself, son!" John's father told him. "Stop yelling at your little sister, just because she put on your jacket."*

get a leg up on one v. phr. To gain an advantage over someone else. ◆*I practiced my Ping-Pong game for several weeks until at last I got a leg up on my best friend Jim, who is actually a champion.*

get a life v. phr., *slang* To decide to look out for oneself, to come out from one's shell, to stop being under the thumb of another. ◆*"All my life I was doing things for my husband, who treated me very shabbily. Too bad that he is dead, but at long last I'll try to get a life," the recently widowed Mrs. Goodman said.*

get a load of v. phr., *slang* **1.** To take a good look at; see (something unusual or interesting.)— Often used to show surprise or admiration. ◆*Get a load of Dick's new car!* **2.** To listen to carefully or with interest, especially exciting news.—Often used as a command. *Get a load of this: Alice got married yesterday!*

get along *also* **get on** v. **1.** To go or move away; move on. ◆*The policeman told the boys on the street corner to get along.* **2.** To go forward; make progress; advance. ◆*John is getting along well in school. He is learning more every day.* **3.** To advance; become old or late. ◆*It is getting along towards sundown.* ◆*Grandmother is 68 and getting along.* **4.** To get or make what you need; manage. ◆*It isn't easy to get along in the jungle.* ◆*We can get along on $100 a week.* **5.** To live or work together in a friendly way; agree; cooperate; not fight or argue. ◆*We don't get along with the Jones family.* ◆*Jim and Jane get along fine together.* ◆*Don't be hard to get along with.*

get a kick out of v. phr. To be greatly thrilled; derive pleasure from. ◆*Tom and Marty get a* kick out of playing four hands on the piano.

get a line on v. phr. To receive special, sometimes even confidential, information about something. ◆Before Bill accepted his new position, he got a line on how the business was being run.

get along or **on in years** v. phr. To age; grow old. ◆My father is getting along in years; he will be ninety on his next birthday.

get a move on informal or slang
get a wiggle on v. phr. To hurry up; get going.—Often used as a command. ◆Get a move on, or you will be late.

get a rise out of v. phr., slang 1. To have some fun with (a person) by making (him) angry; tease. ◆The boys get a rise out of Joe by teasing him about his girl friend. 2. vulgar, avoid To be sexually aroused (said of males). ◆Jim always gets a rise out of watching adult movies.

get around to v. To do (something) after putting it off; find time for. ◆Mr. Lee hopes to get around to washing his car next Saturday.

get at v. 1. To reach an understanding of; find out the meaning. ◆This book is very hard to get at. 2. To do harm to. ◆The cat is on the chair trying to get at the canary. 3. To have a chance to do; attend to. ◆I hope I have time to get at my homework tonight. 4. To mean; aim at; hint at. ◆What the teacher was getting at in this lesson was that it is important to speak correctly.

getaway car n. phr. A vehicle parked near the scene of a crime in which the criminals

escape. ◆The police intercepted the getaway car at a major crossroads.

get away with v., informal To do (something bad or wrong) without being caught or punished. ◆Some students get away without doing their homework.

get away with murder v. phr., informal To do something very bad without being caught or punished. ◆John is scolded if he is late with his homework, but Robert gets away with murder.

get a word in or **get a word in edgewise** also **get a word in edgeways** v. phr. To find a chance to say something when others are talking. ◆Mary talked so much that Jack couldn't get a word in edgewise.

get back at v., informal To do something bad to (someone who has done something bad to you) hurt in return. ◆The elephant waited many years to get back at the man who fed him red pepper.

get back on one's feet v. phr. To once again become financially solvent; regain one's former status and income, or health. ◆Max got back on his feet soon after his open heart surgery. ◆Tom's business was ruined due to the inflation, but he got back on his feet again.

get behind v. 1. To go too slowly; be late; do something too slowly. ◆The post office got behind in delivering Christmas mail. 2. informal To support; help. ◆A club is much better if members get behind their leaders. ◆We got behind Mary to be class president. 3. informal To explain; find out the reason for. ◆The police are questioning *many people to try and get behind the bank robbery.*

get by v., informal **1.** To be able to go past; pass. ♦*The cars moved to the curb so that the fire engine could get by.* **2.** To satisfy the need or demand. ♦*Mary can get by with her old coat this winter.* **3.** Not to be caught and scolded or punished. ♦*The boy got by without answering the teacher's question because a visitor came in.*

get cracking v. phr., slang, informal To hurry up, to start moving fast. (Used mostly as an imperative.) ♦*Come on, you guys, let's get cracking!* (Let's hurry up!)

get down to brass tacks also **get down to cases** v. phr., informal To begin the most important work or business; get started on the most important things to talk about or know. ♦*A busy doctor wants his patients to get down to brass tacks.*

get down to business or **work** v. phr. To start being serious; begin to face a problem to be solved, or a task to be accomplished. ♦*Gentlemen, I'm afraid the party is over and we must get down to business.*

get even v., informal **1.** To owe nothing. ♦*Mr. Johnson has a lot of debts, but in a few years he will get even.* **2.** To do something bad to pay someone back for something bad; get revenge; hurt back. *Jack is waiting to get even with Bill for tearing up his notebook.*

get going v., informal **1.** To excite; stir up and make angry. ♦*Talking about her freckles gets Mary going.* **2.** or chiefly British **get cracking** To begin to move; get started. ♦*The teacher told Walter to get going on his history lesson.* ♦*The foreman told the workmen to get cracking.*

get hitched v. phr. To get married. ♦*After a long period of dating, Fred and Mary finally got hitched.*

get hold of v. **1.** To get possession of. ♦*Little children sometimes get hold of sharp knives and cut themselves.* **2.** To find a person so you can speak with him. ♦*Mr. Thompson spent several hours trying to get hold of his lawyer.*

get in v. phr. **1.** To be admitted. ♦*Andy wants to go to medical school but his grades aren't good enough for him to get in.* **2.** To arrive. ♦*What time does the plane from New York get in?* **3.** To enter. ♦*"Get in the car, and let's go," Tom said in a hurry.* **4.** To put in stock; receive. ♦*The store just got in a new shipment of shoes from China.*

get in on v. phr. To be permitted to participate; become privy to; be included. ♦*This is your chance to get in on a wonderful deal with the new company if you're willing to make an investment.*

get in on the ground floor v. phr. To be one of the first members or employees to participate in the growth of a firm, educational institution, etc. ♦*Mr. Smith, who joined the new college as an instructor, got in on the ground floor, and wound up as its president after twenty years.*

get in with v. phr. To join up with; begin to associate with; be accepted by. ♦*He got in with the wrong gang of boys and wound* *up in jail.* ✦*She got in with her father's firm and made a successful career of it.*

get in wrong *v. phr.* To incur the anger or dislike of someone; come into disfavor. ✦*Although he means well, Fred is always getting in wrong with someone at the office.*

get it *v.* To understand; comprehend; grasp. ✦*"I don't get it," John said. "Why do you spend so much on clothes."*

get it all together *v. phr.* **1.** To be in full possession and control of one's mental faculties; have a clear purpose well pursued. ✦*You've sure got it all together, haven't you?* **2.** Retaining one's self-composure under pressure. ✦*A few minutes after the burglars left he got it all together and called the police.* **3.** To be well built, stacked (said of girls and women). ✦*Sue's sure got it all together, hasn't she?*

get lost *v. phr., slang* Go away!—Used as a command. ✦*Get lost! I want to study.* ✦*John told Bert to get lost.*

get off *v.* **1.** To come down from or out of. ✦*The ladder fell, and Tom couldn't get off the roof.* ✦*The bus stopped, the door opened, and Father got off.* **2.** To take off. ✦*Joe's mother told him to get his wet clothes off.* **3.** To get away; leave. ✦*Mr. Johnson goes fishing whenever he can get off from work.* ✦*William got off early in the morning.* **4.** To go free. ✦*Mr. Andrews got off with a $5 fine when he was caught passing a stop sign.* **5.** To make (something) go. ✦*John got a letter off to his grandmother.* **6.** To tell. ✦*The governor got off several*

jokes at the beginning of his speech. **7.** To write a quick letter or note to someone. ✦*I got off a Christmas card just in time to my relatives.* **8.** *sexual taboo, avoidable* To ejaculate. ✦*If you think administrative work makes me get off, you are sadly mistaken.*

get off one's back *v. phr., slang, colloquial* To stop criticizing or nagging someone. ✦*"Get off my back! Can't you see how busy I am?"*

get off on the wrong foot *v. phr.* To make a bad start; begin with a mistake. ✦*Peggy got off on the wrong foot with her new teacher; she chewed gum in class and the teacher didn't like it.*

get off the ground *v. phr., informal* To make a successful beginning; get a good start; go ahead; make progress. ✦*Our plans for a party didn't get off the ground because no one could come.*

get off to a flying *or* **running start** *v. phr.* To have a promising or successful beginning. ✦*Ron got off to a flying start in business school when he got nothing but A's.*

get on *or* **get onto** *v., informal* **1.** To speak to (someone) roughly about something he did wrong; blame; scold. ✦*Mrs. Thompson got on the girls for not keeping their rooms clean.* ✦*The fans got on the new shortstop after he made several errors.* **2.** To grow older. ✦*Work seems harder these days; I'm getting on, you know.*

get one's act together *v. phr.* To control one's performance at work or in one's personal affairs more efficiently than before. ◆*Democracy would prevail much more easily in many parts of the world if the intelligentsia in the countries concerned could only get their act together.*

get one's back up *v. phr., informal* To become or make angry or stubborn. ◆*Fred got his back up when I said he was wrong.*

get one's brains fried *v. phr., slang also used colloquially* 1. To sit in the sun and sunbathe for an excessive length of time. ◆*Newcomers to Hawaii should be warned not to sit in the sun too long—they'll get their brains fried.* 2. To get high on drugs. ◆*He can't make a coherent sentence anymore—he's got his brains fried.*

get on one's case *v. phr.* To keep checking up on someone; to put pressure on someone; to keep bothering someone. ◆*Peter's parents are always getting on his case to find a nice girl to marry and start a family of his own.*

get one's dander up *or* **get one's Irish up** *v. phr.* To become or make angry. ◆*The boy got his dander up because he couldn't go to the store.* ◆*The children get the teacher's dander up when they make a lot of noise.*

get one's feet wet *v. phr., informal* To begin; do something for the first time.

get one's goat *v. phr., informal* To make a person disgusted or angry. ◆*The boy's laziness all summer got his father's goat.* ◆*The slow service at the cafe got Mr. Robinson's goat.*

get one's rear in gear *v. phr., slang* To hurry up, to get going.

◆*I'm gonna have to get my rear in gear.*

get one's teeth into *or* **sink one's teeth into** *v. phr., informal* To have something real or solid to think about; go to work on seriously; struggle with. ◆*Frank chose a subject for his report that he could sink his teeth into.*

get on one's nerves *v. phr.* To make you nervous. *John's noisy eating habits get on your nerves.* ◆*Children get on their parents' nerves by asking so many questions.*

get over *v.* 1. To finish. ◆*Tom worked fast to get his lesson over.* 2. To pass over. ◆*It was hard to get over the muddy road.* 3. To get well from; recover from. ◆*The man returned to work after he got over his illness.* 4. To accept or forget (a sorrow or surprise). ◆*It is hard to get over the death of a member of your family.*

get real *v. phr., informal* To come to grips with reality; to face facts as they really are. ◆*"Stop daydreaming, my dear," Mike said to his sister. "You'll never win the lottery and your husband isn't coming back. Get real—you need a job!"*

get set *v. phr.* To get ready to start. ◆*The runners got set.* ◆*The seniors are getting set for the commencement.*

get stoned *v. phr., slang* To become very drunk or high on some drug. ◆*Poor Fred was so stoned that Tom had to carry him up the stairs.*

get stuck *v. phr.* 1. To be victimized; be cheated. ◆*The Smiths sure got stuck when they bought that secondhand car; it broke down just two days after they* got it. **2.** To become entrapped or embroiled in a physical, emotional, or social obstacle so as to be unable to free oneself. ♦*Tom and Jane are stuck in a bad marriage.*

get the ax *v. phr., slang* **1.** To be fired from a job. ♦*Poor Joe got the ax at the office yesterday.* **2.** To be dismissed from school for improper conduct, such as cheating. ♦*Joe got caught cheating on his final exam and he got the ax.* **3.** To have a quarrel with one's sweetheart or steady ending in a termination of the relationship. ♦*Joe got the ax from Betsie—they won't see each other again.*

get the ball rolling *or* **set the ball rolling** *or* **start the ball rolling** *informal* To start an activity or action; make a beginning; begin. ♦*George started the ball rolling at the party by telling a new joke.*

get the better of *or* **get the best of** *v. phr.* **1.** To win over, beat; defeat. ♦*Our team got the best of the visitors in the last quarter.* ♦*George got the better of Robert in a game of checkers.* **2.** *or* **have the best of** *or* **have the better of** To win or be ahead in (something); gain most from (something). ♦*Bill traded an old bicycle tire for a horn; he got the best of that deal.*

get the drift *or* **get my drift** *or* **get someone's drift** *v. phr.* To begin to understand what someone else means without being completely specific. ♦*"I think I am beginning to get the drift,"* John said, when his boss explained the ruinous state of the economy. *"No raises next

year, right?" "I'm afraid so,"* his boss answered.

get the eye *v. phr., informal* **1.** To be looked at, especially with interest and liking. ♦*The pretty girl got the eye as she walked past the boys on the street corner.* **2.** To be looked at or stared at, especially in a cold, unfriendly way. ♦*When Mary asked if she could take home the fur coat and pay later, she got the eye from the clerk.*

get the go-ahead *or* **the green light** *v. phr.* To receive the permission or signal to start or to proceed. ♦*We had to wait until we got the go-ahead on our research project.*

get the goods on *or* **have the goods on** *v. phr. slang* To find out true and, often, bad information about; discover what is wrong with; be able to prove the guilt of. ♦*The police had the goods on the burglar before he came to trial.*

get the sack *v. phr., slang* **1.** To be fired or dismissed from work. ♦*John got the sack at the factory last week.* **2.** To be told by one's lover that the relationship is over. ♦*Joanna gave Sam the sack.*

get the show on the road *v. phr., informal* To start a program; get work started. ♦*It was several years before the rocket scientists got the show on the road.*

get through *v. phr.* **1.** To finish. ♦*Barry got through his homework by late evening.* **2.** To pass a course or an examination. ♦*I got through every one of my courses except mathematics.*

get through one's head *v. phr.* **1.** To understand or believe. ♦*Jack couldn't get it through his head *that his father wouldn't let him go to camp if his grades didn't improve.* **2.** To make someone understand or believe. ◆*I'll get it through his head if it takes all night.*

get through to *v.* To be understood by; make (someone) understand. ◆*When the rich boy's father lost his money, it took a long time for the idea to get through to him that he'd have to work and support himself.*

get together *v.* To come to an agreement; agree. ◆*Mother says I should finish my arithmetic lesson, and Father says I should mow the lawn. Why don't you two get together?*

get-together *n.* A party; a gathering. ◆*I hate to break up this nice get-together but we must leave.*

get to the bottom of *v. phr.* To find out the real cause of. ◆*The doctor made several tests to get to the bottom of the man's headaches.*

get under one's skin *v. phr.* To bother; upset. ◆*Children who talk too much in class get under the teacher's skin.*

get up *v.* **1.** To get out of bed. ◆*John's mother told him that it was time to get up.* **2.** To stand up; get to your feet. ◆*A man should get up when a woman comes into the room.* **3.** To prepare; get ready. ◆*Mary got up a picnic for her visitor.* ◆*The students got up a special number of the newspaper to celebrate the school's 50th birthday.* **4.** To dress up. *One of the girls got herself up as a witch for the Halloween party.* **5.** To go ahead. ◆*The wagon driver shouted, "Get up!" to his horses.*

get-up *n.* (stress on *get*) Fancy dress or costume. ◆*Some get-up you're wearing!*

get-up-and-go *also* **get-up-and-get** *n. phr., informal* Energetic enthusiasm; ambitious determination; pep; drive; push. ◆*Joe has a lot of get-up-and-go and is working his way through school.*

get up on the wrong side of the bed *v. phr., informal* To awake with a bad temper. ◆*Henry got up on the wrong side of the bed and wouldn't eat breakfast.*

get up the nerve *v. phr.* To build up your courage until you are brave enough; become brave enough. ◆*Jack got up the nerve to ask Ruth to dance with him.*

get what's coming to one *or slang* **get one's** *v. phr.* To receive the good or bad that you deserve; get what is due to you; get your share. ◆*At the end of the movie the villain got what was coming to him and was put in jail.*

get wind of *v. phr.* To get news of; hear rumors about; find out about. ◆*The police got wind of the plans to rob the bank.*

get wise *v. phr., slang* To learn about something kept secret from you; become alert. ◆*One girl pretended to be sick on gym days when she had athletics, until the teacher got wise and made her go anyway.*

get with it *v. phr., slang* To pay attention; be alive or alert; get busy. ◆*The students get with it just before examinations.* ◆*The coach told the team to get with it.*

ghost of A Least trace of; slightest resemblance to; smallest bit of; a very little. Usually used with *chance* or *idea* in negative sentences, or with *smile.* ♦*There wasn't a ghost of a chance that Jack would win.* ♦*We didn't have the ghost of an idea where to look for John.*

ghost-writer *n.* A writer whose identity remains a secret and who writes for another who receives all the credit. ♦*It is rumored that John Smith's best-selling novel was written by a ghost-writer.*

girlfriend *n., informal* **1.** A female friend or companion. ♦*Jane is spending the night at her girlfriend's house.* **2.** A boy's steady girl; the girl or woman partner in a love affair; girl; sweetheart. ♦*John is taking his girlfriend to the dance.*

give-and-take *n. phr.* **1.** A sharing; giving and receiving back and forth between people; a giving up by people on different sides of part of what each one wants so that they can agree. ♦*There has to be give-and-take between two countries before they can be friends.* **2.** Friendly talking or argument back and forth. Friendly sharing of ideas which may not agree; also: an exchange of teasing remarks. ♦*After the meeting there was a lot of give-and-take about plans for the dance.*

give an ear to *or* **lend an ear to** *v. phr., literary* To listen to. ♦*The king lent an ear to the complaints of his people.*

give away *v.* **1.** To give as a present. ♦*Mrs. Jones has several kittens to give away.* **2.** To hand over (a bride) to her husband at the wedding. ♦*Mr. Jackson gave away his daughter.* **3.** To let (a secret) become known; tell the secret of. ♦*The little boy gave away his hiding place when he coughed.*

giveaway *or* **dead giveaway** *n.* (stress on *give*) **1.** An open secret. ♦*By mid-afternoon, it was a dead giveaway who the new boss would be.* **2.** A forced or sacrifice sale at which items are sold for much less than their market value. ♦*The Simpson's garage sale was actually a big giveaway.* **3.** A gift; something one doesn't have to pay for. ♦*The tickets to the concert were a giveaway.*

give birth to *v. phr.* **1.** To bear live offspring. ♦*The mother gave birth to twin baby girls.* **2.** To bring about; create; occasion. ♦*Beethoven gave birth to a new kind of symphony.*

give chase *v. phr.* To chase or run after someone or something. ♦*The police-man gave chase to the man who robbed the bank.*

give in *v.* To stop fighting or arguing and do as the other person wants; give someone his own way; stop opposing someone. ♦*After Billy proved that he could ride a bicycle safely, his father gave in to him and bought him one.*

give it a rest *v. phr.* To stop trying to achieve something that is doomed to failure. ♦"*Look, John, you'll never be a concert pianist. You're making noise, that's all. Sober up and give it a break!*"

give it one's all *v. phr.* To exert maximum effort in order to achieve a certain goal. ♦*It's too bad John didn't succeed in business; he certainly tried to give it his all.*

give it to one straight *v. phr.* To be direct; be frank. ♦*I asked the* *doctor to give it to me straight how long I have to live.*

give no quarter *v. phr.* To be ruthless and show no mercy. ♦*The enemy soldiers gave no quarter and shot all the prisoners.*

give notice *v. phr.* To inform an employer, an employee, a landlord, or a tenant of the termination of a contractual agreement of service or tenancy. ♦*Max gave notice at the bank where he was working.*

given to *adj. phr.* Having a tendency to; addicted to. ♦*Phil is given to telling fantastic tales about his chateau in France.*

give off *v.* To send out; let out; put forth. ♦*Rotten eggs give off a bad smell.*

give one a lift *v. phr.* 1. To give someone a ride. ♦*Jack gave me a lift in his new car.* 2. To comfort someone. ♦*Talking to my doctor yesterday gave me a lift.*

give one an inch, and he will take a mile If you give some people a little or yield anything, they will want more and more; some people are never satisfied. ♦*If you give him an inch, he'll take a mile.*

give oneself up *v.* To stop hiding or running away; surrender. ♦*The thief gave himself up to the police.*

give oneself up to *v. phr.* Not to hold yourself back from; let yourself enjoy. ♦*Uncle Willie gave himself up to a life of wandering.*

give one some of his or her own medicine *v. phr.* To treat someone the way he or she treats others (used in the negative). ♦*The gangster beat up an innocent old man, so when he resisted*

arrest, a policeman gave him a little of his own medicine.

give one's due *v. phr.* To be fair to (a person), give credit that (a person) deserves. ♦*We should give a good worker his due.*

give one's right arm for *v. phr.* To give something of great value; sacrifice. ♦*During our long hike in the desert, I would have given my right arm for an ice cold drink.*

give one's word *v. phr.* To seriously promise. ♦*"You gave me your word you would marry me," Mary bitterly complained, "but you broke your word."*

give one the eye *v. phr., slang* 1. To look at, especially with interest and liking. ♦*A pretty girl went by and all the boys gave her the eye.* 2. To look or stare at, especially in a cold or unfriendly way. ♦*Mrs. Jones didn't like Mary and didn't speak. She just gave her the eye when they met on the street.*

give or take *v. phr.* To add or subtract. Used with a round number or date to show how approximate it is. ♦*The house was built in 1900, give or take five years.*

give out *v.* 1. To make known; let it be known; publish. ♦*Mary gave out that she and Bob were going to be married.* 2. To let escape; give. ♦*The cowboy gave out a yell.* 3. To give to people; distribute. ♦*The barber gives out free lollipops to all the children.* 4. To fail; collapse. ♦*Tom's legs gave out and he couldn't run any farther.* ♦*The chair gave out under the fat man.* 5. To be finished or gone. ♦*When the food at the party gave out, they bought more.*

The teacher's patience gave out.

give pause *v. phr.* To cause you to stop and think; make you doubt or worry. *The bad weather gave John pause about driving to New York City.*

give rise to *v. phr.* To be the reason for; cause. *A branch floating in the water gave rise to Columbus' hopes that land was near.*

give someone his rights *or* **read someone his rights** *v. phr., informal* 1. The act of advising arrested criminals that they have the right to remain silent and that everything they say can be held against them in a court of law; that they have the right to the presence of an attorney during questioning and that if they can't afford one and request it, an attorney will be appointed for them by the state. *The cops gave Smith his rights immediately after the arrest.* 2. To sever a relationship by telling someone that he or she can go and see a divorce lawyer or the like. *Sue gave Mike his rights before she slammed the door in his face.*

give the ax *v. phr., colloquial* 1. Abruptly to finish a relationship. *She gave me the ax last night.* 2. To fire an employee in a curt manner. *His boss gave John the ax last Friday.*

give the benefit of the doubt *v. phr.* To believe (a person) is innocent rather than guilty when you are not sure. *George's grade was higher than usual and he might have cheated, but his teacher gave him the benefit of the doubt.*

give the devil his due *v. phr.* To be fair, even to someone who is bad; tell the truth about a person even though you don't like him. *I don't like Mr. Jones, but to give the devil his due, I must admit that he is a good teacher.*

give the glad eye *v. phr., slang* To give (someone) a welcoming look as if saying "Come over here, I want to talk to you." *I was surprised when Joe gave me the glad eye.*

give the slip *v.* To escape from (someone); run away from unexpectedly; sneak away from. *Some boys were waiting outside the school to beat up Jack, but he gave them the slip.*

give to understand *v. phr.* To make a person understand by telling him very plainly or boldly. *Frank was given to understand in a short note from the boss that he was fired.*

give up *v.* 1. To stop trying to keep; surrender; yield. *The dog had the ball in his mouth and wouldn't give it up.* 2. To stop doing or having; abandon; quit. *The doctor told Mr. Harris to give up smoking.* *Jane hated to give up her friends when she moved away.* 3. To stop hoping for, waiting for, or trying to do. *Johnny was given up by the doctors after the accident, but he lived just the same.* 4. To stop trying; quit; surrender. *The war will be over when one of the countries gives up.*

give (one) up for *v. phr.* To abandon hope for someone or something. *After Larry had not returned to base camp for three nights, his fellow mountain climbers gave him up for dead.*

give up the ghost v. phr. To die; stop going. ♦After a long illness, the old woman gave up the ghost.

give up the ship v. phr. To stop fighting and surrender; stop trying or hoping to do something. ♦"Don't give up the ship, John," said his father when John failed a test.

give voice v. phr., formal To tell what you feel or think; especially when you are angry or want to object.—Used with to. ♦Willie gave voice to his pain when the dog bit him by crying loudly.

give way v. 1. To go back; retreat. ♦The enemy army is giving way before the cannon fire. 2. To make room, get out of the way. ♦The children gave way and let their mother through the door. 3. To lose control of yourself; lose your courage or hope; yield. ♦Mrs. Jones didn't give way during the flood, but she was very frightened. 4. To collapse; fail. ♦The river was so high that the dam gave way. ♦Mary's legs gave way and she fainted. 5. To let yourself be persuaded; give permission. ♦Billy kept asking his mother if he could go to the movies and she finally gave way.

glad hand n., informal A friendly handshake; a warm greeting. ♦The politician went down the street on election day giving everyone the glad hand.

gloss over v. To try to make what is wrong or bad seem right or not important; try to make a thing look easy; pretend about; hide. ♦John glossed over his mistake by saying that everybody did the same thing.

glutton for punishment n. phr. A greedy person; someone who wants too much of something, such as food or drink, which will make him sick. ♦Fred eats so much red meat that he is a regular glutton for punishment.

go about one's business v. phr. To mind one's own affairs. ♦Fred kept bothering me with his questions all day, so I finally told him to go about his business and leave me alone.

go after v. To try to get. ♦"First find out what job you want and then go after it," said Jim's father.

go ahead v. To begin to do something; not wait. ♦"May I ask you a question?" "Go ahead."

go astray v. phr. To become lost. ♦The letter has obviously gone astray; otherwise it would have been delivered a long time ago.

go ape v. phr., slang To become highly excited or behave in a crazy way. ♦Amy went ape over the hotel and beautiful beaches.

go around v. 1a. To go from one place or person to another. Mr. Smith is going around looking for work. ♦Don't go around telling lies like that. ♦Chicken pox is going around the neighborhood. ♦A rumor is going around school that we will get the afternoon off. 1b. To go together; keep company.—Usually used with with. ♦Bill goes around with boys older than he is because he is big for his age. 2. To be enough to give to everyone; be enough for all. ♦There are not enough desks to go around in the classroom.

go around in circles See IN A CIRCLE.

go at v. **1.** To start to fight with; attack. ♦*The dog and the cat are going at each other again.* **2.** To make a beginning on; approach; tackle. ♦*How are you going to go at the job of fixing the roof?*

go at it hammer and tongs v. phr., informal **1.** To attack or fight with great strength or energy; have a bad argument. ♦*Bill slapped George's face and now they're going at it hammer and tongs in back of the house.* **2.** To start or do something with much strength, energy, or enthusiasm. ♦*The farmer had to chop down a tree and he went at it hammer and tongs.*

go back on one's word v. phr. To renege; break a promise. ♦*Patrick went back on his word when he refused to marry Karen in spite of his earlier promise.*

gobble up v. phr. **1.** To completely devour. ♦*The boys were famished after the steep mountain climb, and gobbled up all the leftovers in the refrigerator.* **2.** To uncritically accept. ♦*The naïve villagers gobbled up all the false news the tyrannical state-run television fed them.*

go broke v. phr., slang To lose all one's money; especially by taking a chance; owe more than you can pay. ♦*The inventor went broke because nobody would buy his machine.*

God forbid interj. May God prevent (something from happening); I hope that will not happen or is not true. ♦*Someone told the worried mother that her son might have drowned. She said, "God forbid!"*

God knows or **goodness knows** or **heaven knows** informal **1.** Maybe God knows but I don't know and no one else knows.— Often used with *only.* ♦*Do you know where Susan is? God only knows!* **2.** Surely; certainly. ♦*Goodness knows, the poor man needs the money.* ♦*Heaven only knows, I have tried hard enough.*

go down v. phr. **1.** To deteriorate in quality. ♦*This hotel, which used to be one of the best, has gone down during the past few years.* **2.** To become lower in price. ♦*It is said that the price of milk is expected to go down soon.* **3.** To sink. ♦*The* Titanic *went down with a lot of people aboard.*

go down in history or **go down in the records** v. phr. To be remembered or recorded for always. ♦*The lives of great men go down in history.* ♦*The boy's straight A's for four years of college went down in the records.* ♦*The president said that the day the war ended would go down in history.*

go Dutch v. phr., informal To go out for fun together but have each person pay for himself. ♦*Sometimes boys and girls go Dutch on dates.* ♦*The girl knew her boyfriend had little money, so she offered to go Dutch.*

go fly a kite v. phr., slang To go away; leave. Usually used as a command, to show that you do not accept someone's ideas. ♦*Harry was tired of John's advice and told him to go fly a kite.*

go from strength to strength v. phr. To move forward, increasing one's fame, power, or fortune in a series of successful achievements. ♦*Our basketball* *team has gone from strength to strength.*

go-getter *n.* A person who works hard to become successful; an active, ambitious person who usually gets what he wants. ♦*The governor of the state has always been a go-getter.*

go-go *adj., slang, informal* **1.** vigorous youthful, unusually active. ♦*Joe is a go-go kind of guy.* **2.** Of a discotheque or the music or dances performed there. **3a.** unrestrained **3b.** very up-to-date, hip. ♦*Mary wore handsome go-go boots to the discotheque last night.*

go hog wild *v. phr., slang* To become extremely agitated and go out of control. ♦*After the soccer game was won, the fans went hog wild.*

go in for *v. phr., informal* To try to do; take part in; take pleasure in. ♦*Most girls do not go in for rough games.* ♦*Mrs. Henry goes in for simple meals.*

going for one *adj. phr.* Working to help; in one's favor. ♦*The young woman surely will get the job; she has everything going for her.*

going on *adv. phr.* Almost; nearly. ♦*Joe is going on six years old.* ♦*It is going on six o'clock.*

going through changes *v. phr., slang, informal* To be in trouble, to have difficulties, to be trapped in unfavorable circumstances. ♦*"What's the matter with Joe?"—"He's going through changes."*

go in one ear and out the other *v. phr., informal* To be not really listened to or understood; be paid no attention. ♦*The teacher's directions to the boy*

went in one ear and out the other.

go into *v.* **1a.** To go or fit inside of; able to be put in. ♦*The table is too big to go into the closet.* **1b.** To be able to be divided into; be divisible into. ♦*Two goes into four two times.* **2.** To enter a state or condition of; pass into. *John went into a fit of temper when he didn't get his own way.* **3.** To be busy or take part in; enter as a job or profession. ♦*The mayor went into politics as a very young man.* **4.** To start to talk about; bring up the subject of; examine. ♦*We'll talk about the dead mouse after dinner, Billy. Let's not go into it now.*

go into a tailspin *or* **go into a nose dive** *v. phr., informal* **1.** To fall or go down badly; collapse; give up trying. ♦*The team went into a tailspin after their captain was hurt, and they were badly beaten.* **2.** *informal* To become very anxious, confused, or mentally sick; give up hope. ♦*The man went into a tailspin after his wife died and he never got over it.*

go into orbit *v. phr., slang* **1.** To become very happy or successful. ♦*Our team has gone into orbit.* **2.** To lose one's temper or control completely; become very angry. ♦*John was afraid his father would go into orbit when he found out about the car accident.*

go jump in the lake *v. phr., informal* To go away and quit being a bother. ♦*George was tired of Tom's advice and told him to go jump in the lake.*

go legit *v. phr.* To start practicing a legitimate business after having been operating outside of the law. ◆*"The old days are over,"* the crime boss said to his friends. *"We are going legit as of right now."*

go native *v. phr.* To behave like a native (said of European Americans in tropical countries). ◆*Mainlanders often go native in Hawaii.*

gone with the wind *adj. phr.* Gone forever; past; vanished. ◆*All the deer that used to live here are gone with the wind.* ◆*Joe knew that his chance to get an "A" was gone with the wind when he saw how hard the test was.*

good buddy *n., slang, citizen's band radio jargon* Salutation used by truckers and automobile drivers who have CB radios. ◆*What's the Smokey situation, good buddy?*

good deal *or* **great deal** *n., informal* A large amount; much.— Used with *a.* ◆*Mrs. Walker's long illness cost her a good deal.* ◆*George spends a great deal of his time watching television.* ◆*George is a good deal like his father; they both love to eat.*

good egg *slang or informal* **good scout** *n. phr.* A friendly, kind, or good-natured person, a nice fellow. ◆*Tommy is such a good egg that everybody wants to be his friend.*

good-for-nothing *adj. phr.* Worthless. ◆*While Janice works hard each day, her good-for-nothing husband hangs around in the bars.*

good grief! *interj., informal* Wow! Indication of surprise, good or bad. ◆*"Good grief,"* Joe cried out loud. *"Is this all you will pay me for my hard work?"*

◆*What a figure Melanie has, good grief! I wonder if she would be willing to go out with me.*

go off the deep end *or* **go overboard** *v. phr., informal* To act excitedly and without careful thinking. ◆*John has gone off the deep end about owning a motorcycle.* ◆*Some girls go overboard for handsome movie and television actors.*

goof off *v., slang* To loaf or be lazy; not want to work or be serious; fool around. ◆*Tom didn't get promoted because he goofed off all the time and never did his homework.*

goose bumps *or* **goose pimples** *n. plural, informal* Small bumps that come on a person's skin when he gets cold or afraid. ◆*Nancy gets goose bumps when she sees a snake.* ◆*Put on your sweater; you're so cold you have goose pimples on your arms.*

go out *v. phr.* **1.** To pass out of date or style. ◆*Short skirts are gradually going out.* **2.** To stop giving off light or burning. ◆*Put more wood on the fire or it will go out.* **3.** To leave. ◆*When I called Sue, her mother said that she had just gone out.*

go out of business *v. phr.* To cease functioning as a commercial enterprise. ◆*The windows of the store are all boarded up because they went out of business.*

go out of one's way *v. phr.* To make an extra effort; do more than usual. ◆*Jane went out of her way to be nice to the new girl.*

go out the window *v. phr., informal* To go out of effect; be abandoned. ◆*During the war, the school dress code went out the window.*

go out with one *v. phr.* To date someone. ◆*"May I ask your daughter for a date, sir?" Fred asked politely. "She is too young to go out with anyone," the father replied. "Why don't you come back next year?"*

go over *v.* 1. To examine; think about or look at carefully. ◆*The teacher went over the list and picked John's name.* ◆*The police went over the gun for fingerprints.* 2. To repeat; do again. *Don't make me go all over it again.* ◆*We painted the house once, then we went over it again.* ◆ 3. To read again; study. ◆*After you finish the test, go over it again to look for mistakes.* ◆*They went over their lessons together at night.* 4. To cross; go to stop or visit; travel. ◆*We went over to the other side of the street.* ◆*I'm going over to Mary's house.* ◆*We went over to the next town to the game.* 5. To change what you believe. ◆*Joe is a Democrat, but he says that he is going over to the Republicans in the next election.* ◆*Many of the natives on the island went over to Christianity after the missionaries came.* 6. To be liked; succeed.—Often used in the informal phrase *go over big.* ◆*Bill's joke went over big with the other boys and girls.* ◆*Your idea went over well with the boss.*

go over like a lead balloon *v. phr., informal* To fail to generate a positive response or enthusiasm; to meet with boredom or disapproval. ◆*The president's* suggested budget cuts went over like a lead balloon.

go over one's head *v. phr.* 1. To be too difficult to understand. ◆*Penny complains that what her math teacher says simply goes over her head.* 2. To do something without the permission of one's superior. ◆*Fred went over his boss's head when he signed the contract on his own.*

go postal *v. phr.* To lose control over oneself and become angry enough to start shooting at innocent bystanders (as was done by a disgruntled employee in a post office in Chicago). ◆*"Oh, I'm so glad I found you, Professor. Here is my term paper. I was stuck in traffic and I thought I was gonna go postal," Ms. Murphy said, handing in her paper at the very last possible moment.*

Gordian knot *n. phr.* Greek antiquity, from Alexander the Great. A very tough and apparently insolvable problem, which, given the right decisive action, can nevertheless be solved. ◆*"I am not going to try to figure out who embezzled the money at this firm," the director said. "I will solve the Gordian knot by firing everybody in one fell swoop and hiring a whole new office staff."*

go somebody one better *v. phr., informal* To do something better than (someone else); do more or better than; beat. ◆*John made a good dive into the water, but Bob went him one better by diving in backwards.*

go stag *v. phr.* 1. To go to a dance or party without a companion of the opposite sex. ◆*When*

Sally turned him down, Tom decided to go stag to the college prom. **2.** To participate in a party for men only. ◆*Mrs. Smith's husband frequently goes stag, leaving her at home.*

go steady *v. phr.* To go on dates with the same person all the time; date just one person. ◆*Jean went steady with Bob for a year; then they had a quarrel and stopped dating each other.*

go straight *v. phr., slang* To become an honest person; lead an honest life. ◆*After the man got out of prison, he went straight.*

got a thing going *v. phr., slang, informal* To be engaged in a pleasurable or profitable activity with someone else as a partner either in romance or in mutually profitable business. ◆*"You two seem to have got a thing going, haven't you?"* ◆*"You've got a good thing going with your travel bureau; why quit now?"*

go the whole hog *or* **go whole hog** *v. phr., informal* To do something completely or thoroughly; to give all your strength or attention to something. ◆*The family went whole hog at the fair, and spent a lot of money.*

go through *v.* **1.** To examine or think about carefully; search. ◆*I went through the papers looking for Jane's letter.* ◆*Mother went through the drawer looking for the sweater.* **2.** To experience; suffer; live through. ◆*Frank went through many dangers during the war.* **3.** To do what you are supposed to do; do what you promised. ◆*I went through my part of the bargain, but you didn't go*

through your part. **4.** To go or continue to the end of; do or use all of. ◆*Jack went through the magazine quickly.* ◆*We went through all our money at the circus.* **5.** To be allowed; pass; be agreed on. ◆*I hope the new law we want goes through Congress.*

go through with *v. phr.* To finish; do as planned or agreed; not stop or fail to do. ◆*The boys don't think Bob will go through with his plans to spend the summer at a camp.*

go to bat for *v. phr., informal* To help out in trouble or need; give aid to. ◆*Mary went to bat for the new club program.*

go to bed with the chickens *v. phr., informal* To go to bed early at night. ◆*On the farm John worked hard and went to bed with the chickens.* ◆*Mr. Barnes goes to bed with the chickens because he has to get up at 5 A.M.*

go together *v.* **1.** To go with the same boy or girl all the time; date just one person. ◆*Herbert and Thelma go together.* **2.** To be suitable or agreeable with each other; match. ◆*Roast turkey and cranberries go together.* ◆*Ice cream and cake go together.*

go to one's head *v. phr.* **1.** To make one dizzy. ◆*Beer and wine go to a person's head.* **2.** To make someone too proud; make a person think he is too important. ◆*The girl's fame as a movie actress went to her head.*

go to pieces *v. phr.* To become very nervous or sick from nervousness; become wild. ◆*The man went to pieces when the* *judge said he would have to go to prison for life.*

go to pot *v. phr., informal* To be ruined; become bad; be destroyed. ◆*The motel business went to pot when the new highway was built.*

go to seed *or* **run to seed** *v. phr.* **1.** To grow seeds. ◆*Onions go to seed in hot weather.* **2.** To lose skill or strength; stop being good or useful. ◆*Mr. Allen was a good carpenter until he became rich and went to seed.*

go to show *or* **go to prove** *v. phr., informal* To seem to prove; act or serve to show (a fact); demonstrate.—Often used after it. ◆*The hard winter at Valley Forge goes to show that our soldiers suffered a great deal to win the Revolution.*

go to the devil *v. phr., informal* To go away, mind your own business.—Used as a command; considered rude. ◆*George told Bob to go to the devil.* ◆*"Go to the devil!" said Jack, when his sister tried to tell him what to do.*

go to the dogs *v. phr., informal* To go to ruin; to be ruined or destroyed. ◆*The man went to the dogs after he started drinking.*

go to the trouble *or* **take the trouble** *v. phr.* To make trouble or extra work for yourself; bother. ◆*John told Mr. Brown not to go to the trouble of driving him home.*

go to town *v. phr., slang* **1.** To do something quickly or with great force or energy; work fast or hard. ◆*The boys went to town on the old garage, and had it torn down before Father came home from work.* **2.** *or* **go places.** To do a good job;

succeed. ◆*Our team is going to town this year; we have won all five games that we played.* ◆*Dan was a good student and a good athlete; we expect him to go places in business.*

go to waste *v. phr.* To be wasted or lost; not used. ◆*Joe's work on the model automobile went to waste when he dropped it.*

go up *v.* **1.** To go or move higher; rise. ◆*Many people came to watch the weather balloon go up.* ◆*The path goes up the hill.* **2.** To be able to become heard; become loud or louder. ◆*A shout went up from the crowd at the game.* **3.** Grow in height while being built; to be built. ◆*The new church is going up on the corner.* **4.** To increase. ◆*Prices of fruit and vegetables have gone up.*

go up in smoke *or* **go up in flames** *v. phr.* **1.** To burn; be destroyed by fire. ◆*The house went up in flames.* ◆*The barn full of hay went up in smoke.* **2.** Disappear; fail; not come true. ◆*Jane's hopes of going to college went up in smoke when her father lost his job.*

go up in the air *v. phr.* To become angry; lose one's temper. ◆*Herb is so irritable these days that he goes up in the air for no reason at all.*

go without saying *v. phr.* To be too plain to need talking about; not be necessary to say or mention. ◆*It goes without saying that children should not be given knives to play with.*

go wrong *v. phr.* **1.** To fail; go out of order. ◆*Something went wrong with our car and we stalled on the road.* **2.** To sink into an immoral or criminal existence. ♦*In a large city many young people go wrong every year.*

grandstand *v., slang, informal* To show off, to perform histrionics needlessly. ♦*Stop grandstanding and get down to honest work!*

grandstander *n., slang, informal* A showoff, a person who likes to engage in histrionics. ♦*Many people think that Evel Knievel is a grandstander.*

grasp at straws *or* **clutch at straws** *v. phr.* To depend on something that is useless or unable to help in a time of trouble or danger; try something with little hope of succeeding. ♦*The robber clutched at straws to make excuses. He said he wasn't in the country when the robbery happened.*

grass is always greener on the other side of the fence *or* **grass is always greener on the other side of the hill** We are often not satisfied and want to be somewhere else; a place that is far away or different seems better than where we are. ♦*John is always changing his job because the grass always looks greener to him on the other side of the fence.*

graveyard shift *n. phr.* The work period lasting from sundown to sunup, when one has to work in the dark or by artificial light. ♦*"Why are you always so sleepy in class?" Professor Brown asked Sam. "Because I have to work the graveyard shift beside going to school," Sam answered.*

gravy train *n., slang, informal* The kind of job that brings in a much higher income than the services rendered would warrant. ♦*Jack's job at the Athletic Club as Social Director is a regular gravy train.*

grease monkey *n., slang, derogatory, avoidable* **1.** A person who greases or works on machinery; a mechanic or worker in a garage or gasoline station. ♦*The grease monkey was all dirty when he came out from under the car.* **2.** Airplane mechanic. ♦*Jack was a grease monkey in the Air Force.*

grease one's palm *or* **grease the palm** *slang* **1.** To pay a person for something done or given, especially dishonestly; bribe. ♦*Some politicians will help you if you grease their palms.* **2.** To give a tip; pay for a special favor or extra help. ♦*We had to grease the palm of the waiter to get a table in the crowded restaurant.*

greasy spoon *n., informal* Any small, inexpensive restaurant patronized by workers or people in a hurry; a place not noted for its excellence of cuisine or its decor. ♦*I won't have time to eat lunch at the club today; I'll just grab a sandwich at the local greasy spoon.*

green around the gills *or* **pale around the gills** *adj. phr., slang* Pale-faced from fear or sickness; sickly; nauseated. ♦*Bill's father took him for a ride in his boat while the waves were rough, and when he came back he was green around the gills.* ♦*The car almost hit Mary crossing the street, and she was pale around the gills because it came so close.*

green thumb *n., informal* A talent for gardening; ability to make things grow. ♦*Mr. Wilson's* neighbors say his flowers grow because he has a green thumb.

green with envy *adj. phr.* Very jealous; full of envy. ◆*The other boys were green with envy when Joe bought a second-hand car.*

grind to a halt *v. phr., informal* To slow down and stop like a machine does when turned off. ◆*The old car ground to a halt in front of the house.*

gross out *v., slang* To commit a vulgar act; to repel someone by saying a disgusting or vulgar thing. ◆*You are going to gross out people if you continue talking like that.*

ground zero *n.* **1.** A place of total devastation. ◆*Hiroshima and Nagasaki were ground zero after the atomic bomb was dropped on them in August 1945.* **2.** After September 11, 2001: The place in New York City where the World Trade Center stood that was brought down by suicide terrorists. ◆*Many tourists come to see ground zero, the place where the World Trade Center once stood.* **3.** A very messy and disorganized place. ◆*"Why must you turn your room into a total ground zero?" Father asked indignantly.*

growing pains *n.* **1.** Pains in children's legs supposed to be caused by changes in their bodies and feelings as they grow. ◆*The little girl's legs hurt, and her mother told her she had growing pains.* **2.** *informal* Troubles when something new is beginning or growing. ◆*The factory has growing pains.*

grow on *or* **grow upon** *v.* **1.** To become stronger in; increase as

a habit of. ◆*The habit of eating before going to bed grew upon John.* **2.** To become more interesting to or liked by. ◆*The more Jack saw Mary, the more she grew on him.*

grow out of *v. phr.* **1.** To outgrow; become too mature for. ◆*As a child he had a habit of scratching his chin all the time, but he grew out of it.* **2.** To result from; arise. ◆*Tom's illness grew out of his tendency to overwork and neglect his health.*

grow up *v.* To increase in size or height; become taller or older; reach full height. **1.** ◆*Johnny is growing up; his shoes are too small for him.* ◆*I grew up on a farm.* ◆*The city has grown up since I was young.* **2.** To become adult in mind or judgment; become old enough to think or decide in important matters. ◆*Tom wants to be a coach when he grows up.*

gum up *v., slang* To cause not to work or ruin; spoil; make something go wrong. ◆*Jimmy has gummed up the typewriter.*

gun for *v., informal* **1.** To hunt for with a gun; look hard for a chance to harm or defeat. ◆*The cowboy is gunning for the man who stole his horse.* **2.** To try very hard to get. ◆*The man is gunning for first prize in the golf tournament.*

gung-ho *adj., colloquial* Enthusiastic, full of eagerness in an uncritical or unsophisticated manner. ◆*Suzie is all gung-ho on equal rights for women, but fails to see the consequences.*

gut feeling *n. phr.* An instinctive reaction. ◆*I have a gut feeling that they will never get married in spite of all they say.*

gut reaction *n. phr.* A mental or physical response that springs from one's depths. ♦*My gut reaction was to get out of here as fast as possible.*

gut talk *n. phr.* Sincere, honest talk. ♦*We admire people who speak gut talk and tell exactly what they think and feel.*

had better *informal* Should; must. ◆*I had better leave now, or I'll be late.*

hail from *v., informal* To have your home in; come from; be from; *especially,* to have been born and raised in. ◆*Mrs. Gardner hails from Mississippi.*

hair stand on end *informal* The hair of your head rises stiffly upwards as a sign or result of great fright or horror. ◆*When he heard the strange cry, his hair stood on end.* ◆*The sight of the dead man made his hair stand on end.*

hale and hearty *adj. phr.* In very good health; well and strong. ◆*Grandfather will be 80 years old tomorrow, but he is hale and hearty.* ◆*That little boy looks hale and hearty, as if he is never sick.*

half-baked *adj., informal* Not thought out or studied thoroughly; not worth considering or accepting. ◆*We cannot afford to put the government in the hands of people with half-baked plans.*

half-hearted *adj.* Lacking enthusiasm or interest. ◆*Phil made several half-hearted attempts to learn word processing, but we could see that he didn't really like it.*

half the battle *n. phr.* A large part of the work. ◆*When you write an essay for class, making the outline is half the battle.* ◆*To see your faults and decide to change is half the battle of self-improvement.*

hammer and tongs *adv. phr.* Violently. ◆*Mr. and Mrs. Smith have been at it all day, hammer and tongs.*

hammer out *v.* 1. To write or produce by hard work. ◆*The President sat at his desk till midnight hammering out his speech for the next day.* 2. To remove, change, or work out by discussion and debate; debate and agree on (something). ◆*Mrs. Brown and Mrs. Green have hammered out their difference of opinion.*

hand down *v.* To arrange to give or leave after death. ◆*In old times, property was usually handed down to the oldest son at his father's death.*

handle with gloves *or* **handle with kid gloves** *v. phr., informal* 1. To treat very gently and carefully. ◆*An atomic bomb is handled with kid gloves.* 2. To treat with great tact and diplomacy. ◆*Aunt Jane is so irritable that we have to treat her with kid gloves.*

hand-me-down *n., informal* Something given away after another person has no more use for it; *especially,* used clothing. ◆*Alice had four older sisters, so all her clothes were hand-me-downs.*

handout *n.* (stress on *hand*) 1. A free gift of food, clothes, etc. ◆*The homeless people were standing in a long line for various handouts.* 2. A typed and photocopied sheet or sheets of paper outlining the main points made by a speaker. ◆*Please look at page three of the handout.*

hand out *v., informal* (stress on *out*) To give (things of the same kind) to several people. ◆*The teacher handed out the examination papers.* ◆*Handing out* *free advice to all your friends will not make them like you.*

hand over *v.* To give control or possession of; give (something) to another person. ♦*When Mr. Jones gets old, he will hand over his business to his son.*

hand over fist *adv. phr., informal* Fast and in large amounts. ♦*Fred may get a pony for Christmas because his father is making money hand over fist.* ♦*Business is so bad that the store on the corner is losing money hand over fist.*

hands-down *adj., informal* 1. Easy. ♦*The Rangers won a hands-down victory in the tournament.* 2. Unopposed; first; clear. ♦*Johnny was the hands-down favorite for president of the class.*

hands down *adv., informal* 1. Without working hard; easily. ♦*The Rangers won the game hands down.* 2. Without question or doubt; without any opposition; plainly. ♦*John was hands down the best writer in the class.*

hands off *informal* Keep your hands off or do not interfere; leave that alone.—Used as a command. ♦*I was going to touch the machine, but the man cried, "Hands off!" and I let it alone.*

hands-off *adj., informal* Leaving alone, not interfering; inactive. ♦*The United States told the European governments to follow a hands-off policy toward Latin America.*

hands up *informal* Hold up your hands! Put your hands up high and keep them there!— Used as a command. ♦*The sheriff point-*

ed his gun at the outlaws and called out, "Hands up!"

hand something to someone on a silver platter *v. phr.* To give a person a reward that has not been earned. ♦*The lazy student expected his diploma to be handed to him on a silver platter.*

hand-to-mouth *adj.* Not providing for the future; living from day to day; not saving for later. ♦*Many native tribes lead a hand-to-mouth existence, content to have food for one day at a time.*

handwriting on the wall *n. phr.* A sign that something bad will happen. ♦*John's employer had less and less work for him; John could read the handwriting on the wall and looked for another job.*

hang around *v., informal* 1. To pass time or stay near without any real purpose or aim; loaf near or in. ♦*The principal warned the students not to hang around the corner drugstore after school.* 2. To spend time or associate. ♦*Jim hangs around with some boys who live in his neighborhood.*

hang by a thread *or* **hang by a hair** *v. phr.* To depend on a very small thing; be in doubt. ♦*For three days Tom was so sick that his life hung by a thread.*

hang on *v.* 1. To hold on to something, usually tightly. ♦*Jack almost fell off the cliff, but managed to hang on until help came.* 2a. To continue doing something; persist. ♦*The grocer was losing money every day, but he hung on, hoping that business would improve.* 2b. To hold a lead in a race or other contest while one's opponents try to rally. ♦*The favorite horse opened an early lead and hung on to win as two other horses almost passed him in the final stretch.* 3. To continue to give trouble or cause suffering. ♦*Lou's cold hung on from January to April.* 4. To continue listening on the telephone. ♦*Jerry asked John, who had called him on the phone, to hang on while he ran for a pencil and a sheet of paper.*

hang out *v.* 1. *slang* To spend your time idly or lounging about. ♦*The teacher complained that Joe was hanging out in poolrooms instead of doing his homework.* 2. *slang* To live; reside. ♦*Two policemen stopped the stranger and asked him where he hung out.* 3. To reach out farther than the part below. ♦*The branches of the trees hung out over the road.* ♦*The upper floor of that house hangs out above the first.*

hang out one's shingle *v. phr., informal* To give public notice of the opening of an office, especially a doctor's or lawyer's office, by putting up a small signboard. ♦*The young doctor hung out his shingle and soon had a large practice.*

hangover *n.* (stress on *hang*) A bad feeling of nausea and/or headache the day after one has had too much to drink. ♦*Boy, did I have a hangover after that party yesterday!*

hang over *v.* (stress on *over*) 1. To be going to happen to; threaten. ♦*Great trouble hangs over the little town because its only factory has closed down.* 2. To remain to be finished or settled.

♦*The committee took up the business that hung over from its last meeting.*

hang up *v.* (stress on *up*) 1. To place on a hook, peg, or hanger. ♦*When the children come to school, they hang up their coats in the cloakroom.* 2a. To place a telephone receiver back on its hook and break the connection. ♦*Carol's mother told her she had talked long enough on the phone and made her hang up.* 2b. To put a phone receiver back on its hook while the other person is still talking.—Used with *on*. ♦*I said something that made Joe angry, and he hung up on me.*

hang-up *n., informal* (stress on *hang*) 1. A delay in some process. ♦*The mail has been late for several days; there must be some hang-up with the trucks somewhere.* 2. A neurotic reaction to some life situation probably stemming from a traumatic shock which has gone unconscious. ♦*Doctor Simpson believes that Suzie's frigidity is due to some hang-up about men.*

happy hour *n., informal* A time in bars or restaurants when cocktails are served at a reduced rate, usually one hour before they start serving dinner. ♦*Happy hour is between 6 and 7 P.M. at Celestial Gardens.*

happy hunting ground *n. phr.* 1. The place where, in American Indian belief, a person goes after death; heaven. ♦*The Indians believed that at death they went to the happy hunting ground.* 2. *informal* A place or area where you can find a rich variety of what you want, and plenty of it. ♦*The forest is a happy hunting ground for scouts who are interested in plants and flowers.*

hard-and-fast *adj.* Not to be broken or changed; fixed; strict. ♦*The teacher said that there was a hard-and-fast rule against smoking in the school.*

hard as nails *adj. phr., informal* **1.** Not flabby or soft; physically very fit; tough and strong. ♦*After a summer of work in the country, Jack was as hard as nails, without a pound of extra weight.* **2.** Not gentle or mild; rough; stern. ♦*John works for a boss who is as hard as nails and scolds John roughly whenever he does something wrong.*

hard feeling *n.* Angry or bitter feeling; enmity.—Usually used in the plural. ♦*Jim asked Andy to shake hands with him, just to show that there were no hard feelings.*

hard going *adj. phr.* Fraught with difficulty. ♦*Dave finds his studies of math hard going.*

hardheaded *adj.* Stubborn; shrewd; practical. ♦*Don is a hardheaded businessman who made lots of money, even during the recession.*

hard line *n. phr.* Tough political policy. ♦*Although modern economists were trying to persuade him to open up to the West, Castro has always taken the hard line approach.*

hard-nosed *adj., slang* Tough or rugged; very strict; not weak or soft; stubborn, especially in a fight or contest. ♦*Joe's father was a hard-nosed army officer who had seen service in two wars.*

hard nut to crack *also* **tough nut to crack** *n. phr., informal* Something difficult to understand or to do. ♦*Tom's algebra lesson was a hard nut to crack.*

hard of hearing *adj.* Partially deaf. ♦*Some people who are hard of hearing wear hearing aids.*

hard-on *n. vulgar, avoidable.* An erection of the male sexual organ.

hard sell *n., informal* A kind of salesmanship characterized by great vigor, aggressive persuasion, and great eagerness on the part of the person selling something; opposed to "soft sell." ♦*Your hard sell turns off a lot of people; try the soft sell for a change, won't you?*

hard up *adj., informal* Without enough money or some other needed thing. ♦*Dick was hard up and asked Lou to lend him a dollar.*

hash out *v., informal* To talk all about and try to agree on; discuss thoroughly. ♦*The teacher asked Susan and Jane to sit down together and hash out their differences.*

hat in hand *adv. phr., informal* In a humble and respectful manner. ♦*They went hat in hand to the old woman to ask for her secret recipe.*

hatchet job *n. phr., slang* **1.** The act of saying or writing terrible things about someone or something, usually on behalf of one's boss or organization. ♦*When Phil makes speeches against the competition, exaggerating their weaknesses, he is doing the hatchet job on behalf of our president.* **2.** A ruthless, wholesale job of editing a script whereby entire paragraphs or pages are omitted. ♦*Don, my editor, did a hatchet job on my new novel.*

hatchet man *n., colloquial* **1.** A politician or newspaper columnist whose job is to write and say unfavorable things about the opposition. ♦*Bill Lerner is the hatchet man for the mayor's party; he smears all the other candidates regularly.* **2.** An executive officer in a firm whose job is to fire superfluous personnel, cut back on the budget, etc., in short, to do the necessary but unpleasant things. ♦*The firm hired Cranhart to be hatchet man; his title is that of executive vice president.*

hate one's guts *v. phr., slang* To feel a very strong dislike for someone. ♦*Dick said that he hated Fred's guts because Fred had been very mean to him.*

have a ball *v. phr., slang* Enjoy yourself very much; have a wonderful time. ♦*Mary and Tim have a ball exploring the town.*

have a beef against one *or* **hold a beef against one** *phrasal idiom* To have a complaint against one. ♦*John behaves very embarrassed around the director; I guess he must have a beef against him.* ♦*Why hold a beef against me? I didn't cause your troubles!*

have a big head *v. phr.* To be conceited; be excessively proud; think too highly of oneself. ♦*Albert is a nice enough guy, but alas, he has a big head.*

have a blast *v. phr.* To have a big celebration, a joyous party; to have a great time. ♦*When Professor Doolittle retired, he invited the entire department to his country house and we all had a blast.*

have a field day *v. phr.* To enjoy great success or unlimited opportunity. ♦*The visiting basketball team was so weak that our school had a field day scoring one point after another.*

have a fit *or* **have fits** *or* **throw a fit** *v. phr.* **1.** To have a sudden illness with stiffness or jerking of the body. ♦*Our dog had a fit yesterday.* **2.** *informal* To become angry or upset. ♦*Father will throw a fit when he sees the dent in the car.* ♦*Howard will have a fit when he learns that he lost the election.*

have a go at *v. phr., informal* To try, especially after others have tried. ♦*She had a go at pottery, but did not do very well.*

have a hand in *v. phr.* To have a part in or influence over; to be partly responsible for. ♦*Ben had a hand in getting ready the Senior play.*

have all one's buttons *or* **have all one's marbles** *v. phr., slang* To have all your understanding; be reasonable.—Usually used in the negative or conditionally. ♦*Mike acts sometimes as if he didn't have all his buttons.* ♦*He would not go to town barefooted if he had all his marbles.*

have an edge on *v. phr., informal* **1.** To have an advantage over someone or something else in the course of an evaluative comparison. ♦*I can't beat you at tennis, but I have an edge on you in ping-pong.* **2.** To be mildly intoxicated; to have had a few drinks. ♦*Joe sure had an edge on when I saw him last night.*

have an eye for v. phr. To be able to judge correctly; have good taste in. ♦She has an eye for color and style in clothes.

have an eye on or **have one's eye on** v. phr., informal To look at or think about (something wanted); have a wish for; have as an aim. ♦John has his eye on a scholarship so he can go to college.

have a screw loose v. phr., slang To act in a strange way; to be foolish. ♦Now I know he has a screw loose—he stole a police car this time.

have a short fuse v. phr. To be impatient; have a hard time taking abuse and irritation. ♦Jack has a very short fuse; it's better not to mess with him.

have a shot at v. phr. To have a chance at succeeding by trying to do something. ♦"Do you think we have a shot at winning the lottery?" Jim asked. "It's very hard to win the lottery. It's a long shot in any event," Peter replied.

have a snowball's chance in hell v. phr. To be condemned to failure; enjoy a zero chance of success. ♦Pessimists used to think that we had a snowball's chance in hell to put a man on the moon; yet we did it in July, 1969.

have a way with v. phr. To be able to lead, persuade, or influence. ♦Ted will be a good veterinarian, because he has a way with animals.

have a word with v. phr. 1. To talk, discuss, or speak briefly with. ♦Robert, I need to have a word with you about tomorrow's exam. 2. To engage in a sincere discussion with the pur-

pose of persuading the other person or letting him or her know of one's dissatisfaction. ♦Our boss has been making funny decisions lately; I think we ought to have a word with him.

have been around v. phr., informal Have been to many places and done many things; know people; have experience and be able to take care of yourself. ♦It's not easy to fool him; he's been around.

have dibs on or **put dibs on** v. phr., slang To demand a share of something or to be in line for the use of an object usable by more than one person. ♦Don't throw your magazine away! I put (my) dibs on it, remember?

have eyes only for v. phr. To see or want nothing else but; give all your attention to; be interested only in. ♦All the girls liked Fred, but he had eyes only for Helen.

have got it up there v. phr. To be intellectually superior; to be smart. ♦John's success is easy to explain; he's really got it up there.

have got to v. phr. Must; be in great need to do something; be obliged to. ♦I am sorry but we have got to leave; otherwise, we'll miss the last train.

have had it v. phr., slang To have experienced or suffered all you can; to have come to the end of your patience or life. ♦"I've had it," said Lou, "I'm resigning from the job of chairman right now."

have in mind v. phr. To plan; intend; select. ♦We don't know whom our boss has in mind for the new position.

have in the palm of one's hand *v. phr.* To completely control; have a project finished, all wrapped up. ◆*Our boss felt that if he could calm his critics he would soon have the entire factory in the palm of his hand.*

have it *v. phr.* 1. To hear or get news; understand. ◆*I have it on the best authority that we will be paid for our work next week.* 2. To do something in a certain way. ◆*Bobby must have it his way and play the game by his rules.* 3. To claim; say. ◆*Rumor has it that the school burned down.* 4. To allow it.—Usually used with *will* or *would* in negative sentences. ◆*Mary wanted to give the party at her house, but her mother wouldn't have it.* 5. To win. ◆*When the senators vote, the ayes will have it.* 6. To get or find the answer; think of how to do something. ◆*"I have it!" said John to Mary. "We can buy Mother a nice comb for her birthday."* 7. *informal* To have an (easy, good, rough, soft) time; have (certain kinds of) things happen to you; be treated in a (certain) way by luck or life. ◆*Everyone liked Joe and he had it good until he got sick.*

have it coming *v. phr.* To deserve the good or bad things that happen to you. ◆*I feel sorry about Jack's failing that course, but he had it coming to him.* ◆*Everybody said that Eve had it coming when she won the scholarship.*

have it in for *v. phr., informal* To wish or mean to harm; have a bitter feeling against. ◆*After John beat Ted in a fight, Ted always had it in for John.*

have it made *v. phr., slang* To be sure of success; have everything you need. ◆*With her fine grades Alice has it made and can enter any college in the country.*

have it out *v. phr.* To settle a difference by a free discussion or by a fight. ◆*The former friends finally decided to have it out in a free argument and they became friends again.*

have on *v.* 1. To be dressed in; wear. ◆*Mary had on her new dress.* 2. To have (something) planned; have an appointment; plan to do. ◆*I'm sorry I can't attend your party, but I have a meeting on for that night.*

have one's ass in a sling *v. phr., slang, vulgar, avoid!* To be in an uncomfortable predicament; to be in the doghouse; to be at a disadvantage. ◆*Al sure had his ass in a sling when the boss found out about his juggling the account.*

have one's cake and eat it too *v. phr.* To enjoy two opposite advantages. ◆*You can either spend your money going to Europe or save it for a down payment on a house, but you can't do both. That would be having your cake and eating it, too.*

have one's hands full *v. phr.* To have as much work as you can do; be very busy. ◆*The plumber said that he had his hands full and could not take another job for two weeks.*

have qualms about *v. phr.* To feel uneasy about; hesitate about something. ◆*Mike had no qualms in telling Sue that he was no longer in love with her.*

have rocks in one's head *v. phr.,* *informal* To be stupid; not have good judgment. ◆*When Mr. James quit his good job with the coal company to begin teaching school, some people thought he had rocks in his head.*

have (someone) by the balls *v. phr., slang, vulgar, avoidable* To have someone at a disadvantage or in one's power. ◆*The kidnappers had the company by the balls for six long weeks.*

have (something) down pat *v. phr.* To know the details of something entirely, in every detail. ◆*"Can we trust Jim with making that deal with our Japanese partners?" the company director asked. "I am sure we can," Jim's supervisor answered. "He has all the details down pat."*

have something on *v. phr., informal* To have information or proof that someone did something wrong. ◆*Although Miss Brown is not a good worker, her boss does not fire her because she has something on him.*

have something on the ball *v. phr., slang, colloquial* To be smart, clever; to be skilled and have the necessary know-how. ◆*You can trust Syd; he's got a lot on the ball* OR *he's got something on the ball.*

have the last laugh *or* **get the last laugh** *v. phr.* To make someone seem foolish for having laughed at you. ◆*Other schools laughed at us when our little team entered the state championship, but we had the last laugh when we won it.*

have to do with *v. phr.* **1.** To be about; be on the subject of or connected with. ◆*The book has to do with airplanes.* **2.** To know or be a friend of; work or have business with.—Usually used in negative sentence. ◆*Tom said he didn't want to have anything to do with the new boy.*

have two strikes against one *or* **have two strikes on one** *v. phr., informal* To have things working against you; be hindered in several ways; be in a difficult situation; be unlikely to succeed. ◆*Children from the poorest parts of a city often have two strikes against them before they enter school.*

head-hunting *n., slang, informal* **1.** The custom of seeking out, decapitating, and preserving the heads of enemies as trophies **2.** A search for qualified individuals to fill certain positions. ◆*The president sent a committee to the colleges and universities to do some head-hunting; we hope he finds some young talent.* **3.** A systematic destruction of opponents, especially in politics. ◆*Billings was hired by the party to do some head-hunting among members of the opposition.*

head off *v.* **1.** To get in front of and stop, turn back, or turn aside. ◆*The sheriff said to head the cattle thieves off at the pass.* **2.** To block; stop; prevent. ◆*He will get into trouble if someone doesn't head him off.*

head-on *adj. or adv. phr.* **1.** With the head or front pointing at; with the front facing; front end to front end. ◆*Our car skidded into a head-on crash with the truck.* ◆*In the fog the boat ran head-on into a log.* **2.** In a way that is exactly opposite; against or opposed to in argument. ◆*If you think a rule should be changed, a head-on attack against it is best.*

head out *v.* **1.** To go or point away. ◆*The ship left port and headed out to sea. The car was parked beside the house. It was headed out towards the street.* **2.** *informal* Leave; start out. ◆*I have a long way to go before dark. I'm going to head out.*

head over heels *also* **heels over head 1a.** In a somersault; upside down; head first. ◆*It was so dark Bob fell head over heels into a big hole in the ground.* **1b.** In great confusion or disorder; hastily. ◆*The children all tried to come in the door at once, head over heels.* **2.** *informal* Completely; deeply. ◆*He was head over heels in debt.* ◆*She was head over heels in love.*

head shrinker *n., slang, informal* A psychoanalyst, also called a *shrink.* ◆*Forrester is falling apart; his family physician sent him to a head shrinker (to a shrink).*

head start *n.* **1.** A beginning before someone; lead or advantage at the beginning. ◆*The other racers knew they couldn't catch Don if he got too big a head start.* **2.** A good beginning. ◆*The teacher gave the class a head start on the exercise by telling them the answers to the first two problems.*

head up *v., informal* **1.** To be at the head or front of. ◆*The elephants headed up the whole parade.* **2.** To be the leader or boss of. ◆*Mr. Jones will head up the new business.*

heap coals of fire on one's head *v. phr., literary* To be kind or helpful to someone who has done wrong to you, so that he is ashamed. ◆*Alice heaped coals of fire on Mary's head by inviting her to a party after Mary had gossiped about her.*

heart goes out to *formal* You feel very sorry for; you feel pity or sympathy for.—Used with a possessive. ◆*Our hearts went out to the young mother whose child had died.*

heart is in the right place *or* **have one's heart in the right place** To be kind-hearted, sympathetic or well-meaning; have good intentions. ◆*Tom looks very rough but his heart is in the right place.*

heart of gold *n. phr.* A kind, generous, or forgiving nature. ◆*John has a heart of gold. I never saw him angry at anyone.* ◆*Mrs. Brown is a rich woman with a heart of gold.*

heart of stone *n. phr.* A nature without pity. ◆*Mr. Smith has a heart of stone. He whipped his horse until it fell down.*

heart skip a beat *or* **heart miss a beat 1.** The heart leaves out or seems to leave out a beat; the heart beats hard or leaps from excitement or strong feeling. ◆*When Paul saw the bear standing in front of him, his heart skipped a beat.* **2.** To be startled or excited from surprise, joy, or fright. ◆*When Linda was told that she had won, her heart missed a beat.*

heart stand still *v. phr.* To be very frightened or worried. ◆*Everybody's heart stood still when the President announced that war was declared.*

heart-to-heart *adj.* Speaking freely and seriously about something private. ♦*The father decided to have a heart-to-heart talk with his son about smoking.*

heavy heart *n. phr.* A feeling of being weighed down with sorrow; unhappiness. ♦*They had very heavy hearts as they went to the funeral.*

hedge about *or* **hedge in 1.** To surround with a hedge or barrier; protect or separate by closing in. ♦*The little garden is hedged in to keep the chickens out.* **2.** To keep from getting out or moving freely; keep from acting freely; block in. ♦*The boys are hedged in today. They can only play in the backyard.*

he laughs best who laughs last A person should go ahead with what he is doing and not worry when others laugh at him. When he succeeds he will enjoy laughing at them for being wrong more than they enjoyed laughing at him.—A proverb. ♦*Everyone laughed at Mary when she was learning to ski. She kept falling down. Now she is the state champion. He laughs best who laughs last.*

hell and high water *n. phr.* Troubles or difficulties of any kind. ♦*After John's father died he went through hell and high water, but he managed to keep the family together.*

hell-on-wheels *n., slang* A short-tempered, nagging, or crabby person especially one who makes another unhappy by constantly criticizing him even when he has done nothing wrong. ♦*Finnegan complains that his wife is hell on wheels;*

he is considering getting a divorce.

he-man *n., informal* A man who is very strong, brave, and healthy. ♦*Larry was a real he-man when he returned from service with the Marines.*

hem and haw *v. phr.* **1.** To pause or hesitate while speaking, often with little throat noises. ♦*The man was a poor lecturer because he hemmed and hawed too much.* **2.** To avoid giving a clear answer; be evasive in speech. ♦*The principal asked Bob why he was late to school, and Bob only hemmed and hawed.*

here goes *interj., informal* I am ready to begin; I am now ready and willing to take the chance; I am hoping for the best.—Said especially before beginning something that takes skill, luck, or courage. ♦ *"Here goes!" said Charley, as he jumped off the high diving board.*

here goes nothing *interj., informal* I am ready to begin, but this will be a waste of time; this will not be anything great; this will probably fail.—Used especially before beginning something that takes skill, luck or courage. ♦ *"Here goes nothing," said Bill at the beginning of the race.*

hide one's head in the sand *or* **bury one's head in the sand** *or* **have one's head in the sand** To keep from seeing, knowing, or understanding something dangerous or unpleasant; to refuse to see or face something. ♦*If there is a war, you cannot just bury your head in the sand.*

hide one's light under a bushel *v. phr.* To be very shy and modest and not show your abilities or talents; be too modest in letting others see what you can do. ◆*All year long Tom hid his light under a bushel and the teacher was surprised to see how much he knew when she read his exam paper.*

high and dry *adv. or adj. phr.* **1.** Up above the water; beyond the reach of splashing or waves. ◆*Mary was afraid she had left her towel where the tide would reach it, but she found it high and dry.* **2.** Without anyone to help; alone and with no help. ◆*When the time came to put up the decorations, Mary was left high and dry.*

high-and-mighty *adj., informal* Feeling more important or superior to someone else; too proud of yourself. ◆*Mary became high-and-mighty when she won the prize, and Joan would not go around with her anymore.*

high gear *n. phr., informal* Top speed; full activity. ◆*Production got into high gear after the vacation.*

high-handed *adj.* Depending on force rather than right; bossy; dictatorial. ◆*Mr. Smith was a high-handed tyrant in his office.*

high seas *n. phr.* The open ocean, not the waters near the coast. ◆*It was a big powerful liner built to sail on the high seas.* ◆*The ships of every country have the right to sail on the high seas.*

high time *adj. phr., used predicatively* (stress on *time*) Dire, necessary, and sufficient circumstances prompting action. ◆*It is high time we sold the*

old house; it will fall apart within a year.

highway robbery *n. phr.* **1.** A hold-up of or theft from a person committed on an open road or street usually by an armed man. ◆*Highway robbery was common in England in Shakespeare's day.* **2.** An extremely high price or charge; a profiteer's excessive charge. ◆*To someone from a small town, the prices of meals and theater tickets in New York often seem to be highway robbery.*

hit-and-run *adj.* **1.** Of or about an accident after which a motorist drives away without giving his name and offering help. ◆*Judges are stern with hit-and-run drivers.* **2.** Striking suddenly and leaving quickly. ◆*The bandits often made hit-and-run attacks on wagon trains.*

hit a nerve *v. phr.* To affect someone strongly and negatively. ◆*When John called his sister a hooker, the remark hit a nerve so strongly that she gave him a slap in the face.*

hit a snag *or* **run into trouble** *v. phr.* To encounter unexpected difficulties or problems. ◆*Sam was repairing my broken computer when he suddenly hit a snag, and said that we needed a new hard disk.* ◆*The construction engineer ran into trouble suddenly when he found that the beams were too weak to hold up the walls.*

hit bottom *or* **touch bottom** *v. phr., informal* **1.** To be at the very lowest. ◆*In August there was a big supply of corn and the price hit bottom.* **2.** To live through the worst; not to be able to go any lower. ◆*When* *they lost all their money they thought they had touched bottom and things would have to get better.*

hitch one's wagon to a star *v. phr.* To aim high; follow a great ambition or purpose. ◆*John hitched his wagon to a star and decided to try to become President.*

hither and thither *or* **hither and yon** *adv. phr., literary* In one direction and then in another. ◆*Bob wandered hither and thither looking for a playmate.*

hit home *v. phr.* To go directly to the mark; strike a vulnerable spot. ◆*His remark hit home when he referred to those who do not contribute sufficiently to the college fund drive.*

hit it off *v. phr., informal* To enjoy one another's company; be happy and comfortable in each other's presence. ◆*Tom and Fred hit it off well with each other.* ◆*Mary and Jane hit it off from the first.*

hit on *or* **hit upon** *v.* To happen to meet, find, or reach; to choose or think by chance. ◆*There seemed to be several explanations of the crime, but the detectives hit on the right one the first time.*

hit on one *v. phr.* To flirt with someone. ◆*"Why are you hitting on me?" Suzie asked, "when your pretty wife is standing just a few feet away from us?"*

hit-or-miss *also* **hit-and-miss** *adj.* Unplanned; uncontrolled; aimless; careless. ◆*John did a lot of hit-or-miss reading, some of it about taxes.* ◆*Mary packed her bag in hurried, hit-or-miss fashion.*

hit the books *v. phr., informal* To study your school assignments, prepare for classes. ◆*Jack broke away from his friends, saying, "I've got to hit the books."*

hit the bull's-eye *v. phr., informal* To go to the important part of the matter; reach the main question. ◆*John hit the bull's-eye when he said the big question was one of simple honesty.*

hit the ceiling *or* **hit the roof** *v. phr., slang* To become violently angry; go into a rage. ◆*When Elaine came home at three in the morning, her father hit the ceiling.*

hit the deck *v. phr.* To get up from bed, to start working. (From sailor's language as in *"All hands on the deck!"*) ◆*OK boys, it's time to hit the deck!*

hit the dirt *v. phr., slang military* To take cover under gunfire by falling on the ground. ◆*We hit the dirt the moment we heard the machine gun fire.*

hit the fan *v. phr., informal* To become a big public problem or controversy. ◆*The whole mess hit the fan when the judge was arrested for drunken driving for the second time.*

hit the hay *or* **hit the sack** *v. phr., slang* To go to bed. ◆*Louis was so tired that he hit the sack soon after supper.*

hit the high spots *v. phr.* To consider, mention, or see only the more important parts of something such as a book, war, or school course. ◆*The first course in general science hits only the high spots of the physical sciences.*

hit the jackpot *v. phr., slang* To be very lucky or successful. ◆*Mr.*

Brown invented a new gadget which hit the jackpot.

hit the nail on the head v. phr. To get something exactly right; speak or act in the most fitting or effective way. ♦*The mayor's talk on race relations hit the nail on the head.*

hit the road v. phr., slang 1. To become a wanderer; to live an idle life; become a tramp or hobo. ♦*When Jack's wife left him, he felt a desire to travel, so he hit the road.* 2. To leave, especially in a car. ♦*It is getting late, so I guess we will hit the road for home.* ♦*He packed his car and hit the road for California.*

hit the sauce v. phr., slang To drink alcoholic beverages—especially heavily and habitually. ♦*When Sue left him, Joe began to hit the sauce.*

hit the spot v. phr., informal To refresh fully or satisfy you; bring back your spirits or strength—used especially of food or drink. ♦*A cup of tea always hits the spot when you are tired.*

hitting skins n. phr., slang Sex. "What is Jim the best at?" the prospective employer asked. "Not much that I know of," Tracy answered, "except for hitting skins."

hit town v. phr. To arrive in town. ♦*Give me a phone call as soon as you hit town.*

hold a candle to also **hold a stick to** v. phr. To be fit to be compared with; be in the same class with. ♦*Henry thought that no modern physicist could hold a candle to Einstein.*

hold all the trumps v. phr. To have the best chance of winning; have all the advantages; have full control. ♦*Fred has $200 and I have no money, so he holds all the trumps and can buy whatever he wants with it.*

hold back v. 1. To stay back or away; show unwillingness. ♦*John held back from social activity because he felt embarrassed with people.* 2. To keep someone in place; prevent from acting. ♦*The police held back the crowd.*

hold court v. phr. 1. To hold a formal meeting of a royal court or a court of law. ♦*Judge Stephens allowed no foolishness when he held court.* 2. informal To act like a king or queen among subjects. ♦*Even at sixteen, Judy was holding court for numbers of charmed boys.*

hold down v. 1. To keep in obedience; keep control of; continue authority or rule over. ♦*Kings used to know very well how to hold down the people.* 2. informal To work satisfactorily at. ♦*John had held down a tough job for a long time.*

hold forth v. 1. To offer; propose. ♦*As a candidate, Jones held forth the promise of a bright future.* 2. To speak in public; preach.—Usually used with little respect. ♦*Senator Smith was holding forth on free trade.*

hold good v. 1. To continue to be good; last. ♦*The coupon on the cereal box offered a free toy, but the offer held good only till the end of the year.* 2. To continue; endure; last. ♦*The agreement between the schools held good for three years.*

hold off v. 1a. To refuse to let (someone) become friendly. ♦*The president's high rank and* *chilly manner held people off.* **1b.** To be rather shy or unfriendly. ♦*Perkins was a scholarly man who held off from people.* **2.** To keep away by fighting; oppose by force. ♦*The kidnapper locked himself in the house and held off the police for an hour.* **3.** To wait before (doing something); postpone; delay. ♦*Jack held off paying for the television set until the dealer fixed it.*

hold on *v.* **1.** To keep holding tightly; continue to hold strongly. ♦*As Ted was pulling on the rope, it began to slip and Earl cried, "Hold on, Ted!"* **2.** To wait and not hang up a telephone; keep a phone for later use. ♦*Mr. Jones asked me to hold on while he spoke to his secretary.* **3.** To keep on with a business or job in spite of difficulties. ♦*It was hard to keep the store going during the depression, but Max held on and at last met with success.* **4.** *informal* To wait a minute; stop.— Usually used as a command. ♦*"Hold on!" John's father said, "I want the car tonight."*

hold one's breath *v. phr.* **1.** To stop breathing for a moment when you are excited or nervous. ♦*The race was so close that everyone was holding his breath at the finish.* **2.** To endure great nervousness, anxiety, or excitement. ♦*John held his breath for days before he got word that the college he chose had accepted him.*

hold one's horses *v. phr., informal* To stop; wait; be patient. ♦*"Hold your horses!" Mr. Jones said to David when David wanted to call the police.*

hold one's own *v. phr.* To keep your position; avoid losing ground; keep your advantage, wealth, or condition without loss. ♦*Mr. Smith could not build up his business, but he held his own.* ♦*The team held its own after the first quarter.* ♦*Mary had a hard time after the operation, but soon she was holding her own.*

hold one's peace *v. phr., formal* To be silent and not speak against something; be still; keep quiet. ♦*I did not agree with the teacher, but held my peace as he was rather angry.*

hold one's tongue *v. phr.* To be silent; keep still; not talk. ♦*The teacher told Fred to hold his tongue.*

hold on to *v. phr.* **1a.** *or* **hold to** To continue to hold or keep; hold tightly. ♦*The old man held on to his job stubbornly and would not retire.* **1b.** To stay in control of. ♦*Ann was so frightened that she had to hold onto her husband in order to not to scream.* **2.** To continue to sing or sound. ♦*The singer held on to the last note of the song for a long time.*

holdout *n.* A rebel who refuses to go with the majority. ♦*Sam was a lone holdout in town; he refused to sell his old lakefront cottage to make place for a skyscraper.*

hold out *v. phr.* **1.** To put forward; reach out; extend; offer. ♦*Mr. Ryan held out his hand in welcome.* **2.** To keep resisting; not yield; refuse to give up. ♦*The city held out for six months under siege.* Compare HANG ON, HOLD ON. **3.** To refuse to agree or settle until one's wishes have been agreed to. ♦*The strikers* *held out for a raise of five cents an hour.* **4.** *slang* To keep something from; refuse information or belongings to which someone has a right. ◆*Mr. Porter's partner held out on him when the big payment came in.*

hold out hope *v. phr.* To give encouragement to people in difficulty. ◆*The U.S. central command held out hope for our prisoners of war.*

holdover *n.* **1.** A successful movie or theater production that plays longer than originally planned. ◆*Because of its great popularity,* Star Wars *was a holdover in most movie theaters.* **2.** A reservation not used at the time intended, but used later. ◆*They kept my seat at the opera as a holdover because I am a patron.*

hold over *v.* **1.** To remain or keep in office past the end of the term. ◆*The new President held the members of the Cabinet over for some time before appointing new members.* **2.** To extend the engagement of; keep longer. ◆*The theater held over the feature film for another two weeks.* **3.** To delay action on; to postpone; to defer. ◆*The directors held over their decision until they could get more information.*

hold still *v. phr.* To remain motionless. ◆*"Hold still," the dentist said. "This won't hurt you at all."*

hold the bag *v. phr.* To be made liable for or victimized. ◆*We went out to dinner together but when it was time to pay I was left holding the bag.*

hold the fort *v. phr.* **1.** To defend a fort successfully; fight off

attackers. ◆*The little group held the fort for days until help came.* **2.** *informal* To keep a position against opposing forces. ◆*Friends of civil liberties held the fort during a long debate.* **3.** *informal* to keep service or operations going ◆*Mother and Father went out and told the children to hold the fort.*

holdup *n.* (stress on *hold*) **1.** Robbery. ◆*John fell victim to a highway holdup.* **2.** A delay, as on a crowded highway. ◆*Boy we're late! What's causing this holdup?*

hold up *v.* (stress on *up*) **1.** To raise; lift. ◆*John held up his hand.* **2.** To support; bear; carry. ◆*The chair was too weak to hold up Mrs. Smith.* **3.** To show; call attention to; exhibit. ◆*The teacher held up excellent models of composition for her class to imitate.* **4.** To check; stop; delay. ◆*The wreck held up traffic on the railroad's main line tracks.* **5.** *informal* To rob at gunpoint. ◆*Masked men held up the bank.* **6.** To keep one's courage or spirits up; remain calm; keep control of oneself. ◆*The grieving mother held up for her children's sake.* **7.** To remain good; not get worse. ◆*Sales held up well.* ◆*Our team's luck held up and they won the game.* ◆*The weather held up and the game was played.* **8.** To prove true. ◆*The police were doubtful at first, but Tony's story held up.* **9.** To delay action; defer; postpone. ◆*The President held up on the news until he was sure of it.*

hold water *v. phr.* **1.** To keep water without leaking. ◆*That* *pail still holds water.* **2.** *informal* To prove true; stand testing; bear examination.— Usually used in negative, interrogative, or conditional sentences. ◆*Ernest told the police a story that wouldn't hold water.*

holier-than-thou *adj.* Acting as if you are better than others in goodness, character, or reverence for God; acting as if morally better than other people. ◆*Most people find holier-than-thou actions in others hard to accept.*

holy cow *or* **holy mackerel** *or* **holy Moses** *interj.*, *informal*— Used to express strong feeling (as astonishment, pleasure, or anger); used in speech or when writing conversation. ◆*"Holy cow! They can't do that!" Mary said when she saw the boys hurting a much smaller boy.*

holy terror *n.*, *informal* A very disobedient or unruly child; brat. ◆*All the children are afraid of Johnny because he's a holy terror.*

honeymoon is over The first happy period of friendship and cooperation between two persons or groups is over. ◆*A few months after a new President is elected, the honeymoon is over and Congress and the President begin to criticize each other.*

hooked on *adj.* **1.** Addicted to a substance such as cigarettes, coffee, tea, drugs, or alcohol. ◆*Fred is hooked on grass, but Tim is only hooked on tea.* **2.** Enthusiastic or very supportive of something. ◆*I am hooked on the local symphony.*

hook, line and sinker *adv. phr.*, *informal* Without question or doubt; completely. ◆*Johnny*

was so easily fooled that he fell for Joe's story, hook, line and sinker.

hookup *n.* (stress on *hook*) A connection, electrical or otherwise, between two instruments or two individuals. ◆*Edwin and Hermione are a perfect couple; they have got the right hookup.*

hook up *v. phr.* (stress on *up*) To connect or fit together. ◆*The company sent a man to hook up the telephone.* ◆*They could not use the gas stove because it had not been hooked up.*

hope against hope *v. phr.* To try to hope when things look black; hold to hope in bad trouble. ◆*The mother continued to hope against hope although the plane was hours late.* ◆*Jane hoped against hope that Joe would call her.*

hopped up *adj.*, *slang* **1.** Doped with a narcotic drug. ◆*Police found Jones hiding in an opium den, among other men all hopped up with the drug.* **2.** Full of eagerness; excited. ◆*Fred was all hopped up about going over the ocean.*

horn in *v.*, *slang* To come in without invitation or welcome; interfere. Often used with *on*. ◆*Jack would often horn in on conversations discussing things he knew nothing about.*

horse around *v.*, *slang* To join in rough teasing; play around. ◆*They were a bunch of sailors on shore leave, horsing around where there were girls and drinks.*

horse of a different color *or* **horse of another color** *n. phr.*, *informal* Something altogether separate and different. ◆*Anyone* can be broke, but to steal is a horse of a different color.

horse sense n., informal A good understanding about what to do in life; good judgment; wisdom in making decisions. ♦Some people are well educated and read many books, but still do not have much horse sense.

horse trade n. **1.** The sale of a horse or the exchange of two horses. ♦It was a horse trade in which the owner of the worse animal gave a rifle to make the trade equal. **2.** informal A business agreement or bargain arrived at after hard and skillful discussion. ♦Party leaders went around for months making horse trades to get support for their candidate.

hot air n., informal Nonsense, exaggerated talk, wasted words characterized by emotion rather than intellectual content. ♦That was just a lot of hot air what Joe said.

hot dog n. phr., informal A frankfurter or wiener in a roll. ♦The boys stopped on the way home for hot dogs and coffee.

hot dog! interj., informal Hurrah!—A cry used to show pleasure or enthusiasm. ♦"Hot dog!" Frank exclaimed when he unwrapped a birthday gift of a small record player.

hot potato n., informal A question that causes strong argument and is difficult to settle. ♦Many school boards found segregation a hot potato in the 1960s.

hot rod n., informal An older automobile changed so that it can gain speed quickly and go very fast. ♦Hot rods are used by young people especially in drag racing.

house of cards n. phr. Something badly put together and easily knocked down; a poorly founded plan, hope, or action. ♦John's business fell apart like a house of cards.

house of ill fame or **of ill repute** n. phr. A bordello; a brothel. ♦At the edge of town there is a house of ill repute run by a Madame who used to be a singer in a bar.

hover over v. phr. **1.** To remain close or above. ♦The rescue helicopter was carefully hovering above the stranded rock climbers. **2.** To watch over; supervise. ♦"Mother!" Phillip cried, "if you don't stop hovering over me, I'll go bananas!"

how come informal also nonstandard **how's come** interrog. How does it happen that? Why? ♦How come you are late? ♦You're wearing your best clothes today. How come?

how does it play? adv. phr. What is the reaction? How do the people evaluate what is happening? ♦"What I need to know is," the public relations director of the famous daily newspaper asked, "how our attempt at liberating Iraq is playing in the Arab streets, now that Baghdad has fallen."

how does that grab you? adv. phr., slang What do you reply to that? What do you think of that? ♦"The income tax cut will have to be less than the president promised before the second Gulf War. Now let me ask you, how does that grab you?"

how do you do? formal greeting How are you?—Usually as a reply to an introduction; it is in the form of a question but no answer is expected. ♦*"Mary, I want you to meet my friend Fred. Fred, this is my wife, Mary." "How do you do, Mary?" "How do you do, Fred?"*

hue and cry *n.* **1.** An alarm and chase after a supposed wrong-doer; a pursuit usually by shouting men. ♦*"Stop, thief," cried John as he ran. Others joined him, and soon there was a hue and cry.* **2.** An excited mass protest, alarm, or outcry of any kind. ♦*The explosion was so terrible that people at a distance raised a great hue and cry about an earthquake.*

hug the road *v. phr.* To stay firmly on the road; ride smoothly without swinging. ♦*A heavy car with a low center of gravity will hug the road. ♦At high speeds a car will not hug the road well.*

hush-hush *adj., informal* Kept secret or hidden; kept from public knowledge; hushed up; concealed. ♦*The company had a new automobile engine that it was developing, but kept it a hush-hush project until they knew it was successful.*

hush up *v.* **1.** To keep news of (something) from getting out; prevent people from knowing about. ♦*It isn't always easy to hush up a scandal.* **2.** *informal* To be or make quiet; stop talking, crying, or making some other noise.—Often used as a command. ♦*"Hush up," Mother said, when we began to repeat ugly gossip.*

icebreaker *n. phr.* A joke or a funny anecdote used at the beginning of a formal presentation or question-and-answer session after a lecture, which puts the participants at ease, allowing a flow of free conversation. ◆*"I always welcome an icebreaker in a formal situation," Sir Randolph Quirk, the president of the British Academy said after a heavily attended and televised conference in Singapore.*

I couldn't agree with you more *v. phr.* meaning: "How right you are!" ◆*"We need a little more love between human beings on planet Earth," the Reverend Blomerly said. "I couldn't agree with you more," his parishioner answered.*

I couldn't care less *v. phr.* It really doesn't matter to me; I am entirely indifferent in the matter. ◆*"The Milky Way Galaxy will definitely collide with the Andromeda Galaxy in a billion year's time," the lecturer in astronomy said, trying to impress Miss Curtis. "That is interesting" the pretty young girl answered, "but I really couldn't care less. My problems are more immediate."*

idiot box *n.* A television set. ◆*Phil has been staring at the idiot box all afternoon.*

if the hill will not come to Muhammad, Muhammad will go to the hill If one person will not go to the other, then the other must go to him.—A proverb. ◆*Grandfather won't come to visit us, so we must go and visit him. If the hill won't come to Muhammad, then Muhammad will go to the hill.*

if the shoe fits, wear it If what is said describes you, you are meant.—A proverb. ◆*I won't say who, but some children are always late. If the shoe fits, wear it.*

if worst comes to worst If the worst thing happens that be imagined; if the worst possible thing happens; if troubles grow worse. ◆*If worst comes to worst and Mr. Jones loses the house, he will send his family to his mother's farm.*

ill at ease *adj. phr.* Not feeling at ease or comfortable; anxious; worried; unhappy. ◆*When Joe first went to dancing school, he was ill at ease, not knowing how to act.*

I'm from Missouri I am skeptical; I don't believe what you said unless you show me.—A proverb. ◆*"I won two air tickets and a week in a hotel in Hawaii," John said. "I hope you're coming." "You know me, John," Mary replied, "I'm from Missouri. I'll believe you when you show them to me."*

in a bind *or* **in a box** *adv. phr., informal* Likely to have trouble whether you do one thing or another. ◆*Sam is in a bind because if he carries home his aunt's groceries, his teacher will be angry because he is late, and if he doesn't, his aunt will complain.*

in a circle *or* **in circles** *adv. phr.* Without any progress; without getting anywhere; uselessly. ◆*The committee debated for two hours, just talking in circles.*

in a family way or **in the family way** adj. phr., informal Going to have a baby. ♦Sue and Liz are happy because their mother is in the family way.

in a fix adv. phr. In trouble. ♦Last night Jack wrecked his car and now he is in a fix.

in a jam adv. phr., informal In a predicament; in a situation fraught with difficulty. ♦If you continue to disregard the university instructions on how to take a test, you'll wind up in a jam with the head of the department.

in a jiffy adv. phr., informal Immediately; right away; in a moment. ♦Wait for me; I'll be back in a jiffy.

in a nutshell adv. phr., informal In a few words; briefly, without telling all about it. ♦We are in a hurry, so I'll give you the story in a nutshell.

in any case also **in any event** or **at all events** adv. phr. **1.** No matter what happens; surely; without fail; certainly; anyhow; anyway. ♦It may rain tomorrow, but we are going home in any case. **2.** Regardless of anything else; whatever else may be true; anyhow; anyway. ♦I don't know if it is a white house or a brown house. At all events, it is a big house on Main Street.

in a pickle adv. phr., informal In a quandary; in a difficult situation. ♦I was certainly in a pickle when my front tire blew out.

in a pig's eye adv., slang, informal Hardly; unlikely; not so. ♦Would I marry him? In a pig's eye.

in a pinch adv. phr., informal In an emergency. ♦Dave is a good friend who will always help out in a pinch.

in arms adv. phr. Having guns and being ready to fight; armed. ♦When our country is at war, we have many men in arms.

in a world of one's own or **in a world by oneself 1.** In the place where you belong; in your own personal surroundings; apart from other people. ♦They are in a little world of their own in their house on the mountain. **2a.** In deep thought or concentration. ♦Mary is in a world of her own when she is playing the piano. **2b.** slang Not caring about or connected with other people in thoughts or actions.—Usually used sarcastically. ♦That boy is in a world all by himself. He never knows what is happening around him.

in case adv. phr., informal In order to be prepared; as a precaution; if there is need.—Usually used in the phrase just in case. ♦The bus is usually on time, but start early, just in case.

in character adv. or adj. phr. **1.** In agreement with a person's character or personality; in the way that a person usually behaves or is supposed to behave; as usual; characteristic; typical; suitable. ♦John was very rude at the party, and that was not in character because he is usually very polite. **2.** Suitable for the part or the kind of part being acted; natural to the way a character in a book or play is supposed to act. ♦It would not have been in character for Robin Hood to steal from a poor man.

in charge adv. or adj. phr. **1.** In authority or control; in a position to care for or supervise;

responsible. ♦*If you have any questions, ask the boss. He's in charge.* 2. Under care or supervision. ♦*During your visit to the library, you will be in the librarian's charge.*

in charge of *prep.* 1. Responsible for; having supervision or care of. ♦*Marian is in charge of selling tickets.* 2. *or* **in the charge of** Under the care or supervision of. ♦*Mother puts the baby in the charge of the baby-sitter while she is out.*

in check *adv. phr.* In a position where movement or action is not allowed or stopped; under control; kept quiet or back. ♦*The soldiers tried to keep the attacking Iraqis in check until help came.* ♦*Mary couldn't hold her feelings in check any longer and began to cry.*

in clover *or* **in the clover** *adv. or adj. phr., informal* In rich comfort; rich or successful; having a pleasant or easy life. ♦*They live in clover because their father is rich.* ♦*When we finish the hard part we'll be in the clover.*

in cold blood *adv. phr.* Without feeling or pity; in a purposely cruel way; coolly and deliberately. ♦*The bank robbers planned to shoot in cold blood anyone who got in their way.*

in common *adv. phr.* Shared together or equally; in use or ownership by all. ♦*Mr. and Mrs. Smith own the store in common.*

in deep *adj. phr.* Seriously mixed up in something, especially trouble. ♦*George began borrowing small sums of money to bet on horses, and before he knew it he was in deep.*

Indian giver *n. phr.* A person who gives one something, but later asks for it back.—An ethnic slur; avoid! ♦*John gave me a beautiful fountain pen, but a week later, like an Indian giver, he wanted it back.*

Indian summer *n. phr.* A dry and warm period of time late in the fall, usually in October. ♦*After the cold and foggy weather, we had a brief Indian summer, during which the temperature was up in the high seventies.*

in fact *also* **in point of fact** *adv. phr.* Really truthfully.—Often used for emphasis. ♦*It was a very hot day; in fact, it was 100 degrees.*

in for *prep., informal* Unable to avoid; sure to get. ♦*On Christmas morning we are in for some surprises.*

in good time *or* **in good season** *adv. phr.* 1. A little early; sooner than necessary. ♦*The school bus arrived in good time.* ♦*We reached the station in good season to catch the 9:15 bus for New York.* 2. *or* **in due course** *or* **in due season** *or* **in due time** In the usual amount of time; at the right time; in the end. ♦*Spring and summer will arrive in due course.*

in hand *adv. or adj. phr.* 1. Under control. ♦*The baby-sitter kept the children well in hand.* 2. In your possession; with you.—Often used in the phrase *cash in hand.* ♦*Tom figured that his cash in hand with his weekly pay would be enough to buy a car.* 3. Being worked on; with you to do. ♦*We should finish the work we have in hand before we begin something new.*

in harm's way *or* **into harm's way** *adv. phr.* In danger of getting wounded or killed either in a war or in the police force. ◆*America worries about sending U.S. troops into harm's way.* ◆*Many reporters during the war lived in harm's way.*

in kind *adv. phr.* In a similar way; with the same kind of thing. ◆*Lois returned Mary's insult in kind.*

in league with *or informal* **in cahoots with** *prep.* In secret agreement or partnership with (someone); working together secretly with, especially for harm. ◆*People once believed that some women were witches in league with the devil.*

in line *adj. phr.* **1.** In a position in a series or after someone else. ◆*John is in line for the presidency of the club next year.* **2.** Obeying or agreeing with what is right or usual; doing or being what people expect or accept; within ordinary or proper limits. ◆*The coach kept the excited team in line.*

in line with *prep.* In agreement with. ◆*In line with the custom of the school, the students had a holiday between Christmas and New Year's Day.*

in love *adj. phr.* Liking very much; loving. ◆*Tom and Ellen are in love.* ◆*Mary is in love with her new wristwatch.*

in luck *adj. phr.* Being lucky; having good luck; finding something good by chance. ◆*Mary dropped her glasses but they did not break. She was in luck.*

in memory of *prep.* As something that makes people remember (a person or thing); as a reminder of; as a memorial to. ◆*Many special ceremonies are in memory of famous people.*

in no time *or* **in nothing flat** *adv. phr., informal* In a very little time; soon; quickly. ◆*When the entire class worked together they finished the project in no time.* ◆*The bus filled with students in nothing flat.*

in on *prep.* **1.** Joining together for. ◆*The children collected money from their classmates and went in on a present for their teacher.* **2.** Told about; having knowledge of. ◆*Bob was in on the secret.*

in one's element *adv. phr.* **1.** In one's natural surroundings. ◆*The deep-sea fish is in his element in deep ocean water.* **2.** Where you can do your best. ◆*John is in his element working on the farm.*

in one's face *adv. phr.* **1.** Against your face. ◆*The trick cigar blew up in the clown's face.* ◆*A cold wind was in our faces as we walked to school.* **2.** In front of you. ◆*I told the boys that they were wrong, but they laughed in my face.*

in one's good graces *or* **in one's good books** *adv. phr.* Approved of by you; liked by someone. ◆*Bill is back in the good graces of his girlfriend because he stopped drinking.*

in one's hair *adj. phr., informal* Bothering you again and again; always annoying. ◆*John got in Father's hair when he was trying to read the paper by running and shouting.*

in one's mind's eye *adv. phr.* In the memory; in the imagination. ◆*In his mind's eye he saw again the house he had lived in when he was a child.*

in one's shell *or* **into one's shell** *adv. or adj. phr., informal* In or into bashfulness; into silence; not sociable; unfriendly. ♦*The teacher tried to get Rose to talk to her, but she stayed in her shell.*

in one's shoes *also* **in one's boots** *adv. phr.* In or into one's place or position. ♦*How would you like to be in a lion tamer's boots?*

in one's tracks *adv. phr., informal* Just where one is at the moment; abruptly; immediately. ♦*Mary stopped dead in her tracks, turned around, and ran back home.*

in order *adv. or adj. phr.* **1.** In arrangement; in the proper way of following one another. ♦*Line up and walk to the door in order.* ♦*Name all the presidents in order.* **2.** In proper condition. ♦*The car was in good working order when I bought it.* **3.** Following the rules; proper; suitable. ♦*Is it in order to ask the speaker questions at the meeting?* ♦*At the end of a program, applause for the performers is in order.*

in part *adv. phr.* To some extent; partly; not wholly.—Often used with *large* or *small.* ♦*We planted the garden in part with flowers. But in large part we planted vegetables.* ♦*Tom was only in small part responsible.*

in particular *adv. phr.* In a way apart from others; more than others; particularly; especially. ♦*The speaker talked about sports in general and about football in particular.*

ins and outs *n. phr.* The special ways of going somewhere or doing something; the different parts. ♦*Jerry's father is a good life insurance salesman; he* knows all the ins and outs of the business.

in short supply *adj. phr.* Not enough; in too small a quantity or amount; in less than the amount or number needed. ♦*We have five people and only four beds, so the beds are in short supply.*

inside dope *n. phr.* Secret information about the inner workings of a business, an organization, or some place of employment. ♦*"How does one get ahead at the Chicago Tool and Die Company?" Peter asked his friend Tom, who had been working there for several years. "I'll give you the inside dope," Tom replied. "Rule number one: never disagree with the boss; he is very vain."*

inside out *adv.* **1.** So that the inside is turned outside. ♦*Mother turns the stockings inside out when she washes them.* **2.** *or* **inside and out** *also* **in and out** In every part; throughout; completely. ♦*We searched the house inside and out for the kitten.*

inside track *n. phr.* **1.** The inside, shortest distance around a curved racetrack; the place that is closest to the inside fence. ♦*A big white horse had the inside track at the start of the race.* **2.** *informal* An advantage due to special connections or information. ♦*I would probably get that job if I could get the inside track.*

in spite of *prep. phr.* Against the influence or effect of; in opposition to; defying the effect of; despite. ♦*In spite of the bad storm John delivered his papers on time.*

in stitches *adj. phr., informal* Laughing so hard that the sides ache; in a fit of laughing hard. ♦*The comedian was so funny that he had everyone who was watching him in stitches.*

in stock *adj. phr.* Having something ready to sell or use; in present possession or supply; to be sold. ♦*The store had no more red shoes in stock, so Mary chose brown ones instead.*

in store *adj. or adv. phr.* 1. Saved up in case of need; ready for use or for some purpose. ♦*The squirrel has plenty of nuts in store for the winter.* 2. Ready to happen; waiting.—Often used in the phrase *hold* or *have in store.* ♦*What does the future hold in store for the boy who ran away?* ♦*There is a surprise in store for Helen when she gets home.*

in the air *adv. phr.* 1. In everyone's thoughts. ♦*Christmas was in the air for weeks before.* ♦*The war filled people's thoughts every day; it was in the air.* 2. Meeting the bodily senses; surrounding you so as to be smelled or felt. ♦*Spring is in the air.*

in the bag *adj. phr., informal* Sure to be won or gotten; certain. ♦*We thought we had the game in the bag.*

in the ballpark *adv. phr.* In roughly the amount mentioned. ♦*"Will the new employee cost us $75,000 a year?" Tom asked the director. "You're in the ballpark," the director replied.*

in the black *adv. or adj. phr., informal* In a successful or profitable way; so as to make money. ♦*A business must stay in the black to keep on.*

in the cards *also* **on the cards** *adj. phr., informal* To be expected; likely to happen; foreseeable; predictable. ♦*It was in the cards for the son to succeed his father as head of the business.*

in the clear *adj. phr.* 1. Free of anything that makes moving or seeing difficult; with nothing to limit action. ♦*The plane climbed above the clouds and was flying in the clear.* ♦*Jack passed the ball to Tim, who was in the clear and ran for a touchdown.* 2. *informal* Free of blame or suspicion; not thought to be guilty. ♦*Steve was the last to leave the locker room, and the boys suspected him of stealing Tom's watch, but the coach found the watch and put Steve in the clear.* 3. Free of debt; not owing money to anyone. ♦*Bob borrowed a thousand dollars from his father to start his business, but at the end of the first year he was in the clear.*

in the clouds *adj. phr.* Far from real life; in dreams; in fancy; in thought. ♦*When Alice agreed to marry Jim, Jim went home in the clouds.*—Often used with *head, mind, thoughts.* ♦*Mary is looking out the window, not at the chalkboard; her head is in the clouds again.*

in the dark *adj. phr.* In ignorance; without information. ♦*John was in the dark about the job he was being sent to.*

in the doghouse *adj. phr., slang* In disgrace or disfavor. ♦*Our neighbor got in the doghouse with his wife by coming home drunk.*

in the hole *adv. or adj. phr., informal* **1a.** Having a score lower than zero in a game, especially a card game; to a score below zero. *John went three points in the hole on the first hand of the card game.* **1b.** Behind an opponent; in difficulty in a sport or game. *We had their pitcher in the hole with the bases full and no one out.* **2.** In debt; behind financially. *John went in the hole with his hot dog stand.*

in the line of duty *adj. phr.* Done or happening as part of a job. *The policeman was shot in the line of duty.*

in the line of fire *adv. phr.* In a dangerous position between two opposing parties. *John is right in the line of fire between the company's director and the vice president, who couldn't agree on John's proposal about the budget.*

in the long run *adv. phr.* In the end; in the final result. *John knew that he could make a success of the little weekly paper in the long run.*

in the market for *adj. phr.* Wishing to buy; ready to buy. *Mr. Jones is in the market for a new car.*

in the nick of time *adv. phr.* Just at the right time; barely soon enough; almost too late. *The doctor arrived in the nick of time to save the child. from choking to death.*

in the red *adv. or adj. phr., informal* In an unprofitable way; so as to lose money. *A large number of American radio stations operate in the red.*

in the running *adj. or adv. phr.* Having a chance to win; not to be counted out; among those who might win. *At the beginning of the last lap of the race,* only two horses were still in the running. *A month before Joyce married Hal, three of Joyce's boyfriends seemed to be still in the running.*

in the saddle *adv. or adj. phr.* In command; in control; in a position to order or boss others. *Getting appointed chief of police put Stevens in the saddle.*

in the same boat *adv. or adj. phr.* In the same trouble; in the same fix; in the same bad situation. *When the town's one factory closed and hundreds of people lost their jobs, all the storekeepers were in the same boat.*

in the short run *adv. phr.* In the immediate future. *We are leasing a car in the short run; later we might buy one.*

in the soup *adj. phr., slang* In serious trouble; in confusion; in disorder. *When his wife overdrew their bank account without telling him, Mr. Phillips suddenly found himself really in the soup.*

in the works *adv. or adj. phr.* In preparation; being planned or worked on; in progress. *John was told that the paving of his street was in the works.*

in time *adv. or adj. phr.* **1.** Soon enough. *We got to Washington in time for the cherry blossoms. *We got to the station just in time to catch the bus.* **2.** In the end; after a while; finally. *Fred and Jim did not like each other at first, but in time they became friends.* **3.** In the right rhythm; in step. *The marchers kept in time with the band.*

into thin air *adv. phr.* Without anything left; completely. *When Bob returned to the room, he was surprised to find *that his books had vanished into thin air.*

in touch *adj. phr.* Talking or writing to each other; giving and getting news. ◆*John kept in touch with his school friends during the summer.* ◆*The man claimed to be in touch with people on another planet.*

in tow *adj. phr.* **1.** Being pulled. ◆*The tugboat had the large ocean liner in tow as they came into the harbor.* **2.** Being taken from place to place; along with someone. ◆*Janet took the new girl in tow and showed her where to go.*

in tune *adv. or adj. phr.* **1.** At the proper musical pitch; high or low enough in sound. ◆*The piano is in tune.* **2.** Going well together; in agreement; matching; agreeable.—Often used with *with.* ◆*In his new job, John felt in tune with his surroundings and his associates.*

in turn *adv. phr.* According to a settled order; each following another. ◆*Each man in turn got up and spoke.*

in two shakes of a lamb's tail *adv., informal* Quickly; in no time at all. ◆*I'll be back in two shakes of a lamb's tail.*

in vain *adv. phr.* Without effect; without getting the desired result; without success. ◆*The drowning man called in vain for help.*

in view *adv. or adj. phr.* **1.** In sight; visible. ◆*We came around a bend and there was the ocean in view.* **2.** As a purpose, hope, or expectation. ◆*John had his son's education in view when he began to save money.*

in view of *prep.* After thinking about; because of. ◆*Schools*

were closed for the day in view of the heavy snowstorm. ◆*In view of rising labor costs, many companies have turned to automation.*

in with *prep.* In friendship, favor, or closeness with; in the trust or liking of. ◆*It took the new family some time to get in with their neighbors.*

I.O.U. *adj. phr.* I owe you, abbreviated; a promissory note. ◆*I had to borrow some money from John and, in order to remind both of us, I wrote him an I.O.U. note for $250.*

iron in the fire *n. phr.* Something you are doing; one of the projects with which a person is busy; job. ◆*John had a number of irons in the fire, and he managed to keep all of them hot.—* Usually used in the phrase *too many irons in the fire.* ◆*"Ed has a dozen things going all the time, but none of them seem to work out." "No wonder. He has too many irons in the fire."*

iron out *v., informal* To discuss and reach an agreement about (a difference); find a solution for (a problem); remove (a difficulty). ◆*The House and Senate ironed out the differences between their two tax bills.*

itching palm *n., slang* A wish for money; greed. ◆*The bellboys in that hotel seem always to have itching palms.*

itchy feet *adj. phr.* Anxious to travel; bitten by wanderlust. ◆*My brother John is constantly traveling somewhere; it seems he can never stop. He's got itchy feet, for sure.*

it's a cinch *informal sentence* It is very easy. ◆*"What about the* *final exam?"* Fred asked. *"It was a cinch,"* Sam answered.

it's a deal *informal sentence* Consider it done; OK; it is agreed. ◆ *"How much for this used car?"* Bill asked. *"Two thousand,"* the man answered. *"I'll give $1,500,"* Bill said. *"It's a deal!"* the owner answered as they sealed the transaction.

it's a go *or* **it's all go** *adj. phrase, informal* Agreed; it's OK; we can proceed. ◆ *Are we going to Europe this summer, or not?"* John's family wanted to know. *"I have good news,"* John replied. *"It's a go!"*

it's a lemon *adj. phr. informal* The thing is badly made; it won't work. ◆ *"I sure bought myself a lemon,"* John said. *"This car will never work."* ◆ *"What's wrong with your watch? You're always late."* *"It is a lemon, I must admit,"* John said.

it's boloney (*or* **bologna** *or* **baloney**)—**no matter how thin you slice it** *adj. phr.* It is sheer nonsense, no matter how hard you try to prove the opposite. ◆ *The members of the UFO cult believed that if they committed suicide, the UFO would gather up their souls and take them to another solar system.*

One should be tolerant toward different religious beliefs, but this one is boloney, no matter how thin you slice it.

it's high time *informal sentence* It is overdue. ◆ *It is high time for John Browning to be promoted to full professor; he has written a great deal, but his books went unnoticed.*

it's not my bag *phrasal idiom, slang* It's not my thing, not my affair, not in my karma. ◆ *"Come on, brother, let's rob that store; it will be a cakewalk,"* the guy in tattered clothes said to John. *"Sorry,"* John replied. *"That sort of thing is not my bag."*

Ivy League *n.* A small group of the older and more famous eastern U.S. colleges and universities. ◆ *Several Ivy League teams play each other regularly each year.* ◆ *Harvard, Yale, and Princeton were the original Ivy League.*

I wasn't born yesterday *v. phr.* I am not naïve or credulous enough to believe what you said.—A proverb. ◆ *So you want me to believe that you're the sister of Princess Anastasia Romanoff? Come on, I wasn't born yesterday.*

jack of all trades *n., informal* (Often followed by the words "master of none.") A person who is knowledgeable in many areas. Can be used as praise, or as a derogatory remark, depending on the context and the intonation. ◆*"How come Joe did such a sloppy job?" Mary asked. "He's a jack of all trades," Sally answered.*

jack up *v.* 1. To lift with a jack. ◆*The man jacked up his car to fit a flat tire.* 2. *informal* To make (a price) higher; raise. ◆*Just before Christmas, some stores jack up their prices.*

jailbait *n., slang* A girl below the legal age of consent for sex; one who tempts you to intimacy, which is punishable by imprisonment. ◆*Stay away from Arabella; she is jailbait.*

jailbird *n., informal* A convict; someone who is in jail or has been recently released from prison. ◆*Because Harry was a jailbird, it was understandably hard for him to find a job after being imprisoned.*

jawbreaker *n.* 1. A large piece of hard candy or bubblegum. ◆*Billy asked his mother for a quarter to buy some jawbreakers and a chocolate bar.* 2. *informal* A word or name that is hard to pronounce. ◆*His name, Nissequogue, is a real jawbreaker.*

jazz up *v., slang* To brighten up; add more noise, movement, or color; make more lively or exciting. ◆*The party was very dull until Pete jazzed it up with his drums.*

John Hancock *or* **John Henry** *n., informal* Your signature; your name in writing. ◆*The man said, "Put your John Hancock on this paper."* ◆*Joe felt proud when he put his John Henry on his very first driver's license.*

Johnny-come-lately *n.* Someone new in a place or group; newcomer; *also:* a new person who takes an active part in group affairs before the group has accepted him; upstart. ◆*Everybody was amazed when a Johnny-come-lately beat the old favorite in the race.*

Johnny-on-the-spot *adj. phr.* At the right place when needed; present and ready to help; very prompt; on time. ◆*A good waterboy is always Johnny-on-the-spot.*

jump at *v.* To take or accept quickly and gladly. ◆*Johnny jumped at the invitation to go swimming with his brother.*

jump bail *or* **skip bail** *v. phr., informal* To run away and fail to come to trial, and so to give up a certain amount of money already given to a court of law to hold with the promise that you would come. ◆*The robber paid $2000 bail so he wouldn't be put in jail before his trial, but he jumped bail and escaped to Mexico.*

jump ball *n.* The starting of play in basketball by tossing the ball into the air between two opposing players, each of whom jumps and tries to hit the ball to a member of his own team. ◆*Two players held onto the ball at the same time and the referee called a jump ball.*

jump down one's throat *v. phr.* To suddenly become very angry at someone; scold severely or angrily. ♦*The teacher jumped down Billy's throat when Billy admitted he did not do his homework.*

jumping-off place *n. phr.* **1.** A place so far away that it seems to be the end of the world. ♦*Columbus' sailors were afraid they would arrive at the jumping-off place if they sailed farther west.* **2.** The starting place of a long, hard trip or of something difficult or dangerous. ♦*The jumping-off place for the explorer's trip through the jungle was a little village.*

jump on *or* **jump all over** *or* **land on** *or* **land all over** *v. phr., informal* To scold; criticize; blame. ♦*Tom's boss jumped all over Tom because he made a careless mistake.* ♦*Janice landed on Robert for dressing carelessly for their date.* ♦*"I don't know why Bill is always jumping on me; I just don't understand him," said Bob.*

jump on the bandwagon *or* **get on the bandwagon** *v. phr., informal* To join a popular cause or movement. ♦*At the last possible moment, the senator jumped on the winning candidate's bandwagon.*

jump out of one's skin *v. phr., informal* To be badly frightened; be very much surprised. ♦*The lightning struck so close to Bill that he almost jumped out of his skin.*

jump-start *v. phr.* To restart an enterprise or business with vigorous action. ♦*The president of the United States decided to jump-start the economy with a tax cut stimulus package.*

jump the gun *also* **beat the gun** *v. phr.* **1.** To start before the starter's gun in a race. ♦*The runners were called back because one of them jumped the gun.* **2.** *informal* To start before you should; start before anyone else. ♦*The new students were not supposed to come before noon, but one boy jumped the gun and came to school at eight in the morning.*

jump the track *v. phr.* **1.** To go off rails; go or run the wrong way. ♦*The train jumped the track and there was a terrible accident.* **2.** *informal* To change from one thought or idea to another without plan or reason; change the thought or idea you are talking about to something different. ♦*Bob didn't finish his algebra homework because his mind kept jumping the track to think about the new girl in class.*

jump through a hoop *v. phr., informal* To do whatever you are told to do; obey any order. ♦*Bob would jump through a hoop for Mary.*

jump to a conclusion *v. phr.* To decide too quickly or without thinking or finding the facts. ♦*Jerry saw his dog limping on a bloody leg and jumped to the conclusion that it had been shot.*

junked up *adj. or v. phr., slang, drug culture* To be under the influence of drugs, especially heroine. ♦*You can't talk to Billy, he's all junked up.*

junk food *n. phr.* The name given to hamburgers, hot dogs, french fries, and the like available at fast-food restaurants. ♦*"Eat a regular home-cooked meal," Dr. Gordon suggested. "Stay away from junk food."*

junk mail *n. phr.* Unwanted and unsolicited mail stuffed into one's mailbox both at home and at work, usually advertisements of one sort or another. ♦*"Did you check the mailbox, honey?" Ted asked his wife. "Yes, but it's only junk mail," she answered.*

just about *adv., informal* Nearly; almost; practically. ♦*Just about everyone in town came to hear the mayor speak.*

just in case *adv. phr.* For an emergency; in order to be protected. ♦*"Here are my house keys,* Sue," Tom said. "I'll be back in two weeks, but you should have them, just in case...."

just the other way *or* **the other way around** *adv. phr.* Just the opposite. ♦*One would have thought that Goliath would defeat David, but it was the other way around.*

just what the doctor ordered *n. phr., informal* Exactly what is needed or wanted. ♦*"Ah! Just what the doctor ordered!" exclaimed Joe when Mary brought him a cold soda.*

kangaroo court n. A self-appoint-ed group that decides what to do to someone who is supposed to have done wrong. ♦*The Chicago mob held a kangaroo court and shot the gangster who competed with Al Capone.*

keel over v. **1.** To turn upside down; tip over; overturn.—Usually refers to a boat. ♦*The strong wind made the sailboat keel over and the passengers fell into the water.* **2.** informal To fall over in a faint; faint. ♦*When the principal told the girl her father died, she keeled right over.*

keen about or **on** adj. phr. Very enthusiastic about someone or something. ♦*It is well known that Queen Elizabeth is keen on horses.*

keep abreast (of) someone or **something** v. phr. To be informed of the latest developments. ♦*It is difficult to keep abreast of all the various wars that are being waged on planet Earth.*

keep after v., informal To speak to (someone) about something again and again; remind over and over again. ♦*Sue's mother had to keep after her to clean her bedroom.*

keep an eye on or **keep one's eye on** or **have one's eye on** v. phr. **1.** To watch carefully; not stop paying attention to. ♦*A good driver keeps his eye on the road.* ♦*The teacher had her eye on me because she thought I was cheating.* **2.** To watch and do what is needed; mind. ♦*Mother told Jane to keep an eye on the baby while she was in the store.*

keep a stiff upper lip v. phr. To be brave; face trouble bravely. ♦*John was very much worried about his sick daughter, but he kept a stiff upper lip.*

keep at v. To continue to do; go on with. ♦*Mary kept at her home-work until she finished it.*

keep body and soul together v. phr. To keep alive; survive. ♦*John was unemployed most of the year and hardly made enough money to keep body and soul together.*

keep books v. phr. To keep records of money gained and spent; do the work of a bookkeeper. ♦*Miss Jones keeps the compa-ny's books.*

keep down v. Keep from progress-ing or growing; keep within limits; control. ♦*You can't keep a good man down.*

keep house[1] v. phr. To do the nec-essary things in a household; do the cooking and cleaning. ♦*Since their mother died, Mary and her brother keep house for their father.*

keep house[2] also **play house** v. phr., informal To live together without being married. ♦*Bob and Nancy keep house these days.*

keep on v. **1.** To go ahead; not stop; continue. ♦*Columbus kept on until he saw land.*—Often used before a present participle. ♦*Relentlessly, the boy kept on asking about outer space.* **2.** To allow to continue working for you. ♦*The new owner kept Fred on as gardener.*

keep one's chin up v. phr. To be brave; be determined; face trou-ble with courage. ♦*He didn't think that he would ever get out of the jungle alive, but he kept his chin up.*

keep one's eye on the ball v. phr., informal To be watchful and ready; be wide-awake and ready to win or succeed; be smart. ◆*Tom is just starting on the job but if he keeps his eye on the ball, he will be promoted.*

keep one's head *also* **keep one's wits about one** v. phr. To stay calm when there is trouble or danger. ◆*When Tim heard the fire alarm he kept his head and looked for the nearest exit.*

keep one's head above water v. phr. To remain solvent; manage to stay out of debt. ◆*Herb's income declined so drastically that he now has difficulty keeping his head above water.*

keep one's nose clean v. phr., slang To stay out of trouble; do only what you should do. ◆*The policeman warned the boys to keep their noses clean unless they wanted to go to jail.*

keep one's nose to the grindstone *or* **have one's nose to the grindstone** *or* **hold one's nose to the grindstone** v. phr., informal To work hard all the time; keep busy with boring or tiresome work. ◆*Sarah keeps her nose to the grindstone and saves as much as possible to start her own business.*

keep one's own counsel v. phr., formal To keep your ideas and plans to yourself. ◆*John listened to what everyone had to say in the discussion, but he kept his own counsel.*

keep one's shirt on v. phr., slang To calm down; keep from losing your temper or getting impatient or excited. ◆*John said to Bob, "Keep your shirt on."*

keep pace v. phr. To go as fast; go at the same rate; not get behind. ◆*When Bill was moved to a more advanced class, he had to work hard to keep pace.*

keep tab on *or* **keep tabs on** v. phr., informal 1. To keep a record of. ◆*The government tries to keep tabs on all the animals in the park.* 2. To keep a watch on; check. ◆*The house mother kept tabs on the girls to be sure they were clean and neat.*

keep the ball rolling v. phr., informal To keep up an activity or action; not allow something that is happening to slow or stop. ◆*Clyde kept the ball rolling at the party by telling funny jokes.*

keep the home fires burning v. phr. To keep things going as usual while someone is away; wait at home to welcome someone back. ◆*While John was in the army, Mary kept the home fires burning.*

keep the wolf (wolves) from the door v. phr. To avoid hunger, poverty, and/or creditors. ◆*"I don't like my job," Mike complained, "but I must do something to keep the wolves from the door."*

keep track v. phr. To know about changes; stay informed or up-to-date; keep a count or record. ◆*What day of the week is it? I can't keep track.*

keep under one's hat v. phr., informal To keep secret; not tell. Often used as a command. ◆*Keep it under your hat.*

keep up v. 1a. To go on; not stop; continue. ◆*The rain kept up for two days and the roads were flooded.* 1b. To go on with (something); continue steadily; never stop. ◆*Mrs. Smith told John to keep up the good work.* 2a. To go at the same rate as others. ♦*John had to work hard to keep up.* **2b.** To keep (something) at the same level or rate or in good condition. ♦*Grandfather was too poor to keep up his house.* **3.** To keep informed.—Usually used with *on* or *with*. ♦*Mary is interested in politics and always keeps up with the news.*

keep up with the Joneses *v. phr.* To follow the latest fashion; try to be equal with your neighbors. ♦*Mrs. Smith kept buying every new thing that was advertised. Finally Mr. Smith told her to stop trying to keep up with the Joneses and to start thinking for herself.*

keep watch *v. phr.* To be vigilant; be alert; guard. ♦*The police have asked the neighborhood to keep watch against an escaped convict.*

kettle of fish *v. phr., informal* Something to be considered; how things are; a happening; business. ♦*He had two flat tires and no spare on a country road at night, which was certainly a pretty kettle of fish.*

keyed up *adj., informal* Excited; nervous; anxious to do something. ♦*Mary was all keyed up about the exam.*

kick around *v., informal* **1.** To act roughly or badly; to treat badly; bully. ♦*John likes to kick around the little boys.* **2.** To lie around or in a place; be treated carelessly; be neglected. ♦*The letter kicked around on my desk for days.* **3.** *slang* To talk easily or carelessly back and forth about; examine in a careless and easygoing way. ♦*Bob and I kicked around the idea of going*

swimming, but it was hot and we were too lazy.

kick back *v., slang, informal* (stress on *back*) To pay money illegally for favorable contract arrangements. ♦*I will do it if you kick back a few hundred for my firm.*

kickback *n., slang, informal* (stress on *kick*) Money paid illegally for favorable treatment. ♦*He was arrested for making kickback payments.*

kick it *v. phr., slang* To end a bad or unwanted habit such as drinking, smoking, or drug addiction. ♦*Farnsworth finally kicked it; he's in good shape.*

kickoff *n.* (stress on *kick*) The start of something, like a new venture, a business, a sports event, or a concert season. ♦*Beethoven's Ninth will be the kickoff for this summer season at Ravinia.*

kick off *v. phr.* (stress on *off*) **1.** *informal* To begin; launch; start. ♦*The candidate kicked off his campaign with a speech on television.* **2.** *slang* To die. ♦*Mr. Jones was almost ninety years old when he kicked off.*

kick oneself *v. phr., informal* To be sorry or ashamed; regret. ♦*Mary could have kicked herself for letting the secret out before it was announced officially.*

kick out *or* **boot out** *v., informal* To make (someone) go or leave; get rid of; dismiss. ♦*The boys made so much noise at the movie that the manager kicked them out.* ♦*The chief of police was booted out of office because he was a crook.*

kick over *v.* **1.** Of a motor: To begin to work. ♦*He had not* *used his car for two months and when he tried to start it, the motor would not kick over.* **2.** *slang* To pay; contribute. ◆*The gang forced all the storekeepers on the block to kick over $500 a week.* **3.** *slang* To die. ◆*Mrs. O'Leary's cow kicked over this morning.*

kick the bucket *v. phr., slang* To die. ◆*Old Mr. Jones kicked the bucket just two days before his ninety-fourth birthday.*

kick up a fuss *or* **kick up a row** *or* **raise a row** *also* **kick up a dust** *v. phr., informal* To make trouble; make a disturbance. ◆*When the teacher gave the class five more hours of homework, the class kicked up a fuss.* ◆*When the teacher left the room, two boys kicked up a row.*

kick up one's heels *v. phr., informal* To have a merry time; celebrate.◆*When exams were over the students went to town to kick up their heels.*

kill off *v.* To kill or end completely; destroy. ◆*The factory dumped poisonous wastes into the river and killed off the fish.*

kill the goose that laid the golden egg To spoil something that is good or something that you have, by being greedy.—A proverb. ◆*Communist China decided to keep Capitalism alive in Hong Kong. They don't want to kill the goose that laid the golden egg.*

kill time *v. phr.* To cause the time to pass more rapidly; waste time. ◆*The plane trip to Hong Kong was long and tiring, but we managed to kill time by watching several movies.*

kill two birds with one stone *v. phr.* To succeed in doing two

things by only one action; get two results from one effort. ◆*Mother stopped at the supermarket to buy bread and then went to get Jane at dancing class; she killed two birds with one stone.*

kiss off *v. phr., slang* Go away, leave me alone! ◆*"Kiss off, Buster," the bartender said, when the neighborhood drunk, who didn't have any money, asked for another glass of whiskey.*

kiss of death *n. phr.* A curse, a very bad thing. ◆*Having unsafe sex with a stranger can often be the kiss of death.*

kiss someone *or* **something good-bye** *v. phr.* To lose or give up someone or something forever. ◆*"If you won't marry Jane," Peter said to Tom, "you might as well kiss her goodbye."* ◆*People who bet on a losing horse at the races might as well kiss their money goodbye.*

knock about *or* **knock around** *v.* To travel without a plan; go where you please. ◆*After he graduated from college, Joe knocked about for a year seeing the country before he went to work in his father's business.*

knocked out *adj., slang* Intoxicated; drugged; out of one's mind. ◆*Jim sounds so incoherent, he must be knocked out.*

knock it off *v. phr., slang, informal* **1.** To stop talking about something considered not appropriate or nonsensical by the listener.—Used frequently as an imperative. ◆*Come on, Joe, knock it off, you're not making any sense at all!* **2.** To cease doing something; to quit.—Heavily favored in the imperative. ◆*Come on boys, knock it off, you're breaking the furniture in my room!*

knock off *v. phr., slang* **1.** To burglarize someone. ◆*They knocked off the Manning residence.* **2.** To murder someone. ◆*The gangsters knocked off Herman.*

knock off one's feet *v. phr.* To surprise (someone) so much that he does not know what to do. ◆*When Charlie was given the prize, it knocked him off his feet for a few minutes.*

knock one up *v. phr. vulgar, avoidable* To get a woman pregnant. ◆*Did you hear that poor Suzie got knocked up by her careless boyfriend when they were vacationing together in the mountains?*

knock one's block off *v. phr., slang* To hit someone very hard; beat someone up. ◆*Stay out of my yard or I'll knock your block off.*

knock oneself out *v. phr., informal* To work very hard; make a great effort. ◆*Mrs. Ross knocked herself out planning her daughter's wedding.*

knock on wood *v. phr.* To knock on something made of wood to keep from having bad luck.—Many people believe that you will have bad luck if you talk about good luck or brag about something, unless you knock on wood; often used in a joking way. ◆*Charles said, "I haven't been sick all winter." Grandfather said, "You'd better knock on wood when you say that."*

knockout *n., slang* (stress on *knock*) **1.** Strikingly beautiful woman. ◆*Sue is a regular knockout.* **2.** A straight punch in boxing that causes one's opponent to fall and lose consciousness. ◆*The champion won the fight with a straight knockout.*

knock out *v. phr.* (stress on *out*) To make helpless, unworkable, or unusable. ◆*The soldier knocked out two enemy tanks with his bazooka.*

know-it-all *n.* A person who acts as if he knows all about everything; someone who thinks no one can tell him anything new. ◆*After George was elected class president, he wouldn't take suggestions from anyone; he became a know-it-all.*

know where one stands *v. phr.* To be aware of one's monetary or social position. ◆*"Excuse me, sir!" Ted said to the company director, "I hate to bother you, but I'd really like to know where I stand. Will I get a pay raise next year?"*

know which side one's bread is buttered on *v. phr.* To know who can help you and try to please him; know what is for your own gain. ◆*Dick was always polite to the boss; he knew which side his bread was buttered on.*

knuckle under *v. phr.* To do something because you are forced to do it. ◆*Bobby refused to knuckle under to the bully.*

labor of love n. phr. Something done for personal pleasure and not pay or profit. ◆Building the model railroad was a labor of love for the retired engineer.

lady friend n. 1. A woman friend. ◆His aunt stays with a lady friend in Florida during the winter. 2. A woman who is the lover of a man. ◆The lawyer took his lady friend to dinner.

lady-killer n., informal 1. Any man who has strong sex appeal toward women. ◆Joe is a regular lady-killer. 2. A man who relentlessly pursues amorous conquests, is successful at it, and then abandons his heartbroken victims. ◆The legendary Don Juan of Spain is the most famous lady-killer of recorded history.

lady's man n. A man or boy who likes to be with women or girls very much and is popular with them. ◆Charlie is quite a lady's man now.

laid up adj. Sick; confined to bed. ◆I was laid up for a couple of weeks with an ear infection.

lame duck n., informal An elected public official who has been either defeated in a new election or whose term cannot be renewed, but who has a short period of time left in office during which he can still perform certain duties, though with somewhat diminished powers. ◆In the last year of their second terms, American presidents are lame ducks.

landing ship n. A ship built to land troops and army equipment on a beach for an invasion. ◆The landing ship came near the beach, doors in the bow opened, and marines ran out.

landslide n. An overwhelming victory during a political election. ◆Ronald Reagan won the election of 1980 in a landslide.

lap up v. 1. To eat or drink with the tip of the tongue. ◆The kitten laps up its milk. 2. informal To take in eagerly. ◆She flatters him all the time and he just laps it up.

lash out v. 1. To kick. ◆The horse lashed out at the man behind him. 2. To try suddenly to hit. ◆The woman lashed out at the crowd with her umbrella. 3. To attack with words. ◆The senator lashed out at the administration.

last but not least adv. phr. In the last place but not the least important. ◆Billy will bring sandwiches, Alice will bring cake, Susan will bring cookies, John will bring potato chips, and last but not least, Sally will bring the lemonade.

last ditch n. The last place that can be defended; the last resort. ◆They will fight reform to the last ditch.

last-ditch adj. Made or done as a last chance to keep from losing or failing. ◆He threw away his cigarettes in a last-ditch effort to stop smoking.

last straw or **straw that breaks the camel's back** n. phr. A small trouble which follows other troubles and makes one lose patience and be unable to bear them. ◆Bill had a bad day in school yesterday. He lost his knife on the way home, then he fell down, and when he broke a *shoelace, that was the last straw and he began to swear.*

last word *n.* **1.** The last remark in an argument. *I never win an argument with her. She always has the last word.* **2.** The final say in deciding something. *The superintendent has the last word in ordering new desks.* **3.** *informal* The most modern thing. *Mr. Green's Jaguar is the last word in cars.*

laugh off *v.* To dismiss with a laugh as not important or not serious; not take seriously. *He had a bad fall while ice skating but he laughed it off.*

laundry list *n. phr.* A list of things to buy or to do. *The government has a whole laundry list of things to accomplish before U.S. troops can be withdrawn from Iraq.*

lay a finger on *v. phr.* To touch or bother, even a little.—Used in negative, interrogative, and conditional sentences. *Don't you dare lay a finger on the vase! If you so much as lay a finger on my boy, I'll call the police.*

lay an egg *v. phr., slang* To fail to win the interest or favor of an audience. *His joke laid an egg. Sometimes he is a successful speaker, but sometimes he lays an egg.*

lay away *v.* **1.** To save. *She laid a little of her pay away each week.* **2.** To bury (a person).—Used to avoid the word *bury,* which some people think is unpleasant. *He was laid away in his favorite spot on the hill.*

lay-away plan *n.* A plan for buying something that you can't pay cash for; a plan in which you pay some money down and

pay a little more when you can, and the store holds the article until you have paid the full price. *She could not afford to pay for the coat all at once, so she used the lay-away plan.*

lay into *or* **light into** *v., informal* **1.** To attack physically; go at vigorously. *The two fighters laid into each other as soon as the bell rang. John loves Italian food and he really laid into the spaghetti.* **2.** *slang* To attack with words. *The senator laid into the opponents of his bill.*

lay it on *or* **lay it on thick** *also* **put it on thick** *or* **spread it on thick** *or* **lay it on with a trowel** *v. phr., informal* To persuade someone by using very much flattery; flatter. *Bob wanted to go to the movies. He laid it on thick to his mother.*

layoff *n.* (stress on *lay*) A systematic or periodical dismissal of employees from a factory or a firm. *Due to the poor economy, the car manufacturer announced a major layoff starting next month.*

lay off *v. phr.* (stress on *off*) **1.** To mark out the boundaries or limits. *He laid off a baseball diamond on the vacant lot.* **2.** To put out of work. *The company lost the contract for making the shoes and laid off half its workers.* **3.** *slang* To stop bothering; leave alone.—Usually used in the imperative. *Lay off me, will you?* **4.** *slang* To stop using or taking. *His doctor told him to lay off cigarettes.*

lay out *v. phr.* **1.** To prepare (a dead body) for burial. *The corpse was laid out by the undertaker.* **2.** *slang* To knock down flat; to hit unconscious. ◆*A stiff blow to the jaw laid the boxer out in the second round.* **3.** To plan. ◆*Come here, Fred, I have a job laid out for you.* **4.** To mark or show where work is to be done. ◆*The foreman laid out the job for the new machinist.* **5.** To plan the building or arrangement of; design. ◆*The architect laid out the interior of the building.* **6.** *slang* To spend; pay. ◆*How much did you have to lay out for your new car?*

layout *n.* General situation; arrangement; plan. ◆*The layout of their apartment overlooking Lake Michigan was strikingly unusual.*

layover *n.* A stopover, usually at an airport or in a hotel due to interrupted air travel. ◆*There were several layovers at O'Hare last month due to bad weather.*

lay over *v.* **1.** To put off until later; delay; postpone. ◆*We voted to lay the question over to our next meeting for decision.* **2.** To arrive in one place and wait some time before continuing the journey. ◆*We had to lay over in St. Louis for two hours waiting for a plane to Seattle.*

lay up *v.* **1.** To collect a supply of; save for future use; store. ◆*Bees lay up honey for the winter.* **2.** To keep in the house or in bed because of sickness or injury; disable. ◆*Jack was laid up with a twisted knee and couldn't play in the final game.* **3.** To take out of active service; put in a boat dock or a garage. ◆*Bill had to lay up his boat when school started.*

lay waste *v. phr., literary* To cause wide and great damage to; destroy and leave in ruins; wreck. ◆*Enemy soldiers laid waste the land.*

lead a dog's life *v. phr., informal* To live a hard life, work hard, and be treated unkindly. ◆*Some poorer college students led a dog's life.*

lead a merry chase *v. phr.* To delay or escape capture by (someone) skillfully; make (a pursuer) work hard. ◆*Valerie is leading her boyfriend a merry chase.*

lead by the nose *v. phr., informal* To have full control of; make or persuade (someone) to do anything whatever. ◆*Don't let anyone lead you by the nose; use your own judgment and do the right thing.*

lead off *v.* To begin; start; open. ◆*Richard led off the chess game with a knight.* ◆*We always let Henry lead off.* ◆*Mr. Jones led off with the jack of diamonds.*

lead on *v. phr.* To encourage you to believe something untrue or mistaken. ◆*We were led on to think that Jeanne and Jim were engaged to be married.*

lead the way *v. phr.* To go before and show how to go somewhere; guide. ◆*The boys need someone to lead the way on their hike.* ◆*That school led the way in finding methods to teach reading.*

lean on *v. phr., slang, informal* To pressure (someone) by blackmailing, threats, physical violence, or the withholding of some favor in order to make the person comply with a wish or request. ◆*I would gladly do what you ask if you only stopped leaning on me so hard!*

leave a bad taste in one's mouth *v. phr.* To feel a bad impression; make you feel disgusted. ♦*His rudeness to the teacher left a bad taste in my mouth.*

leave hanging *or* **leave hanging in the air** *v. phr.* To leave undecided or unsettled. ♦*Because the committee could not decide on a time and place, the matter of the spring dance was left hanging.*

leave holding the bag *or* **leave holding the sack** *v. phr., informal* **1.** To cause (someone) not to have something needed; leave without anything. ♦*In the rush for seats, Joe was left holding the bag.* **2.** To force (someone) to take the whole responsibility or blame for something that others should share. ♦*After the party, the other girls on the clean-up committee went away with their dates, and left Mary holding the bag.*

leave no stone unturned *v. phr.* To try in every way; miss no chance; do everything possible.—Usually used in the negative. ♦*The police will leave no stone unturned in their search for the bank robbers.*

leave off *v.* To come or put to an end; stop. ♦*Marion put a marker in her book so that she would know where she left off.*

left-handed compliment An ambiguous compliment which is interpretable as an offense. ♦*I didn't know you could look so pretty! Is that a wig you're wearing?*

leg man *n., informal* **1.** An errand boy; one who performs messenger services, or the like. ♦*Joe hired a leg man for the office.* **2.**

Slang, semi-vulgar, avoid! A man who is particularly attracted to good looking female legs and pays less attention to other parts of the female anatomy. ♦*Herb is a leg man.*

leg to stand on *n. phr.* A firm foundation of facts; facts to support your claim.—Used in the negative. ♦*Jerry's answering speech left his opponent without a leg to stand on.*

leg work *n., informal* The physical end of a project, such as the typing of research reports; the physical investigating of a criminal affair; the carrying of books to and from libraries; etc. ♦*Joe, my research assistant, does a lot of leg work for me.*

lemon law *n. phr.* A law in effect in some states that allows customers to return a faulty product for a full refund, after they have proven that they tried to fix the item more than once. ♦*"Dad, our car is a lemon," Mark and Sylvia bitterly complained. "I think Wisconsin has a lemon law," Sylvia's father answered. "See if they will give you a refund."*

let bygones be bygones *v. phr.* To let the past be forgotten. ♦*We should let bygones be bygones and try to get along with each other.*

letdown *n.* A disappointment; a heartbreak. ♦*It was a major letdown for John when Mary refused to marry him.*

let down *v. phr.* **1.** To allow to descend; lower. ♦*Harry let the chain saw down on a rope and then climbed down himself.* **2.** To relax; stop trying so hard; take it easy. ♦*The horse let down near the end of the race* and lost. **3.** To fail to do as well as (someone) expected; disappoint. ♦*The team felt they had let the coach down.*

let down easy *v. phr.* To refuse or say no to (someone) in a pleasant manner; to tell bad news about a refusal or disappointment in a kindly way. ♦*The boss tried to let Jim down easy when he had to tell him he was too young for the job.*

let go *v.* **1a.** To stop holding something; loosen your hold; release. ♦*The boy grabbed Jack's coat and would not let go.*—Often used with *of.* ♦*When the child let go of her mother's hand, she fell down.* **1b.** To weaken and break under pressure. ♦*The old water pipe suddenly let go and water poured out of it.* **2.** To pay no attention to; neglect. ♦*Robert let his teeth go when he was young and now he has to go to the dentist often.* **3.** To allow something to pass; do nothing about. ♦*The children teased Frank, but he smiled and let it go.* **4.** To discharge from a job; fire. ♦*Mr. Wilson got into a quarrel with his boss and was let go.* **5.** To make (something) go out quickly; shoot; fire. ♦*Robin Hood let go an arrow at the deer.* **6.** *or* **let oneself go** *informal* To be free in one's actions or talk; relax. ♦*The cowboys worked hard all week, but on Saturday night they went to town and let themselves go.*

let go of *v. phr.* To release one's grasp. ♦*As soon as Sally let go of the leash, her dog ran away.*

let grass grow under one's feet *v. phr.* To be idle; be lazy; waste time.—Used in negative, conditional, and interrogative sentences. ♦*The new boy joined the football team, made the honor roll, and found a girlfriend during the first month of school. He certainly did not let any grass grow under his feet.*

let it all hang out *v. phr., slang, informal* Not to disguise anything; to let the truth be known. ♦*Sue can't deceive anyone; she just lets it all hang out.*

let it lay *v. phr., used imperatively, slang* Forget it; leave it alone; do not be concerned or involved. ♦*Don't get involved with Max again—just let it lay.*

let it rip *v. phr., used imperatively, slang* **1.** Don't be concerned; pay no attention to what happens. ♦*Why get involved? Forget about it and let it rip.* **2.** (Imperatively) Do become involved and make the most of it; get in there and really try to win. ♦*Come on man, give it all you've got and let it rip!*

let know *v. phr.* To inform. ♦*Please let us know the time of your arrival.*

let loose *v.* **1a.** *or* **set loose** *or* **turn loose** To set free; loosen or give up your hold on. ♦*The farmer opened the gate and let the bull loose in the pasture.* **1b.** *or* **turn loose** To give freedom (to someone) to do something; to allow (someone) to do what he wants. ♦*The children were turned loose in the toy store to pick the toys they wanted.* **1c.** To stop holding something; loosen your hold. ♦*Jim caught Ruth's arm and would not let loose.* **2a.** *informal* To let or make (something) move fast or hard; release. ♦*The fielder let loose a long throw to home plate after catching the ball.*

2b. *informal* To release something held. ◆*Those dark clouds are going to let loose any minute.* **3.** *informal* To speak or act freely; disregard ordinary limits. ◆*The boss told Jim that some day she was going to let loose and tell him what she thought of him.*

let off *v.* **1.** To discharge (a gun); explode; fire. ◆*Willie accidentally let off his father's shotgun and made a hole in the wall.* **2.** To permit to go or escape; excuse from a penalty, a duty, or a promise. ◆*Two boys were caught smoking in school but the principal let them off with a warning.* **3.** *or informal* **let off the hook** To miss a chance to defeat or score against, especially in sports or games. ◆*The boxer let his opponent off the hook many times.*

let off steam *or* **blow off steam** *v. phr.* **1.** To let or make steam escape; send out steam. ◆*The janitor let off some steam because the pressure was too high.* **2.** *informal* To get rid of physical energy or strong feeling through activity; talk or be very active physically after forced quiet. ◆*After the long ride on the bus, the children let off steam with a race to the lake.*

let on *v. informal* **1.** To tell or admit what you know.—Used in the negative. ◆*Frank lost $50 but he didn't let on to his mother.* **2.** To try to make people believe; pretend. ◆*The old man likes to let on that he is rich.*

let one in on *v. phr.* To reveal a secret to; permit someone to share in. ◆*If I let you in on something big we're planning,* will you promise not to mention it to anyone?

let one's hair down *or* **let down one's hair** *v. phr., informal* Act freely and naturally; be informal; relax. ◆*Kings and queens can seldom let their hair down.*

let out *v.* **1a.** To allow to go out or escape. ◆*The guard let the prisoners out of jail to work in the garden.* ◆*Mother won't let us out when it rains.* **1b.** *informal* To make (a sound) come out of the mouth; utter. ◆*A bee stung Charles. He let out a yell and ran home.* ◆*Father told Betty to sit still and not let out a peep during church.* **2.** To allow to be known; tell. ◆*I'll never tell you another secret if you let this one out.* **3.** To make larger (as clothing) or looser; allow to slip out (as a rope). ◆*Father hooked a big fish on his line. He had to let the line out so the fish wouldn't break it.* **4.** *informal* To allow to move at higher speed. ◆*The rider let out his horse to try to beat the horse ahead of him.* **5.** *informal* To dismiss or be dismissed. ◆*The coach let us out from practice at 3 o'clock.* ◆*I'll meet you after school lets out.*

let sleeping dogs lie Do not make (someone) angry and cause trouble or danger; do not make trouble if you do not have to.— A proverb. ◆*Don't tell Father that you broke the window. Let sleeping dogs lie.*

let the cat out of the bag *v. phr., informal* To tell about something that is supposed to be a secret. ◆*We wanted to surprise Mary with a birthday gift, but Allen let the cat out of the bag by asking her what she would* *like.*—Sometimes used in another form. ◆*Well, the cat is out of the bag—everybody knows about their marriage.*

let the chips fall where they may *v. phr.* To pay no attention to the displeasure caused others by your actions. ◆*The senator decided to vote against the bill and let the chips fall where they may.*

let up *v., informal* **1.** To become less, weaker, or quiet; become slower or stop. ◆*It's raining as hard as ever. It's not letting up at all.* **2.** To do less or go slower or stop; relax; stop working or working hard. ◆*Let up for a minute. You can't work hard all day.* ◆*Jim ran all the way home without letting up once.* **3.** To become easier, kinder, or less strict.—Usually used with *on.* ◆*Let up on Jane. She is sick.*

let well enough alone *or* **leave well enough alone** *v. phr.* To be satisfied with what is good enough; not try to improve something because often that might cause more trouble. ◆*Ethel made a lot of changes in her test paper after she finished. She should have let well enough alone, because she made several new mistakes.*

level playing field *n. phr.* Equal opportunity; fair chance for both competitors in a game or employment. ◆*In a democracy people should be afforded a level playing field in all walks of life.*

lie in state *v. phr.* Of a dead person: To lie in a place of honor, usually in an open coffin, and be seen by the public before burial. ◆*When the president died, thousands of people saw his body lying in state.*

lie in wait *v. phr.* To watch from hiding in order to attack or surprise someone; to ambush. ◆*The driver of the stagecoach knew that the thieves were lying in wait somewhere along the road.*

lie low *or nonstandard* **lay low** *v., informal* **1.** To stay quietly out of sight; try not to attract attention; hide. ◆*After holding up the bank, the robbers lay low for a while.* **2.** To keep secret one's thoughts or plans. ◆*I think he wants to be elected president, but he is lying low and not saying anything.*

life of Riley *n. phr., informal* A soft easy life; pleasant or rich way of living. ◆*He's living the life of Riley. He doesn't have to work anymore.*

lift a finger *or* **lift a hand** *also* **raise a hand** *v. phr.* To do something; do your share; to help.—Usually used in the negative. ◆*We all worked hard except Joe. He wouldn't lift a finger.*

light up *v.* Suddenly to look pleased and happy. ◆*Martha's face lit up when she saw her old friend.*

like father, like son A son is usually like his father in the way he acts.—A proverb. ◆*Mr. Jones and Tommy are both quiet and shy. Like father, like son.*

like hell *adv., slang, vulgar, avoid!* **1.** With great vigor. ◆*As soon as they saw the cops, they ran like hell.* **2.** *interj.* Not so; untrue; indicates the speaker's lack of belief in what he heard. ◆*Like hell you're gonna bring me my dough!*

like two peas in a pod *adj. phr.* Closely similar; almost exactly alike. ♦*The twin sisters Eve and Agnes are like two peas in a pod.*

like water off a duck's back *adv. phr., informal* Without changing your feelings or opinion; without effect. ♦*Advice and correction roll off him like water off a duck's back.*

lineup *n.* (stress on *line*) **1.** An alignment of objects in a straight line. ♦*A lineup of Venus and the moon can be a very beautiful sight in the night sky.* **2.** An arrangement of suspects through a one-way mirror so that the victim or the witness of a crime can identify the wanted person. ♦*She picked out her attacker from a police lineup.*

line up *v. phr.* (stress on *up*) **1.** To take places in a line or formation; stand side by side or one behind another; form a line or pattern. ♦*The boys lined up and took turns diving off the springboard.* **2.** To put in line. ♦*John lined up the pool balls.* **3.** To adjust correctly. ♦*The garage man lined up the car's wheels.* **4a.** *informal* To make ready for action; complete a plan or agreement for; arrange. ♦*The superintendent lined up all the new teachers he needed before he went on vacation.* **4b.** *informal* To become ready for action; come together in preparation or agreement. ♦*Larry wanted to go to the seashore for the family vacation, but the rest of the family lined up against him.*

lip service *n.* Support shown by words only and not by actions; a show of loyalty that is not proven in action.—Usually used with *pay.* ♦*By holding elections, communism pays lip service to democracy, but it offers only one candidate per office.*

little frog in a big pond *or* **small frog in a big pond** *n. phr.* An unimportant person in a large group or organization. ♦*In a large company, even a fairly successful man is likely to feel like a little frog in a big pond.*

little pitchers have big ears Little children often overhear things they are not supposed to hear, or things adults do not expect they would notice.—A proverb. ♦*Be especially careful not to swear in front of little children. Little pitchers have big ears.*

live and let live *v. phr.,* To live in the way you prefer and let others live as they wish without being bothered by you. ♦*Father scolds Mother because she wears her hair in curlers and Mother scolds Father because he smokes a smelly pipe. Grandfather says it's her hair and his pipe; live and let live.*

live down *v.* To remove (blame, distrust or unfriendly laughter) by good conduct; cause (a mistake or fault) to be forgiven or forgotten by not repeating it. ♦*John's business failure hurt him for a long time, but in the end he lived it down.*

live from hand to mouth *v. phr.* To live on little money and spend it as fast as it comes in; live without saving for the future; have just enough. ♦*Mr. Johnson got very little pay, and the family lived from hand to mouth when he had no job.*

live in the fast lane *v. phr., informal* To live a full and very active life pursuing wealth and success. ◆*They have been living in the fast lane ever since they arrived in New York City.*

live it up *v. phr., informal* To pursue pleasure; enjoy games or night life very much; have fun at places of entertainment. ◆*Joe had had a hard winter in lonesome places; now he was in town living it up.*

live off someone *v. phr.* To be supported by someone. ◆*Although Eric is already 40 years old, he has no job and continues to live off his elderly parents.*

live up to *v.* To act according to; come up to; agree with; follow. ◆*So far as he could, John had always tried to live up to the example he saw in Lincoln.*

living end *adj., slang* Great; fantastic; the ultimate. ◆*That show we saw last night was the living end.*

lock, stock, and barrel *n. phr.* Everything; completely. ◆*The robbers emptied the whole house—lock, stock, and barrel.*

lock the barn door after the horse is stolen To be careful or try to make something safe when it is too late.—A proverb. ◆*After Mary failed the examination, she said she would study hard. She wanted to lock the barn door after the horse was stolen.*

log in *v. phr.* To register at work at the beginning. ◆*All employees at this firm are required to log in at the start of their workday.*

log off *v. phr.* To finish using the e-mail or the Internet on one's computer. ◆*Every evening I finish my work at the computer and I log off.*

log on *v. phr.* To start work on the Internet or one's e-mail on a computer. ◆*I log on twice a day to see if I have e-mail.*

log out *v. phr.* To register at the end of one's work day. ◆*All employees are required to log out at the end of the work day, just as they logged in when they started.*

long face *n.* A sad look; disappointed look. ◆*He told the story with a long face.*

long for *v. phr.* To desire greatly; miss someone or something badly. ◆*All I am longing for is a little peace and quiet after a hard day's work.* ◆*John was longing for Suzie even after they had been divorced for three years.*

long haul *or* **long pull** *n., informal* 1. A long distance or trip. ◆*It is a long haul to drive across the country.* 2. A long length of time during which work continues or something is done; a long time of trying. ◆*A boy crippled by polio may learn to walk again, but it may be a long haul.*—Used in the phrase *over the long haul.* ◆*Over the long haul, an expensive pair of shoes may save you money.*

long shot *n.* A bet or other risk taken though not likely to succeed. ◆*The horse was a long shot, but it came in and paid well.*

look a gift horse in the mouth To complain if a gift is not perfect.—A proverb. Used with a negative. ◆*John gave Joe a baseball but Joe complained that the ball was old. His father* told him not to *look a gift horse in the mouth.*

look at the world through rose-colored glasses *or* **see with rose-colored glasses** *v. phr.* To see everything as good and pleasant; not see anything hard or bad. ◆*If you see everything through rose-colored glasses, you will often be disappointed.*

look down on *also* **look down upon** *v.* To think of (a person or thing) as less good or important; feel that (someone) is not as good as you are, or that (something) is not worth having or doing; consider inferior. ◆*Mary looked down on her classmates because she was better dressed than they were.*

look down one's nose at *v. phr., informal* To think of as worthless; feel scorn for. ◆*The banker's wife has beautiful china cups, and she looked down her nose at the plastic cups that Mrs. Brown used.*

look for *v.* 1. To think likely; expect. ◆*We look for John to arrive any day now.* 2. To try to find; search for; hunt. ◆*Fred spent all day looking for a job.* 3. To do things that cause (your own trouble); make (trouble) for yourself; provoke. ◆*Joe often gets into fights because he is always looking for trouble.*

look forward to *v.* 1. To expect. ◆*At breakfast, John looked forward to a difficult day.* 2. To expect with hope or pleasure. ◆*Frank was looking forward to that evening's date.*

look into *v.* To find out the facts about; examine; study; inspect. ◆*Mr. Jones said he was looking into the possibility of buying a house.*

look like a million dollars *v. phr., informal* To look well and prosperous; appear healthy and happy and lucky; look pretty and attractive. ◆*John came back from Florida driving a fine new car, tanned and glowing with health. He looked like a million dollars.*

look like the cat that ate the canary *or* **look like the cat that swallowed the canary** *v. phr.* To seem very self-satisfied; look as if you had just had a great success. ◆*When she won the prize, she went home looking like the cat that swallowed the canary.*

look out *or* **watch out** *v.* 1. To take care; be careful; be on guard.—Usually used as a command or warning. ◆*"Look out!" John called, as the car came toward me.* ◆*"Look out for the train," the sign at the railroad crossing warns.* 2. To be alert or watchful; keep watching. ◆*A collector of antique cars asked Frank to look out for a 1906 gas head lamp.* 3. *informal* To watch or keep (a person or thing) and do what is needed; provide protection and care. —Used with *for.* ◆*Lillian looked out for her sister's children one afternoon a week.*

look to *v.* 1. To attend to; get ready for; take care of. ◆*The president assigned a man to look to our needs.* 2. To go for help to; depend on. ◆*The child looks to his mother to cure his hurts.*

look up *v.* 1. *informal* To improve in future chances; promise more success. ◆*The first year was tough, but business looked up after that.* 2. To search for; hunt for information about;

find. ♦*It is a good habit to look up new words in a dictionary.* 3. To seek and find. ♦*While he was in Chicago, Henry looked up a friend of college days.*

look up to v. To think of (someone) as a good example to copy; honor; respect. ♦*Young children look up to older ones, so older children should be good examples.*

lord it over v. phr. To act as the superior and master of; dominate; be bossy over; control. ♦*The office manager lorded it over the clerks and typists.*

lose face v. To be embarrassed or shamed by an error or failure; lose dignity, influence or reputation; lose self-respect or the confidence of others. ♦*Many Japanese soldiers were killed in World War II because they believed that to give up or retreat would make them lose face.*

lose ground 1. To go backward; retreat. ♦*The soldiers began to lose ground when their leader was killed.* 2. To become weaker; get worse; not improve. ♦*The sick man began to lose ground when his cough grew worse.*

lose heart v. phr. To feel discouraged because of failure; to lose hope of success. ♦*The team had won no games and it lost heart.*

lose one's heart v. phr. To fall in love; begin to love. ♦*She lost her heart to the soldier with the broad shoulders and the deep voice.*

lose one's marbles v. phr. To go mad; become crazed. ♦*Stan must have lost his marbles; he is hopelessly pursuing a happily married woman.*

lose one's shirt v. phr., slang To lose all or most of your money. ♦*Mr. Matthews lost his shirt betting on the horses.*

lose out v. To fail to win; miss first place in a contest; lose to a rival. ♦*John lost out in the rivalry for Mary's hand in marriage.*

lose touch v. phr., informal To fail to keep in contact or communication.—Usually used with *with.* ♦*After she moved to another town, she lost touch with her childhood friends.*

lose track v. phr. To forget about something; not stay informed; fail to keep a count or record. ♦*What's the score now? I've lost track.*—Used with *of.* ♦*John lost track of the money he spent at the circus.*

loud mouth or **big mouth** n., slang A noisy, boastful, or foolish talker. ♦*Fritz is a loud mouth who cannot be trusted with secrets.*

louse up v., slang To throw into confusion; make a mess of; spoil; ruin. ♦*The rain loused up the picnic.*

lovers' lane n. A hidden road or walk where lovers walk or park in the evening. ♦*A parked car in a lonely lovers' lane often is a chance for holdup men.*

lowbrow n. A person of limited culture; a nonintellectual. ♦*Some people claim that only lowbrows read the comics.*

lowdown n., slang, informal The inside facts of a matter; the total truth. ♦*Nixon never gave the American people the lowdown on Watergate.*

lower the boom v. phr., informal To punish strictly; check or stop fully. ♦*The police lowered the boom on open gambling.*

low-key *adj.* Relaxed and easygoing. ♦*Surprisingly, dinner with the governor was a low-key affair.*

luck out *v. phr., slang, informal* **1.** Suddenly to get lucky when in fact the odds are against one's succeeding. ♦*I was sure I was going to miss the train as I was three minutes late, but I lucked out; the train was five minutes late.* **2.** To be extraordinarily fortunate. ♦*Catwallender really lucked out at Las Vegas last month; he came home with $10,000 in cash.* **3.** (By sarcastic opposition) to be extremely unfortunate; to be killed. ♦*Those poor marines sure lucked out in Saigon, didn't they?*

lucky star *n.* A certain star or planet which, by itself or with others, is seriously or jokingly thought to bring a person good luck and success in life. ♦*Ted was unhurt in the car accident, for which he thanked his lucky stars.*

lump in one's throat *n. phr.* A feeling (as of grief or pride) so strong that you almost sob. ♦*The bride's mother had a lump in her throat.*

lump sum *n.* The complete amount; a total agreed upon and to be paid at one time. ♦*The case was settled out of court with the plaintiff receiving a lump sum of half a million dollars for damages.*

lust for *v. phr.* To physically yearn for; hanker after; want something very strongly. ♦*Ed has been lusting after Meg for a very long time.*

mad about adj. phr. 1. Angry about. ◆What is Harriet so mad about? 2. Enthusiastic about. ◆Dan is mad about pop music.

mad as a hornet or **mad as a wet hen** adj. phr., informal In a fighting mood; very angry. ◆When my father sees the dent in his fender, he'll be mad as a hornet. ◆Mrs. Harris was mad as a wet hen when the rabbits ate her tulips.

magic carpet n. 1. A rug said to be able to transport a person through the air to any place he wishes. ◆The caliph of Baghdad flew on his magic carpet to Arabia. 2. Any form of transportation that is comfortable and easy enough to seem magical. ◆Mr. Smith's new car drove so smoothly it seemed like a magic carpet.

main drag n., colloquial 1. The most important street or thoroughfare in a town. ◆Lincoln Avenue is the main drag of our town. 2. The street where the dope pushers and the prostitutes are. ◆Wells Street is the main drag of Chicago, actionwise.

main squeeze n., slang 1. The top ranking person in an organization or in a neighborhood; an important person, such as one's boss. ◆Mr. Bronchard is the main squeeze in this office. 2. The top person in charge of an illegal operation, such as drug sales, etc. ◆Before we can clean up this part of town, we must arrest the main squeeze. 3. One's principal romantic or sexual partner. ◆The singer's main squeeze is a member of the band.

make a beeline for v. phr. To go in a straight line toward. ◆When the bell rang Ted made a beeline for the door of the classroom.

make a big deal about v. phr., informal To exaggerate an insignificant event. ◆Jeff said, "I'm sorry I banged into you in the dark. Don't make a big deal out of it."

make a day of it v. phr., informal To do something all day. ◆When they go to the beach they take a picnic lunch and make a day of it.

make a dent in v. phr., informal To make less by a very small amount; reduce slightly.—Usually used in the negative or with such qualifying words as hardly or barely. ◆Mary studied all afternoon and only made a dent in her homework.

make a go of v. phr. To turn into a success. ◆He is both energetic and highly skilled at trading; he is sure to make a go of any business that holds his interest.

make a hit v. phr., informal To be successful; be well-liked; get along well. ◆Mary's new red dress made a hit at the party.

make a mountain out of a molehill To think a small problem is a big one; try to make something unimportant seem important. ◆You're not hurt badly, Johnny. Stop trying to make a mountain out of a molehill with crying.

make a move v. phr. 1. To budge; change places. ◆"If you make a move," the masked gangster said, "I'll start shooting." 2. To go home after dinner or a party. ◆"I guess it's time to make a *move," Roy said at the end of the party.*

make a play for *v. phr., slang* To try to get the interest or liking of; flirt with; attract. ◆*Bob made a play for the pretty new girl.*

make a point *v. phr.* To try hard; make a special effort.—Used with *of* and a verbal noun. ◆*He made a point of remembering to get his glasses fixed.*

make away with *v., informal* Take; carry away; cause to disappear. ◆*Two masked men held up the clerk and made away with the payroll.*

make-believe *n.* False; untrue; created by illusion. ◆*The creatures of* Star Wars *are all make-believe.*

make believe *v.* To act as if something is true while one knows it is not; pretend. ◆*Let's make believe we have a million dollars.*

make book *v. phr.* To serve as a bookmaker taking bets on the horse races. ◆*The police were out to prosecute anybody who made book illegally.*

make do *v. phr.* To use a poor substitute when one does not have the right thing. ◆*Many families manage to make do on very little income.*

make ends meet *v. phr.* To have enough money to pay one's bills; earn what it costs to live. ◆*Both husband and wife had to work to make ends meet.*

make eyes at *v. phr., informal* To look at a girl or boy in a way that tries to attract her/him to you; flirt. ◆*The other girls disliked her way of making eyes at their boyfriends instead of finding one of her own.*

make for *v.* To go toward; start in the direction of. ◆*The children took their ice skates and made for the frozen pond.*

make free with *v.* 1. To take or use (things) without asking. ◆*Bob makes free with his roommate's clothes.* 2. To act toward (someone) in a rude or impolite way. ◆*The girls don't like Ted because he makes free with them.*

make fun of *or* **poke fun at** *v. phr., informal* To joke about; laugh at; tease; mock. ◆*Men like to make fun of the trimmings on women's hats.* ◆*James poked fun at the new pupil because her speech was not like the other pupils.*

make good *v. phr.* 1. To do what one promised to do; make something come true. ◆*Joe made good his boast to swim across the lake.* 2. To compensate; pay for loss or damage. ◆*The policeman told the boy's parents that the boy must make good the money he had stolen or go to jail.* 3. To do good work at one's job; succeed. ◆*Kate wanted to be a nurse. She studied and worked hard in school. Then she got a job in the hospital and made good as a nurse.*

make hay while the sun shines *v. phr.* To do something at the right time; not wait too long. ◆*Dick had a free hour so he made hay while the sun shone and got his lesson for the next day.*

make head or tail of *v. phr., informal* To see the why of; finding a meaning in; understand.—Used in negative, conditional, and interrogative sentences.

♦*Can you make head or tail of the letter?*

make it with *v. phr., slang, informal* **1.** To be accepted by a group. ♦*Joe finally made it with the in crowd in Hollywood.* **2.** *vulgar* To have sex with (someone). ♦*I wonder if Joe has made it with Sue.*

make light of *v. phr.* To treat an important matter as if it were trivial. ♦*One ought to know which problems to make light of and which ones to handle seriously.*

make love *v. phr.* **1.** To be warm, loving, and tender toward someone of the opposite sex; try to get him or her to love you too. ♦*There was moonlight on the roses and he made love to her in the porch swing.* **2.** To have sexual relations with (someone). ♦*It is rumored that Alfred makes love to every girl he hires as a secretary.*

make mincemeat (out) of *v. phr.* To destroy completely. ♦*The defense attorney made mincemeat of the prosecution's argument.*

make neither head nor tail of *v. phr.* To be unable to figure something out. ♦*This puzzle is so complicated that I can make neither head nor tail of it.*

make no bones *v. phr., informal* **1.** To have no doubts; not to worry about right or wrong; not to be against.—Used with *about*. ♦*The boss made no bones about hiring extra help for the holidays.* **2.** To make no secret; not keep from talking; admit.—Used with *about* or *of* the fact. ♦*John thinks being poor is no disgrace and he makes no bones of the fact.*

make of *v. phr.* To interpret; understand. ♦*What do you make of his sudden decision to go to Africa?*

make off *v.* To go away; run away; leave. ♦*A thief stopped John on a dark street and made off with his wallet.*

make one's bed and lie in it To be responsible for what you have done and so to have to accept the bad results. ♦*Billy smoked one of his father's cigars and now he is sick. He made his bed, now let him lie in it.*

make one's blood boil *or* **make the blood boil** *v. phr., informal* To make someone very angry. ♦*When someone calls me a liar it makes my blood boil.*

make oneself scarce *v. phr., slang* To leave quickly; go away. ♦*The boys made themselves scarce when they saw the principal coming to stop their noise.*

make one's head spin *v. phr.* To be bewildered; be confused. ♦*It makes my head spin to think about the amount of work I still have to do.*

make one's mark *v. phr.* To become known to many people; do well the work you started to do; make a reputation. ♦*Shakespeare made his mark as a playwright.*

make one's mouth water *v. phr.* **1.** To look or smell very good; make you want very much to eat or drink something you see or smell. ♦*The pies in the store window made Dan's mouth water.* **2.** To be attractive; make you want to have something very much. ♦*Judy loves Swiss chocolates, and the ones in the store window made her mouth water.*

make out v. **1.** To write the facts asked for (as in an application blank or a report form); fill out. ♦*The teacher made out the report cards and gave them to the students to take home.* **2.** To see, hear, or understand by trying hard. ♦*It was dark, and we could not make out who was coming along the road.* **3.** *informal* To make someone believe; show; prove. ♦*Charles and Bob had a fight, and Charles tried to make out that Bob started it.* **4.** *informal* Do well enough; succeed. ♦*John's father wanted John to do well in school and asked the teacher how John was making out.* **5.** To kiss or pet. ♦*What are Jack and Jill up to?—They're making out on the back porch.*

make over v. **1.** To change by law something from one owner to another owner; change the name on the title (lawful paper) from one owner to another. ♦*Mr. Brown made over the title to the car to Mr. Jones.* **2.** To make something look different; change the style of. ♦*He asked the tailor to make over his pants.*

make the grade v. phr., informal **1.** To make good; succeed. ♦*It takes hard study to make the grade in school.* **2.** To meet a standard; qualify. ♦*That whole shipment of cattle made the grade as prime beef.*

makeup n. (stress on *make*) **1.** Cosmetics. ♦*All the actors and actresses put on a lot of makeup.* **2.** Attributive auxiliary in lieu of, or belated. ♦*The professor gave a makeup to the sick students.*

make up v. (stress on *up*) **1.** To make by putting things or parts together. ♦*A car is made up of many different parts.* **2.** To invent; think and say something that is new or not true. ♦*Jean makes up stories to amuse her little brother.* **3a.** To do or provide (something lacking or needed); do or supply (something not done, lost, or missed); get back; regain; give back; repay. ♦*I have to make up the test I missed last week.* **3b.** To do what is lacking or needed; do or give what should be done or given; get or give back what has been lost, missed, or not done; get or give instead; pay back.—Used with *for*. ♦*We made up for lost time by taking an airplane instead of a train.* **4.** To put on lipstick and face paint powder. ♦*Clowns always make up before a circus show.* ♦*Tom watched his sister make up her face for her date.* **5.** To become friends again after a quarrel. ♦*Mary and Joan quarreled, but made up after a while.* **6.** To try to make friends with someone; to win favor.—Followed by *to*. ♦*The new boy made up to the teacher by sharpening her pencils.*

make up one's mind v. phr. To choose what to do; decide. ♦*They made up their minds to sell the house.*

make waves v. phr., informal Make one's influence felt; create a disturbance, a sensation. ♦*Joe Catwallender is the wrong man for the job; he is always trying to make waves.*

make way v. phr. To move from in front so someone can go through; stand aside. ♦*When older men retire they make way* *for younger men to take their places.*

man in the street *n. phr.* The man who is just like most other men; the average man; the ordinary man. ♦*The newspaper took a poll of the man in the street.*

mark time *v. phr.* **1.** To move the feet up and down as in marching, but not going forward. ♦*The officer made the soldiers mark time as a punishment.* **2.** To be idle; waiting for something to happen. ♦*The teacher marked time until all the children were ready for the test.* **3.** To seem to be working or doing something, but really not doing it. ♦*It was so hot that the workmen just marked time.*

matter of course *n. phr.* Something always done; the usual way; habit; rule. ♦*Bank officers ask questions as a matter of course when someone wants to borrow money.*

matter of fact *n. phr.* Something that is really true; something that can be proved. ♦*The town records showed that it was a matter of fact that the two boys were brothers.* Used for emphasis in the phrase *as a matter of fact.* ♦*I didn't go yesterday, and as a matter of fact, I didn't go all week.*

matter-of-fact *adj.* **1.** Simply telling or showing the truth; not explaining or telling more. ♦*The newspaper gave a matter-of-fact account of the murder trial.* **2.** Showing little feeling or excitement or trouble; seeming not to care much. ♦*He was a very matter-of-fact person.*

mean business *v. phr., informal* To decide strongly to do what you plan to do; really mean it; be

serious. ♦*The boss said he would fire us if we didn't work harder and he means business.*

measure up *v.* To be equal; be of fully high quality; come up. ♦*Lois' school work didn't measure up to her ability.*

meet one's Waterloo *v. phr.* To be defeated; lose an important contest. ♦*After seven straight victories the team met its Waterloo.*

meet up with *v. phr.* To meet by accident; come upon without planning or expecting to.♦*The family would have arrived on time, but they met up with a flat tire.*

melt in one's mouth *v. phr.* **1.** To be so tender as to seem to need no chewing. ♦*The chicken was so tender that it melted in your mouth.* **2.** To taste very good; be delicious. ♦*Mother's apple pie really melts in your mouth.*

mend one's fences *v. phr., informal* To do something to make people like or follow you again; strengthen your friendships or influence. ♦*John saw that his friends did not like him, so he decided to mend his fences.*

mend one's ways *v. phr.* To reform; change one's behavior from negative to positive. ♦*He had better mend his ways or he'll wind up in jail.*

mess around *v. phr.* **1.** To engage in idle or purposeless activity. ♦*Come on, you guys,—start doing some work, don't just mess around all day!* **2.** *vulgar* To be promiscuous; to indulge in sex with little discrimination as to who the partner is. ♦*Allen needs straightening out; he's been messing around with the whole female population of his class.*

mess up v. phr., slang, informal 1. To cause trouble; to spoil something. ◆What did you have to mess up my accounts for? 2. To cause someone emotional trauma. ◆Sue will never get married; she got messed up when she was a teenager. 3. To beat up someone physically. ◆When Joe came in after the fight with the boys, he was all messed up.

middle of the road n. phr. A way of thinking which does not favor one idea or thing too much; being halfway between two different ideas. ◆The teacher did not support the boys or the girls in the debate, but stayed in the middle of the road.

middle-of-the-road adj. Favoring action halfway between two opposite movements or ideas; with ideas halfway between two opposite sides; seeing good on both sides. ◆The men who wrote the Constitution followed a middle-of-the-road plan on whether greater power belonged to the United States government or to the separate states.

mind one's p's and q's v. phr. To be very careful what you do or say; not make mistakes. ◆When the principal of the school visited the class, the students all minded their p's and q's.

mind over matter n. phr. The power of the mind over physical matters, such as illness, fear, etc.—A proverb. ◆Advocates of alternative medicine discourage the taking of too many drugs and point out that since most illnesses are psychosomatic, one might as well use "mind over matter" to cure oneself.

mind you v. phr., informal I want you to notice and understand. ◆Mind you, I am not blaming him.

miss out v., informal To fail; lose or not take a good chance; miss something good. ◆You missed out by not coming with us; we had a great time.

miss the boat also **miss the bus** v. phr., informal To fail through slowness; to put something off until too late; do the wrong thing and lose the chance. ◆Ted could have married Lena but he put off asking her and missed the boat.

miss the point v. phr. To be unable to comprehend the essence of what was meant. ◆The student didn't get a passing grade on the exam because, although he wrote three pages, he actually missed the point.

mixed up adj. phr. 1. informal Confused in mind; puzzled. ◆Bob was all mixed up after the accident. 2. Disordered; disarranged; not neat. ◆The papers on his desk were mixed up. 3. informal Joined or connected (with someone or something bad). ◆Harry was mixed up in a fight after the game.

mix up v. To confuse; make a mistake about. ◆Jimmy doesn't know colors yet; he mixes up purple with blue. ◆Even the twins' mother mixes them up.

monkey business n., slang, informal 1. Any unethical, illegitimate, or objectionable activity that is furtive or deceitful, e.g., undercover sexual advances, cheating, misuse of public funds, etc. ◆There is a lot of monkey business going on in that firm; you'd better watch out who you deal with! 2. Comical or silly actions;

goofing off. ♦*Come on boys, let's cut out the monkey business and get down to work!*

monkey love *n. phr.* An exaggerated show of affection often covering up true and meaningful fondness and caring, which may include occasional punishment. ♦*The Chisolms are guilty of showering their children with monkey love. It would be far better for the two teenagers to be told occasionally that they are out of line.*

monkey on one's back *n. phr., informal* An unsolved or nagging problem. ♦*"My math course is a real monkey on my back,"* Jack complained.

more the merrier *n. phr.* The more people who join in the fun, the better it will be.—Used in welcoming more people to join others in some pleasant activity. ♦*Come with us on the boat ride; the more the merrier.*

morning after *n., slang* The effects of drinking liquor or staying up late as felt the next morning; a hangover. ♦*One of the troubles of drinking too much liquor is the morning after.* ♦*Jack woke up with a big headache and knew it was the morning after.*

mouse click *or* **mouse clicks away** *adj. phr.* Easy to gain access to; just as easy as to make a click with one's "mouse" at a home personal computer. ♦*You can find anything you need in our store; we are just a mouse click away.*

move heaven and earth *v. phr.* To try every way; do everything you can. ♦*Joe moved heaven and earth to be sent to Washington.*

move in on *v. phr., slang, colloquial* To take over something that belongs to another. ♦*He moved in on my girlfriend and now we're not talking to each other.*

mug shot *n. phr.* A police photograph showing the arrested person's full face and profile. ♦*"Go over these mug shots,"* Sergeant O'Malley said, *"and tell me if you find the person who held up the liquor store!"*

mum is the word You must keep the secret; keep silent; don't tell anyone.—Often used as an interjection. ♦*We are planning a surprise party for John and mum is the word.*

muscle in on *v. phr.* To intrude; penetrate; force oneself into another's business or territory. ♦*The eastern Mafia muscled in on the western Mafia's turf and a shooting war was started.*

musical chairs *n. phr.* (Originally the name of a children's game.) The transfer of a number of officers in an organization into different jobs, especially each other's jobs. ♦*The boss regularly played musical chairs with department heads to keep them fresh on the job.*

music to one's ears *n. phr.* Something one likes to hear. ♦*When the manager phoned to say I got the job, it was music to my ears.*

my God *or* **my goodness** *interj.* Used to express surprise, shock, or dismay. ♦*My God! What happened to the car?*

my lips are sealed *informal sentence* A promise that one will not give away a secret. ♦*"You can tell me what happened,"* Helen said. *"My lips are sealed."*

nail down v. phr., informal To make certain; make sure; settle. ◆Joe had a hard time selling his car, but he finally nailed the sale down when he got his friend Sam to give him $300.

namedropper n. phr. A person who is always mentioning well-known names. ◆Since her move to Hollywood she has become a regular namedropper.

name is mud informal (You) are in trouble; a person is blamed or no longer liked.—Used in the possessive. ◆If you tell your mother I spilled ink on her rug my name will be mud.

name of the game n., informal The crux of the matter; that which actually occurs under the disguise of something else. ◆Getting medium income families to support the rest of society—that's the name of the game!

neck of the woods n. phr., informal Part of the country; place; neighborhood; vicinity. ◆We visited Illinois and Iowa last summer; in that neck of the woods the corn really grows tall.

needle in a haystack n. phr., informal Something that will be very hard to find. ◆"I lost my class ring somewhere in the front yard," said June. Jim answered, "Too bad. That will be like finding a needle in a haystack."

neither fish nor fowl also **neither fish, flesh, nor fowl** Something or someone that does not belong to a definite group or known class; a strange person or thing; someone or something odd or hard to understand. ◆The man is neither fish nor fowl; he votes Democrat or Republican according to which will do him the most good.

neither here nor there adj. phr. Not important to the thing being discussed; off the subject; not mattering. ◆The boys all like the coach but that's neither here nor there; the question is, "Does he know how to teach football?"

Nervous Nellie n., informal A timid person who lacks determination and courage. ◆I say we will never win if we don't stop being Nervous Nellies!

nest egg n. Savings set aside to be used in the future. ◆Herb says he doesn't have to worry about his old age because he has a nest egg in the bank.

never mind v. phr. Don't trouble about it; don't worry about it; forget it; skip it.—Usually used in speaking or when writing dialogue. ◆"What did you say?" "Oh, never mind." ◆"What about money?" "Never mind that. I'll take care of it."

new blood n. Something or someone that gives new life or vigor, fresh energy or power. ◆New blood was brought into the company through appointment of younger men to important positions.

new broom sweeps clean A new person makes many changes.—A proverb. ◆The new superintendent has changed many of the school rules. A new broom sweeps clean.

new deal n., informal 1. A complete change; a fresh start. ◆People had been on the job too long; a new deal was needed to get things out of the old bad *habits.* 2. Another chance. ♦*The boy asked for a new deal after he had been punished for fighting in school.*

newfangled *adj.* Newly invented or contrived; excessively complex. ♦*Dorothy felt that many newfangled gadgets in Kate's all-electric kitchen weren't really necessary.*

new money *n. phr.* People who have become rich recently. ♦*Since Bob's father invented a new computer component, Bob and his family are new money.*

nightcap *n.* A good-night drink; a drink taken just before bedtime. ♦*Would you like to come up to my place for a nightcap?*

night owl *n. phr.* One who sleeps during the day and stays up or works during the night. ♦*Tom hardly ever sleeps at night; he prefers to work by lamp light and has become a regular night owl.*

nip and tuck *adj. or adv., informal* Evenly matched; hard fought to the finish. ♦*The game was nip and tuck until the last minute.*

nip in the bud *v. phr.* To check at the outset; prevent at the start; block or destroy in the beginning. ♦*The police nipped the plot in the bud.*

nobody home *slang* 1. Your attention is somewhere else, not on what is being said or done here; you are absent-minded. ♦*The teacher asked him a question three times but he still looked out the window. She gave up, saying, "Nobody home."* 2. You are feeble-minded or insane. ♦*He pointed to the woman, tapped his head, and said, "Nobody home."*

nobody's fool *n. phr.* A smart person; a person who knows what he is doing; a person who can take care of himself. ♦*In the classroom and on the football field, Henry was nobody's fool.*

no-brainer *n. phr.* Something easy to do or solve that requires little or no thinking. ♦*How do we decide the salary raises for next year? I tell you how; it's a no-brainer—nobody gets any, because the state cut our budget.*

no deal *or* **no dice** *or* **no go** *or* **no sale** *slang* Not agreed to; refused or useless; without success or result; no; certainly not.—Used in the predicate or to refuse something. ♦*Billy wanted to let Bob join the team, but I said that it was no deal because Bob was too young.* ♦*"Let me have a dollar." "No dice!" answered Joe.* ♦*I tried to get Mary on the telephone but it was no go.* ♦*"Let's go to the beach tomorrow." "No sale; I have my music lesson tomorrow."*

no doubt *adv.* 1. Without doubt; doubtless; surely; certainly. ♦*No doubt Susan was the smartest girl in her class.* 2. Probably. ♦*John will no doubt telephone us if he comes to town.*

no end *adv., informal* 1. Very much; exceedingly. ♦*Jim was no end upset because he couldn't go swimming.* 2. Almost without stopping; continually. ♦*The baby cried no end.*

no end to *or informal* **no end of** So many, or so much of, as to seem almost endless; very many or very much. ♦*There was no end to the letters pouring into the post office.*

no frills *n. phr.* A firm or product that offers no extras; a generic product that carries no expensive label. ◆*We went on a no frills trip to Europe with few luxuries.*

no kidding *n. phr.* Without jokes or teasing; honestly spoken. ◆*"You actually won the lottery?" Dick asked. "No kidding," Joe replied. "I really did."*

no love lost *n. phr.* Bad feeling; ill will. ◆*Bob and Dick both wanted to be elected captain of the team, and there was no love lost between them.*

no matter 1. Not anything important. ◆*I wanted to see him before he left but it's no matter.* **2.** It makes no difference; regardless of. ◆*She was going to be a singer no matter what difficulties she met.*

nose about *or* **nose around** *v. phr., informal* To look for something kept private or secret; poke about; explore; inquire; pry. ◆*In Grandmother's attic, Sally spent a while nosing about in the old family pictures.*

nose down *v., of an aircraft* To head down; bring down the nose of. ◆*The big airliner began to nose down for a landing.*

nose in[1] *or* **nose into**[1] *informal* Prying or pestering interest in; unwelcome interest in; impolite curiosity. ◆*He always had his nose in other people's business.*

nose in[2] *or* **nose into**[2] *v.* To move in close; move slowly in with the front first. ◆*The ship nosed into the pier.* ◆*The car nosed into the curb.*

nose out *v., informal* **1.** To learn by effort (something private or secret); uncover. ◆*The principal nosed out the truth about the stolen examination.* **2.** To defeat by a nose length; come in a little ahead of in a race or contest. ◆*The horse we liked nosed out the second horse in a very close finish.*

nose out of *informal* Curious attention; bothering.—Usually used with a possessive and usually used with *keep*. ◆*When Billy asked his sister where she was going she told him to keep his nose out of her business.*

no sweat[1] *adj., slang, informal* Easily accomplished; uncomplicated. ◆*That job was no sweat.*

no sweat[2] *adv.* Easily. ◆*We did it no sweat.*

not a leg to stand on *n. phr., informal* No good proof or excuse; no good evidence or defense to offer. ◆*The man with a gun and $300 in his pocket was accused of robbing an oil station. He did not have a leg to stand on.*

not bad *or* **not so bad** *or* **not half bad** *adj., informal* Pretty good; all right; good enough. ◆*The party last night was not bad.* ◆*It was not so bad, as inexpensive vacations go.* ◆*The show was not half bad.*

not for the world *or* **not for worlds** *adv. phr.* Not at any price; not for anything. ◆*I wouldn't hurt his feelings for the world.* ◆*Not for worlds would he let his children go hungry.*

nothing doing *adv. phr., informal* I will not do it; certainly not; no indeed; no. ◆*"Will you lend me a dollar?" "Nothing doing!"*

nothing if not *adv. phr.* Without doubt; certainly. ◆*With its* *bright furnishings, flowers, and sunny windows, the new hospital dayroom is nothing if not cheerful.*

not one iota *(n. phr.) from the Bible referring to the Greek letter "i."* Not at all; not in the least. *◆Not an iota must be changed or omitted in that valuable, ancient manuscript while you try deciphering it.*

not on your life *adv. phr., informal* Certainly not; not ever; not for any reason.—Used for emphasis. *◆I wouldn't drive a car with brakes like that—not on your life.*

not to give one the time of day *v. phr., slang, informal* To dislike someone strongly enough so as to totally ignore him. *◆Sue wouldn't give Helen the time of day.*

not to give quarter *v. phr.* **1.** To be utterly unwilling to show mercy; not to allow a weaker or defeated party the chance to save themselves through escape. *◆The occupying foreign army gave no quarter—they took no prisoners, shot everyone, and made escape impossible.* **2.** To argue so forcefully during a negotiation or in a court of law as to make any counter-argument or counter-proposal impossible. *◆The District Attorney hammered away at the witnesses and gave no quarter to the attorney for the defense.*

not to know chalk from cheese To be very stupid; to be unable to distinguish valuable things from rubbish.—A proverb. *◆Poor Jerry will never amount to much; the poor guy doesn't even know chalk from cheese.*

not to know one from Adam *v. phr.* To not know a person; be

unable to recognize someone. *◆I have no idea who that guy is that Jane just walked in with; I don't know him from Adam.*

not to know shit from shinola *vulgar, avoidable* To be ignorant enough to confuse things of unequal value.—A proverb. *◆Algernon talks big, but he doesn't know shit from shinola about money matters.*

not to lift a finger *v. phr.* To not help in the slightest degree. *◆ "My husband won't lift a finger to help me," she complained, "although we have 12 people coming for dinner."*

not to miss a beat *v. phr. negative only* To do without hesitation; go on undisturbed. *◆John is the most clever and most poised engineer we ever had at this auto plant; he simply never misses a beat. ◆Ervin is a terrific pianist with a phenomenal memory; he just never misses a beat.*

not to see the forest for the trees *v. phr. negative only* To be unable to see the total picture in a situation because of being lost in the details. *◆Ernie is a great toolmaker, but sometimes he needs reminding what the whole project is about; otherwise he doesn't see the forest for the trees.*

not to touch (something) with a ten-foot pole *v. phr.* To consider something completely undesirable or uninteresting. *◆Some people won't touch spinach with a ten-foot pole.*

nuke a tater *v. phr.* **1.** To bake a potato in a microwave oven. *◆ "We have no time for standard*

baked potatoes in the oven,"
she said. "We'll just have to
nuke a tater."

number one¹ or Number One¹ *n.
phr., informal* Yourself; your
own interests; your private or
selfish advantage. Usually used
in the phrase *look out for number one.* ♦*He was well known
for his habit of always looking
out for number one.*

number one² *adj. phr.* **1.** Of first
rank or importance; foremost;
principal. ♦*Tiger Woods is easily America's number one golfer.*
2. Of first grade; of top quality;
best. ♦*That is number one western steer beef.*

nurse a drink *v. phr., informal* To
hold a drink in one's hand at a
party, pretending to be drinking
it or taking extremely small sips
only. ♦*John's been nursing that
drink all evening.*

nurse a grudge *v. phr.* To keep a
feeling of envy or dislike
toward some person; remember
something bad that a person
said or did to you, and dislike
the person because of that.
♦*Mary nursed a grudge against
her teacher because she
thought she deserved a better
grade in English.*

nut case *n. phr.* A very silly, crazy,
or foolish person. ♦*I am going
to be a nut case if I don't go on
a vacation pretty soon.*

nuts and bolts of *n. phr.* The basic
facts or important details of
something. ♦*"Ted will be an
excellent trader," his millionaire grandfather said, "once he
learns the nuts and bolts of the
profession."*

nutty as a fruitcake *adj. phr.,
slang* Very crazy; entirely mad.
♦*He looked all right, as we
watched him approach, but
when he began to talk, we saw
that he was as nutty as a fruitcake.*

oddball *n., slang, informal* An eccentric person; one who doesn't act like everyone else. ◆*John is an oddball—he never invites anyone.*

of age *adj. phr.* **1a.** Old enough to be allowed to do or manage something. ◆*Mary will be of driving age on her next birthday.* **1b.** Old enough to vote; having the privileges of adulthood. ◆*The age at which one is considered of age to vote, or of age to buy alcoholic drinks, or of age to be prosecuted as an adult, varies within the United States.* **2.** Fully developed; mature. ◆*Education for the foreign born came of age when bilingual education was accepted as a necessary part of the public school system.*

of course *adv. phr.* **1.** As you would expect; naturally. ◆*Bob hit Herman, and Herman hit him back, of course.* **2.** Without a doubt; certainly; surely. ◆*Of course you know that girl; she's in your class.*

off balance *adj. phr.* **1.** Not in balance; not able to stand up straight and not fall; not able to keep from turning over or falling; unsteady. ◆*Never stand up in a canoe; it will get off balance and turn over.* **2.** Not prepared; not ready; unable to meet something unexpected. ◆*The teacher's surprise test caught the class off balance, and nearly everyone got a poor mark.*

off base *adj. phr., informal* Not agreeing with fact; wrong. ◆*The idea that touching a toad causes warts is off base.*

offbeat *adj., informal* Nonconventional; different from the usual; odd. ◆*Linguistics used to be an offbeat field, but nowadays every self-respecting university has a linguistics department.*

off center *adv. phr.* Not exactly in the middle. ◆*Mary hung the picture off center, because it was more interesting that way.*

off-center *adj., informal* Different from the usual pattern; not quite like most others; odd. ◆*Roger's sense of humor was a bit off-center.*

off-color *or* **off-colored** *adj.* **1.** Not of the proper hue or shade; not matching a standard color sample. ◆*The librarian complained that the painter had used an off-color green on the walls.* **2.** *informal* Not of the proper kind for polite society; in bad taste; dirty. ◆*When Joe told his off-color story, no one was pleased.*

off duty *adj.* Not supposed to be at work; having free time; not working. ◆*Sailors like to go sightseeing when they are off duty in a foreign port.*

off guard *adj.* In a careless attitude; not alert to coming danger; not watching. ◆*Tim's question caught Jean off guard, and she told him the secret before she knew it.*

off one's back *adj. phr., informal* Stopped from bothering one; removed as an annoyance or pest. ◆*"Having a kid brother always following me is a nuisance," Mary told her mother. "Can't you get him off my back?"*

off one's chest *adj. phr., informal* Told to someone and so not bothering you anymore; not making you feel worried or upset, because you have talked about it. ♦*After Dave told the principal that he had cheated on the test, he was glad because it was off his chest.*

off one's hands *adv. phr.* No longer in your care or possession. ♦*Ginny was glad to have the sick dog taken off her hands by the doctor.*

off one's high horse *adj. phr., informal* Not acting proud and scornful; humble and agreeable. ♦*The girls were so kind to Nancy after her mother died that she came down off her high horse and made friends with them.*

off one's rocker *or* **off one's trolley** *adj. phr., informal* Not thinking correctly; crazy; silly; foolish. ♦*Tom is off his rocker if he thinks he can run faster than Bob can.* ♦*If you think you can learn to figure skate in one lesson, you're off your trolley.*

off the beam *adv. or adj. phr.* **1.** *(Of an airplane)* Not in the radio beam that marks the path to follow between airports; flying in the wrong direction. ♦*A radio signal tells the pilot of an airplane when his plane is off the beam.* **2.** *slang* Wrong; mistaken. ♦*Maud was off the beam when she said that the girls didn't like her.*

off the beaten track *adv. phr.* Not well known or often used; not gone to or seen by many people; unusual. ♦*We are looking for a vacation spot that is off the beaten track.*

off the cuff *adv. phr., informal* Without preparing ahead of time what you will say; without

preparation. ♦*Some presidents like to speak off the cuff to newspaper reporters but others prefer to think questions over and write their answers.*

off-the-cuff *adj., informal* Not prepared ahead of time.—Used of a speech or remarks. ♦*Jack was made master of ceremonies because he was a good off-the-cuff speaker.*

off the hook *adv. phr.* Out of trouble; out of an awkward or embarrassing situation. ♦*Thelma found she had made two dates for the same night; she asked Sally to get her off the hook by going out with one of the boys.*

off the record[1] *adv. phr.* Confidentially. ♦*"Off the record," the boss said, "you will get a good raise for next year, but you'll have to wait for the official letter."*

off the record[2] *adj. phr.* Not to be published or told; secret; confidential. ♦*The president told the reporters his remarks were strictly off the record.*—Sometimes used with hyphens, before the noun. ♦*The governor was angry when a newspaper printed his off-the-record comments.*

off the top of one's head *adv. or adj. phr., informal* Without thinking hard; quickly. ♦*Vin answered the teacher's question off the top of his head.*

off the wagon *adj. phr., slang* No longer refusing to drink whiskey or other alcoholic beverages; drinking liquor again, after stopping for a while. ♦*When a heavy drinker quits, he must really quit. One little drink of whiskey is enough to drive him off the wagon.*

off-the-wall *adj. phr.* Strange; out of the ordinary; stupid. ♦*He has been making off-the-wall remarks all day; something must be the matter with him.*

old as the hills *adj. phr.* Very old; ancient. ♦*"Why didn't you laugh?" she asked. "Because that joke is as old as the hills," he answered.*

old maid *n. phr.* A spinster; a woman who has never married. ♦*Because my old maid aunt is a terrific cook as well as a good-looking woman, nobody understands why she never married.*

on an even keel *adv. phr., informal* In a well-ordered way or condition; orderly. ♦*When the football rally became a riot, the principal stepped to the platform and got things back on an even keel.*

on a pedestal *adv. phr.* Lovingly honored and cared for. ♦*Bill is always waiting on his fiancee and bringing her flowers and candy. He has certainly put her on a pedestal.*

on a shoestring *adv. phr.* With little money to spend; on a very low budget. ♦*The couple was seeing Europe on a shoestring.*

on board[1] *prep.* On (a ship). ♦*Joan was not on board the ship when it sailed.*

on board[2] *adv. or adj. phr.* On a ship. ♦*A ship was leaving the harbor, and we saw the people on board waving.*

on call *adj. phr.* **1.** Having to be paid on demand. ♦*Jim didn't have the money ready even though he knew the bill was on call.* **2.** Ready and available. ♦*This is Dr. Kent's day to be on call at the hospital.*

once and for all *adv. phr.* **1.** One time and never again; without any doubt; surely; certainly; definitely. ♦*For once and for all, I will not go swimming with you.* **2.** Permanently. ♦*The general decided that two bombs would destroy the enemy and end the war once and for all.*

once in a blue moon *adv. phr.* Very rarely; very seldom; almost never. ♦*Coin collecting is interesting, but you find a valuable coin only once in a blue moon.*

once in a while *adv. phr.* Not often; not regularly; sometimes; occasionally. ♦*We go for a picnic in the park once in a while.*

once-over *n., slang* **1.** A quick look; a swift examination of someone or something.— Usually used with *give* or *get*. ♦*The new boy got the once-over from the rest of the class when he came in.* **2.** or **once-over-lightly** A quick or careless job, especially of cleaning or straightening; work done hastily for now. ♦*Ann gave her room a quick once-over-lightly with the broom and dust cloth.*

once upon a time *adv. phr.* Sometime before now, long ago. Used at the beginning of fairy stories. ♦*Once upon a time there lived a king who had an ugly daughter.*

on cloud nine *adj. phr., slang* Too happy to think of anything else; very happy. ♦*Ada has been on cloud nine since the magazine printed the story she wrote.*

on easy street *adj. phr., informal* Having enough money to live very comfortably; rather rich. ♦*After years of hard work, the*

Grants found themselves on easy street.

on edge *adj. phr.* Excited or nervous; impatient. ◆*The magician kept the children on edge all through his show.*

one eye on *informal* Watching or minding (a person or thing) while doing something else; part of your attention on.— Used after *have, keep,* or *with.* ◆*Jane had one eye on the baby as she ironed.*

one foot in the grave *n. phr.* Near to death. ◆*The dog is fourteen years old, blind, and feeble. He has one foot in the grave.*

one for the books *n. phr., informal* Very unusual; a remarkable something. ◆*The newspaper reporter turned in a story that was one for the books.*

on end *adj. phr.* Seemingly endless.—Used with plural nouns of time. ◆*Judy spent hours on end writing and rewriting her essay.*

one-night stand *n. phr.* **1.** A single performance given by a traveling company while on a tour. ◆*After they went bankrupt in the big cities, the traveling jazz quartet played one-night stands in the country.* **2.** A brief affair or sexual encounter. ◆*"With AIDS all around us," said Jane, "nobody is having one-night stands anymore."*

one on the city *n., slang* A glass of water (which is provided free of charge, as a free gift from the city). ◆*What will you have?— Oh, just give me one on the city.*

one-two *n.* **1.** A succession of two punches, the first a short left, followed by a hard right punch, usually in the jaw. ◆*Ali gave Frazier the one-two.* **2.** Any

quick or decisive action which takes the opposition by surprise, thereby ensuring victory. ◆*He gave us the old one-two and won the game.*

one up *adj. phr.* Having an advantage; being one step ahead. ◆*John graduated from high school; he is one up on Bob, who dropped out.*

one-upmanship *v., informal* Always keeping ahead of others; trying to keep an advantage. ◆*No matter what I do, I find that Jim has already done it better. He's an expert at one-upmanship.*

on faith *adv. phr.* Without question or proof. ◆*He looked so honest that we accepted his story on faith.*

on file *adv. phr.* Placed in a written or electronic file; on record. ◆*We are sorry we cannot hire you right now but we will keep your application on file.*

on hand *adv. phr.* **1a.** Nearby; within reach. ◆*Always have your dictionary on hand when you study.* **1b.** Here. ◆*Soon school will end and vacation will be on hand.* **2.** Present. ◆*Mr. Blake's secretary is always on hand when he appears in public.* **3.** In your possession; ready. ◆*The Girl Scouts have plenty of cookies on hand.*

on ice *adv. or adj. phr., slang* **1.** The same as won; sure to be won. ◆*The score was 20–10 in the last inning, and our team had the game on ice.* **2.** Away for safekeeping or later use; aside. ◆*The senator was voted out of office. He is on ice until the next election.*

on one's back *adj. phr., informal* Making insistent demands of you; being an annoyance or bother. ♦*My wife has been on my back for weeks to fix the front door screen.*

on one's coattails *adv. phr.* Because of another's merits, success, or popularity. ♦*Bob and Jim are best friends. When Jim was invited to join a fraternity, Bob rode in on his coattails.*

on one's feet *adv. phr.* **1.** Standing or walking; not sitting or lying down; up. ♦*Before the teacher finished asking the question, George was on his feet ready to answer it.* **2.** Recovering; getting better from sickness or trouble. ♦*Jack is back on his feet after a long illness.*

on one's head *or* **upon one's head** *adv. phr.* On one's self. ♦*When the school board fired the superintendent of schools, they brought the anger of the parents upon their heads.*

on one's high horse *adj. phr., informal* **1.** Acting as if you are better than others; being very proud and scornful. ♦*Martha was chairman of the picnic committee, and at the picnic she was on her high horse, telling everyone what to do.* **2.** Refusing to be friendly because you are angry; in a bad temper. ♦*Joe was on his high horse because he felt Mary wasn't giving him enough attention.*

on one's knees *adj. phr.* **1.** Pleading; begging very hard. ♦*The boys were on their knees for hours before their parents agreed to their camping plans.* **2.** In a very weak condition; near failure. ♦*When the gradu-ates of the school heard that it was on its knees they gave money generously so that it would not close.*

on one's last legs *adj. phr.* Failing; near the end. ♦*The blacksmith's business is on its last legs.*

on one's toes *adj. phr., informal* Alert; ready to act. ♦*The successful ball player is always on his toes.*

on pins and needles *adj. phr., informal* Worried; nervous. ♦*Many famous actors are on pins and needles before the curtain opens for a play.*

on purpose *adv. phr.* For a reason; because you want to; not accidentally. ♦*Jane did not forget her coat; she left it in the locker on purpose.*

on sale *adj. phr.* Selling for a special low price. ♦*Tomato soup that is usually sold for ninety cents a can is now on sale for seventy cents.*

on schedule[1] *adv. phr.* As planned or expected; at the right time. ♦*The school bus arrived at school on schedule.*

on schedule[2] *adj. phr.* Punctual; as planned. ♦*The new airline claims to have more on schedule arrivals than the competition.*

on tenterhooks *adv. phr.* To be in a state of painful suspense; to feel anxious and impatient to receive some news, good or bad. ♦*When Rose's father was near death, her husband told me, "We are on tenterhooks waiting for the phone call every day."* ♦*The young poet was on tenterhooks until his new manuscript was accepted by Princeton University Press.*

on the air *adj. or adv. phr.* Broadcasting or being broadcast on radio or TV. ♦*His show is on the air at six o'clock.*

on the ball *adj. phr., informal* 1. Paying attention and doing things well.—Used after *is* or *get.* ♦*The coach told Jim he must get on the ball or he cannot stay on the team.* 2. That is a skill or ability; making you good at things.—Used after *have.* ♦*John will succeed in life; he has a lot on the ball.*

on the bandwagon *adj. phr., informal* In or into the newest popular group or activity; in or into something you join just because many others are joining it.—Often used after *climb, get,* or *jump.* ♦*When all George's friends decided to vote for Bill, George climbed on the bandwagon too.*

on the beam *adv. or adj. phr.* 1. (Of an airplane) In the radio beam that marks the path to follow between airports; flying in the right direction. ♦*A radio signal tells the pilot of an airplane when he is flying on the beam.* 2. *slang* Doing well; just right; good or correct. ♦*Kenneth's answer was right on the beam.*

on the blink *adj. phr.* Faulty; malfunctioning; inoperative. ♦*I need to call a competent repairman because my computer is on the blink again.*

on the block *adj. phr.* To be sold; for sale. ♦*The vacant house was on the block.*

on the dole *adv. phr.* Drawing unemployment benefits. ♦*When Jim lost his job he got on the dole and is still on it.*

on the dot *also* **on the button** *adv. phr., informal* Exactly on time; not early and not late. ♦*Susan arrived at the party at 2:00 P.M. on the dot.*

on the double! *adv. phr.* Hurry up! ♦*"Let's go! On the double!" the pilot cried, as he started up the engine of the small plane.*

on the fly[1] *adv. phr.* 1. While in the air; in flight. ♦*The bird caught a bug on the fly.* 2. *informal* Between other activities; while busy with many things. ♦*The president was so busy that he had to dictate letters on the fly.*

on the fly[2] *adj. phr., informal* Busy; going somewhere in a hurry; going about doing things. ♦*Getting the house ready for the visitors kept Mother on the fly all day.*

on the go *adj. phr., informal* Active and busy. ♦*Successful businessmen are on the go most of the time.*

on the house *adj. phr., informal* Paid for by the owner. ♦*At the opening of the new hotel, the champagne was on the house.*

on the level *adj. phr., informal* Honest and fair; telling the whole truth. ♦*Our teacher respects the students who are on the level with her.*

on the loose *adj. phr., informal* Free to go; not shut in or stopped by anything. ♦*The zookeeper forgot to close the gate to the monkey cage and the monkeys were on the loose.*

on the make *adj., slang* 1. Promiscuous or aggressive in one's sexual advances. ♦*I can't stand Murray; he's always on the make.* 2. Pushing to get ahead in one's career; doing anything to succeed. ♦*The new department head is a young man on the make, who expects to be company president in ten years.*

on the market *adj. phr.* For sale. ♦*In the summer many fresh vegetables are on the market.*

on the mend *adj. phr.* Healing; becoming better. ♦*John's broken leg is on the mend.*

on the money *adv. phr.* Exactly right; exactly accurate. ♦*Algernon won the lottery; the numbers he picked were right on the money.*

on the move *adj. or adv. phr.* 1. Moving around from place to place; in motion. ♦*It was a very cold day, and the teacher watching the playground kept on the move to stay warm.* 2. Moving forward; going somewhere. ♦*The candidate promised that if people would make him president, he would get the country on the move.*

on the nose *adv. phr., informal* Just right; exactly. ♦*The airplane pilot found the small landing field on the nose.*

on the other hand *adv. phr.* Looking at the other side; from another point of view.—Used to introduce an opposite or different fact or idea. ♦*Jim wanted to go to the movies; his wife, on the other hand, wanted to stay home and read.*

on the Q.T. *adv. phr., informal* Secretly; without anyone's knowing. ♦*The teachers got the principal a present strictly on the Q.T.*

on the road *adv. or adj. phr.* 1. Traveling; moving from one place to another. ♦*When we go on vacation, we take a lunch to eat while on the road.* 2. Changing; going from one condition to another. ♦*Mary was very sick for several weeks, but now she is on the road to recovery.*

on the rocks *adj. phr.* 1. *informal* Wrecked or ruined. ♦*Mr. Jones' business and marriage were both on the rocks.* 2. With ice only. ♦*At the restaurant, Sally ordered orange juice on the rocks.*

on the run *adv. or adj. phr.* 1. In a hurry; hurrying. ♦*Jane called "Help!" and Tom came on the run.* 2. Going away from a fight; in retreat; retreating. ♦*The enemy soldiers were on the run.*

on the safe side *adv. phr.* Provided for against a possible emergency; well prepared. ♦ *"Please double-check these proofs, Mr. Brown," the printer said, "just to be on the safe side."*

on the same page with *adv. phr.* In agreement with someone; subscribing to the same values. ♦*It will be interesting to see if the European Union and the United States can be on the same page as far as the war against terrorism is concerned.*

on the sly *adv. phr.* So that other people won't know; secretly. ♦*The boys smoked on the sly.*

on the spot *adv. or adj. phr.* 1. *or* **upon the spot** At that exact time and at the same place; without waiting or leaving. ♦*The news of important events is often broadcast on the spot over television.* 2. *informal also* **in a spot** In trouble, difficulty, or embarrassment. ♦*Mr. Jones is on the spot because he cannot pay back the money he borrowed.* 3. *slang* In danger of murder; named or listed for death. ♦*After he talked to the police, the gangsters put him on the spot.*

on the spur of the moment *adv. phr.* On a sudden wish or decision; suddenly; without thought or preparation. ♦*John had not planned to take the trip; he just left on the spur of the moment.*

on the tip of one's tongue *adv. phr.* About to say something, such as a name, a telephone number, etc., but unable to remember it for the moment. ♦*"His name is on the tip of my tongue," Tom said. "It will come to me in a minute."*

on the up and up *adj. phr., informal* Honest; trustworthy; sincere. ♦*We felt that he was honest and could be trusted. This information is on the up and up.*

on the wagon *adv. phr.* Participating in an alcohol addiction program; not touching any alcoholic beverage. ♦*Jim's doctor and his family finally managed to convince him that he was an alcoholic and should go on the wagon.*

on time *adv. or adj. phr.* 1. At the time arranged; not late; promptly. ♦*The train left on time.* ♦*Mary is always on time for an appointment.* 2. On the installment plan; on credit, paying a little at a time. ♦*John bought a car on time.*

on top *adv. or adj. phr., informal* In the lead; with success; with victory. ♦*The horse that everyone had expected would be on top actually came in third.*

on top of *prep.* 1. On the top of; standing or lying on; on. ♦*When the player on the other team dropped the ball, Bill fell on top*

of it. 2. *informal* Very close to. 3. *informal* In addition to; along with. ♦*Mary worked at the store all day and on top of that she had to baby-sit with her brother.* 4. *informal* Managing very well; in control of. ♦*Although his new job was very complicated, John was on top of it within a few weeks.* 5. Knowing all about; not falling behind in information about; up-to-date on. ♦*Mary stays on top of the news by reading newspapers and magazines.*

open heart *n.* 1. No hiding of your feelings; frankness; freedom. ♦*She spoke with an open heart of her warm feelings for her pupils.* 2. Kindness; generosity. ♦*She contributed to the fund with an open heart.*

open one's heart *v. phr.* 1. To talk about your feelings honestly; confide in someone. ♦*John felt much better after he opened his heart to Betty.* 2. To be sympathetic to; give love or help generously. ♦*Mrs. Smith opened her heart to the poor little boy.*

other fish to fry *n. phr., informal* Other things to do; other plans. ♦*They wanted John to be the secretary, but he had other fish to fry.*

outback *n.* 1. The remote and uncultivated wilderness areas of Australia or New Zealand, with very few inhabitants. ♦*Mike and Barbara roughed it in the Australian outback for nearly two years.* 2. Any remote, sparsely populated region. ♦*Tom's old ranch in Texas is next to an arid outback.*

out cold *adv. or adj., informal* Unconscious; in a faint. ♦*The ball hit Dick in the head and* *knocked him out cold for ten minutes.*

out in force *adv. phr.* Present in very large numbers; en masse. ♦*On the Fourth of July the police cars are out in force in the Chicago area.*

out in left field *adj. phr., informal* **1.** Far from the right answer; wrong; astray. ♦*Johnny tried to answer the teacher's question but he was way out in left field.* **2.** Speaking or acting very queerly; crazy. ♦*The girl next door was always queer, but after her father died, she was really out in left field and had to go to a hospital.*

out in the cold *adj. phr., informal* Alone; not included. ♦*All the other children were chosen for parts in the play, but John was left out in the cold.*

out of *prep.* **1a.** From the inside to the outside of. ♦*John took the apple out of the bag.* **1b.** In a place away from. ♦*No, you can't see Mr. Jones; he is out of the office today.* **2.** From a particular condition or situation; not in; from; in a way changed from being in. ♦*The drugstore is going out of business.* **3.** Beyond the range of. ♦*The plane is out of sight now.* **4.** From (a source). ♦*Mother asked Billy who started the fight, but she couldn't get anything out of him.* **5.** Because of; as a result of. ♦*Mary scolded Joan out of jealousy.* **6.** Without; not having. ♦*The store is out of coffee.* **7.** From (a material). ♦*The house is built out of stone.* **8.** From among. ♦*The man picked Joe out of the crowd.*

out of circulation *adj. phr., informal* Not out in the company of friends, other people, and groups; not active; not joining in what others are doing. ♦*John has a job after school and is out of circulation with his friends.*

out of hand *adv. phr.* **1.** Out of control. ♦*Bobby's birthday party got out of hand and the children were naughty.* **2.** Suddenly, quickly without examination of possible truth or merit; without any consideration.—Often used after *dismiss* or *reject.* ♦*The senator rejected out of hand the critics' call for his resignation.*

out of keeping *adj. phr.* Not going well together; not agreeing; not proper. ♦*Loud talk was out of keeping in the library.*

out of kilter *adj. phr., informal* **1.** Not balanced right; not in a straight line or lined up right. ♦*The wheels of my bicycle were out of kilter after it hit the tree.* **2.** Needing repair; not working right. ♦*My watch runs too slowly; it must be out of kilter.*

out of line *adj. phr.* Not obeying or agreeing with what is right or usual; doing or being what people do not expect or accept; outside ordinary or proper limits; not usual, right, or proper. ♦*Mrs. Green thought the repair man's charge was out of line.*

out of line with *prep.* Not in agreement with. ♦*The price of the bicycle was out of line with what Bill could afford.*

out of luck *adj. phr.* Being unlucky; having bad luck; having something bad happen to you. ♦*All of the girls had dates so Ben was out of luck.*

out of one's element *adv. phr.* Outside of your natural surroundings; where you do not belong or fit in. ♦*Wild animals are out of their element in cages.*

out of one's hair *adj. phr., informal* Rid of as a nuisance; relieved of as an annoyance. ♦*Harry got the boys out of his hair so he could study.*

out of one's shell *adv. phr., informal* Out of one's bashfulness or silence; into friendly conversation—Usually used after *come*. ♦*The other girls tried to draw Ella out of her shell, but without success.*

out of order *adv. or adj. phr.* **1.** In the wrong order; not coming after one another in the right way. ♦*Peter wrote the words of the sentence out of order.* **2.** In poor condition; not working properly. ♦*Our television set is out of order.* **3.** Against the rules; not suitable. ♦*The judge told the people in the courtroom that they were out of order because they were so noisy.*

out of place *adj. phr.* In the wrong place or at the wrong time; not suitable; improper. ♦*Joan was the only girl who wore a formal at the party, and she felt out of place.*

out of print *adj. phr.* No longer obtainable from the publisher because the printed copies have been sold out; no longer printed. ♦*The book is out of print. An edition of one thousand copies was sold and no more copies were printed.*

out of range *adv. phr.* Unreachable socially, financially, or intellectually. ♦*"I'd like to date the college beauty queen, but she is out of range for me," John sighed sadly.* ♦*"I'd like to buy a new Mercedes Benz," Ted said, "but it is out of range for us right now."* ♦*"Medical school is out of range for me now," Mike said, after he took a look at the tuition costs.*

out of sight *adv. phr.* **1.** Not within one's field of vision. ♦*The sailboat disappeared out of sight over the horizon.* **2.** Extremely expensive. ♦*The builder's estimate was so high that it was out of sight.* **3.** Unbelievable; fantastic; incredible (both in the positive and the negative sense; an exaggeration.) ♦*Roxanne is such a stunning beauty, it's simply out of sight.* **4.** Unreachable; unrealizable; belonging to the world of fiction and fantasy. ♦*Max's dreams about winning the Senatorial election are really out of sight; he admits it himself.*

out of sight, out of mind If one doesn't see something for an extended period of time, one tends to forget about it.—A proverb. ♦*After Caroline moved out of town, Ray soon found other women to date. As the saying goes, "out of sight, out of mind."*

out of sorts *adj. phr.* In an angry or unhappy mood; in a bad temper; grouchy. ♦*Bob was out of sorts because he didn't get a bicycle for his birthday.*

out of step *adv. or adj. phr.* **1.** Not in step; not matching strides or keeping pace with another or others. ♦*George always marches out of step with the music.* **2.** Out of harmony; not keeping up.—Often followed by *with*. ♦*Just because you don't smoke, it doesn't mean you are out of* *step with other boys and girls your age.*

out of stock *adj. phr.* Having none for sale or use; no longer in supply; sold out. ◆*When Father tried to get tires for an old car, the man in the store said that size was out of stock and were not sold anymore.*

out of the blue *or* **out of a clear sky** *or* **out of a clear blue sky** *adv. phr., informal* Without any warning; by surprise; unexpectedly. ◆*The cowboy thought he was alone but suddenly out of a clear sky there were bandits all around him.*

out of the frying pan into the fire Out of one trouble into worse trouble; from something bad to something worse.—A proverb. ◆*The policeman was out of the frying pan into the fire. After he escaped from the gang, he was captured by terrorists.*

out of thin air *adv. phr.* Out of nothing or from nowhere. ◆*The teacher scolded Dick because his story was made out of thin air.*

out of this world *adj. phr., slang* Wonderfully good or satisfying; terrific; super. ◆*The dress in the store window was out of this world!*

out of touch *adj. phr.* Not writing or talking with each other; not getting news anymore. ◆*On his island Robinson Crusoe was out of touch with world news.*

out of tune *adv. or adj. phr.* **1.** Out of proper musical pitch; too low or high in sound. ◆*The band sounded terrible, because the instruments were out of tune.* **2.** Not in agreement; in disagreement; not going well together.—Often used with *with.*

◆*What Jack said was out of tune with how he looked; he said he was happy, but he looked unhappy.*

out of turn *adv. phr.* **1.** Not in regular order; at the wrong time. ◆*By taking a day off out of turn, Bob got the schedule mixed up.* **2.** Too hastily or wrongly; at the wrong time or place; so as to annoy others. ◆*Dick loses friends by speaking out of turn.*

out of whack *adj. phr., slang* **1.** Needing repair; not working right. ◆*Ben was glad the lawn mower got out of whack, because he didn't have to mow the lawn.* **2.** Not going together well; not in agreement. ◆*The things Mr. Black does are out of whack with what he says.*

out of work *adv. phr.* Having no income-producing job; unemployed. ◆*When too many people are out of work, it is a sign that the economy is in a recession.*

out on a limb *adv. phr.* With your beliefs and opinions openly stated; in a dangerous position that can't be changed. ◆*The president went out on a limb and supported a foreign aid bill that many people were against.*

out to lunch *adj., slang, informal* **1.** Gone for the midday meal. **2.** Inattentive; daydreaming; inefficient; stupid. ◆*Neil Bender is just out to lunch today; he's in a fog.*

over one's head *adv. or adj. phr.* **1.** Not understandable; beyond your ability to understand; too hard or strange for you to understand. ◆*The lesson today was hard; it went over my head.* **2.** To a more important person in charge; to a higher official. *When Mary's supervisor said no, Mary went over her head to the person in charge of the whole department.*

over the hill *adj., informal* Past one's prime; unable to function as one used to; senile. *Poor Mr. Jones is sure not like he used to be; well, he's over the hill.*

over the top *adv. phr.* 1. Out of the trenches and against the enemy. *The plan was to spend the night in the trenches and go over the top at dawn.* 2. Over the goal. *Our goal was to collect a half million dollars for the new school building, but we went over the top.*

over with[1] *prep.* At the end of; finished with; through with. *They were over with the meeting by ten o'clock.*

over with[2] *adj., informal* At an end; finished. *After the hard test, Jerry said, "I'm glad that's over with!"*

pack rat n., *informal* A person who cannot part with old, useless objects; an avid collector of useless things; a junk hoarder. ◆*"Why are there so many things in this room?" John asked. "It is my brother's room, and he is a pack rat; he is unable to throw stuff away."*

pack of lies n. phr. An unbelievable story; unprovable allegations. ◆*What Al told us about his new girlfriend was nothing but a pack of lies.*

paddy wagon n., *informal* A police van used for transporting prisoners to jail or the police station. ◆*The police threw the demonstrators into the paddy wagon.*

pain in the ass or **pain in the neck** n., *slang, vulgar with ass* An obnoxious or bothersome person or event. ◆*Phoebe Hochrichter is a regular pain in the neck/ass.*

palm off v., *informal* **1.** To sell or give (something) by pretending it is something more valuable; to sell or give by trickery. ◆*He palmed off his own painting as a Rembrandt.* **2.** To deceive (someone) by a trick or lie. ◆*He palmed his creditors off with a great show of prosperity.* **3.** To introduce someone as a person he isn't; present in a false pretense. ◆*He palmed the girl off as a real Broadway actress.*

pan out v., *informal* To have a result, especially a good result; result favorably; succeed. ◆*Edison's efforts to invent an electric light bulb did not pan out until he used tungsten wires.*

par for the course n. phr., *informal* Just what was expected; nothing unusual; a typical happening.—Usually refers to things going wrong. ◆*When John came late again, Mary said, "That's par for the course."*

part and parcel n. phr. A necessary or important part; something necessary to a larger thing.—Usually followed by of. ◆*Freedom of speech is part and parcel of the liberty of a free man.*

pass away v. **1.** To slip by; go by; pass. ◆*Forty years had passed away since they had met.* **2.** To cease to exist; end; disappear; vanish ◆*When automobiles became popular, the use of the horse and buggy passed away.* **3.** To have your life stop; die. ◆*He passed away at eighty.*

pass muster v. phr., *informal* To pass a test or check-up; be good enough. ◆*His work was done carefully, so it always passed muster.*

pass off v. **1.** To sell or give (something) by false claims; offer (something fake) as genuine. ◆*The dishonest builder passed off a poorly built house by pretending it was well constructed.* **2.** To claim to be someone you are not; pretend to be someone else. ◆*He passed himself off as a doctor until someone checked his record.* **3.** To go away gradually; disappear. ◆*Tom's morning headache had passed off by that night.* **4.** To reach an end; run its course from beginning to end. ◆*The party passed off well.*

pass on v. **1.** To give an opinion about; judge; settle. ◆*The college passed on his application and found him acceptable.* ◆*The committee recommended *three people for the job and the president passed on them.* **2.** To give away (something that has been outgrown). *As he grew up, he passed on his clothes to his younger brother.* **3.** To die. *Mary was very sorry to hear that her first grade teacher had passed on.*

pass out *v., informal* **1.** To lose consciousness; faint. *She went back to work while she was still sick, and finally she just passed out.* **2.** *or slang* **pass out cold** To drop into a drunken stupor; become unconscious from drink. *After three drinks, the man passed out.*

pass the buck *v. phr., informal* To make another person decide something or accept a responsibility or give orders instead of doing it yourself; shift or escape responsibility or blame; put the duty or blame on someone else. *If you break a window, do not pass the buck; admit that you did it.*—**buck-passer** *n. phr.* A person who passes the buck. *Mr. Jones was a buck-passer even at home, and tried to make his wife make all the decisions.*—**buck-passing** *n. or adj.* *Buck-passing clerks in stores make customers angry.*

patch up *v.* **1.** To mend a hole or break; repair; fix. *The lovers patched up their quarrel.* **2.** To put together in a hurried or shaky way. *They patched up a hasty peace.*

pay attention *v. phr.* To listen to someone; hear and understand someone alertly. *"Pay attention, children!" the teacher cried. "Here is your homework for next week!"*

pay a visit *v. phr.* To visit someone, usually by previous arrangement. *"It's your turn to pay me a visit," John said, "I've been to your place several times."*

pay dirt *n., slang* **1.** The dirt in which much gold is found. *The man searched for gold many years before he found pay dirt.* **2.** *informal* A valuable discovery.—Often used in the phrase *strike pay dirt.* *When Bill joined the team, the coach struck pay dirt.*

pay down *v. phr.* **1.** To give as a deposit on some purchase, the rest of which is to be paid in periodic installments. *"How much can you pay down on the house, sir?" the realtor asked.* **2.** To decrease a debt with periodical payments. *I'd like to pay down the charges on my credit cards.*

pay off *v. phr.* (stress on *off*) **1.** To pay the wages of. *The men were paid off just before quitting time, the last day before the holiday.* **2.** To pay and discharge from a job. *When the building was completed he paid off the laborers.* **3.** To hurt (someone) who has done wrong to you; get revenge on. *When Bob tripped Dick, Dick paid Bob off by punching him in the nose.* **4.** *informal* To bring a return; make profit. *At first Mr. Harrison lost money on his investments, but finally one paid off.* **5.** *informal* To prove successful, rewarding, or worthwhile. *John studied hard before the examination, and it paid off. He made an A.*

pay through the nose *v. phr., informal* To pay at a very high rate; pay too much. ♦*There was a shortage of cars; if you found one for sale, you had to pay through the nose.*

pecking order n. The way people are ranked in relation to each other (for honor, privilege, or power); status classification; hierarchy. ♦*After the president was in office several months, his staff developed a pecking order.*

peeping Tom n. A man or boy who likes sly peeping. ♦*He was picked up by the police as a peeping Tom.*

penny for one's thoughts Please tell me what you are thinking about; what's your daydream. ♦*"A penny for your thoughts!" he exclaimed.*

penny wise and pound foolish Wise or careful in small things but not careful enough in important things.—A proverb. ♦*Mr. Smith's fence is rotting and falling down because he wouldn't spend money to paint it. He is penny wise and pound foolish.*

pen pal n. A friend who is known to someone through an exchange of letters. ♦*John's pen pal writes him letters about school in Alaska.*

people who live in glass houses should not throw stones Do not complain about other people if you are as bad as they are.—A proverb. ♦*Mary says that Betty is promiscuous, but Mary is a call girl. People who live in glass houses should not throw stones.*

peter out v., *informal* To fail or die down gradually; grow less; become exhausted. ♦*The mine once had a rich vein of silver, but it petered out.*

pick-me-up n. phr. Something you take when you feel tired or weak. ♦*Mary always carried a bar of chocolate in her pocketbook for a pick-me-up.*

pickpocket n. A thief; a petty criminal who steals things and money out of people's pockets on a bus, train, etc. ♦*In some big cities many poor children become pickpockets out of poverty.*

pick on v. 1. *informal* To make a habit of annoying or bothering (someone); do or say bad things to (someone). ♦*Other boys picked on him until he decided to fight them.* 2. To single out; choose; select. ♦*He visited a lot of colleges, and finally picked on Stanford.*

pick out v. 1. To choose. ♦*It took Mary a long time to pick out a dress at the store.* 2. To see among others; recognize; tell from others. ♦*We could pick out different places in the city from the airplane.* 3. To find by examining or trying; tell the meaning. ♦*The box was so dirty we couldn't pick out the directions on the label.*

pick the brains of v. phr. To get ideas or information about a particular subject by asking an expert. ♦*If you have time, I'd like to pick your brains about home computers.*

pickup n., (stress on pick) 1. A rugged, small truck. ♦*When he got into the lumber business, Max traded in his comfortable two-door sedan for a pickup.* 2. Scheduled meeting in order to transfer merchandise or stolen goods. ♦*The dope pushers usu-*

ally make their pickup on Rush Street. **3.** A person who is easy to persuade to go home with the suitor. *◆Sue is said to be an easy pickup.*

pick up *v.* (stress on *up*) **1.** To take up; lift. *◆During the morning Mrs. Carter picked up sticks in the yard.* **2.** *informal* To pay for someone else. *◆After lunch, in the restaurant, Uncle Bob picked up the check.* **3.** To take on or away; receive; get. *◆At the next corner the bus stopped and picked up three people.* **4.** To get from different places at different times; a little at a time; collect. *◆He had picked up rare coins in seaports all over the world.* **5.** To get without trying; get accidentally. *◆He picked up knowledge of radio just by staying around the radio station.* **6a.** To gather together; collect. *◆When the carpenter finished making the cabinet, he began picking up his tools.* **6b.** To make neat and tidy; tidy up; put in order. *◆Pick up your room before Mother sees it.* **6c.** To gather things together; tidy a place up. *◆It's almost dinner time, children. Time to pick up and get ready.* **7.** To catch the sound of. *◆He picked up Chicago on the radio.* **8.** To get acquainted with (someone) without an introduction; make friends with (a person of the other sex). *◆Mother told Mary not to walk home by herself from the party because some stranger might try to pick her up.* **9.** *informal* To take to the police station or jail; arrest. *◆Police picked the man up for burglary.* **10.** To recognize the trail of a hunted person or ani-mal; find. *◆State police picked up the bandit's trail.* **11.** To make (someone) feel better; refresh. *◆A little food will pick you up.* **12a.** To increase (the speed); make (the speed) faster. *◆The teacher told her singing class to pick up the tempo.* **12b.** To become faster; become livelier. *◆The speed of the train began to pick up.* **13.** To start again after interruption; go on with. *◆The class picked up the story where they had left it before the holiday.* **14.** *informal* To become better; recover; gain. *◆He picked up gradually after a long illness.*

piece of cake *adj., slang* Easy. *◆The final exam was a piece of cake.*

pie in the sky *n. phr., informal* An unrealistic wish or hope. *◆Our trip to Hawaii is still only a pie in the sky.*

piggy bank *n.* A small bank, sometimes in the shape of a pig, for saving coins. *◆John's father gave him a piggy bank.*

pig in a poke *n. phr.* An unseen bargain; something accepted or bought without looking at it carefully. *◆Buying land by mail is buying a pig in a poke: sometimes the land turns out to be under water.*

pig out *v. phr.* **1.** To eat a tremendous amount of food. *◆"I always pig out on my birthday," she confessed.* **2.** To peruse; have great fun with; indulge in for a longer period of time. *◆"Go to bed and pig out on a good mystery story," the doctor recommended.*

pile up *v. phr.* (stress on *up*) **1.** To grow into a big heap. *◆He didn't go into his office for three* *days and his work kept piling up.* **2.** To run aground. ◆*Boats often pile up on the rocks in the shallow water.* **3.** To crash. ◆*One car made a sudden stop and the two cars behind it piled up.*

pile-up *n.* (stress on *pile*) **1.** A heap; a deposit of one object on top of another. ◆*There is a huge pile-up of junked cars in this vacant lot.* **2.** A large number of objects in the same place, said of traffic. ◆*I was late because of the traffic pile-up on the high-way.*

pin down *v.* **1a.** To keep (someone) from moving; make stay in a place or position; trap. ◆*Mr. Jones' leg was pinned down under the car after the accident.* **1b.** To keep (someone) from changing what (he) says or means; make (someone) admit the truth; make (someone) agree to something. ◆*Mary didn't like the book but I couldn't pin her down to say what she didn't like about it.* **2.** To tell clearly and exactly; explain so that there is no doubt. ◆*The police tried to pin down the blame for the fire in the school.*

pipe dream *n., informal* An unrealizable, financially unsound, wishful way of thinking; an unrealistic plan. ◆*Joe went through the motions of pretending that he wanted to buy that $250,000 house, but his wife candidly told the real estate lady that it was just a pipe dream.*

pipe up *v., informal* To speak up; to be heard. ◆*Everyone was afraid to talk to the police, but a small child piped up.*

pip-squeak *n., informal* A small, unimportant person. ◆*If the club is really democratic, then every little pip-squeak has the right to say what he thinks.*

piss off *v., slang, vulgar, avoid!* To bother; annoy; irritate. ◆*You really piss me off when you talk like that.*—**pissed off** *adj.* ◆*Why act so pissed off just because I made a pass at you?*

pitch in *v., informal* **1.** To begin something with much energy; start work eagerly. ◆*Pitch in and we will finish the job as soon as possible.* **2.** To give help or money for something; contribute. ◆*Everyone must pitch in and work together.*

play ball *v. phr. informal* To join in an effort with others; cooperate. ◆*To get along during Prohibition, many men felt that they had to play ball with gangsters.*

play by ear *v. phr.* **1.** To play a musical instrument by remembering the tune, not by reading music. ◆*Mary does not know how to read music. She plays the piano by ear.* **2.** *informal* To decide what to do as you go along; to fit the situation.— Used with *it.* ◆*It was her first job and she didn't know what to expect, so she had to play it by ear.*

play cat and mouse with *v. phr.* To tease or fool (someone) by pretending to let him go free and then catching him again. ◆*The policeman decided to play cat and mouse when he saw the woman steal the dress in the store.*

play down *v.* To give less emphasis to; make (something) seem less important; divert attention

from; draw notice away from.
♦*A salesman's job is to emphasize the good points of his merchandise; he must play down
any faults it has.*

played out *adj. phr.* Tired out;
worn out; finished; exhausted.
♦*It had been a hard day, and by
night he was played out.*

play footsie *v. phr., slang, informal* 1. Touch the feet of a member of the opposite sex under
the table as an act of flirtation.
♦*Have you at least played footsie with her?* 2. To engage in
any sort of flirtation or collabo-
ration, especially in a political
situation. ♦*The mayor was suspected of playing footsie with
the Syndicate.*

play hooky *v. phr., informal* To
stay out of school to play. ♦*Carl
is failing in school because he
has played hooky so many times
during the year.*

play off *v.* 1. To match opposing
persons, forces, or interests so
that they balance each other.
♦*Britain tried to play off
European nations against each
other so that she would have a
balance of power.* 2. To finish
the playing of (an interrupted
contest.) ♦*The visitors came
back the next Saturday to play
off the game stopped by rain.* 3.
To settle (a tie score) between
contestants by more play.
♦*When each player had won
two matches, the championship
was decided by playing off the
tie.*

play on *or* **play upon** *v.* 1. To
cause an effect on; influence.
♦*A heavy dose of television
drama played on his feelings.* 2.
To work upon for a planned
effect; excite to a desired action

by cunning plans; manage.
♦*The makeup salesman played
on the woman's wish to look
beautiful.*

play one's cards right *or* **play
one's cards well** *v. phr., informal* To use abilities and opportunities so as to be successful;
act cleverly; make the best use
of your place or skills. ♦*People
liked Harold, and he played his
cards well—and soon he began
to get ahead rapidly.*

play the field *v. phr., informal* To
date many different people; not
always have dates with the
same person. ♦*Al had a steady
girlfriend, but John was playing
the field.*

play up *v.* To call attention to; talk
more about; emphasize. ♦*The
coach played up the possibilities, and kept our minds off our
weaknesses.*

play up to *v. phr., slang* 1. To try
to gain the favor of, especially
for selfish reasons; act to win
the approval of; try to please.
♦*He played up to the boss.*
2. To use (something) to gain an
end; to attend to (a weakness).
♦*He played up to the old lady's
vanity to get her support.*

play with fire *v. phr.* To put oneself in danger; to take risks.
♦*Leaving your door unlocked in
New York City is playing with
fire.*

plow into *v.* 1. To attack vigorously. ♦*He plowed into his work
and finished it in a few hours.* 2.
To crash into with force. ♦*A
truck plowed into my car and
smashed the fender.*

point out *v.* 1. To show by pointing with the finger; point to;
make clear the location of. ♦*The
guide pointed out the principal*

sights of the city. **2.** To bring to notice; call to attention; explain. ◆*The policeman pointed out that the law forbids public sale of firecrackers.*

poison-pen *adj.* Containing threats or false accusations; written in spite or to get revenge, and usually unsigned. ◆*Mrs. Smith received a poison-pen letter telling her that her husband was untrue.*

polish off *v., informal* **1.** To defeat easily. ◆*The Dodgers polished off the Yankees in four straight games in the 1963 World Series.* **2.** To finish completely; finish doing quickly, often in order to do something else. ◆*The boys were hungry and polished off a big steak.* ◆*Mary polished off her homework early so that she could watch TV.*

polish the apple *v. phr., slang* To try to make someone like you; to try to win favor by flattery. ◆*Susan is the teacher's pet because she always polishes the apple.*—**apple-polisher** *n., slang* A person who is nice to the one in charge in order to be liked or treated better; a person who does favors for a superior. ◆*Joe is an apple-polisher. He will do anything for the boss.*—**apple-polishing** *n., slang* Trying to win someone's goodwill by small acts currying favor; the behavior of an apple-polisher. ◆*When John brought his teacher flowers, everyone thought he was apple-polishing.*

pooped out *adj., slang* Worn out; exhausted. ◆*The heat made them feel pooped out.*

pop in *v. phr.* To suddenly appear without announcement. ◆*"Just*

pop into my office any time you're on campus," Professor Brown said.

pop up *v.* **1.** *or* **bob up** To appear suddenly or unexpectedly; show up; come out. ◆*After no one had heard from him for years, John popped up in town again.*

pot calling the kettle black *informal* The person who is criticizing someone else is as guilty as the person he or she accuses; the charge is as true of the person who makes it as of the one he or she makes it against. ◆*Bill said John was cheating at a game but John replied that the pot was calling the kettle black.*

pour oil on troubled waters *v. phr.* To quiet a quarrel; say something to lessen anger and bring peace. ◆*The troops were nearing a bitter quarrel until the leader poured oil on the troubled waters.*

pour out *v.* **1.** To tell everything about; talk all about. ◆*Mary poured out her troubles to her pal.* **2.** To come out in great quantity; stream out. ◆*The people poured out of the building when they heard the fire alarm.*

powder room *n.* The ladies' rest room. ◆*When they got to the restaurant, Mary went to the powder room to wash up.*

power behind the throne *n. phr.* The person with the real power backing up the more visible partner (usually said about the wives of public figures). ◆*It is rumored that the First Lady is the power behind the throne in the White House.*

prey on *or* **prey upon** *v.* **1.** To habitually kill and eat; catch for food. ◆*Cats prey on mice.* **2.** To capture or take in spoils of war or robbery. ◆*Pirates preyed on American ships in the years just after the Revolutionary War.* **3.** To cheat; rob. ◆*Gangsters preyed on businesses of many kinds while the sale of liquor was prohibited.* **4.** To have a tiring and weakening effect on; weaken. ◆*Ill health had preyed on him for years.*

promise the moon *v. phr.* To promise something impossible. ◆*I can't promise you the moon, but I'll do the best job I can.*

proof of the pudding is in the eating Only through actual experience can the value of something be tested.—A proverb. ◆*He was intrigued by the ads about the new high mileage sports cars. "Drive one, sir," the salesman said. "The proof of the pudding is in the eating."*

psyched up *adj., informal* Mentally alert; ready to do something. ◆*The students were all psyched up for their final exams.*

psych out *v. phr., slang, informal* **1.** To find out the real motives of (someone). ◆*Sue sure has got Joe psyched out.* **2.** To go berserk; to lose one's nerve. ◆*Joe says he doesn't ride his motorcycle on the highway anymore because he's psyched out.*

pull a fast one *v. phr.* To gain the advantage over one's opponent unfairly; deceive; trick. ◆*When Smith was told by his boss that he might be fired, he called the company president, who was his father-in-law, and pulled a fast one by having his boss demoted.*

pull one's leg *v. phr., informal* To get someone to accept a ridiculous story as true; fool someone with a humorous account of something; trick. ◆*For a moment, I actually believed that his wife had royal blood. Then I realized he was pulling my leg.*

pull one's punches *v. phr., informal* **1.** Not to hit as hard as you can. ◆*Jimmy pulled his punches and let Paul win the boxing match.* **2.** To hide unpleasant facts or make them seem good.—Usually used in the negative. ◆*The mayor spoke bluntly; he didn't pull any punches.*

pull one's weight *v. phr.* To do your full share of work; do your part. ◆*When Mother was sick in the hospital, Father said each child must pull his own weight.*

pull out of a hat *v. phr., informal* To get as if by magic; invent; imagine. ◆*Let's see you pull an excuse out of your hat.*

pull over *v.* To drive to the side of the road and stop. ◆*The policeman told the speeder to pull over.*

pull rank *v. phr., slang, informal* To assert one's superior position or authority on a person of lower rank as in exacting a privilege or a favor. ◆*How come you always get the night duty? The boss pulled rank on me.*

pull strings *or* **pull wires** *v. phr., informal* To secretly use influence and power, especially with people in charge or in important jobs to do or get something; make use of friends to gain your wishes. ◆*If you want to see the governor, Mr. Root can pull strings for you.* ◆*Jack pulled wires and got us a room at the crowded hotel.*

pull the chestnuts out of the fire *v. phr.* To perform a difficult, dangerous, or illicit work on behalf of someone else. ◆*The new boss is using his colleagues to pull the chestnuts out of the fire for him.*

pull the plug on *v. phr., slang* To expose (someone's) secret activities. ◆*The citizens' committee pulled the plug on the mayor, and he lost his election.*

pull the rug out from under *v. phr., informal* To withdraw support unexpectedly from; to spoil the plans of. ◆*Bill thought he would be elected, but his friends pulled the rug out from under him and voted for John.*

pull the wool over one's eyes *v. phr., informal* To fool someone into thinking well of you; deceive. ◆*The businessman had pulled the wool over his partner's eyes about their financial position.*

pull through *v.* **1.** To help through; bring safely through a difficulty or sudden trouble; save. ◆*A generous loan showed the bank's faith in Father and pulled him through the business trouble.* **2.** To recover from an illness or misfortune; conquer a disaster; escape death or failure. ◆*By a near-miracle, he pulled through after the smashup.*

push around *v., informal* To be bossy with; bully. ◆*Don't try to push me around!*

push comes to shove *v. phr.* Often heard when a bad situation, which is difficult to tolerate, suddenly comes to a head and steady, slow pressure is replaced by a sudden explosion of events.—A proverb. ◆*I am afraid that when push comes to*

shove during the present economic slump, many of us will be fired.

push the envelope *v. phr.* To strain a delicate situation to the utmost; engage in exaggerated demands. ◆*If you want to succeed with these difficult peace negotiations, you had better stop pushing the envelope.* ◆*"You're pushing the envelope!" John warned his colleague. "The boss will not listen to you if you won't stop."*

pushover *n.* (stress on *push*) **1.** Something easy to accomplish or overcome. ◆*For Howard steering a boat is a pushover as he was raised on a tropical island.* **2.** A person easily seduced. ◆*It is rumored that she is a pushover when she has a bit to drink.*

push over *v. phr.* (stress on *over*) To upset; overthrow. ◆*She is standing on her feet very solidly; a little criticism from you certainly won't push her over.*

put across *v.* **1.** To explain clearly; make yourself understood; communicate. ◆*He knew how to put his ideas across.* **2.** *informal* To get (something) done successfully; bring to success; make real. ◆*He put across a big sales campaign.*

put all one's eggs in one basket *v. phr.* To place all your efforts, interests, or hopes in a single person or thing. ◆*To buy stock in a single company is to put all your eggs in one basket.*

put away *v.* **1.** To put in the right place or out of sight. ◆*She put away the towels.* **2.** To lay aside; stop thinking about. ◆*He put his worries away for the weekend.* **3.** *informal* To eat or drink. ◆*He put away a big supper and three cups of coffee.* 4. *informal* To put in a mental hospital. ◆*He had to put his wife away when she became mentally ill.* 5. To put to death for a reason; kill. ◆*He had his dog put away when it became too old and unhappy.*

putdown *n.* (stress on *put*) An insult. ◆*It was a nasty putdown when John called his sister a fat cow.*

put down *v. phr.* (stress on *down*) 1. To stop by force; crush. ◆*In 24 hours the general had entirely put down the rebellion.* 2. To put a stop to; check. ◆*She had patiently put down unkind talk by living a good life.* 3. To write a record of; write down. ◆*He put down the story while it was fresh in his mind.* 4. To write a name in a list as agreeing to do something. ◆*The banker put himself down for $1000.* 5. To decide the kind or class of; characterize. ◆*He put the man down as a bum.* 6. To name as a cause; attribute. ◆*He put the odd weather down to nuclear explosions.* 7. To dig; drill; sink. *He put down a new well.*

put in *v.* 1. To add to what has been said; say (something) in addition to what others say. ◆*My father put in a word for me and I got the job.* 2. To buy and keep in a store to sell. ◆*He put in a full stock of drugs.* 3. To spend (time). ◆*He put in many years as a printer.* 4. To plant. ◆*He put in a row of radishes.* 5. To stop at a port on a journey by water. ◆*After the fire, the ship put in for repairs.* 6. To apply; ask.—Used with *for.* ◆*When a*

better job was open, he put in for it.

put in a word for *v. phr.* To speak in favor of someone; recommend someone. ◆*"Don't worry about your job application," Sam said to Tim. "I'll put in a word for you with the selection committee."*

put off *v.* 1. *informal* To cause confusion in; embarrass; displease. ◆*I was rather put off by the shamelessness of his proposal.* 2. To wait and have (something) at a later time; postpone. ◆*They put off the picnic because of the rain.* 3. To make (someone) wait; turn aside. ◆*When he asked her to name a day for their wedding, she put him off.* 4. To draw away the attention; turn aside; distract. ◆*Little Jeannie began to tell the guests some family secrets, but Father was able to put her off.* 5. To move out to sea; leave shore. ◆*They put off in small boats to meet the coming ship.*

put on *v. phr.* 1. To dress in. ◆*The boy took off his clothes and put on his pajamas.* 2a. To pretend; assume; show. ◆*The child was putting on airs.* 2b. To exaggerate; make too much of. ◆*That's rather putting it on.* 3. To begin to have more (body weight); gain (weight). ◆*Mary was thin from sickness, and the doctor said she must put on ten pounds.* 4a. To plan and prepare; produce; arrange; give; stage. ◆*The senior class put on a dance.* ◆*The actor put on a fine performance.* 4b. To make (an effort). ◆*The runner put on an extra burst of speed and won the race.* 5. To choose to send; employ on a job. ◆*The school* *put on extra men to get the new building ready.*

put-on *n.* An act of teasing; the playing of a practical joke on someone. ♦*Eric didn't realize that it was a put-on when his friends phoned him that he won the lottery.*

put on the dog *v. phr.* To behave ostentatiously in terms of dress and manner. ♦ *"Stop putting on the dog with me," Sue cried at Roy. "I knew the real you from way back!"*

put on the map *v. phr.* To make (a place) well known. ♦*The first successful climb of Mount Matterhorn put Zermatt, Switzerland, on the map.*

put out *v.* **1.** To make a flame or light stop burning; extinguish; turn off. ♦*Please put the light out when you leave the room.* ♦*The firemen put out the blaze.* **2.** To prepare for the public; produce; make. ♦*For years he had put out a weekly newspaper.* ♦*It is a small restaurant, which puts out an excellent dinner.* **3.** To invest or loan money. ♦*He put out all his spare money at 4 percent or better.* **4.** To make angry; irritate; annoy. ♦*It puts the teacher out to be lied to.* **5.** *informal* To cause inconvenience to; bother. ♦*He put himself out to make things pleasant for us.* **6.** To retire from play in baseball. ♦*The runner was put out at first base.* **7.** To go from shore; leave. ♦*A Coast Guard boat put out through the waves.* **8.** *vulgar, avoidable* Said of women easy and ready to engage in sexual intercourse. ♦*It is rumored that Hermione gets her promotions as fast as she does because she puts out.*

put over *v.* **1.** To wait to a later time; postpone. ♦*They put over the meeting to the following Tuesday.* **2.** *informal* To make a success of; complete. ♦*He put over a complex and difficult business deal.* **3.** *informal* To practice deception; trick; fool. —Used with *on.* ♦*George thought he was putting something over on the teacher when he said he was absent the day before because his mother was sick.*

put the bite on *v. phr., slang* To ask (for money, favors, etc.). ♦*John put the bite on his friend for several tickets to the dance.*

put two and two together *v. phr.* To make decisions based on available proofs; reason from the known facts; conclude; decide. ♦*He had put two and two together and decided where they had probably gone.*

put up *v.* **1a.** To make and pack (especially a lunch or medicine); get ready; prepare. ♦*Every morning Mother puts up lunches for the three children.* **1b.** To put food into jars or cans to save; can. ♦*Mother is putting up peaches in jars.* **1c.** To store away for later use. ♦*The farmer put up three tons of hay for the winter.* **2.** To put in place; put (something) where it belongs. ♦*After he unpacked the car, John put it up.* **3.** To suggest that (someone) be chosen a member, officer, or official. ♦*The club decided to take in another member, and Bill put up Charles.*—Often used with *for.* ♦*The Republicans put Mr. Williams up for mayor.* **4.** To put (hair) a special way; arrange. ◆*Aunt May puts up her hair in curlers every night.* **5.** To place on sale; offer for sale. ◆*She put the house up for sale.* **6a.** To provide lodging for; furnish a room to. ◆*The visitor was put up in the home of Mr. Wilson.* **6b.** To rent or get shelter; take lodging; stay in a place to sleep. ◆*The traveler put up at a motel.* ◆*We put up with friends on our trip to Canada.* **7.** To make; engage in. *He put up a good fight against his sickness.* **8.** To furnish (money) or something needed; pay for. ◆*He put up the money to build a hotel.*

put-up *adj.* Artificially arranged; plotted; phony; illegal. ◆*The FBI was sure that the bank robbers worked together with an insider and that the whole affair was a put-up job.*

put up to *v. phr., informal* To talk to and make do; persuade to; get to do. ◆*Older boys put us up to painting the statue red.*

put up with *v.* To accept patiently; bear. ◆*We had to put up with Jim's poor table manners because he refused to change.*

put wise *v., slang* To tell (someone) facts that will give him an advantage over others or make him alert to opportunity or danger. ◆*The new boy did not know that Jim was playing a trick on him, so I put him wise.*

put words into one's mouth *v. phr.* To say without proof that another person has certain feelings or opinions; claim a stand or an idea is another's without asking; speak for another without right. ◆*When he said "John here is in favor of the idea," I told him not to put words in my mouth.*

quality time *n. phr.* A good leisure time spent with friends in conversation as during a major holiday; a serious time spent with one's children or other family members. ◆*"Come over after dinner, and let's have some quality time together," Bob said to his friends.* ◆*Parents ought to spend some quality time with their children every day and not just send them to bed in a hurry.*

queer fish *n.* A strange or unusual person who does odd things. ◆*Uncle Algernon dresses in heavy furs in the summer and short-sleeved shirts in the winter. No wonder everyone considers him a queer fish.*

quick fix *or* **stopgap** *n. phr.* A simple short-term solution to a problem. ◆*Putting duct tape on a broken car bumper is just a quick fix that won't last very long.* ◆*To hire a substitute lecturer to teach English grammar instead of hiring a permanent faculty member is just a stopgap solution.*

quick on the trigger *or* **trigger happy** *adj. phr.* Ready to shoot without warning; fast with a gun. ◆*He's a dangerous criminal quick on the trigger.* **2.** *informal* Fast at answering questions or solving problems. ◆*In class discussions John is always quick on the trigger.*

quick on the uptake *adj. phr.* Smart; intelligent. ◆*Eleanor is very witty and quick on the uptake.*

quick study *n. phr.* One who acquires new skills and habits in record time. ◆*Sue is new at her job but people have confidence in her because she is a quick study.*

quite a bit *also formal* **not a little** *n. or adj. phr.* Rather a large amount; rather much; more than a little. ◆*Six inches of snow fell today, and quite a bit more is coming tonight.*—Sometimes used like an adverb. ◆*Harry was sick quite a bit last winter.*

quite a few *or* **quite a number** *also formal* **not a few** *n. or adj. phr.* Rather a large number; more than a few. ◆*Quite a few went to the game.* ◆*The basket had quite a few rotten apples in it.*—The phrase *quite a number* is used like an adjective only before *less, more.* ◆*Few people saw the play on the first night but quite a number more came on the second night.*—Sometimes used like an adverb. ◆*We still have quite a few more miles to go before we reach New York.*

quite the thing *n. phr.* The socially proper thing to do. ◆*In polite society it is quite the thing to send a written thank you note to one's host or hostess after a dinner party.*

rack and ruin *n. phr.* Complete decay; condition of decline. ◆*The entire house had been so neglected that it had gone to rack and ruin.*

railroad *v.* To force through; push through by force. ◆*The bill was railroaded through the state legislature due to the influence of some very wealthy sponsors.*

rain cats and dogs *or* **rain buckets** *or* **rain pitchforks** *v. phr., informal* To rain very hard; come down in torrents. ◆*In the middle of the picnic it started to rain cats and dogs, and everybody got soaked.* ◆*Terry looked out of the window and said, "It's raining pitchforks, so we can't go out to play right now."*

raincheck *n.* **1.** A special free ticket to another game or show that will be given in place of one canceled because of rain. ◆*When the drizzle turned into a heavy rain the manager announced that the baseball game would be replayed the next day. He told the crowd that they would be given rainchecks for tomorrow's game as they went out through the gates.* **2.** *informal* A promise to repeat an invitation at a later time. ◆*Bob said, "I'm sorry you can't come to dinner this evening, Dave. I'll give you a raincheck."*

rained out *adj.* Stopped by rain. ◆*The ball game was rained out in the seventh inning.*

raise Cain *v. phr., slang* To be noisy; cause trouble. ◆*When John couldn't go on the basketball trip with the team he raised Cain.*

raise eyebrows *v. phr.* To shock people; cause surprise or disapproval. ◆*The news that the princess was engaged to a commoner raised eyebrows all over the kingdom.*

raise the roof *v. phr., informal* **1.** To make a lot of noise; be happy and noisy. ◆*The gang raised the roof with their singing.* **2.** To scold loudly. ◆*Mother raised the roof when she saw the dog's muddy footprints on her new bedspread.*

rake in *v. phr.* To realize great profits; take in money. ◆*Because of the heavy snowfall, ski lodge operators in the Rocky Mountains have been raking in the dough this winter season.*

rat race *n., slang* A very confusing, crowded, or disorderly rush; a confusing scramble, struggle, or way of living that does not seem to have a purpose. ◆*This job is a rat race. The faster you work, the faster the boss wants you to work.*

reach for the sky *v. phr., slang* **1.** To put your hands high above your head or be shot.—Usually used as a command. ◆*A holdup man walked into a gas station last night and told the attendant "Reach for the sky!"* **2.** To set one's aims high. ◆*"Why medical technician?" asked her father. "Reach for the sky! Become a physician!"*

read one one's rights *v. phr.* To give to an arrested person the legally required statement regarding the rights of such a person. ◆*"Read him his rights, Sergeant," the captain said, "and book him for breaking and entering."*

read one's mind *v. phr.* To know what someone else is thinking.

◆*I have known John so long that I can read his mind.*—**mind reader** *n.* ◆*That's exactly what I was going to say. You must be a mind reader!*

read the riot act *v. phr.* To give someone a strong warning or scolding. ◆*Three boys were late to class and the teacher read the riot act to them.*

ready money *n. phr.* Cash on hand. ◆*Frank refuses to buy things on credit, but, if he had the ready money, he would buy that lovely old house.*

red eye *adj. phr.* Bloodshot eyes that are strained from too much reading. ◆*Poor Tim has a red eye; he must have been studying too late again.*

red eye *n. phr., informal* A night flight. ◆*The company refused to pay for him to take a more expensive daytime flight, so he had to come in on the red eye.*

red-handed *adj.* In the very act; while committing a crime or evil action. ◆*The criminal was caught red-handed while holding up the neighborhood bank at gunpoint.*

red herring *n. phr.* A false scent laid down in order to deceive; a phony or misleading story designed to cause confusion. ◆*That story about the president having an affair was a red herring created by the opposition in order to discredit him.*

red tape *n. phr.* Unnecessary bureaucratic routine; needless but official delays. ◆*If you want to get anything accomplished in a hurry, you have to find someone in power who can cut through all that red tape.*

regular guy *or* **regular fellow** *n., informal* A friendly person who is easy to get along with; a good sport. ◆*You'll like Tom. He's a regular guy.*

rest room *n.* A room or series of rooms in a public building which has things for personal comfort and grooming, such as toilets, washbowls, mirrors, and often chairs or couches. ◆*Sally went to the rest room to powder her nose.*

rev up *v. phr., informal, slang* **1.** To press down sharply several times on the accelerator of an idling car in order to get maximum acceleration. ◆*The race driver revved up his car by pumping his accelerator.* **2.** To get oneself ready in order to accomplish a demanding or difficult task. ◆*The boys were getting all revved up for the football game.*

rhyme or reason *n. phr.* A good plan or reason; a reasonable purpose or explanation.—Used in negative, interrogative, or conditional sentences. ◆*Don could see no rhyme or reason to the plot of the play.*

ride herd on *v. phr.* **1.** To patrol on horseback around a herd of animals to see that none of them wanders away. ◆*Two cowboys rode herd on the cattle being driven to market.* **2.** *informal* To watch closely and control; take care of. ◆*A special legislative assistant rides herd on the bills the president is anxious to have congress pass.*

ride out *v.* To survive safely; endure. ◆*The captain ordered all sails lowered so the ship could ride out the storm.*

riding high *adj.* Attracting attention; enjoying great popularity. ◆*After scoring the winning* *touchdown, John is riding high with his classmates.*

rid of Free of; away from; without the care or trouble. ◆*I wish you'd get rid of that cat!*

right on *adj., interj., slang, informal* **1.** Exclamation of animated approval: "Yes," "That's correct," "You're telling the truth," "We believe you," etc. ◆*Orator: And we shall see the promised land! Crowd: Right on!* **2.** Correct; to the point; accurate. ◆*The reverend's remark was right on!*

right out *or* **straight out** *adv.* Plainly; in a way that hides nothing; without waiting or keeping back anything. ◆*When Ann entered the beauty contest her little brother told her straight out that she was crazy.*

ring a bell *v. phr.* To make you remember something; sound familiar. ◆*When Ann told Jim the name of the new teacher it rang a bell, and Jim said, "I went to school with John Smith."*

ring in the New Year *v. phr.* To clink with glasses filled with champagne and wish one another a happy New Year at midnight on December 31. ◆*We rang in the New Year and wished one another peaceful and worry-free times.*

ring up *v.* **1.** To add and record on a cash register. ◆*The supermarket clerk rang up Mrs. Smith's purchases and told her she owed $33.* ◆*Business was bad Tuesday; we didn't ring up a sale all morning.* **2.** *informal* To telephone. ◆*Sally rang up Sue and told her the news.*

rip off *v., slang* (stress on *off*) Steal. ◆*The hippies ripped off the grocery store.*

rip-off *n., slang* (stress on *rip*) An act of stealing or burglary. ◆*Those food prices are so high, it's almost a rip-off.*

road hog *n., informal* A car driver who takes more than his share of the road. ◆*A road hog forced John's car into the ditch.*

rob one blind *v. phr.* To take everything away from someone in a holdup or by dishonest court action. ◆*When John was divorced from Melanie, she robbed him blind.*

rob Peter to pay Paul *v. phr.* To change one duty or need for another; take from one person or thing to pay another. ◆*Trying to study a lesson for one class during another class is like robbing Peter to pay Paul.*

rob the cradle *v. phr., informal* To have dates with or marry a person much younger than yourself. ◆*When the old woman married a young man, everyone said she was robbing the cradle.*

rock the boat *v. phr., informal* To make trouble and risk losing or upsetting something; cause a disturbance that may spoil a plan. ◆*Politicians don't like to rock the boat around election time.*

roll around *v., informal* To return at a regular or usual time; come back. ◆*When winter rolls around, out come the skis and skates.*

roller coaster ride *n. phr.* Extreme emotional upheaval, due to ups and down's in one's life. ◆*Poor Mary has been on an emotional roller coaster ride. First her* *husband died; then she met a wonderful new man, who also died. She doesn't know what to do next.*

rolling stone gathers no moss A person who changes jobs or where he lives often will not be able to save money or things of his own.—A proverb. ♦*Uncle Willie was a rolling stone that gathered no moss. He worked in different jobs all over the country.*

roll out the red carpet *v. phr.* 1. To welcome an important guest by putting a red carpet down for him to walk on. ♦*They rolled out the red carpet for the Queen when she arrived in Australia.* 2. To greet a person with great respect and honor; give a hearty welcome. ♦*Margaret's family rolled out the red carpet for her teacher when she came to dinner.*

roll up one's sleeves To get ready for a hard job; prepare to work hard or seriously. ♦*When Paul took his science examination, he saw how little he knew about science. He rolled up his sleeves and went to work.*

root for *v. phr.* To cheer for; applaud; support. ♦*During the Olympics one usually roots for the team of one's own country.*

rope in *v., informal* 1. To use a trick to make (someone) do something; deceive; fool. ♦*The company ropes in high school students to sell magazine subscriptions by telling them big stories of how much money they can earn.* 2. To get (someone to join or help); persuade to do something. ♦*Martha roped in Charles to help her decorate the gym for the party.*

rope into *v., informal* 1. To trick into; persuade dishonestly. ♦*Jerry let the big boys rope him into stealing some apples.* 2. To get (someone) to join in; persuade to work at. ♦*It was Sue's job to bathe the dog but she roped Sam into helping her.*

rough-and-ready *adj.* 1. Not finished in detail; not perfected; rough but ready for use now. ♦*We asked Mr. Brown how long it would take to drive to Chicago and his rough-and-ready answer was two days.* 2. Not having nice manners but full of energy and ability. ♦*Jim is a rough-and-ready character; he'd rather fight than talk things over.*

rough up *v.* To attack or hurt physically; treat roughly; beat. ♦*Three boys were sent home for a week because they roughed up a player on the visiting team.*

round off *v.* 1. To make round or curved. ♦*John decided to round off the corners of the table he was making so that no one would be hurt by bumping them.* 2. To change to the nearest whole number. ♦*The teacher said to round off the averages.* 3. To end in a satisfactory way; put a finishing touch on; finish nicely. ♦*We rounded off the dinner with mixed nuts.*

round robin *n. phr.* A contest or games in which each player or team plays every other player or team in turn.—Often used like an adjective. ♦*The tournament will be a round robin for all the high school teams in the city.*

roundup *n.* (stress on *round*) A muster; an inspection; a gathering together. ♦*The police* *roundup of all suspected drug dealers took place early in the morning.*

round up *v.* (stress on *up*) **1.** To bring together (cattle or horses). ◆*Cowboys round up their cattle in the springtime to brand the new calves.* **2.** *informal* To collect; gather. ◆*Dave rounded up many names for his petition.*

rub elbows *also* **rub shoulders** *v. phr.* To be in the same place (with others); meet and mix. ◆*On a visit to the United Nations Building in New York, you may rub elbows with people from faraway lands.*

rub it in *v. phr., slang* To remind a person again and again of an error or shortcoming; tease; nag. ◆*I know my black eye looks funny. You don't need to rub it in.*

rub off *v.* To pass to someone near as if by touching. ◆*Jimmy is very lucky; I wish some of his luck would rub off on me.*

rub out *v. slang* To destroy completely; kill; eliminate. ◆*The gangsters told the storekeeper that if he did not pay them to protect him, someone would rub him out.*

rub the wrong way *v. phr., informal* To make (someone) a little angry; do something not liked by (someone); annoy; bother. ◆*John's bragging rubbed the other boys the wrong way.*

rule out *v.* **1.** To say that (something) must not be done; not allow; *also:* decide against. ◆*The principal ruled out dances on school nights.* **2.** To show that (someone or something) is not a possibility; make it unnecessary to think about; remove (a chance). ◆*The doctor took X rays to rule out the chance of*

broken bones. **3.** To make impossible; prevent. ◆*Father's illness seems to rule out college for Jean.*

run a risk *or* **take a risk** *v. phr.* To be open to danger or loss; put yourself in danger; be unprotected. ◆*I was afraid to run the risk of betting on the game.*

run around in circles *v. phr.* To waste time in repetitious movements; be confused. ◆*There was such a crowd in the lobby that I ran around in circles trying to find my group.*

run around *or* **chase around** *v., informal* To go to different places for company and pleasure; be friends. ◆*Tim hasn't been to a dance all year; with school work and his job, he hasn't time to run around.*

run away with *v.* **1.** To take hold of; seize. ◆*The boys thought they saw a ghost in the old house last night; they let their imagination run away with them.* **2.** To be much better or more noticeable than others; win easily. ◆*Our team ran away with the game in the last half.*

run down *v.* (stress on *down*) **1.** To crash against and knock down or sink. ◆*Jack rode his bicycle too fast and almost ran down his little brother.* **2a.** To chase until exhausted or caught. ◆*The dogs ran down the wounded deer.* **2b.** To find by hard and thorough search; *also:* trace to its cause or beginning. ◆*The policeman ran down proof that the burglar had robbed the store.* **3.** *informal* To say bad things about; criticize. ◆*Suzy ran down the club because the girls wouldn't let her join.* **4.** To stop working; not run or go.

◆*The battery in Father's car ran down this morning.* **5.** To get into poor condition; look bad. ◆*A neighborhood runs down when the people don't take care of their houses.*

run-down *adj.* (stress on *run*) In poor health or condition; weak or needing much work. ◆*Grandma caught a cold because she was very run-down from loss of sleep.*

run for it *or* **make a run for it** *v. phr.* To dash for safety; make a speedy escape. ◆*The bridge the soldiers were on started to fall down and they had to run for it.*

run in *v. phr.* (stress on *in*) **1.** *informal* To take to jail; arrest. ◆*The policeman ran the man in for peddling without a license.* **2.** To make a brief visit. ◆*The neighbor boy ran in for a minute to see Bob's newest model rocket.*

run-in *n.* (stress on *run*) **1.** A traffic accident. ◆*My car was wrecked when I had a run-in with a small truck.* **2.** A violent quarrel. ◆*John had a nasty run-in with his boss and was fired.*

run in the blood *or* **run in the family** *v. phr.* To be a common family characteristic; be learned or inherited from your family. ◆*Red hair runs in the family.*

run into *v.* **1.** To mix with; join with. ◆*If the paint brush is too wet, the red paint will run into the white on the house.* ◆*This small brook runs into a big river in the valley below.* **2.** To add up to; reach; total. ◆*Car repairs can run into a lot of money.* ◆*A good dictionary may run into several editions.* **3a.** Bump; crash into; hit. ◆*Joe lost control of his bike and ran into a tree.* **3b.** To meet by chance.

◆*I ran into Joe yesterday on Main Street.* **3c.** Be affected by; get into. ◆*I ran into trouble on the last problem on the test.*

run into the ground *v. phr., informal* **1.** To do or use (something) more than is wanted or needed. ◆*It's all right to borrow my hammer once in a while, but don't run it into the ground.* **2.** To win over or defeat (someone) completely. ◆*We lost the game today, but tomorrow we'll run them into the ground.*

run its course *v. phr.* To fulfill a normal development; terminate a normal period. ◆*Your flu will run its course; in a few days you'll be back on your feet.*

run off *v., phr.* (stress on *off*) **1.** To produce with a printing press or duplicating machine. ◆*The print shop ran off a thousand copies of the newspaper.* **2.** To drive away. ◆*The boys saw a dog digging in mother's flower bed, and they ran him off.*

run-off *n.* (stress on *run*) A second election held to determine the winner when the results of the first one were inconclusive. ◆*The senatorial race was so close that the candidates will have to hold a run-off.*

run-of-the-mill *adj.* Of a common kind; ordinary; usual. ◆*It was just a run-of-the-mill movie.*

runner-up *n.* The person who finishes second in a race or contest; the one next after the winner. ◆*Sylvia was runner-up in the Miss Illinois contest.*

run out *v.* **1a.** To come to an end; be used up. ◆*We'd better do our Christmas shopping; time is running out.* **1b.** To use all of the supply; be troubled by not having enough. ◆*The car ran* *out of gas three miles from town.* **2.** *informal* To force to leave; expel. ✦*Federal agents ran the spies out of the country.*

run out on *v. phr.* To leave someone in the lurch; abandon another. ✦*When Ted ran out on Delores, she got so angry that she sued him for divorce.*

run over *v.* **1.** To be too full and flow over the edge; spill over. ✦*Billy forgot he had left the water on, and the tub ran over.* **2.** To try or go over (something) quickly; practice briefly. ✦*During the lunch hour, Mary ran over her history facts so she would remember them for the test.* **3.** To drive on top of; ride over. ✦*At night cars often run over small animals that are blinded by the headlights.*

run scared *v. phr.* To expect defeat, as in a political campaign. ✦*The one-vote defeat caused him to run scared in every race thereafter.*

run short *v. phr.* **1.** To not have enough. ✦*We are running short of sugar.* **2.** To be not enough in quantity. ✦*We are out of potatoes and the flour is running short.*

run that by me again! *v. phr., informal command* Repeat what you just said, as I couldn't understand you. ✦*"Run that by me again," Ted cried. "This telephone connection is very bad."*

run the gauntlet *v. phr.* **1.** To be made to run between two lines of people facing each other and be hit by them with clubs or other weapons. ✦*Joe had to run the gauntlet as part of his initiation into the club.* **2.** To face a hard test; bear a painful experience. ✦*Ginny had to run the gauntlet of her mother's ques-*

tions about how the ink spot got on the dining room rug.

run through *v.* **1.** To make a hole through, especially with a sword; pierce. ✦*The pirate was a good swordsman, but the hero finally ran him through.* **2.** To spend recklessly; use up wastefully. ✦*The rich man's son quickly ran through his money.* **3.** To read or practice from beginning to end without stopping. ✦*The visiting singer ran through his numbers with the orchestra just before the program.*

run up *v. phr.* **1.** To add to the amount of; increase. ✦*Karl ran up a big bill at the bookstore.* **2.** To pull (something) upward on a rope; put (something) up quickly. ✦*The pirates ran up the black flag.*

run wild *v. phr.* To be or go out of control. ✦*The students ran wild during spring vacation.*

rush hour *n. phr.* The time roughly from 7 to 9 A.M., and 3 to 6 P.M. in major American cities, when cars can only go slowly; the busiest commuting time. ✦*It's a bad idea to try driving during rush hour, when everyone is trying to get to work or home from work.*

rush off *v. phr.* To depart in great haste. ✦*I have no time to eat breakfast this morning; there is a special meeting so I must rush off to work.*

Russian roulette *n.* A game of chance in which one bullet is placed in a revolver, the cartridge cylinder is spun, and the player aims the gun at his own head and pulls the trigger. ✦*Only a fool would risk playing Russian roulette.*

sack in/out v., slang To go to sleep for a prolonged period (as in from night to morning). ◆*Where are you guys going to sack in/sack out?*

sack rat n. phr., slang A person who sleeps too much. ◆*My roommate John in a regular sack rat; it takes a major effort to wake him up for breakfast.*

sacred cow n. A person or thing that is never criticized, laughed at, or insulted even if it deserves such treatment. ◆*Motherhood is a sacred cow to most politicians.*

sail into v., informal 1. To attack with great strength; begin hitting hard. ◆*George grabbed a stick and sailed into the dog.* 2. To scold or criticize very hard. ◆*The coach really sailed into Bob for dropping the pass.*

salt of the earth n. phr., informal One who helps to make society good and wholesome; a basically good or valuable person. ◆*Everyone here considers Syd and Susan the salt of the earth because they are so generous.*

save face v. phr. To save your good reputation, popularity, or dignity when something has happened or may happen to hurt you; hide something that may cause you shame. ◆*The colonel who lost the battle saved face by showing his orders from the general.*

save one's breath v. phr., informal To keep silent because talking will not help; not talk because it will do no good. ◆*Save your breath; the boss will never give you the day off.*

save the day v. phr. To bring about victory or success, especially when defeat is likely. ◆*The forest fire was nearly out of control when suddenly it rained heavily and saved the day.*

save up v. phr. To put away for future use; keep as savings; save. ◆*John was saving up for a new bicycle.*

say a mouthful 1. v. phr., slang To say something of great importance or meaning; say more by a sentence than the words usually mean.—Usually in past tense. ◆*Tom said a mouthful when he guessed that company was coming to visit. A dozen people came.* 2. v. phr., informal To vent one's honest opinion, even in anger. ◆*He sure said a mouthful when he told his boss what was wrong with our business.*

say one's peace or **speak one's piece** v. phr. To say openly what you think; say, especially in public, what you usually say or are expected to say. ◆*Every politician got up and said his piece about how good the mayor was and then sat down.*

say the word v. phr., informal To say or show that you want something or agree to something; show a wish, willingness, or readiness; give a sign; say yes; say so. ◆*Just say the word and I will lend you the money.*

say uncle also **cry uncle** v. phr., informal To say that you surrender; admit that you have lost; admit a defeat; give up. ◆*The bully twisted Jerry's arm and said, "Cry uncle."*

scare out of one's wits or **scare stiff** or **scare the daylights out of** v. phr., informal To frighten very much. ◆*The owl's hooting* scared him out of his wits. ♦The child was scared stiff in the dentist's chair. ♦Pete's ghost story scared the daylights out of the smaller boys.

scot-free adj. phr. Without punishment; completely free. ♦In spite of his obvious guilt, the jury acquitted him and he got off scot-free.

scrape the bottom of the barrel v. phr., informal To use or take whatever is left after the most or the best has been taken; accept the leftovers. ♦The garage owner had to scrape the bottom of the barrel to find a qualified mechanic to work for him.

scratch one's back v. phr., informal To do something kind and helpful for someone or to flatter him in the hope that he will do something for you. Usually used in the expression "You scratch my back and I'll scratch yours." ♦Mary asked Jean to introduce her to her brother. Jean said, "You scratch my back and I'll scratch yours."

scratch the surface v. phr. To learn or understand very little about something.—Usually used with a limiting adverb (as only, hardly). ♦We thought we understood Africa but when we made a trip there we found we had only scratched the surface.

scream bloody murder v. phr., informal To yell or protest as strongly as one can. ♦When the thief grabbed her purse, the woman screamed bloody murder.

screw around v. phr., vulgar, avoidable To hang around idly without accomplishing anything, to loaf about, to beat or hack around. ♦You guys are no longer welcome here; all you do is screw around all day.

screw up v. phr., slang, semi-vulgar, best avoided (stress on up) 1. To make a mess of, to make an error which causes confusion. ♦The treasurer screwed up the accounts of the Society so badly that he had to be fired. 2. To cause someone to be neurotic or maladjusted. ♦Her divorce screwed her up so badly that she had to go to a shrink.

screw-up n. (stress on screw) A mistake; an error; a confusing mess. ♦ "What a screw-up!" the manager cried when he realized that the bills were sent to the wrong customers.

search me informal I don't know; how should I know?—May be considered rude. ♦When I asked her what time it was, she said, "Search me, I have no watch."

search one's heart or **search one's soul** v. phr., formal To study your reasons and acts; try to discover if you have been fair and honest. ♦The teacher searched his heart trying to decide if he had been unfair in failing Tom.—**heart-searching** or **soul-searching** n. or adj. ♦The minister preached a soul-searching sermon about the thoughtless ways people hurt each other.

second-guess v. phr. 1. To criticize another's decision with advantage of hindsight. ♦The losing team's coach is always second-guessed. 2. To guess what someone else intends or would think or do. ♦Television planners try to second-guess the public.

second thought *n.* A change of ideas or opinions resulting from more thought or study. ♦*Your second thoughts are very often wiser than your first ideas.*

second wind *also* **second breath** *n.* **1.** The easier breathing that follows difficult breathing when one makes a severe physical effort, as in running or swimming. ♦*We climbed with labored breathing for half an hour, but then got our second wind and went up more easily.* **2.** *informal* The refreshed feeling you get after first becoming tired while doing something and then becoming used to it. ♦*Tom became very tired of working at his algebra, but after a while he got his second wind and began to enjoy it.*

security blanket *n., slang, colloquial* An idea, person, or object that one holds on to for psychological reassurance or comfort as infants usually hang on to the edge of a pillow, a towel, or a blanket. ♦*Sue has gone to Aunt Mathilda for a chat; she is her security blanket.*

see about *v.* **1.** To find out about; attend to. ♦*If you are too busy, I'll see about the train tickets.* **2.** *informal* To consider; study. ♦*I cannot take time now but I'll see about your plan when I have time.*

see fit *or* **think fit** *v. phr.* To decide that an action is necessary, wise, or advisable; choose. ♦*Jim asked "Dad, what time should I come home after the dance?" His father answered, "You may do as you see fit."*

see off *v.* To go to say or wave goodbye to. ♦*When Marsha* *flew to Paris, Flo saw her off at the airport.*

see out *v.* **1.** To go with to an outer door. ♦*A polite man sees his company out after a party.* **2.** To stay with and finish; not quit. ♦*Pete's assignment was hard but he saw it out to the end.*

see red *v. phr., informal* To become very angry. ♦*Whenever anyone teased John about his weight, he saw red.*

see stars *v. phr., informal* To imagine you are seeing stars as a result of being hit on the head. ♦*When Ted was hit on the head by the ball, he saw stars.*

see the light *v. phr., informal* To understand or agree, often suddenly; accept another's explanation or decision. ♦*Mary thought it was fun to date older boys but when they started drinking, she saw the light.*

see the light at the end of the tunnel *v. phr., informal* To anticipate the happy resolution of a prolonged period of problems. ♦*We've been paying on our house mortgage for many years, but at long last we can see the light at the end of the tunnel.*

see the light of day *v. phr.* To be born or begun. ♦*The children visited the old house where their great-grandfather first saw the light of day.*

see things *v. phr., informal* To imagine sights which are not real; think you see what is not there. ♦*She woke her husband to tell him she had seen a face at the window, but he told her she was seeing things.*

see to *also* **look to** *v.* To attend to; take care of; do whatever needs to be done about. ♦*While*

Donna bought the theatre tickets, I saw to the parking of the car.

see to it *v. phr.* To take care; take the responsibility; make sure. Used with a noun clause. ◆*We saw to it that the child was fed and bathed.*

seed money *n. phr.* A small grant or donation for others to be able to start a new venture. ◆*All you need is some seed money and you can set up your own desktop publishing firm.*

sell down the river *v. phr.* To give harmful information about someone or something to one's enemies; betray. ◆*The traitor sold his country down the river to the enemy army.*

sell off *v. phr.* To liquidate one's holdings of certain set items. ◆*The retired professor had to sell off his rare butterfly collection to meet his health expenses.*

sellout *n.* (stress on *sell*) **1.** A betrayal or act of treason. ◆*The spy's behavior during the Cold War was a classical sellout.*

sell out *v.* (stress on *out*) **1a.** To sell all of a certain thing which a store has in stock. ◆*In the store's January white sale the sheets and pillowcases were sold out in two days.* **1b.** To sell all the stock and close the store; go out of business. ◆*The local hardware store sold out last month and was replaced by a cafe.* **2.** *informal* To be unfaithful to your country for money or other reward; be disloyal; sell a secret; accept a bribe. ◆*In the Revolutionary War, Benedict Arnold sold out to the British.*

send up *v. phr., colloquial* To sentence (someone) to prison. ◆*Did you know that Milton Shaeffer was sent up for fifteen years?*

set about *v.* To begin; start. ◆*Benjamin Franklin set about learning the printer's trade at an early age.*

set aside *v.* **1.** To separate from the others in a group or collection. ◆*She set aside the things in the old trunk which she wanted to keep.* **2.** To select or choose from others for some purpose. ◆*The governor set aside a day for thanksgiving.* **3.** To pay no attention to (something); leave out. ◆*The complaint was set aside as of no importance.* **4.** *formal* To refuse to accept; annul; cancel as worthless or wrong. ◆*The Supreme Court set aside the decision of the lower courts.*

setback *n.* (stress on *set*) A disadvantage; a delay. ◆*We suffered a major setback when my wife lost her job.*

set back *v.* (stress on *back*) **1.** To cause to put off or get behind schedule; slow up; check. ◆*The cold weather set back the planting by two weeks.* **2.** *informal* To cause to pay out or to lose (a sum of money); cost. ◆*His new car set him back over $3000.*

set forth *v., formal* **1.** To explain exactly or clearly. ◆*The President set forth his plans in a television talk.* **2.** To start to go somewhere; begin a trip. ◆*The troop set forth on their ten-mile hike early.*

set in *v.* To begin; start; develop. ◆*He did not keep the cut clean and infection set in.* ◆*The wind set in from the east.*

set in one's ways *adj. phr.* Stubborn; opinionated; unchangeable. ◆*My grandfather is so old and set in his ways that he'll eat nothing new.*

set off *v.* **1.** To decorate through contrast; balance by difference. ◆*A small gold pin set off her plain dark dress.* **2.** To balance; make somewhat equal. ◆*Her great wealth, as he thought, set off her plain face.* **3a.** To begin to go. ◆*They set off for the West in a covered wagon.* **3b.** To cause to begin. ◆*An atomic explosion is created by setting off a chain reaction in the atom.* **3c.** To cause to explode. ◆*On July 4 we set off firecrackers in many places.*

set one's heart on *v. phr.* To want very much. ◆*He set his heart on that bike.*

set out *v.* **1.** To leave on a journey or voyage. ◆*The Pilgrims set out for the New World.* **2.** To decide and begin to try; attempt. ◆*George set out to improve his pitching.* **3.** To plant in the ground. ◆*The gardener set out some tomato seedlings.*

set sail *v. phr.* To begin a sea voyage; start sailing. ◆*The ship set sail for Europe.*

set store by *v. phr., informal* To like or value; want to keep. Used with a qualifying word between *set* and *store.* ◆*Pat doesn't set much store by Mike's advice.*

set the pace *v. phr.* To decide on a rate of speed of travel or rules that are followed by others. ◆*Louise set the pace in selling tickets for the school play.*

set the world on fire *v. phr., informal* To do something outstand-

ing; act in a way that attracts much attention or makes you famous. ◆*John works hard, but he will never set the world on fire.*

settle a score *also* **wipe out an old score** *v. phr.* To hurt (someone) in return for a wrong or loss. ◆*John settled an old score with Bob by beating him.*

settle down *v.* **1.** To live more quietly and sensibly; have a regular place to live and a regular job; stop acting wildly or carelessly, especially by growing up. ◆*John will settle down after he gets a job and gets married.* **2.** To become quiet, calm, or comfortable. ◆*Father settled down with the newspaper.*

settle for *v.* To be satisfied with (less); agree to; accept. ◆*Jim wanted $200 for his old car, but he settled for $100.*

settle up *v. phr.* To pay up; conclude monetary or other transactions. ◆*"Let's settle up,"* Carol's attorney said when she sued Don for a hefty sum of money after their divorce.*

set up *v.* **1.** To provide the money for the necessities for. ◆*When he was twenty-one, his father set him up in the clothing business.* **2.** To establish; start. ◆*The government has set up many hospitals for veterans of the armed forces.* **3.** To make ready for use by putting the parts together or into their right place. ◆*The men set up the new printing press.* **4.** To bring into being; cause. ◆*Ocean tides are set up by the pull between earth and the moon.* **5.** To claim; pretend. ◆*He set himself up to be a graduate of a medical school, but he was not.* **6.** To harm someone by entrapment or some other ruse. ♦*Joe was actually innocent of the robbery, but his "trusted friends" set him up, so the police found the gun in his car.*

setup *n. phr.* (stress on *set*) **1.** Arrangement, management, circumstances. ♦*Boy, you really have a wonderful setup in your office!* **2.** Financial arrangement. ♦*It is a fairly generous setup sending your uncle $1,000 a month.*

sewed up *adj. phr., informal* Won or arranged as you wish; decided. ♦*Dick thought he had the job sewed up, but another boy got it.*

sexual harassment *n. phr.* The act of constantly making unwanted advances of a sexual nature for which the offended party may seek legal redress. ♦*The court fined Wilbur Catwallender $750,000 for sexual harassment of two of his female employees.*

shack up with *v. phr., slang* To move in with (someone) of the opposite sex without marrying the person. ♦*Did you know that Ollie and Sue aren't married? They just decided to shack up for a while.*

shaggy dog (story) *n. phr.* A special kind of joke whose long and often convoluted introduction and development delay the effect of the punch line. ♦*Uncle Joe only seems to bore his audiences with his long shaggy dog jokes, for when he comes to the long-awaited punch line, he gets very few laughs.*

shake a leg *v. phr., slang* To go fast; hurry. ♦*Shake a leg! The bus won't wait.*

shakedown *n.* (stress on *shake*) **1.** A test. ♦*Let's take the new car out and give it a shakedown.* **2.** An act of extorting money by threatening. ♦*It was a nasty shakedown to get $500 from the old man, promising to protect him.*

shake down *v. phr.* (stress on *down*) **1.** To cause to fall by shaking. ♦*He shook some pears down from the tree.* **2.** *informal* To test, practice, get running smoothly (a ship or ship's crew). ♦*The captain shook down his new ship on a voyage to the Mediterranean Sea.* **3.** *slang* To get money from by threats. ♦*The gangsters shook the store owner down every month.*

shake up *v., informal* (stress on *up*) To bother; worry; disturb. ♦*The notice about a cut in pay shook up everybody in the office.*

shake-up *n.* (stress on *shake*) A change; a reorganization. ♦*After the scandal there was a major shake-up in the Cabinet.*

shape up *v. phr., informal* **1.** To begin to act or work right; get along satisfactorily. ♦*"How is the building of the new gym coming along?" "Fine. It's shaping up very well."* **2.** To show promise. ♦*Plans for our picnic are shaping up very well.*

shell out *v., informal* To pay or spend. ♦*Dick had to shell out a lot of money for his new car.*

shine up to *v., slang* To try to please; try to make friends with. ♦*Smedley shines up to all the pretty girls.*

shoe on the other foot The opposite is true; places are changed. ♦*He was my captain in the* *army but now the shoe is on the other foot.*

shoo-in *n., informal* Someone or something that is expected to win; a favorite; sure winner. ◆*Chris is a shoo-in to win a scholarship.* ◆*This horse is a shoo-in. He can't miss winning.*

shoot one's wad *v. phr. slang, colloquial* **1.** To spend all of one's money. ◆*We've shot our wad for the summer and can't buy any new garden furniture.* **2.** To say everything that is on one's mind. ◆*Joe feels a lot better now that he's shot his wad at the meeting.*

shoot out *v.* **1.** To fight with guns until one person or side is wounded or killed; settle a fight by shooting.—Used with *it.* ◆*The cornered bank robbers decided to shoot it out with the police.*

shoot questions at *v. phr.* To interrogate rapidly and vigorously. ◆*The attorney for the prosecution shot one question after another at the nervous witness.*

shoot straight *or* **shoot square** *v., informal* To act fairly; deal honestly. ◆*You can trust that salesman; he shoots straight with his customers.* ◆*We get along well because we always shoot square with each other.*—**straight shooter** *or* **square shooter** *n., informal* Bill is a square-shooter.—**straightshooting** *adj.* ◆*The boys all liked the straight-shooting coach.*

shoot the breeze *or* **bat the breeze** *or* **fan the breeze** *or* **shoot the bull** *v. phr., slang* To talk. ◆*Jim shot the breeze with his neighbor while the children were playing.* ◆*The fishermen*

were shooting the bull about the school of sailfish they had seen.

shoot the works *v. phr., slang* **1.** To spare no expense or effort; get or give everything. ◆*Billy shot the works when he bought his bicycle; he got a bell, a light, a basket, and chrome trimmings on it, too.* **2.** To go the limit; take a risk. ◆*The motor of Tom's boat was dangerously hot, but he decided to shoot the works and try to win the race.*

shoot up *v.* **1.** To grow quickly. ◆*Billy had always been a small boy, but when he was thirteen years old he began to shoot up.* **2.** To arise suddenly. ◆*As we watched, flames shot up from the roof of the barn.* **3.** *informal* To shoot or shoot at recklessly; shoot and hurt badly. ◆*The cowboys got drunk and shot up the bar room.* ◆*The soldier was shot up very badly.* **4.** To take drugs by injection. ◆*A heroin addict will shoot up as often as he can.*

shore up *v.* To add support to (something) where weakness is shown; make (something) stronger where support is needed; support. ◆*When the flood waters weakened the bridge, it was shored up with steel beams and sandbags until it could be rebuilt.*

short end *n.* The worst or most unpleasant part. ◆*The new boy got the short end of it because all the comfortable beds in the dormitory had been taken before he arrived.*

shorthanded *adj.* Understaffed; short on workers. ◆*With several employees gone for the holiday weekend and two dozen people* *in line, the rent-a-car agency suddenly found itself terribly shorthanded.*

shot in the arm *n. phr., informal* Something inspiring or encouraging. ♦*We were ready to quit, but the coach's talk was a shot in the arm.*

showdown *n.* (stress on *show*) A final challenge or confrontation during which both sides have to use all of their resources. ♦*You cannot know a country's military strength until a final showdown occurs.*

showoff *n.* (stress on *show*) A boastful person. ♦*Jim always has to be the center of attention; he is an insufferable showoff.*

show off *v. phr.* (stress on *off*) 1. To put out nicely for people to see; display; exhibit. ♦*The Science Fair gave Julia a chance to show off her shell collection.* 2. *informal* To try to attract attention; *also,* try to attract attention to. ♦*Joe hasn't missed a chance to show off his muscles since that pretty girl moved in next door.*

show up *v.* (stress on *up*) 1. To make known the real truth about (someone). ♦*The man said he was a mind reader, but he was shown up as a fake.* 2. To come or bring out; become or make easy to see. ♦*This test shows up your weaknesses in arithmetic.* 3. *informal* To come; appear. ♦*We had agreed to meet at the gym, but Larry didn't show up.*

shrug off *v.* To act as if you are not interested and do not care about something; not mind; not let yourself be bothered or hurt by. ♦*Alan shrugged off our ques-*

tions; he would not tell us what had happened.

shut off *v.* 1. To make (something like water or electricity) stop coming. ♦*Please shut off the hose before the grass gets too wet.* 2. To be apart; be separated from; *also* to separate from. ♦*Our camp is so far from the highway we feel shut off from the world when we are there.*

shut out *v.* 1. To prevent from coming in; block. ♦*During World War II, Malta managed to shut out most of the Italian and German bombers by throwing up an effective antiaircraft screen.* 2. To prevent (an opposing team) from scoring throughout an entire game. ♦*The Dodgers shut out the Reds, 5–0.*

shut up *v.* 1. *informal* To stop talking. ♦*Shut up and let Joe say something.* ♦*If you'll shut up for a minute, I'll tell you our plan.* 2. To close the doors and windows of. ♦*We got the house shut up only minutes before the storm hit.* 3. To close and lock for a definite period of time. ♦*The Smiths always spend Labor Day shutting up their summer home for the year.* ♦ 4. To confine. ♦*That dog bites. It should be shut up.*

sick and tired *adj.* 1. Feeling strong dislike for something repeated or continued too long; exasperated; annoyed. ♦*John is sick and tired of having his studies interrupted.* ♦*I've been studying all day, and I'm sick and tired of it.*

sidekick *n.* A companion; a close friend of lesser status. ♦*Wherever you see Dr. Howell, Dr. Percy, his* *youthful sidekick, is sure to be present as well.*

sign up v. **1.** To promise to do something by signing your name; join; sign an agreement. ◆*We will not have the picnic unless more people sign up.* **2.** To write the name of (a person or thing) to be in an activity; also, to persuade (someone) to do something. ◆*Betty decided to sign up her dog for obedience training.*

signed, sealed, and delivered adj. phr. Finished; completed; in a state of completion. ◆*"How is the campus renovation plan for the governor's office coming along?" the dean of the college asked. "Signed, sealed, and delivered," his assistant answered.*

simmer down v., informal To become less angry or excited; become calmer. ◆*Tom got mad, but soon simmered down.*

sing a different tune or **whistle a different tune** also **sing a new tune** v. phr., informal To talk or act in the opposite way; contradict something said before. ◆*Charles said that all smokers should be expelled from the team but he sang a different tune after the coach caught him smoking.*

sink in or **soak in** v., informal To be completely understood; be fully realized or felt. ◆*Everybody laughed at the joke but Joe; it took a moment for it to sink in before he laughed too.*

sit back v. **1.** To be built a distance away; stand away (as from a street). ◆*Our house sits back from the road.* **2.** To relax; rest, often while others are working; take time out. ◆*Sit back for a*

minute and think about what you have done.

sit by v. **1.** To stay near; watch and care for. ◆*Mother sat by her sick baby all night.* **2.** To sit and watch or rest especially while others work ◆*Don't just sit idly by while the other children are all busy.*

sit in v. (stress on *in*) **1.** To be a member; participate. ◆*We're having a conference and we'd like you to sit in.* also **sit in on:** To be a member of; participate in. ◆*We want you to sit in on the meeting.* **2.** To attend but not participate. Often used with *on*. ◆*Our teacher was invited to sit in on the conference.*

sit on v. **1.** To be a member of (a jury, board, commission), etc. ◆*Mr. Brown sat on the jury at the trial.* **2.** informal To prevent from starting or doing something; squelch. ◆*The teacher sat on Joe as soon as he began showing off.*

sitting duck n. phr. Someone in a vulnerable position, who doesn't know what danger he or she is facing. ◆*Many a widow is a sitting duck for men seeking a quick adventure.* ◆*Unsuspecting tourists, who leave their car doors open in national parks, may be sitting ducks for thieves and robbers.*

sit up v. (stress on *up*) **1.** To move into a sitting position. ◆*Joe sat up when he heard the knock on his bedroom door.* **2.** To stay awake instead of going to bed. ◆*Mrs. Jones will sit up until both of her daughters get home from the dance.* **3.** informal To be surprised. ◆*Janice really sat up when I told her the gossip about Tom.*

sit-up n. (stress on *sit*) A vigorous exercise in which the abdominal muscles are strengthened by locking one's feet in a fastening device and sitting up numerous times. ◆*Do a few sit-ups if you want to reduce your waist.*

skin off one's nose n. phr., slang Matter of interest, concern, or trouble to you. Normally used in the negative. ◆*Go to Jake's party if you wish. It's no skin off my nose.* ◆*Grace didn't pay any attention to our argument. It wasn't any skin off her nose.* ◆*You could at least say hello to our visitor. It's no skin off your nose.*

skip it v. phr., informal To forget all about it. ◆*When Jack tried to reward him for returning his lost dog, the man said to skip it.*

slap one's wrist v. phr. To receive a light punishment. ◆*She could have been fired for contradicting the company president in public, but all she got was a slap on the wrist.*

sleep around v. phr, slang, vulgar, avoidable To be free with one's sexual favors; to behave promiscuously. ◆*Sue Catwallender is a nice girl but she sleeps around an awful lot with all sorts of guys.*

sleep a wink v. phr. To get a moment's sleep; enjoy a bit of sleep.—Used in negative and conditional statements and in questions. ◆*I didn't sleep a wink all night.*

sleep like a log v. phr. To sleep very deeply and soundly. ◆*Although I am usually a light sleeper, I was so exhausted from the sixteen-hour transpacific flight that, once we got home, I slept like a log for twelve hours.*

sleep off v. phr. To sleep until the effect of too much alcohol or drugs passes. ◆*George had too many beers last night and he is now sleeping off the effects.*

sleep on v. To postpone a decision about. ◆*We will have to sleep on your invitation until we know whether we will be free Monday night.*

sleep with v. phr. To have a sexual affair with someone; have sex; copulate. ◆*It has been rumored in the office that the boss sleeps with all the girls he hires.*

slip of the pen n. phr. The mistake of writing something different from what you should or what you planned. ◆*That was a slip of the pen. I meant to write September, not November.* ◆*I wish you would forget it. That was a slip of the pen.*

slip of the tongue also **slip of the lip** n. phr. The mistake of saying something you had not wanted or planned to say; an error of speech. ◆*She didn't mean to tell our secret; it was a slip of the lip.*

slip one's mind v. phr. To forget something. ◆*I meant to mail those letters but it entirely slipped my mind.*

slipup n. (stress on *slip*) A mistake. ◆*"I'm sorry, sir. That was an unfortunate slipup," the barber said when he scratched the client's face.*

slip up v. phr. (stress on *up*) To make a mistake. ◆*Someone at the bank slipped up. There are only 48 pennies in this 50¢ roll of coins.*

slowdown n. (stress on *slow*) A period of lesser activity, usually in the economic sphere. ◆*We all* *hope the current slowdown in the economy will soon be over.*

slow down v. phr. (stress on *down*) To go more slowly than usual. ◆*The road was slippery, so Mr. Jones slowed down the car.* ◆*Pat once could run a mile in five minutes, but now that he's older he's slowing down.*

small fry n. 1. Young children. ◆*In the park, a sandbox is provided for the small fry.* 2. Something or someone of little importance. ◆*Large dairies ignore the competition from the small fry who make only a few hundred pounds of cheese a year.*

smash hit n., informal A very successful play, movie or opera. ◆*The school play was a smash hit.*

smell a rat v. phr., informal To be suspicious; feel that something is wrong. ◆*Every time Tom visits me, one of my ashtrays disappears. I'm beginning to smell a rat.*

smoke out v. phr. (stress on *out*) 1. To force out with smoke. ◆*The boys smoked a squirrel out of a hollow tree.* ◆*The farmer tried to smoke some gophers out of their burrows.* 2. informal To find out the facts about. ◆*It took the reporter three weeks to smoke out the whole story.*

smoke-out n. (stress on *smoke*) A successful conclusion of an act of investigative journalism revealing some long-kept secrets. ◆*Journalist Bob Woodward was the hero of the Watergate smoke-out.*

smoke screen n. phr. A camouflage; a veil; something used to cover or hide something. ◆*June hides her commercial interests*

behind a smoke screen of religious piety.

smoking gun n. phr. Material proof or crucial testimony that some crime has been committed. ◆*A DNA examination was the smoking gun that proved beyond any doubt that the accused rapist was indeed guilty.*

snake in the grass n. phr., informal A person who cannot be trusted; an unfaithful traitor; rascal. ◆*Some snake in the grass told the teacher our plans.*

snap out of v., informal To change quickly from a bad habit, mood, or feeling to a better one.— Often used with *it*. ◆*The coach told the lazy player to snap out of it.*

snapshot n. A small photograph, unlike a professional portrait. ◆*We took several snapshots of the scenery while driving around the island.*

sneeze at v., informal To think of as not important; not take seriously.—Used with negative or limiting words and in questions. ◆*Is a thousand dollars anything to sneeze at?* ◆*John finished third in a race with twenty other runners. That is nothing to sneeze at.*

snow job n., slang, informal 1. Insincere or exaggerated talk designed to gain the favors of someone. ◆*Joe gave Sue a snow job and she believed every word of it.* 2. The skillful display of technical vocabulary and prestige terminology in order to pass oneself off as an expert in a specialized field without really being a knowledgeable worker in that area. ◆*That talk* *by Nielsen on pharmaceuticals sounded very impressive, but I will not hire him because it was essentially a snow job.*

snow under v. 1. To cover over with snow. ♦*The doghouse was snowed under during the blizzard.* 2. *informal* To give so much of something that it cannot be taken care of; to weigh down by so much of something that you cannot do anything about it.—Usually used in the passive. ♦*The factory received so many orders that it was snowed under with work.*

soak up v. 1. To take up water or other liquid as a sponge does. ♦*The rag soaked up the water that I spilled.* 2. To use a sponge or something like a sponge to take up liquid. ♦*John soaked up the water with the rag.* 3. *informal* To take up into yourself in the way a sponge takes up water. ♦*Mary was lying on the beach soaking up the sun.*

sob story n. A story that makes you feel pity or sorrow; a tale that makes you tearful. ♦*The beggar told us a long sob story before he asked for money.*

sock it v. phr., also interj., slang, informal To give one's utmost; everything one is capable of; to give all one is capable of. ♦*Right on, Joe, sock it to 'em!* ♦*I was watching the debate on television and more than once Bill Buckley really socked it to them.*

so far, so good *informal* Until now things have gone well. ♦*So far, so good; I hope we keep on with such good luck.*

so long interj., informal Goodbye.—Used when you are leaving someone or he is leaving

you. ♦*So long, I will be back tomorrow.*

something else adj., slang, informal So good as to be beyond description; the ultimate; stupendous. ♦*Janet Hopper is really something else.*

song and dance n., informal 1. Foolish or uninteresting talk; dull nonsense. Usually used with give. ♦*I met Nancy today and she gave me a long song and dance about her family.* 2. A long lie or excuse, often meant to get pity. Usually used with give. ♦*Billy gave the teacher a song and dance about his mother being sick as an excuse for being late.*

son of a bitch or **sunuvabitch** also **S.O.B.** n. phr., vulgar, avoidable (but becoming more and more acceptable, especially if said with a positive or loving intonation). Fellow, character, guy, individual. Negatively: ♦*Get out of here you filthy, miserable sunuvabitch!* Positively: ♦*So you won ten million dollars at the lottery, you lucky son of a bitch (or sunuvabitch)!*

son of a gun n. phr., slang 1. A bad person; a person not liked. ♦*I don't like Charley; keep that son of a gun out of here.* 2. A mischievous rascal; a lively guy.—Often used in a joking way. ♦*The farmer said he would catch the son of a gun who let the cows out of the barn.* 3. Something troublesome; a hard job. ♦*The test today was a son of a gun.*

sound off v. 1. To say your name or count "One! Two! Three! Four!" as you march.—Used as orders in U.S. military service. ♦*"Sound off!" said the ser-*

geant, and the soldiers shouted, "One! Two! Three! Four!" with each step as they marched. **2.** *informal* To tell what you know or think in a loud clear voice, especially to brag or complain. ◆*If you don't like the way we're doing the job, sound off!*

sound out *v.* To try to find out how a person feels about something, usually by careful questions. ◆*Alfred sounded out his boss about a day off from his job.*

souped-up *adj., informal* More powerful or faster because of changes and additions. ◆*Many teen-aged boys like to drive souped-up cars.*

spaced out *adj., slang, informal* Having gaps in one's train of thought, confused, incoherent; resembling the behavior of someone who is under the influence of drugs. ◆*Joe's been acting funny lately—spaced out, you might say.*

speak of the devil (and he appears) *or* **talk of the devil** A person comes just when you are talking about him.—A proverb. ◆*We were just talking about Bill when he came in the door. Speak of the devil (and he appears).*

speak out *or* **speak up** *v.* **1.** To speak in a loud or clear voice. ◆*The trucker told the shy boy to speak up.* **2.** To speak in support of or against someone or something. ◆*Willie spoke up for Dan as club president.*

speak up *v. phr.* **1.** To speak louder. ◆*Would you please speak up? We can't hear you in the back row.* **2.** To complain; voice one's opposition to something. ◆*If you think you are not treat-*

ed properly at work, don't be shy—speak up!

speed up *v.* To go faster than before; to make go faster. ◆*The car speeded up when it reached the country.*

spell out *v.* **1.** To say or read aloud the letters of a word, one by one; spell. ◆*John could not understand the word the teacher was saying, so she spelled it out on the blackboard.* **2.** To read slowly, have trouble in understanding. ◆*The little boy spelled out the printed words.* **3.** *informal* To explain something in very simple words; explain very clearly. ◆*The class could not understand the problem, so the teacher spelled it out for them.*

spill one's guts *v. phr.* To confess under interrogation; completely relate a story; name accomplices. ◆*After two hours of intensive interrogation the accused criminal spilled his guts, and led the police to the arrest of his fellow criminals.*

spill the beans *v. phr., informal* To tell a secret to someone who is not supposed to know about it. ◆*John's friends were going to have a surprise party for him, but Tom spilled the beans.*

spin a yarn *v. phr.* To tell a story of adventure with some exaggeration mixed in; embellish and protract such a tale. ◆*Uncle Fred, who used be a sailor, knows how to spin a fascinating yarn, but don't always believe everything he says.*

spine-chilling *adj.* Terrifying; causing great fear. ◆*Many children find the movie "Frankenstein" spine-chilling.*

spinoff n. (stress on *spin*) A byproduct of something else. ♦*The television soap opera "Knot's Landing" was considered a spinoff of "Dallas," with many of the same characters featured in both.*

spin off v. phr. (stress on *off*) To bring something into existence as a byproduct of something that already exists. ♦*When Dr. Catwallender opened his medical practice, he also spun off a small dispensary beside it where patients could get their prescriptions filled.*

spin one's wheels v. phr. **1.** Said of cars stuck in snow or mud whose wheels are turning without the car moving forward. ♦*There was so much snow on the driveway that my car's wheels were spinning in it and we couldn't get going.* **2.** To exert effort in a job without making any progress. ♦*I've been working for the firm for two decades, but I feel I am merely spinning my wheels.*

spitting image n. spit and image *informal* An exact likeness; a duplicate. ♦*John is the spitting image of his grandfather.*

split hairs v. phr. To find and argue about small and unimportant differences as if the differences are important. ♦*John is always splitting hairs; he often starts an argument about something small and unimportant.*

split the difference v. phr., *informal* To settle a money disagreement by dividing the difference, each person giving up half. ♦*Bob offered $25 for Bill's bicycle and Bill wanted $35; they split the difference.*

split ticket n. A vote for candidates from more than one party. ♦*Mr. Jones voted a split ticket.*

split up v. phr. (stress on *up*) **1.** To separate; get a divorce. ♦*After three years of marriage, the unhappy couple finally split up.* **2.** To separate something; divide into portions. ♦*The brothers split up their father's fortune among themselves after his death.*

split-up n. (stress on *split*) A separation or division into two or many smaller parts. ♦*The split-up of our company was due to the founder's untimely death.*

spoken for adj. Occupied; reserved; taken; already engaged or married. ♦*"Sorry, my boy," Mr. Jones said condescendingly, "but my daughter is already spoken for. She will marry Fred Wilcox next month."*

spoon-feed v. **1.** To feed with a spoon. ♦*Mothers spoon-feed their babies.* **2a.** To make something too easy for (a person). ♦*Bill's mother spoon-fed him and never let him think for himself.* **2b.** To make (something) too easy for someone. ♦*Some students want the teacher to spoon-feed the lessons.*

spring chicken n., *slang* A young person.—Usually used with *no*. ♦*Mr. Brown is no spring chicken, but he can still play tennis well.*

square away v. phr. **1.** To arrange the sails of a ship so that the wind blows from behind. ♦*The captain ordered the crew to square away and sail before the wind.* **2.** *informal* To put right for use or action. Used in the passive or participle. ♦*The liv-*

ing room was squared away for the guests. **3.** *informal* To stand ready to fight; put up your fists. ♦*Jack and Lee squared away.*

stab in the back[1] *v. phr., slang* To say or do something unfair that harms (a friend or someone who trusts you). ♦*Owen stabbed his friend Max in the back by telling lies about him.*

stab in the back[2] *n. phr., slang* An act or a lie that hurts a friend or trusting person; a promise not kept, especially to a friend. ♦*John stabbed his own friend in the back by stealing from his store.*

stab in the dark *n. phr.* A random attempt or guess at something without previous experience or knowledge of the subject. ♦*"You're asking me who could have hidden grandpa's will,"* Fred said. *"I really have no idea, but let me make a stab in the dark—I think my sister Hermione has it."*

stack the cards *v. phr.* **1.** To arrange cards secretly and dishonestly for the purpose of cheating. ♦*The gambler had stacked the cards against Bill.* **2.** To arrange things unfairly for or against a person; have things so that a person has an unfair advantage or disadvantage; make sure in an unfair way that things will happen.—Used in the passive with "in one's favor" or "against one." ♦*A tall basketball player has the cards stacked in his favor.*

stamping ground *n., informal* A place where a person spends much of his time. ♦*Pete's soda fountain is an after-school stamping ground.*

stamp out *v.* To destroy completely and make disappear. ♦*In the last few years, we have nearly stamped out polio by using vaccine.*

stand by *v.* **1.** To be close beside or near. ♦*Mary could not tell Jane the secret with her little brother standing by.* **2.** To be near, waiting to do something when needed. ♦*The policeman in the patrol car radioed the station about the robbery, and then stood by for orders.* **3.** To follow or keep (one's promise). *He is a boy who always stands by his promises.* **4.** To be loyal to; support; help. *When three big boys attacked Bill, Ed stood by him.* ♦*Some people blamed Harry when he got into trouble, but Joe stood by him.*

stand down *v. phr.* To stop being in a state of emergency. ♦*After the danger had passed, the commanding general ordered the troops to stand down.*

stand for *v.* **1.** To be a sign of; make you think of; mean. ♦*The letters "U.S.A." stand for "United States of America."* ♦*The written sign "=" in an arithmetic problem stands for "equals."* **2.** To speak in favor of something, or show that you support it. ♦*The new president stood for honest government.* **3.** *Chiefly British* To try to be elected for. ♦*Three men from London are standing for Parliament.* **4.** *informal* To allow to happen or to be done; permit.—Usually used in the negative. ♦*The teacher will not stand for fooling in the classroom.*

stand in awe of *v. phr.* To look upon with wonder; feel very respectful to. ♦*The soldier stood in awe of his officers.*

stand in for *v. phr.* To substitute for someone. ♦*The famous brain surgeon was called out of town, so his assistant had to stand in for him during the operation.*

standoffish *adj.* Stiff; aloof; reserved in manner. ♦*The famous chess player is hard to get to know because he is so standoffish.*

stand out *v.* 1. To go farther out than a nearby surface; project. ♦*A mole stood out on her cheek.* 2. To be more noticeable in some way than those around you; be higher, bigger, or better. ♦*Fred was very tall and stood out in the crowd.*

stand pat *v., informal* To be satisfied with things and be against a change. ♦*Bill had made up his mind on the question, and when his friends tried to change his mind, he stood pat.*

stand to reason *v. phr.* To seem very likely from the known facts. ♦*Joe is intelligent and studies hard; it stands to reason that he will pass the examination.*

stand trial *v. phr.* To submit to a trial by court. ♦*The case has been postponed and he may not have to stand trial until next April.*

stand up *v.* 1. To be strong enough to use hard or for a long time. ♦*A rocket must be built strongly to stand up under the blast-off.* 2. *informal* To make a date and then fail to keep it. ♦*June cried when Bill stood her up on their first date.*

stand up and be counted *v. phr.* To be willing to say what you

think in public; let people know that you are for or against something. ♦*The equal rights movement needs people who are willing to stand up and be counted.*

stand up to *v.* To meet with courage. ♦*Mary stood up to the snarling dog that leaped toward her.*

stand up with *v., informal* To be best man or maid of honor at a wedding. ♦*A groom often chooses his brother to stand up with him.*

stars in one's eyes *n. phr.* 1. An appearance or feeling of very great happiness or expectation of happiness. ♦*Mary gets stars in her eyes when she thinks of her boyfriend.* 2. A belief in the possibility of quick and lasting reforms in people and life and an eagerness to make such changes. ♦*Some inexperienced people get stars in their eyes when they think of improving the world.*—**starry-eyed** *adj.* Very happy and excited, perhaps with little reason; eager and self-confident about improving human nature and general conditions of life. ♦*Young people are often starry-eyed and eager to improve the world; they do not know how hard it is.*

start in *v., informal* 1. To begin to do something; start. ♦*Fred started in weeding the garden. The family started in eating supper.* 2. To begin a career. ♦*Bob started in as an office boy and became president.* 3. To give a first job to. ♦*The bank started him in as a clerk.*

start up *v.* 1. To begin operating. ♦*The driver started up the* *motor of the car.* **2.** To begin to play (music). ◆*The conductor waved his baton, and the band started up.* **3.** To rise or stand suddenly. ◆*When he heard the bell, he started up from his chair.*

stash bag *or* **stuff bag** *n., slang, informal* **1.** A small bag containing marijuana cigarettes or the ingredients for making them. ◆*The police are holding John because they found a stash bag full of the stuff on him.* **2.** Any small bag resembling a stash bag used for small personal items such as lipstick, driver's license, etc. ◆*Do you have any room for my keys in your stash bag?*

stay put *v. phr.* To stay in place; not leave. ◆*Harry's father told him to stay put until he came back.*

steal a march on *v. phr.* To get ahead of someone by doing a thing unnoticed; get an advantage over. ◆*The army stole a march on the enemy by marching at night and attacking them in the morning.*

steal one's thunder *v. phr.* To do or say something, intentionally or not, that another person has planned to say or do. ◆*Fred intended to nominate Bill for president, but John got up first and stole Fred's thunder.*

steal the show *v. phr.* To act or do so well in a performance that you get most of the attention and the other performers are unnoticed. ◆*Mary was in only one scene of the play, but she stole the show from the stars.*

steal the spotlight *v. phr.* To attract attention away from a person or thing that people

should be watching. ◆*When the maid walked on the stage and tripped over a rug, she stole the spotlight from the leading players.*

step in *v.* **1.** To go inside for a quick visit. ◆*It was a cold night, and when the policeman passed, we invited him to step in for a cup of coffee.* **2.** To begin to take part in a continuing action or discussion, especially without being asked. ◆*When the dogs began to fight, John stepped in to stop it before they were hurt.*

step on it *or* **step on the gas** *v. phr.* **1.** To push down on the gas pedal to make a car go faster. ◆*Be very careful when you step on the gas. Don't go too fast.* **2.** *informal* To go faster; hurry. ◆*Step on it, or we'll be late for school.*

step out on *v. phr.* To be unfaithful to one's marriage partner or steady lover. ◆*It is rumored that he has been stepping out on his wife. That's why she's so upset.*

stepped up *adj.* Carried on at a faster or more active rate; increased. ◆*To fill the increase in orders, the factory had to operate at a stepped-up rate.*

step up *v.* **1.** To go from a lower to a higher place. ◆*John stepped up onto the platform and began to speak.* **2.** To come towards or near; approach. ◆*The sergeant called for volunteers and Private Jones stepped up to volunteer.* **3.** To go or to make (something) go faster or more actively. ◆*When John found he was going to be late, he stepped up his pace.* **4.** To rise to a higher or more important position; be promoted. ◆*This year Mary* *is secretary of the club, but I am sure she will step up to president next year.*

step up to the plate *v. phr. from baseball* To face a challenge, to shoulder a responsibility. ◆*Eventually both the Palestinians and the Israelis will have to step up to the plate and start working in earnest on a viable peace plan.*

stick-in-the-mud *n., informal* An overcareful person; someone who is old-fashioned and fights change. ◆*Mabel said her mother was a real stick-in-the-mud to make a rule that she must be home by 10 o'clock on weeknights and 11:30 Saturdays.*

stick one's neck out *or* **stick one's chin out** *v. phr., informal* To do something dangerous or risky. ◆*When I was in trouble, Paul was the only one who would stick his neck out to help me.* ◆*John is always sticking his chin out by saying something he shouldn't.*

stick up *v., informal* (stess on *up*) To rob with a gun. ◆*In the old West, outlaws sometimes stuck up the stagecoaches.*

stick-up *n., informal* (stress on *stick*) A robbery by a man with a gun. ◆*Mr. Smith was the victim of a stick-up last night.*

stick with *v., informal* **1.** *or* **stay with** To continue doing; not quit. ◆*Fred stayed with his homework until it was done.* **2.** To stay with; not leave. ◆*Stick with me until we get out of the crowd.* **3.** To sell (someone) something poor or worthless; cheat. ◆*Father said that the man in the store tried to stick him with a bad TV set.* **4.** To leave (someone) with (something unpleasant); force to do or

keep something because others cannot or will not.—Used in the passive. ◆*Mr. Jones bought a house that is too big and expensive, but now he's stuck with it.*

stick with *v. phr.* To unfairly thrust upon; encumber one with. ◆*In the restaurant my friends stuck me with the bill although it was supposed to be Dutch treat.*

sticky fingers *n. phr., slang* **1.** The habit of stealing things you see and want. ◆*Don't leave money in your locker; some of the boys have sticky fingers.*

stir up *v.* **1.** To bring (something) into being, often by great exertion or activity; cause. ◆*It was a quiet afternoon, and John tried to stir up some excitement.* **2.** To cause (someone) to act; incite to action or movement; rouse. ◆*The coach's pep talk stirred up the team to win.*

stir up a hornet's nest *v. phr.* To make many people angry; do something that many people don't like. ◆*The principal stirred up a hornet's nest by changing the rules at school.*

stop off *v.* To stop at a place for a short time while going somewhere. ◆*We stopped off after school at the soda fountain before going home.*

straight from the horse's mouth *slang* Directly from the person or place where it began; from a reliable source or a person that cannot be doubted. ◆*They are going to be married. I got the news straight from the horse's mouth—their minister.*

straw in the wind *n. phr.* A small sign of what may happen. ◆*The doctor's worried face was a straw in the wind.*

straw poll *n. phr.* An informal survey taken in order to get an opinion. ◆*The results of our straw poll show that most faculty members prefer to teach between 9 and 11 A.M.*

strike a bargain *v. phr.* To arrive at a price satisfactory to both the buyer and the seller. ◆*After a great deal of haggling, they managed to strike a bargain.*

strike a chord *v. phr.* To find oneself in agreement with someone else's feelings and ideas. ◆*John's proposal to expand the firm's foreign trade struck a chord with the vice president, who had been thinking along similar lines on his own.*

strike it rich *v. phr., informal* **1.** To discover oil, or a large vein of minerals to be mined, or a buried treasure. ◆*The old prospector panned gold for years before he struck it rich.* **2.** To become rich or successful suddenly or without expecting to. ◆*John did not know that he had a rich Uncle John in Australia. John struck it rich when his uncle left his money to John.*

strike one funny *v. phr.* To appear or seem laughable, curious, ironic, or entertaining. ◆*"It strikes me funny," he said, "that you should refuse my invitation to visit my chateau in France. After all, you love both red wine and old castles."*

strike out *v.* **1.** To destroy something that has been written or drawn by drawing a line or cross through it or by erasing it. ◆*John misspelled "corollary." He struck it out and wrote it correctly.* **2.** To begin to follow a new path or a course of action

that you have never tried. ◆*The boy scouts struck out at daybreak over the mountain pass.* **3.** To put (a batter) out of play by making him miss the ball three times; *also:* To be put out of play by missing the ball three times. ◆*The pitcher struck out three men in the game.*

strike up *v.* **1a.** To start to sing or play. ◆*The President took his place on the platform, and the band struck up the national anthem.* **1b.** To give a signal to start (a band) playing. ◆*When the team ran on the field, the band director struck up the band.* **2.** To bring about; begin; start. ◆*It did not take Mary long to strike up acquaintances in her new school.*

string along *v., informal* **1.** To deceive; fool; lead on dishonestly. ◆*Mary was stringing John along for years but she didn't mean to marry him.* **2.** To follow someone's leadership; join his group. ◆*Those of you who want to learn about wild flowers, string along with Jake.*

string out *v.* To make (something) extend over a great distance or a long stretch of time. ◆*The city and county needed to string out the telephone poles for several miles.*

strings attached *adv. phr.* With some special proviso or condition that is a handicap. ◆*John inherited a large fortune but with the string attached that he could not touch a penny of it before his 28th birthday.*

strung out *adj., slang, colloquial* **1.** Nervous, jittery, jumpy; generally ill because of drug use or withdrawal symptoms. ◆*The only explanation I can think of* *for Max's behavior is that he must be strung out.* 2. To suffer because of a lack of something previously accustomed to, such as the love and affection of someone. ◆*Sue is all strung out for Jim; they've just split up.*

stuck on *slang* Very much in love with; crazy about. ◆*Judy thinks she is very pretty and very smart. She is stuck on herself.* ◆*Lucy is stuck on the football captain.*

stuck-up *adj., informal* Acting as if other people are not as good as you are; conceited; snobbish. ◆*Mary is very stuck-up, and will not speak to the poor children in her class.*

stuck with *adj. phr.* Left in a predicament; left having to take care of a problem caused by another. ◆*Our neighbors vanished without a trace and we got stuck with their cat and dog.*

sucker list *n., slang* A list of easily fooled people, especially people who are easily persuaded to buy things or give money. ◆*The crook got hold of a sucker list and started out to sell his worthless stock.*

suck in *v.* 1. *informal* To pull in by taking a deep breath and tightening the muscles; flatten. ◆*"Suck in those abdominal muscles," the gym teacher said.* 2. *slang* To make a fool of; cheat. ◆*The uneducated farmer was sucked in by a clever crook.*

sugar daddy *n., slang, semi-vulgar, avoidable* An older, well-to-do man, who gives money and gifts to a younger woman or girls, usually in exchange for sexual favors. ◆*Betty Morgan got a mink coat from her sugar daddy.*

sum up *v.* To put something into a few words; shorten into a brief summary; summarize. ◆*The teacher summed up the lesson in three rules.*

sunbelt *n., informal* A portion of the southern United States where the winter is very mild in comparison to other states. ◆*The Simpsons left Chicago for the sunbelt because of Jeff's rheumatism.*

sunny-side up *adj.* Fried on one side only. ◆*Barbara likes her eggs sunny-side up.*

sure thing 1. *n., informal* Something sure to happen; something about which there is no doubt. ◆*It's no fun betting on a sure thing.*—**sure thing** 2. *adv.* Of course; certainly. ◆*Sure thing, I'll be glad to do it for you.*

surf the Web *v. phr.* To look through information on the Internet. ◆*John can find answers for most of your questions; he can surf the Web like a professional.*

swallow one's pride *v. phr.* To bring your pride under control; humble yourself. ◆*After Bill lost the race, he swallowed his pride and shook hands with the winner.*

swallow one's words To speak unclearly; fail to put enough breath into your words. ◆*Phyllis was hard to understand because she swallowed her words.*

swear by *v.* 1. To use as the support or authority that what you are saying is truthful; take an oath upon. ◆*A witness swears by the Bible that he will tell the truth.* 2. To have complete confidence in; be sure of; trust completely. ♦*We can be sure that Fred will come on time, since his friend Tom swears by him.*

swear in *or* **swear into** *v.* To have a person swear or promise to do his duty as a member or an officer of an organization, government department, or similar group.—*Swear into* is used when the name of the group is given. ♦*At the inauguration, the Chief Justice of the Supreme Court swears in the new president.*

swear off *v., informal* To give up something you like or you have got in the habit of using by making a promise. ♦*Mary swore off candy until she lost ten pounds.*

swear out *v.* To get (a written order to do something) by swearing that a person has broken the law. ♦*The police swore out a warrant for the suspect's arrest.*

sweat blood *v. phr., slang* **1.** To be very much worried. ♦*The engine of the airplane stopped, and the pilot sweated blood as he glided to a safe landing.* **2.** To work very hard. ♦*Jim sweated blood to finish his composition on time.*

sweat out *v., informal* To wait anxiously; worry while waiting. ♦*Karl was sweating out the results of the college exams.*

sweep off one's feet *v. phr.* To make (someone) have feelings (as love or happiness) too strong to control; overcome with strong feeling; win sudden and complete acceptance by (someone) through the feelings. ♦*The handsome football captain swept Joan off her feet*

when he said so many things to her at the dance.

sweep under the rug *v. phr.* To hide or dismiss casually (something one is ashamed of or does not know what to do about). ♦*In many places, drug abuse by school children is swept under the rug.*

sweetie pie *n., informal* A person who is loved; darling; sweetheart. ♦*Arnold blushed with pleasure when Annie called him her sweetie pie.*

sweet on *adj. phr., informal* In love with; very fond of. ♦*John is sweet on Alice.*

sweet talk 1. *n., informal* Too much praise; flattery. ♦*Sometimes a girl's better judgment is overcome by sweet talk.* **2.** *v., informal* To get what you want by great praise; flatter. ♦*Polly could sweet talk her husband into anything.*

sweet tooth *n. phr.* A great weakness or predilection for sweets. ♦*Sue has such a sweet tooth that she hardly eats anything else but cake.*

swelled head *n., informal* A feeling that you are very important or more important than you really are. ♦*When John won the race, he got a swelled head.* ♦*Pretty girls shouldn't get a swelled head about it.*—**swell-headed** *adj. phr.*

swim against the current *or* **swim against the stream** *v. phr.* To do the opposite of what most people want to do; go against the way things are happening; struggle upstream. ♦*The boy who tries to succeed today without an education is swimming against the stream.*

switched on *adj., slang* **1.** In tune with the latest fads, ideas, and fashions. ◆*I dig Sarah, she is really switched on.* **2.** Stimulated; as if under the influence of alcohol or drugs. ◆*How come you're talking so fast? Are you switched on or something?*

sword of Damocles *n. phr., from Greek mythology* A constant threat or imminent danger. ◆*Nuclear war hangs over modern humanity's head like the sword of Damocles.*

tail wags the dog Said of situations in which a minor part is in control of the whole. ♦*He is just a minor employee at the firm, yet he gives everyone orders, a case of the tail wagging the dog.*

take a back seat *v. phr., informal* To accept a poorer or lower position; be second to something or someone else. ♦*During the war all manufacturing had to take a back seat to military needs.*

take a bath *v. phr., informal* To come to financial ruin. ♦*Boy, did we ever take a bath on that merger with Brown & Brown, Inc.*

take a crack at *v. phr.* To try doing something. ♦*It was a difficult challenge to reorganize our antiquated campus, but the resident architect decided to take a crack at it.*

take a dig at *v. phr.* To attack verbally; offend; denigrate. ♦*If you keep taking digs at me all the time, our relationship will be a short one.*

take a dim view of *v. phr.* **1.** To have doubts about; feel unsure or anxious about. ♦*Tom took a dim view of his chances of passing the exam.* **2.** To be against; disapprove. ♦*The teacher took a dim view of the class's behavior.*

take advantage of *v. phr.* **1.** To make good use of. ♦*The cat took advantage of the high grass to creep up on the bird.* ♦*Jim took advantage of Tracy's innocence, got her drunk, and raped her.* **2.** To treat (someone) unfairly for your own gain or help; make unfair use of.

take after *v.* To be like because of family relationship; to have the same looks or ways as (a parent or ancestor). ♦*She takes after her father's side of the family in looks.*

take a shot at *v. phr.* To try casually; attempt to do. ♦*"Can you handle all these new book orders?" Tom asked. "I haven't done it before," Sally replied, "but I can sure take a shot at it."*

take a stand *v. phr.* To assert one's point of view; declare one's position. ♦*It is time for American society to take a stand against crime.*

take a turn *v. phr.* To become different; change. ♦*Mary's fever suddenly took a bad turn.* Used with *for the better* or *for the worse.* ♦*In the afternoon the weather took a turn for the better.*

take back *v.* **1.** To change or deny something offered, promised, or stated. ♦*I take back my offer to buy the house now that I've had a good look at it.* **2.** admit to making a wrong statement. ♦*I want you to take back the unkind things you said about Kenneth.*

take by storm *v. phr.* **1.** To capture by a sudden or very bold attack. ♦*The army did not hesitate. They took the town by storm.* **2.** To win the favor or liking of; make (a group of people) like or believe you. ♦*John gave Jane so much attention that he took her by storm, and she said she would marry him.*

take care of *v. phr.* **1.** To attend to; supply the needs of. ♦*She stayed home to take care of the* *baby.* 2. *informal* To deal with; do what is needed with. ♦*I will take care of that letter.*

take down *v.* 1. To write or record (what is said). ♦*I will tell you how to get to the place; you had better take it down.* 2. To pull to pieces; take apart. ♦*It will be a big job to take that tree down.* ♦*In the evening the campers put up a tent, and the next morning they took it down.* 3. *informal* To reduce the pride or spirit of; humble. ♦*Bob thought he was a good wrestler, but Henry took him down.*

take down a notch *or* take down a peg *v. phr., informal* To make (someone) less proud or sure of himself. ♦*The team was feeling proud of its record, but last week the boys were taken down a peg by a bad defeat.*

take effect *v. phr.* 1. To have an unexpected or intended result; cause a change. ♦*It was nearly an hour before the sleeping pill took effect.* 2. To become lawfully right, or operative. ♦*The new tax law will not take effect until January.*

take exception to *v. phr.* To speak against; find fault with; be displeased or angered by; criticize. ♦*There was nothing in the speech that you could take exception to.*

take for *v.* To suppose to be; mistake for. ♦*Do you take me for a fool?*

take for a ride *v. phr., slang* 1. To take out in a car intending to murder. ♦*The gang leader decided that the informer must be taken for a ride.* 2. To play a trick on; fool. ♦*The girls told Linda that a movie star was visiting the school, but she did not*

believe them; she thought they were taking her for a ride. 3. To take unfair advantage of; fool for your own gain. ♦*His girlfriend really took him for a ride before he stopped dating her.*

take for granted *v. phr.* 1. To suppose or understand to be true. ♦*A teacher cannot take it for granted that students always do their homework.* 2. To accept or become used to (something) without noticing especially or saying anything. ♦*No girl likes to have her boyfriend take her for granted; instead, he should always try to make her like him better.*

take heart *v. phr.* To be encouraged; feel braver and want to try. ♦*The men took heart from their leader's words and went on to win the battle.*

take ill *or* take sick *v.* To become sick. ♦*Father took sick just before his birthday.*—Used in the passive with the same meaning. ♦*The man was taken ill on the train.*

take in *v.* 1. To include. ♦*The country's boundaries were changed to take in a piece of land beyond the river.* 2. To go and see; visit. ♦*We planned to take in Niagara Falls and Yellowstone Park on our trip.* 3. To make smaller. ♦*This waistband is too big; it must be taken in about an inch.* 4. To grasp with the mind; understand. ♦*He didn't take in what he read because his mind was on something else.* 5a. To deceive; cheat; fool. ♦*The teacher was taken in by the boy's innocent manner.* 5b. To accept without question; believe. ♦*The magician did many tricks, and the children took it all in.* **6a.** To receive; get. ◆*The senior class held a dance to make money and took in over a hundred dollars.* **6b.** Let come in; admit. ◆*When her husband died, Mrs. Smith took in boarders.* **7.** To see or hear with interest; pay close attention to. ◆*When Bill told about his adventures, the other boys took it all in.*

take in stride *v. phr.* To meet happenings without too much surprise; accept good or bad luck and go on. ◆*He learned to take disappointments in stride.*

take it *v. phr.* **1.** To get an idea or impression; understand from what is said or done.—Usually used with *I.* ◆*I take it from your silence that you don't want to go.* **2.** *informal* To bear trouble, hard work, criticism; not give up or weaken. ◆*Bob lost his job and his girl in the same week, and we all admired the way he took it.*

take it on the chin *v. phr., informal* **1.** To be badly beaten or hurt. ◆*Our football team really took it on the chin today. They are all bumps and bruises.* **2.** To accept without complaint something bad that happens to you; accept trouble or defeat calmly. ◆*A good chess player can take it on the chin when he loses.*

take it out on *v. phr., informal* To be unpleasant or unkind to (someone) because you are angry or upset; get rid of upset feelings by being mean to. ◆*The teacher was angry and took it out on the class.*

take its toll *v. phr.* To cause loss or damage. ◆*The bombs had taken their toll on the town.*

take kindly to *v.* To be pleased by; like.—Usually used in negative, interrogative, and conditional sentences. ◆*He doesn't take kindly to any suggestions about running his business.*

take leave of one's senses *v. phr.* To go mad; become crazy. ◆*"Have you taken leave of your senses?" Jake cried when he saw Andy swallow a live goldfish.*

take liberties *v. phr.* To act toward in too close or friendly a manner; use as you would use a close friend or something of your own. ◆*Mary would not let any boy take liberties with her.*

taken aback *also* **taken back** *adj.* Unpleasantly surprised; suddenly puzzled or shocked. ◆*When he came to pay for his dinner he was taken aback to find that he had left his wallet at home.*

takeoff *n.* (stress on *take*) **1.** Departure of an airplane; the act of becoming airborne. ◆*The nervous passenger was relieved that we had such a wonderfully smooth takeoff.* **2.** Imitation; a parody. ◆*Vaughn Meader used to do a wonderful takeoff on President Kennedy's speech.*

take off *v. phr.* (stress on *off*) **1a.** To leave fast; depart suddenly; run away. ◆*The dog took off after a rabbit.* **1b.** *informal* To go away; leave. ◆*The six boys got into the car and took off for the movies.* **2.** To leave on a flight, begin going up. ◆*A helicopter is able to take off and land straight up or down.* **3.** *informal* To imitate amusingly; copy another person's habitual actions or speech. ◆*He made a career of taking off famous peo-*

ple for nightclub audiences. **4.** To take (time) to be absent from work. ♦*When his wife was sick he took off from work.*

take off one's hat to *v. phr.* To give honor, praise, and respect to. ♦*He is my enemy, but I take off my hat to him for his courage.*

take offense at *v. phr.* To become indignant; become angry. ♦*Why do you always take offense at everything I say?*

take off one's hands *v. phr.* **1.** To abdicate one's responsibility of a person or matter. ♦*"I am herewith taking my hand off your affairs," Lou's father said. "See how you succeed on your own."* **2.** To buy; relieve someone of something. ♦*He offered to take my old car off my hands for $350.*

take on *v.* **1.** To receive for carrying; be loaded with. ♦*A big ship was at the dock taking on automobiles in crates to carry overseas for sale.* **2.** To begin to have (the look of); take (the appearance of). ♦*Others joined the fistfight until it took on the look of a riot.* **3a.** To give a job to; hire; employ. ♦*The factory has opened and is beginning to take on new workers.* **3b.** To accept in business or a contest. ♦*The big man took on two opponents at once.*

take one's time *v. phr.* To avoid haste; act in an unhurried way. ♦*It is better to take your time at this job than to hurry and make mistakes.*

take one's word *v. phr.* To believe one's promise. ♦*Herb took Eric's word when he promised to pay up his debt.*

take one up on something *v. phr.* To make someone keep a promise. ♦*I will take you up on your promise to take me to Hawaii next winter.*

take out *v. phr.* **1.** To ask for and fill in. ♦*Mary and John took out a marriage license.* **2.** To aim at and shoot to kill. ♦*The police sharpshooters took out the wanted kidnapper with a telescopic rifle.*

take over *v.* **1a.** To take control or possession of. ♦*He expects to take over the business when his father retires.* **1b.** To take charge or responsibility. ♦*The airplane pilot fainted and his co-pilot had to take over.* **2.** To borrow, imitate, or adopt. ♦*The Japanese have taken over many European ways of life.*

take place *v. phr.* To happen; occur. ♦*The accident took place only a block from his home.*

take sides *v. phr.* To join one group against another in a debate or quarrel. ♦*Switzerland refused to take sides in the two World Wars.*

take someone for a ride *v. phr., informal* **1.** To cheat or swindle someone. ♦*Poor Joe Catwallender was taken for a ride.* **2.** To kill someone after kidnapping. ♦*The criminals took the man for a ride.*

take steps *v. phr.* To begin to make plans or arrangements; make preparations; give orders.— Usually used with *to* and an infinitive. ♦*The city is taking steps to replace its streetcars with busses.*

take stock *v. phr.* **1.** To count exactly the items of merchandise or supplies in stock; take inventory. ♦*The grocery store* took stock every week on Monday mornings. **2.** To study carefully a situation, or a number of possibilities or opportunities. ◆*During the battle the commander paused to take stock of the situation.*

take stock in *v. phr., informal* To have faith in; trust; believe.—Usually used in the negative. ◆*He took no stock in the idea that women were worse politicians.*

take the bull by the horns *v. phr., informal* To take definite action and not care about risks; act bravely in a difficulty. ◆*He decided to take the bull by the horns and demand a raise in salary even though it might cost him his job.*

take the edge off *also* **take off the edge** *v. phr.* To lessen, weaken, soften, or make dull. ◆*Eating a candy bar before dinner has taken the edge off Becky's appetite.*

take the fifth *v. phr., informal* **1.** Taking refuge behind the Fifth Amendment of the Constitution of the United States, which guarantees any witness the right not to incriminate himself while testifying at a trial. ◆*Alger Hiss took the Fifth when asked whether he was a member of the Communist Party.* **2.** Not to answer any question in an informal setting. ◆*Have you been married before?—I take the Fifth.*

take the words out of one's mouth *v. phr.* To say what another is just going to say; to put another's thought into words. ◆*"Let's go to the beach tomorrow." "You took the words*

right out of my mouth; I was thinking of that."

take to *v.* **1.** To go to or into; get yourself quickly to. Used in the imperative. ◆*Take to the hills! The bandits are coming!* **2.** To begin the work or job of; make a habit of. ◆*He took to repairing watches in his spare time.* **3.** To learn easily; do well at. ◆*Father tried to teach John to swim, but John didn't take to it.* **4.** To like at first meeting; be pleased by or attracted to; accept quickly. ◆*Our dog always takes to children quickly.*

take to the cleaners *v. phr., slang* **1.** To win all the money another person has (as in poker). ◆*Watch out if you play poker with Joe; he'll take you to the cleaners.* **2.** To cheat a person out of his money and possessions by means of a crooked business transaction or other means of dishonest conduct. ◆*I'll never forgive myself for becoming associated with Joe; he took me to the cleaners.*

take turns *v. phr.* To do something one after another instead of doing it all at the same time. ◆*In class we should not talk all at the same time; we should take turns.*

take up *v.* **1.** To remove by taking in. ◆*When the vacuum cleaner bag is full, it will not take up dirt from the rug.* **2.** To fill or to occupy. ◆*The oceans take up the greater part of the earth's surface.* **3.** To gather together; collect. ◆*We are taking up a collection to buy flowers for John because he is in the hospital.* **4.** To begin; start. ◆*The teacher took up the lesson where she left off yesterday.* **5.**

To begin to do or learn; go into as a job or hobby. ◆*He recently took up gardening.* **6.** To pull and make tight or shorter; shorten. ◆*The tailor took up the legs of the trousers.* **7.** To take or accept something that is offered. ◆*I took John up on his bet.*

take up arms *v. phr., literary.* To get ready to fight; fight or make war. ◆*The people were quick to take up arms to defend their freedom.*

take with a grain of salt *also* **take with a pinch of salt** *v. phr.* To accept or believe only in part; not accept too much. ◆*We took Uncle George's stories of the war with a pinch of salt.*

talk back *also* **answer back** *v., informal* To answer rudely; reply in a disrespectful way; be fresh. ◆*When the teacher told the boy to stop smoking, he talked back to her and said she couldn't make him.*

talk big *v., informal* To talk boastfully; brag. ◆*He talks big about his pitching, but he hasn't won a game.*

talk down *v.* **1.** To make (someone) silent by talking louder or longer. ◆*Sue tried to give her ideas, but the other girls talked her down.* **2.** To use words or ideas that are too easy. ◆*The speaker talked down to the students, and they were bored.*

talk into *v.* **1.** To get (someone) to agree to; make (someone) decide on (doing something) by talking; persuade to.—Used with a verbal noun. ◆*Bob talked us into walking home with him.* **2.** To cause to be in or to get into by talking. ◆*You talked us into this mess. Now get us out!*

talk out *v.* To talk all about and leave nothing out; discuss until everything is agreed on; settle. ◆*After their quarrel, Jill and John talked things out and reached full agreement.*

talk out of *v.* **1.** To persuade not to; make agree or decide not to.—Used with a verbal noun. ◆*Mary's mother talked her out of quitting school.* **2.** To allow to go or get out by talking; let escape by talking. ◆*Johnny is good at talking his way out of trouble.*

talk over *v.* **1.** To talk together about; try to agree about or decide by talking; discuss. ◆*Tom talked his plan over with his father before he bought the car.* **2.** To persuade; make agree or willing; talk and change the mind of. ◆*Fred is trying to talk Bill over to our side.*

talk shop *v. phr., informal* To talk about things in your work or trade. ◆*Two chemists were talking shop, and I hardly understood a word they said.*

talk through one's hat *v. phr., informal* To say something without knowing or understanding the facts; talk foolishly or ignorantly. ◆*John said that the earth is nearer the sun in summer, but the teacher said he was talking through his hat.*

talk up *v.* **1.** To speak in favor or support of. ◆*Let's talk up the game and get a big crowd.*

tan one's hide *v. phr., informal* To give a beating to; spank hard. ◆*Bob's father tanned his hide for staying out too late.*

taper down *adj. phr.* To decrease; reduce. ◆*He has tapered down his drinking from three martinis to one beer a day.*

taper off v. **1.** To come to an end little by little; become smaller toward the end. ♦*The river tapers off here and becomes a brook.* **2.** To stop a habit gradually; do something less and less often. ♦*Robert gave up smoking all at once instead of tapering off.*

tar and feather v. To pour heated tar on and cover with feathers as a punishment. ♦*In the Old West bad men were sometimes tarred and feathered and driven out of town.*

tear into v. phr. To attack vigorously, physically or verbally. ♦*The anxious school children tore into the new Harry Potter book on sale at the bookstore.*

tearjerker n. A sentimental novel or movie that makes one cry. ♦*Love Story, both in its novel form and as a movie, was a famous tearjerker.*

tell it like it is v. phr., slang, informal To be honest, sincere; to tell the truth. ♦*Joe is the leader of our commune; he tells it like it is.*

tell it to the marines or **tell it to Sweeney** slang I don't believe you; stop trying to fool me. ♦*John said, "My father knows the president of the United States." Dick answered, "Tell it to the marines."*

tell off v. informal To speak to angrily or sharply; attack with words; scold. ♦*Mr. Black got angry and told off the boss.*

tell on v. To tell someone about another's wrong or naughty acts.—Used mainly by children. ♦*Andy cheated on the test and John told the teacher on Andy.*

tempest in a teapot n. phr. Great excitement about something not important. ♦*Bess tore her skirt a little and made a tempest in a teapot.*

thank one's lucky stars v. phr., informal To be thankful for good luck; think oneself lucky. ♦*You can thank your lucky stars you didn't fall in the hole.*

the creeps n., informal **1.** An uncomfortable tightening of the skin caused by fear or shock. ♦*Reading the story of a ghost gave Joe the creeps.* **2.** A strong feeling of fear or disgust. ♦*The cold, damp, lonely swamp gave John the creeps.*

the lid n., slang Something that holds back or holds out of sight. ♦*The police blew the lid off the gambling operations.*

the pits n., slang **1.** A low class, blighted, and ill-maintained place, motel room, or apartment. ♦*Max, this motel is the pits; I will not sleep here!* **2.** The end of the road, the point of no return, the point of total ruin of one's health (from the drug anticulture referring to the armpits as the only place that had veins for injections). ♦*John flunked high school this year for the third time; he will never get to college; it's the pits for him.* **3.** A very depressed state of mind. ♦*Poor Marcy is down in the pits over her recent divorce.*

the ropes n. plural, informal Thorough or special knowledge of a job; how to do something; the ways of people or the world. ♦*When you go to a new school it takes a while to learn the ropes.*

the score *n., slang* The truth; the real story or information; what is happening; the way people and the world really are. ◆*Very few people know the score in politics.*

the tracks *n.* The line between the rich or fashionable part of town and the poor or unfashionable part of town. ◆*The poor children knew they would not be welcome on the other side of the tracks.*

the works *n., plural, slang* **1.** Everything that can be had or that you have; everything of this kind, all that goes with it. ◆*When the homeless man found $100, he went into a fine restaurant and ordered the works with a steak dinner.* **2.** Rough handling or treatment; a bad beating or scolding; killing; murder.—Usually used with *get* or *give.* ◆*The gangster told his accomplice he would give him the works if he double-crossed him.*

think aloud *or* **think out loud** *v.* To say what you are thinking. ◆ *"I wish I had more money for Christmas presents," Father thought aloud. "What did you say?" said Mother. Father answered, "I'm sorry. I wasn't talking to you. I was thinking out loud."*

think better of *v.* To change your mind about; to consider again and make a better decision about. ◆*John told his mother he wanted to leave school, but later he thought better of it.*

think little of *v. phr.* Think that (something or someone) is not important or valuable. ◆*Joan thought little of walking two miles to school.*

think nothing of *v. phr.* To think or consider easy, simple, or usual. ◆*Jim thinks nothing of hiking ten miles in one day.*

think over *v.* To think carefully about; consider; study. ◆*When Charles asked Betty to marry him, she asked him for time to think it over.*

think piece *n., slang* **1.** The human brain. ◆*Lou's got one powerful think piece, man.* **2.** Any provocative essay or article that, by stating a strong opinion, arouses the reader to think about it and react to it by agreeing or disagreeing. ◆*That article by Charles Fenyvesi on Vietnamese refugees in the Washington Post sure was a think piece!*

think twice *v.* To think again carefully; reconsider; hesitate. ◆*The teacher advised Lou to think twice before deciding to quit school.*

think up *v.* To invent or discover by thinking; have a new idea of. ◆*Mary thought up a funny game for the children to play.*

third world *n.* **1.** The countries not aligned with either the former U.S.S.R.-dominated Communist bloc or the U.S.A.-dominated capitalist countries. ◆*New Zealand made a move toward third country status when it disallowed American nuclear submarines in its harbors.* **2.** The developing nations of the world where the industrial revolution has not yet been completed. ◆*Africa and the rest of the third world must be freed from starvation and illiteracy.*

three sheets in the wind *or* **three sheets to the wind** *adj. phr., informal* Unsteady from too much liquor; drunk. ♦*The sailor came down the street, three sheets in the wind.*

through the grapevine *adv. phr.* As a matter of gossip from colleagues, acquaintances, etc. ♦*"I heard through the grapevine that we will be downsizing our inventory next year," Ted said. "I hope it isn't true," Fred replied.*

through the mill *adv. phr.* **1.** Experienced. ♦*You could tell immediately that the new employee had been through the mill.* **2.** Through real experience of the difficulties of a certain way of life. ♦*Poor Jerry has had three operations in one year, and now he's back in the hospital. He's really gone through the mill.*

through thick and thin *adv. phr.* Through all difficulties and troubles; through good times and bad times. ♦*George stayed in college through thick and thin, because he wanted an education.*

throw a curve *v. phr., slang, informal* **1.** To mislead or deceive someone; to lie. ♦*John threw me a curve about the hiring.* **2.** To take someone by surprise in an unpleasant way. ♦*Mr. Weiner's announcement threw the whole company a curve.*

throw a monkey wrench *or* **throw a wrench** *v. phr., informal* To cause something that is going smoothly to stop. ♦*The game was going smoothly until you threw a monkey wrench into the works by fussing about the rules.*

throw away *v.* **1.** To get rid of as unwanted or not needed; junk. ♦*Before they moved they threw away everything they didn't want to take with them.* **2.** To waste. ♦*The senator criticized the government for throwing away billions on the space program.* **3.** To fail to make use of. ♦*She threw away a good chance for a better job.*

throw down the gauntlet *v. phr.* To challenge, especially to a fight. ♦*Another candidate for the presidency has thrown down the gauntlet.*

throw in the sponge *or* **throw up the sponge** *or* **throw in the towel** *v. phr., informal* To admit defeat; accept loss. ♦*When Harold saw his arguments were not being accepted, he threw in the towel and left.*

throw off *v.* **1.** To get free from. ♦*He was healthy enough to throw off his cold easily.* **2.** To mislead; confuse; fool. ♦*They went by a different route to throw the hostile bandits off their track.*

throw one's hat in the ring *or* **toss one's hat in the ring** *v. phr., informal* To announce that you are going to try to be elected to an official position; become a candidate for office. ♦*The senator threw his hat in the ring for president.*

throw one's weight around *v. phr., informal* To use one's influence or position in a showy or noisy manner. ♦*Bob was stronger than the other boys, and he threw his weight around.*

throw *or* **feed one to the wolves** *v. phr.* To turn someone into a scapegoat. ♦*In order to explain the situation to the media, the governor blamed the mayor and threw him to the wolves.*

throw up one's hands *v. phr.* To give up trying; admit that you cannot succeed. ◆*Mrs. Jones threw up her hands when the children messed up the living room for the third time.*

thumb a ride *v. phr., informal* To get a ride by hitchhiking; hitchhike. ◆*Not having much money, Carl decided to thumb a ride to New York.*

thus and so *also* **thus and thus** *adv. phr.* In a particular way; according to directions that have been given. ◆*The teacher is very fussy about the way you write your report. If you don't do it thus and so, she gives you a lower mark.*

tickle one's funny bone *v. phr.* To amuse one; make one laugh. ◆*It tickles my funny bone listening to Sam; he is full of the most amazing humorous anecdotes.*

tickle pink *v. phr., informal* To please very much; thrill; delight. Usually used in the passive participle. ◆*Agnes was tickled pink with the great reviews about her first book of short stories.*

tick off *v.* **1.** To mention one after the other; list. ◆*The teacher ticked off the assignments that Jane had to do.* **2.** To scold; rebuke. ◆*The boss ticked off the waitress for dropping her tray.* **3.** To anger or upset. Usually used as *ticked off.* ◆*She was ticked off at him for breaking their dinner date again.*

tide over *v.* To carry past a difficulty or danger; help in bad times or in trouble. ◆*An ice cream cone in the afternoon tided her over until supper.*

tie down *v.* To keep (someone) from going somewhere or doing something; prevent from leaving; keep in. ◆*The navy tied the enemy down with big gunfire while the marines landed on the beach.*

tied to one's mother's apron strings Not independent of your mother; not able to do anything without asking your mother. ◆*Even after he grew up he was still tied to his mother's apron strings.*

tie in *v.* To connect with something else; make a connection for. Used with *with.* ◆*The teacher tied in what she said with last week's lesson.* ◆*The detectives tied in the fingerprints on the man's gun with those found on the safe, so they knew that he was the thief.*

tie-in *n.* A connection; a point of meeting. ◆*John's essay on World War II provides a perfect tie-in with his earlier work on World War I.*

tie in knots *v. phr.* To make (someone) very nervous or worried. ◆*The thought of having her tooth pulled tied Joan in knots.*

tie one's hands *v. phr.* To make (a person) unable to do anything.—Usually used in the passive. ◆*Father hoped Jim would not quit school, but his hands were tied; Jim was old enough to quit if he wanted to.*

tie the knot *v. phr., informal* To get married; *also* to perform a wedding ceremony. ◆*Diane and Bill tied the knot yesterday.*

tie up *v. phr.* (stress on *up*) **1.** To show or stop the movement or action of; hinder; tangle. ◆*The crash of the two trucks tied up all traffic in the center of town.* **2.** To take all the time of. ◆*The meeting will tie the President* up until noon. **3.** To limit or prevent the use of. ◆*His money is tied up in a trust fund and he can't take it out.* **4.** To enter into an association or partnership; join. ◆*Our company has tied up with another firm to support the show.* **5.** To dock. ◆*The ships tied up at New York.* **6.** To finish; complete. ◆*We've talked long enough; let's tie up these plans and start doing things.*

tie-up *n.* (stress on *tie*) A congestion; a stoppage of the normal flow of traffic, business, or correspondence. ◆*There was a two-hour traffic tie-up on the highway.*

tighten one's belt *v. phr.* To live on less money than usual; use less food and other things. ◆*When father lost his job we had to tighten our belts.* ◆*When the husband lost his job, the Smiths had to do without many things, but when their savings were all spent, they had to tighten their belts another notch.*

tighten the screws *v. phr.* To try to make someone do something by making it more and more difficult not to do it; apply pressure. ◆*When many students still missed class after he began giving daily quizzes, the teacher tightened the screws by failing anyone absent four times.*

tilt at windmills *v. phr., literary* To do battle with an imaginary foe. ◆*John is a nice guy, but when it comes to departmental meetings he wastes everybody's time by constantly tilting at windmills.*

time and again *or* **time and time again** *adv.* Many times; repeatedly; very often. ◆*Children are*

forgetful and must be told time and time again how to behave.

time and a half *n. phr.* Pay given to a worker at a rate half again as much as he usually gets. ◆*Tom gets one dollar for regular pay and a dollar and a half for time and a half.*

time out *n. phr.* Time during which a game, a lecture, a discussion, or other activity is stopped for a while for some extra questions or informal discussion, or some other reason. ◆*"Time out!"—The students said, "Could you explain that again?"*

tip off *v., informal* To tell something not generally known; tell secret facts to; warn. ◆*The thieves did not rob the bank as planned because someone tipped them off that it was being watched by the police.*

tip the scales *v. phr., informal* **1.** To weigh. ◆*Martin tips the scales at 180 pounds.* **2.** *or* **tip the balance** To have important or decisive influence; make a decision go for or against you; decide. ◆*John's vote tipped the scales in our favor, and we won the election.*

tit for tat *n. phr.* Equal treatment in return; a fair exchange. ◆*I told him if he did me any harm I would return tit for tat.* ◆*They had a warm debate and the two boys gave each other tit for tat.*

to all intents and purposes *adv. phr.* In most ways; in fact. ◆*The president is called the head of state, but the prime minister, to all intents and purposes, is the chief executive.*

to a man *adv. phr.* Without exception; with all agreeing. ◆*The* *workers voted to a man to go on strike.*

to and fro *adv. phr.* Forward and back again and again. ♦*Busses go to and fro between the center of the city and the city limits.*

to a T *or* **to a turn** *adv. phr.* Just right; to perfection; exactly. ♦*The roast was done to a turn.* ♦*His nickname, Tiny, suited him to a T.*

to-be *adj.* That is going to be; about to become.—Used after the noun it modifies. ♦*Bob kissed his bride-to-be.*

to be sure *adv. phr.* Without a doubt; certainly; surely. ♦*"Didn't you say Mr. Smith would take us home?" "Oh, yes. To be sure, I did."*

to blame *adj. phr.* Having done something wrong; to be blamed; responsible. ♦*The teacher tried to find out who was to blame in the fight.*

to boot *adv. phr.* In addition; besides; as something extra. ♦*He not only got fifty dollars, but they bought him dinner to boot.*

to date *adv. or adj. phr.* Up to the present time; until now. ♦*To date twenty students have been accepted into the school.*

to death *adv. phr., informal* To the limit; to the greatest degree possible.—Used for emphasis with verbs such as *scare, frighten, bore.* ♦*Cowboy stories bore me to death, but I like mysteries.*

Tom, Dick, and Harry *n. phr.* People in general; anyone; everyone.—Usually preceded by *every* and used to show scorn or disrespect. ♦*The drunk told his troubles to every Tom, Dick and Harry who passed by.*

tone down *v.* To make softer or quieter; make less harsh or strong; moderate. ♦*She wanted the bright colors in her house toned down.*

tongue-in-cheek *adj. phr.* In an ironic or insincere manner. ♦*When the faculty complained about the poor salary increments, the university's president said that he was not a psychiatrist, thus making an inappropriate tongue-in-cheek remark.*

tongue-lashing *n.* A sharp scolding or criticism. ♦*Jim's mother gave him a tongue-lashing for telling family secrets.*

to no avail *or* **of no avail** *adj. phr., formal* Having no effect; useless, unsuccessful. ♦*Tom's practicing was of no avail. He was sick on the day of the game.*

too many cooks spoil the broth *or* **stew** A project is likely to go bad if managed by a multiplicity of primary movers.—A proverb. ♦*When several people acted all at once in trying to reshape the company's investment policy, Tom spoke up and said, "Let me do this by myself! Don't you know that too many cooks spoil the broth?"*

to one's face *adv. phr.* Directly to you; in your presence. ♦*I called him a coward to his face.*

to one's heart's content *adv. phr.* To the extent of one's wishes; one's complete satisfaction. ♦*There is a wonderful small restaurant nearby where you can eat to your heart's content.*

to order *adv. phr.* According to directions given in an order in the way and size wanted. ♦*A very big man often has his suits made to order.*

tooth and nail *adv. phr.* Very forcefully; vehemently; at almost any cost. ◆*John stuck to his decision to become a pianist tooth and nail, but he would have been better off choosing some other profession.*

top-drawer *adj., informal* Of the best; or most important kind. ◆*Mr. Rogers is a top-drawer executive and gets a very high salary.*

to pieces *adv. phr.* **1.** Into broken pieces or fragments; destroyed. ◆*The cannon shot the town to pieces.* **2.** *informal* So as not to work; into a state of not operating. ◆*After 100,000 miles the car went to pieces.* **3.** *informal* Very much; greatly; exceedingly. ◆*Joan was thrilled to pieces to see Mary.* ◆*The shooting scared Bob to pieces.*

top off *v.* To come or bring to a special or unexpected ending; climax. ◆*George had steak for dinner and topped it off with a fudge sundae.*

to speak of *adj. phr., informal* Important; worth talking about; worth noticing.—Usually used in negative sentences. ◆*Judy's injuries were nothing to speak of; just a few scratches.*

to the manner born *adj. phr.* At ease with something because of lifelong familiarity with it. ◆*She says her English is the best because she is to the manner born.*

to the nth degree *adv. phr.* To the greatest degree possible; extremely; very much so. ◆*His choice of words was exactly to the nth degree.*

to the tune of *adv. phr., informal* To the amount or extent of; in the amount of. ◆*When she left the race track she had profited to the tune of ten dollars.*

to the wall *adv. phr.* Into a place from which there is no escape; into a trap or corner. Used after *drive* or a similar word. ◆*John's failing the last test drove him to the wall.*

to this day *adv. phr.* Up till the present; until now. ◆*Although I have traveled all over the world, to this day I can't think of a nicer place to be than Hawaii.*

touch and go *adj. phr.* Very dangerous or uncertain in situation. ◆*Our team won the game, all right, but it was touch and go for a while.*

touch down *v. phr.* (stress on *down*) To alight; land on the ground. ◆*Everyone felt relieved when the 747 jumbo jet finally touched down at Kennedy International Airport after a bumpy ride due to strong wind.*

touchdown *n. phr.* (stress on *touch*) A goal scored during the game of American football. ◆*Yale won easily over Harvard at the annual Ivy League sports contest by scoring several unexpected touchdowns.*

touch off *v.* To start something as if by lighting a fuse. ◆*The president's resignation touched off a national panic.*

touch on *or* **touch upon** *v.* To speak of or write of briefly. ◆*The speaker touched on several other subjects in the course of his talk.*

touchup *n.* (stress on *touch*) **1.** A small repair; a small amount of paint. ◆*Just a small touchup here and there and your novel may be publishable.* **2.** Redoing the color of one's hair. ◆*My* *roots are showing; I need a touchup.*

touch up v. (stress on *up*) **1.** To paint over (small imperfections.) ◆*I want to touch up that scratch on the fender.* **2.** To improve with small additions or changes. ◆*He touched up the photographic negative to make a sharper print.* **3.** slang To talk into lending; wheedle from. ◆*He touched George up for five bucks.*

tough act to follow n. phr. A speech, performance, or activity of such superior quality that the person next in line feels and thinks that it would be very difficult to match it in quality. ◆*Sir Lawrence Olivier's performance of* Hamlet *was a tough act to follow in every sense.*

tough cookie n. phr. An extremely determined, hardheaded person, or someone with whom it is unusually difficult to deal. ◆*Marjorie is a very pretty girl, but when it comes to business she sure is one tough cookie.*

track down v. To find by or as if by following tracks or a trail. ◆*The hunters tracked down game in the forest.*

trade in v. To give something to a seller as part payment for another thing of greater value. ◆*The Browns traded their old car in on a new one.*

trade-in n. Something given as part payment on something better. ◆*The dealer took our old car as a trade-in.*

trade on v. To use as a way of helping yourself. ◆*The senator's son traded on his father's name when he ran for mayor.*

trial and error n. A way of solving problems by trying different possible solutions until you find one that works. ◆*John found the short circuit by trial and error.*

trial balloon n. A hint about a plan of action that is given out to find out what people will say. ◆*John mentioned the presidency to Bill as a trial balloon to see if Bill might be interested in running.*

trick of the trade n. phr., usually in plural, informal **1.** A piece of expert knowledge; a smart, quick, or skillful way of working at a trade or job. ◆*Mr. Olson spent years learning the tricks of the trade as a carpenter.* **2.** A smart and sometimes tricky or dishonest way of doing something in order to succeed or win. ◆*The champion knows all the tricks of the boxing trade; he knows many ways to hurt his opponent and to get him mixed up.*

trick or treat n. The custom of going from house to house on Halloween asking for small gifts and playing tricks on people who refuse to give. ◆*When Mrs. Jones answered the doorbell, the children yelled "Trick or treat." Mrs. Jones gave them all some candy.*

tripped out adj., slang, informal Incoherent, confused, faulty of speech, illogical; as if under the influence of drugs or alcohol. ◆*It was hard to make sense of anything Fred said yesterday, he sounded so tripped out.*

trip up v. **1.** To make (someone) unsteady on the feet; cause to miss a step, stumble, or fall. ◆*A root tripped Billy up while he was running in the woods, and he fell and hurt his ankle.* **2.** To cause (someone) to make a mistake. ♦*The teacher asked tricky questions in the test to trip up students who were not alert.*

trump card *n.* Something kept back to be used to win success if nothing else works. ♦*Mary had several ways to get Joan to come to her party. Her trump card was that the football captain would be there.*

trump up *v.* (stress on *up*) To make up (something untrue); invent in the mind. ♦*Every time Tom is late getting home he trumps up some new excuse.* ♦*The Russians were afraid he was a spy, so they arrested him on a trumped-up charge and made him leave the country.*

try on *v.* To put (clothing) on to see if it fits. ♦*The clerk told him to try the coat on.*

try one's hand *v. phr.* To make an inexperienced attempt (at something unfamiliar.) ♦*I thought I would try my hand at bowling, although I had never bowled before.*

tryout *n.* (stress on *try*) An audience at a theater or opera for would-be actors and singers. ♦*The Civic Opera is holding tryouts throughout all of next week. Maybe I'll go and see if I can sing in the chorus.*

try out *v. phr.* (stress on *out*) **1.** To test by trial or by experimenting. ♦*The scientists tried out thousands of chemicals before they found the right one.* **2.** To try for a place on a team or in a group. ♦*Shirley will try out for the lead in the play.*

tug-of-war *n.* **1.** A game in which two teams pull on opposite ends of a rope, trying to pull the other team over a line marked on the ground. ♦*The tug-of-war*

ended when both teams tumbled in a heap. **2.** A contest in which two sides try to defeat each other; struggle. ♦*The tug of war between the union men and management ended in a long strike.*

tune in To adjust a radio or television set to pick up a certain station. ♦*Tom tuned in to Channel 11 to hear the news.*

tune out *v. phr.* To not listen to something. ♦*"How can you work in such a noisy environment?" Jane asked Sue. "Well, I simply tune it out," she answered.*

tune up *v.* (stress on *up*) **1a.** To adjust (a musical instrument) to make the right sound. ♦*Before he began to play, Harry tuned up his banjo.* **1b.** To adjust a musical instrument or a group of musical instruments to the right sound. ♦*The orchestra came in and began to tune up for the concert.* **2.** To adjust many parts of (car engine) which must work together so that it will run properly. ♦*He took his car to the garage to have the engine tuned up.*

tune-up *n.* (stress on *tune*) **1.** The adjusting or fixing of something (as a motor) to make it work safely and well. ♦*Father says the car needs a tune-up before winter begins.* **2.** Exercise or practicing for the purpose of getting ready; a trial before something. ♦*The team went to the practice field for their last tune-up before the game tomorrow.*

turn a blind eye *v. phr.* To pretend not to see; not pay attention. ♦*The corrupt police chief* *turned a blind eye to the open gambling in the town.*

turn a deaf ear to *v. phr.* To pretend not to hear; refuse to hear; not pay attention. *The teacher turned a deaf ear to Bob's excuse.*

turn down *v.* **1.** To reduce the loudness, brightness, or force of. *The theater lights were turned down.* **2.** To refuse to accept; reject. *His request for a raise was turned down.*

turn in *v.* **1.** *or* **hand in** To give to someone; deliver to someone. *I want you to turn in a good history paper.* **2.** To inform on; report. *She turned them in to the police for breaking the street light.* **3.** To give in return for something. *We turned our car in on a new model.* **4.** *informal* To go to bed. *We were tired, so we turned in about nine o'clock.*

turn in one's grave *or* **turn over in one's grave** *v. phr.* To be so grieved or angry that you would not rest quietly in your grave. *If your grandfather could see what you're doing now, he would turn over in his grave.*

turn off *v.* (stress on *off*) **1.** To stop by turning a knob or handle or by working a switch; to cause to be off. *He turned the water off.* **2.** To leave by turning right or left onto another way. *Turn off the highway at exit 5.* **3.** To disgust, bore, or repel (someone) by being intellectually, emotionally, socially, or sexually unattractive. *I won't date Linda Bell anymore—she just turns me off.*

turn on *v.* **1.** To start by turning a knob or handle or working a switch; cause to be on. *Who*

turned the lights on? **2.** *informal* To put forth or succeed with as easily as turning on water. *She really turns on the charm when that new boy is around.* **3.** To attack. *The lion tamer was afraid the lions would turn on him.* **4.** *slang* The opposite of turning someone off; to become greatly interested in an idea, person, or undertaking; to arouse the senses pleasantly. *Mozart's music always turns me on.* **5.** Introducing someone to a new experience or set of values. *Syd turned me on to transcendental meditation, and ever since I've been feeling great!*

turn one's back on *v. phr.* To refuse to help (someone in trouble or need.) *He turned his back on his own family when they needed help.*

turn one's head *v. phr., informal* To make you lose your good judgment. *The first pretty girl he saw turned his head.*

turn one's nose up at *v. phr.* To scorn; snub; look down at somebody or something. *I don't understand why Sue has to turn her nose up at everyone who didn't go to an Ivy League college.*

turn on one's heel *v. phr.* To turn around suddenly. *When John saw Fred approaching him, he turned on his heel.*

turnout *n.* (stress on *turn*) The number of people in attendance at a gathering. *This is a terrific turnout for Tim's poetry reading.*

turn out *v.* (stress on *out*) **1.** To make leave or go away. *His father turned him out of the house.* **2.** To turn inside out;

empty. ♦*He turned out his pockets looking for the money.* **3.** To make; produce. ♦*The printing press turns out a thousand books an hour.* **4.** *informal* To get out of bed. ♦*At camp the boys had to turn out early and go to bed early too.* **5.** *informal* To come or go out to see or do something. ♦*Everybody turned out for the big parade.* **6.** To prove to be; be in the end; be found to be. ♦*The noise turned out to be just the dog scratching at the door.* **7.** To make (a light) go out. ♦*Please turn out the lights.*

turnover *n.* (stress on *turn*) **1.** The proportion of expenditure and income realized in a business; the volume of traffic in a business. ♦*Our turnover is so great that in two short years we tripled our original investment and are expanding at a great rate.* **2.** Triangular baked pastry filled with some fruit. ♦*John's favorite dessert is apple turnovers.* **3.** The number of employees coming and going in a company. ♦*The boss is so strict in our office that the turnover in personnel is very large.*

turn over *v.* (stress on *over*) **1.** To roll, tip, or turn from one side to the other; overturn; upset. ♦*The bike hit a rock and turned over.* **2.** To think about carefully; to consider. ♦*He turned the problem over in his mind for three days before he did anything about it.* **3.** To give to someone for use or care. ♦*I turned my library books over to the librarian.* **4.** Of an engine or motor; to start. ♦*The battery is dead and the motor won't turn over.* **5a.** To buy and then sell to customers. ♦*The store turned over $5,000 worth of skiing equipment in January.* **5b.** To be bought in large enough amounts; sell. ♦*In a shoe store, shoes of medium width turn over quickly, because many people wear that size.*

turn over a new leaf *v. phr.* To start afresh; to have a new beginning. ♦*"Don't be sad, Jane," Sue said. "A divorce is not the end of the world. Just turn over a new leaf and you will soon be happy again."*

turn tail *v. phr., informal* To run away from trouble or danger. ♦*When the bully saw my big brother, he turned tail and ran.*

turn the clock back *v. phr.* To return to an earlier period. ♦*Mother wished she could turn the clock back to the days before the children grew up and left home.*

turn the other cheek *v. phr.* To let someone do something to you and not to do it in return; not hit back when hit; be patient when injured or insulted by someone; not try to get even. ♦*Joe turned the other cheek when he was hit with a snowball.*

turn the tables *v. phr.* To make something happen just the opposite of how it is supposed to happen. ♦*The boys turned the tables on John when they took his squirt gun away and squirted him.*

turn the tide *v. phr.* To change what looks like defeat into victory. ♦*We were losing the game until Jack got there. His coming turned the tide for us, and we won.*

turn the trick *v. phr., informal* To bring about the result you want; succeed in what you plan to do. ♦*Jerry wanted to win both the swimming and diving contests, but he couldn't quite turn the trick.*

turn thumbs down *v. phr.* To disapprove or reject; say no. ♦*The company turned thumbs down on Mr. Smith's sales plan.*

turn turtle *v. phr.* To turn upside down. ♦*The car skidded on the ice and turned turtle.*

turn up *v.* **1.** To find; discover. ♦*The police searched the house hoping to turn up more clues.* **2.** To appear or be found suddenly or unexpectedly. ♦*The missing boy turned up an hour later.*

turn up one's nose at *v. phr.* To refuse as not being good enough for you. ♦*He thinks he should only get steak, and he turns up his nose at hamburger.*

twiddle one's thumbs *v. phr.* To do nothing; be idle. ♦*I'd rather work than stand around here twiddling my thumbs.*

twist one around one's little finger *also* **turn one around one's little finger** *or* **wrap one around one's finger** *v. phr.* To have complete control over; to be able to make (someone) do anything you want. ♦*Sue can twist any of the boys around her little finger.*

twist one's arm *v. phr., informal* To force someone; threaten someone to make him do something. ♦*I had to twist Tom's arm to make him accept our dinner invitation.*

two bits *n., slang* Twenty-five cents; a quarter of a dollar. ♦*A haircut only cost two bits when Grandfather was young.*

two cents *n. informal* **1.** Something not important or very small; almost nothing. ♦*When John saw that the girl he was scolding was lame, he felt like two cents.* **2.** *or* **two cents worth** Something you want to say; opinion.—Used with a possessive. ♦*If we want your two cents, we'll ask for it.*

two-faced *adj.* Insincere; disloyal; deceitful. ♦*Don't confide too much in him as he has the reputation of being two-faced.*

two strikes against one *n. phr.* Two opportunities wasted in some undertaking, so that only one chance is left. ♦*Poor John has two strikes against him when it comes to his love for Frances: first, he is too fat, and, second, he is bald.*

two-time *v., slang* To go out with a second boy or girlfriend and keep it a secret from the first. ♦*Mary cried when she found that Joe was two-timing her.*

U.F.O. n. phr. Unidentified Flying Object. ◆Some people think that the U.F.O.s are extraterrestrial beings of higher than human development who pay periodic visits to Earth to warn us of our self-destructive tendencies.

ugly duckling n. An ugly or plain child who grows up to be pretty and attractive. ◆Mary was the ugly duckling in her family, until she grew up.

under a cloud adj. phr. 1. Under suspicion; not trusted. ◆The butcher is under a cloud because the inspectors found his scales were not honest. 2. Depressed, sad, discouraged. ◆Joe has been under a cloud since his dog died.

under age adj. phr. Too young; not old enough; below legal age. ◆He could not enlist in the army because he was under age.

under arrest adj. phr. Held by the police. ◆The three boys were seen breaking into the school building and soon found themselves under arrest.

under cover adv. or adj. phr. Hidden; concealed. ◆The prisoners escaped under cover of darkness.

under fire adv. phr. Being shot at or being attacked; hit by attacks or accusations; under attack. ◆The principal was under fire for not sending the boys home who stole the car.

under one's belt adv. phr., informal 1. In your stomach; eaten; or absorbed. ◆Jones is talkative when he has a few drinks under his belt. 2. In your experience, memory or possession; learned or gotten successfully; gained by effort and skill. ◆Jim has to get a lot of algebra under his belt before the examination.

under one's breath adv. phr. In a whisper; with a low voice. ◆The teacher heard the boy say something under his breath and she asked him to repeat it aloud.

under one's nose or **under the nose of** adv. phr., informal In sight of; in an easily seen or noticeable place. ◆The thief walked out of the museum with the painting, right under the nose of the guards.

under one's own steam adv. phr., informal By one's own efforts; without help. ◆We didn't think he could do it, but Bobby finished his homework under his own steam.

under one's thumb or **under the thumb** adj. or adv. phr. Obedient to you; controlled by you; under your power. ◆The mayor is so popular that he has the whole town under his thumb.

under one's wing adv. phr. Under the care or protection of. ◆The boys stopped teasing the new student when Bill took him under his wing.

under the hammer adv. phr. Up for sale at auction. ◆The picture I wanted to bid on came under the hammer soon after I arrived.

under the sun adj. or adv. phr. On earth; in the world.—Used for emphasis. ◆The president's assassination shocked everyone under the sun.

under wraps adv. or adj. phr. Not allowed to be seen until the right time; not allowed to act or speak freely; in secrecy; hidden. ♦*What the President is planning will be kept under wraps until tomorrow.*

until hell freezes over *adv. phr., slang* Forever, for an eternity. ♦*He can argue until hell freezes over; nobody will believe him.*

up against *prep. phr.* Blocked or threatened by. ♦*When she applied to medical school, the black woman wondered whether she was up against barriers of sex and race prejudice.*

up and at them 1. *adv. phr.* Actively engaged in a task as if doing combat. ♦*"You want to know whether he will make a diligent worker?" Dick asked. "Well, I can tell you that most of the time he is up and at them like no one else I know."* **2.** *v. phr.* To become aggressively engaged in doing something. ♦*Come on, up and at them, you guys. We still have a lot of work to get done.*

up-and-coming *adj. phr.* Bound toward success; upwardly mobile; progressive; ambitious. ♦*The newly elected state senator is an up-and-coming young politician.*

up a tree *adv. or adj. phr.* **1.** Hunted or chased into a tree; treed. ♦*The dog drove the coon up a tree so the hunter could shoot him.* **2.** *informal* In trouble; having problems; in a difficulty that it is hard to escape or think of a way out of. ♦*John's father has him up a tree in the checker game.*

up for grabs *adj. phr., informal* Available for anyone to try to get; ready to be competed for; there for the taking. ♦*When the captain of the football team*

moved out of town, his place was up for grabs.

up front[1] *n., slang, informal* The managerial section of a corporation or firm. ♦*Joe Catwallender finally made it (with them) up front.*

up front[2] *adj., slang, informal* Open, sincere, hiding nothing. ♦*Sue was completely up front about why she didn't want to see him anymore.*

up in arms *adj. phr.* **1.** Equipped with guns or weapons and ready to fight. ♦*All of the American colonies were up in arms against the British.* **2.** Very angry and wanting to fight. ♦*The students were up in arms over the new rule against food in the dormitory.*

up in the air *adj. or adv. phr.* **1.** *informal* In great anger or excitement. ♦*My father went straight up in the air when he heard I damaged the car.* **2.** *also* **in midair** Not settled; uncertain; undecided. ♦*Plans for the next meeting have been left up in the air until Jane gets better.*

up one's sleeve *or* **in one's sleeve** *adv. phr.* **1.** Hidden in the sleeve of one's shirt or coat and ready for secret or wrongful use. ♦*The crooked gambler hid aces up his sleeve during the card game so that he would win.* **2.** *informal* Kept secretly ready for the right time or for a time when needed. ♦*Jimmy knew that his father had some trick up his sleeve because he was smiling to himself during the checker game.*

upper hand *or* **whip hand** *n.* Controlling power; advantage. ♦*The cowboy trained the wild* *horse so that he finally got the whip hand and tamed the horse.*

ups and downs *n. phr.* Vicissitudes; alternating periods between good and bad times; changes in fortune. *He is now a wealthy stock trader, but at the beginning of his career he, too, had many ups and downs.*

upset the applecart *or* **upset one's applecart** *v. phr., informal* To ruin a plan or what is being done, often by surprise or accident; change how things are or are being done, often unexpectedly; ruin or mix up another person's success or plan for success. *We are planning a surprise party for Bill, so don't let Mary upset the applecart by telling him before the party.*

upside down *adv. phr.* Overturned so that the bottom is up and the top is down. *The problem with this company is that everything is upside down; we need a new C.E.O.*

up the creek *or* **up the creek without a paddle** *adj. phr., informal* In trouble or difficulty and unable to do anything about it; stuck. *Father said that if the car ran out of gas in the middle of the desert, we would be up the creek without a paddle.*

up tight *or* **uptight** *adj., slang, informal* Worried, irritated, excessively eager or anxious. *Why are you so uptight about getting that job? The more you worry, the less you'll succeed.*

up to *prep.* **1.** As far as, as deep as, or as high as. *The water in the pond was only up to John's knees.* **2.** Close to; approaching. *The team did not play up to its best today.* **3.** As high as; not more than; as much or as many as.

Pick any number up to ten. **4.** *or* **up till** *or* **up until**—Until; till. *Up to her fourth birthday, the baby slept in a crib.* **5.** Capable of; fit for; equal to; strong or well enough for. *We chose Harry to be captain because we thought he was up to the job.* **6.** Doing or planning secretly; ready for mischief. *What are you up to with the matches, John?* **7.** Facing as a duty; to be chosen or decided by; depending on. *It's up to you to get to school on time.*

up-to-date *adj.* Modern; contemporary; the latest that technology can offer. *"I want an up-to-date dictionary of American idioms," Mr. Lee said, "that has all the latest Americanisms in it."*

up to no good *adv. phr.* Intending to do something bad; perpetrating an illicit act. *We could tell from the look on Dennis the Menace's face that he was once again up to no good.*

up to par *or informal* **up to scratch** *or informal* **up to snuff** **1.** In good or normal health or physical condition. *I have a cold and don't feel up to par.* *The boxer is training for the fight but he isn't up to scratch yet.* **2.** *or* **up to the mark** As good as usual; up to the usual level or quality. *John will have to work hard to bring his grades up to snuff.*

up to the chin in *or* **in———up to the chin** *adj. phr., informal* Used also with *ears, elbows, eyes* or *knees* instead of *chin,* and with a possessive instead of *the.* **1.** Having a big or important part in; guilty of; not innocent of; deeply in. *Was Tom* *mixed up in that trouble last night? He was up to his ears in it.* **2.** Very busy with; working hard at. ♦*Bob is up to his neck in homework.* **3.** Having very much or many of; flooded with. ♦*Mary was up to her knees in invitations to go to parties.*

used to[1] *adj. phr.* In the habit of or familiar with. ♦*People get used to smoking and it is hard for them to stop.*

used to[2] *or* **did use to** *v. phr.* Did formerly; did in the past.— Usually used with an infinitive to tell about something past. ♦*Uncle Henry used to have a beard, but he shaved it off.* ♦*I don't go to that school any more, but I used to.* ♦*We don't visit Helen as much as we used to.*

used to be *or* **did use to be** *v. phr.* Formerly or once was. ♦*Dick used to be the best student in our class last year; now two other students are better than he is.*

use every trick in the book *v. phr., informal* To avail oneself of any means at all in order to achieve one's goal, not exclusive of possibly immoral or illegal acts. ♦*Algernon used every trick in the book to get Maxine to go out with him, but she kept refusing.*

user-friendly *adj. phr., computer jargon* A machine, such as a personal computer, a video recorder, a cell phone, etc., which is easy to run even by nonexperts. ♦*Word 2000 is quite a user-friendly program; anyone can learn it in less than a week.* ♦*Some video recorders are not very user-friendly, so people often need to ask for help in programming them.*

use up *v. phr.* **1.** To use until nothing is left; spend or consume completely. ♦*Don't use up all the soap. Leave me some to wash with.*

vanishing cream *n.* A cosmetic cream for the skin that is used chiefly before face powder. ◆*Mrs. Jones spread vanishing cream on her face before applying her face powder.*

variety store *n.* A store that sells many different kinds of things, especially items that are fairly small and in everyday use. ◆*I went into a variety store and bought some paint.*

verbal diarrhea *n. phr.* The inability to keep silent; overtalkativeness. ◆*Archibald is a nice guy but he's got verbal diarrhea and he can't shut up for a single minute.*

Vietnam syndrome *n., informal* An attitude in government circles that diplomacy may be more effective in solving local political problems in other countries than the use of military force, stemming from the failure of the U.S. military intervention in Vietnam. ◆*The pundits of Foggy Bottom display the Vietnam syndrome these days when it comes to Iran.*

virgin page *n. phr.* An empty page with no writing on it. ◆*In the middle of the new book there were a couple of virgin pages, probably due to a printing error.*

visible to the naked eye *adj. phr.* **1.** Perceivable without glasses, binoculars, microscope, or telescope. ◆*The stars are distant objects, but on a clear summer night they are visible to the naked eye.* **2.** Obvious, clear-cut. ◆*After the books were audited, it became visible to the naked eye that Carwallender*

embezzled the company's retirement fund.

visiting nurse *n.* A nurse who goes from home to home taking care of sick people or giving help with other health problems. ◆*After John returned home from the hospital, the visiting nurse came each day to change his bandages.*

voice an opinion *v. phr.* To go on record by uttering an opinion in speech, especially in public, or by writing an article in a newspaper or giving a radio or television interview. ◆*Ms. Bevilaqua keeps voicing the opinion, both verbally and in writing, that it was a mistake to repeal Prohibition.* ◆*Antiabortion advocates voice the opinion that a woman has no choice whether to give birth or not.*

voice box *n.* The part of the throat where the sound of your voice is made; the larynx. ◆*Mr. Smith's voice box was taken out in an operation, and he could not talk after that.*

voiceprint *n., technological, colloquial* The graphic pattern derived from converting an individual's voice into a visible graph used by the police for identification purposes, much as fingerprints. ◆*They have succeeded in identifying the murderer by using a voiceprint.*

vote a straight ticket *v. phr.* To not differentiate one's ballot according to individual names and posts, but to vote for all candidates for all positions of the same party. ◆*"I never have time to study the ballot in detail," Marie said, "and so I tend to vote a straight Democratic ticket."*

vote in *v. phr.* To elevate to the status of "Law of the Land" by special or general ballot. ♦*Congress has finally voted in the Brady Law that requires that prospective gun owners wait a special period of time before making their purchase.*

vote one out *v. phr.* To terminate one's elected office by casting a negative vote about that person (judge, congressman, etc.), mostly so that someone else might occupy the same position. ♦*Congressman Smith was voted out last November in favor of Congresswoman Bradley.*

wade in *or* **wade into** *v.*, *informal* **1.** To go busily to work. ◆*The house was a mess after the party, but Mother waded in and soon had it clean again.* **2.** To attack. ◆*Jack waded into the boys with his fists flying.*

wait at table *or* **wait on table** *or* **wait table** *v. phr.* To serve food. ◆*Mrs. Lake had to teach her new maid to wait on table properly.* ◆*The girls earn spending money by waiting at table in the school dining rooms.*

waiting list *n.* A list of persons waiting to get into something (as a school). ◆*The landlord said there were no vacant apartments available, but that he would put the Rogers' name on the waiting list.*

waiting room *n. phr.* The sitting area in a doctor's, lawyer's, accountant's, etc. office, or in a hospital, or other workplace, where people wait their turn. ◆*Some doctor's offices have elegantly furnished waiting rooms with magazines, newspapers, and coffee for the patients.*

wait on *or* **wait upon** *v.* **1.** To serve. ◆*The clerk in the store asked if we had been waited upon.* **2.** *formal* To visit as a courtesy or for business. ◆*John waited upon the President with a letter of introduction.* **3.** To follow. ◆*Success waits on hard work.*

wait on hand and foot *v. phr.* To serve in every possible way; do everything for (someone). ◆*Sally is spoiled because her mother waits on her hand and foot.*

wait up *v. phr.* To not go to bed until a person one is worried about comes home (said by parents and marriage partners). ◆*She always waits up for her husband when he's out late.*

walk a tightrope *v. phr.* To be in a dangerous or awkward situation where one cannot afford to make a single mistake. ◆*"When we landed on the moon in 1969," Armstrong explained, "we were walking a tightrope till the very end."*

walk away with *or* **walk off with** *v.* **1.** To take and go away with; take away; *often:* steal. ◆*When Father went to work, he accidentally walked off with Mother's umbrella.* ◆**2.** To take, get, or win easily. ◆*Jim walked away with all the honors on Class Night.* ◆*Our team walked off with the championship.*

walking papers *or* **walking orders** *also* **walking ticket** *n.*, *informal* A statement that you are fired from your job; dismissal. ◆*The boss was not satisfied with Paul's work and gave him his walking papers.*

walk in the park *n. phr.* Something very easy to do or to accomplish. ◆*"Is it difficult to surf the net?" six-year-old Tommy asked of his twelve-year-old brother. "No, not at all, it's a walk in the park."*

walk of life *n. phr.* Way of living; manner in which people live. ◆*People from every walk of life enjoy television.*

walk the plank *v. phr.* **1.** To walk off a board extended over the side of a ship and be drowned. ◆*The pirates captured the ship and forced the crew to walk the plank.* **2.** *informal* To resign from a job because someone makes you do it. ♦*When a new owner bought the store, the manager had to walk the plank.*

wallflower *n.* A girl who has to sit out dances because nobody is asking her to dance. ♦*"I used to be a wallflower during my high school days,"* Valerie complained, *"but my luck changed for better once I got into college."*

war baby *n., informal* A person born during a war. ♦*War babies began to increase college enrollments early in the 1960s.*

warm one's blood *v. phr.* To make you feel warm or excited. ♦*When the Bakers came to visit on a cold night, Mr. Harmon offered them a drink to warm their blood.*

warm up *v.* (stress on *up*) **1.** To reheat cooked food. ♦*Mr. Jones was so late that his dinner got cold; his wife had to warm it up.* **2.** To become friendly or interested. ♦*It takes an hour or so for some children to warm up to strangers.* **3.** To get ready for a game or other event by exercising or practicing. ♦*The coach told us to warm up before entering the pool.*

warm-up *n.* (stress on *warm*) A period of exercise or practice in preparation for a game or other event. ♦*Before the television quiz program, there was a warm-up to prepare the contestants.*

wash and wear *adj.* Not needing to be ironed.—Refers especially to synthetic and synthetic blend fabrics. ♦*Sally's dress is made of a wash and wear fabric.*

wash one's hands of *v. phr.* To withdraw from or refuse to be responsible for. ♦*We washed our hands of politics long ago.*

waste away *v.* To become more thin and weak every day. ♦*Jane is wasting away with tuberculosis.*

waste one's breath *v. phr.* To speak or to argue with no result; do nothing by talking. ♦*I know what I want. You're wasting your breath.*

watch one's language *v. phr.* To be careful of how one speaks; avoid saying impolite or vulgar things. ♦*"You boys watch your language,"* Mother said, *"or you won't be watching television for a whole week!"*

watch one's step *v. phr.* To mend one's ways; exercise prudence, tact, and care. ♦*I have to watch my step with the new boss as he is a very proud and sensitive individual.*

water down *v.* To change and make weaker; weaken. ♦*The teacher had to water down the course for a slow-learning class.*

watered down *adj.* Weakened; diluted. ♦*The play was a disappointing, watered down version of Shakespeare's Othello.*

water over the dam *or* **water under the bridge** *n. phr.* Something that happened in the past and cannot be changed. ♦*Since the sweater is too small already, don't worry about its shrinking; that's water over the dam.*

way the wind blows *or* **how the wind blows** *n. phr.* The direction or course something may go; how things are; what may happen. ♦*Most senators find out which way the wind blows in* *their home state before voting on bills in Congress.*

way to go *adj. phr., informal* An exclamation of praise given to one who has done or achieved something out of the ordinary. ♦*"Way to go, Charlie," his friends exclaimed, when, after beating an apparently terminal case of cancer, he not only graduated with honors, but also won the gold medal for diving in the Olympics.*

wear down, wear off *or* **wear away** *v.* **1.** To remove or disappear little by little through use, time, or the action of weather. ♦*Time and weather have worn off the name on the gravestone.* **2.** To lessen; become less little by little. ♦*John could feel the pain again as the dentist's medicine wore away.* **3.** To exhaust; tire out, win over or persuade by making tired. ♦*Mary wore her mother down by begging so that she let Mary go to the movies.*

wear on *v.* **1.** To anger or annoy; tire. ♦*Having to stay indoors all day long is tiresome for the children and wears on their mother's nerves.* **2.** To drag on; pass gradually or slowly; continue in the same old way. ♦*As the years wore on, the man in prison grew old.*

wear one's heart on one's sleeve *also* **pin one's heart on one's sleeve** *v. phr.* To show your feelings openly; show everyone how you feel; not hide your feelings. ♦*Sometimes it is better not to pin your heart on your sleeve.*

wear out *v.* **1a.** To use or wear until useless. ♦*The stockings are so worn out that they can't*

be mended any more. **1b.** To become useless from use or wear. ♦*One shoe wore out before the other.* **2.** *or* **tire out** To make very tired; weaken. ♦*When Dick got home from the long walk, he was all worn out.* ♦*Don't wear yourself out by playing too hard.* **3.** To make by rubbing, scraping, or washing. ♦*The waterfall has worn out a hole in the stone beneath it.*

wear out one's welcome *v. phr., informal* To visit somewhere too long or come back too often so that you are not welcome any more. ♦*The Smith children have worn out their welcome at our house because they are so loud.*

wear the trousers *or* **wear the pants** *v. phr., informal* To have a man's authority; be the boss of a family or household. ♦*Mr. Wilson is henpecked by his wife; she wears the trousers in that family.*

wear thin *v.* **1.** To become thin from use, wearing, or the passing of time. ♦*My old pair of pants has worn thin at the knees.* **2.** To grow less, or less interesting; decrease. ♦*The joke began to wear thin when you heard it too many times.*

wear well *v.* **1.** To continue to be satisfactory, useful, or liked for a long time. ♦*Their marriage has worn well.* **2.** To carry, accept, or treat properly or well. ♦*Grandfather wears his years well.*

weasel out *v. phr.* To renege on a previous promise; not keep an obligation for some not always straight reason. ♦*I'm so tired I think I am going to weasel my* way out of going to that meeting this afternoon.

weasel word *n., informal* A word which has more than one meaning and may be used to deceive others. ◆*When the thief was being questioned by the police, he tried to fool them with weasel words.*

weigh down *also* **weight down 1.** To make heavy; cause to go down or bend with weight; overload. ◆*The evergreens are weighed down by the deep snow.* **2a.** To overload with care or worry; make sad or low in spirits.—Used in the passive. ◆*The company is weighed down by debt.* **2b.** To make heavy, hard, or slow; make dull or uninteresting.—Often in the passive used with *by* or *with*. ◆*The book is weighted down with footnotes.*

weigh in *v.* **1a.** To take the weight of; weigh. ◆*The man at the airport counter weighed in our bags and took our plane tickets.* **1b.** To have yourself or something that you own weighed.—Often used with *at*. ◆*We took our bags to the airport counter to weigh in.* **1c.** To have yourself weighed as a boxer or wrestler by a doctor before a match.—Used with *at.* ◆*The champion weighed in at 160 pounds.* **2.** *slang* To join or interfere in a fight, argument, or discussion. ◆*We told Jack that if we wanted him to weigh in with his opinion we would ask him.*

weigh on *or* **weigh upon** *v.* **1.** To be a weight or pressure on; be heavy on. ◆*The pack weighed heavily on the soldier's back.* **2.** To make sad or worried; trouble; disturb; upset. ◆*John's*

wrongdoing weighed upon his conscience. **3.** To be a burden to. ◆*His guilt weighed heavily upon him.*

weigh one's words *v. phr.* To choose your words carefully; be careful to use the right words. ◆*In a debate, a political candidate has little time to weigh his words, and may say something foolish.*

weight of the world on one's shoulders *or* **world on one's shoulders** *or* **world on one's back** *n. phr.* A very heavy load of worry or responsibility; very tired or worried behavior, as if carrying the world; behavior as if you are very important. ◆*John acts as if he were carrying the world on his back because he has a paper route.*

welcome mat *n.* **1.** A mat for wiping your shoes on, often with the word *welcome* on it, that is placed in front of a door. ◆*Mother bought a welcome mat for our new house.* **2.** *informal* A warm welcome; a friendly greeting.—Used in such phrases as *the welcome mat is out* and *put out the welcome mat.* ◆*Our welcome mat is always out to our friends.*

well and good *adj. phr.* Good; satisfactory. ◆*If my daughter finishes high school, I will call that well and good.*—Used without a verb to show agreement or understanding. ◆*Well and good; I will come to your house tomorrow.*

wet behind the ears *adj. phr., informal* Not experienced; not knowing how to do something; new in a job or place. ◆*The new student is still wet behind the ears; he has not yet learned the* *tricks that the boys play on each other.*

wet blanket *n. informal* A person or thing that keeps others from enjoying life. ◆*The weatherman throws a wet blanket on picnic plans when he forecasts rain.*

wet one's whistle *v. phr., slang* To have a drink, especially of liquor. ◆*Uncle Willie told John to wait outside for a minute while he went in to the cafe to wet his whistle.*

what have you *or* **what not** *n. phr., informal* Whatever you like or want; anything else like that. ◆*We found suits, coats, hats and what not in the closet.*

what if What would, or will, happen if; what is the difference if; suppose that. ◆*What if we paint it red. How will it look?*

what of it *or* **what about it** *interj., informal* What is wrong with it; what do you care. ◆*"John missed the bus." "What of it?"*

what's up *or* **what's cooking** *also* **what's doing** *slang* What is happening or planned; what is wrong. ◆*"What's up?" asked Bob as he joined his friends. "Are you going to the movies?" ◆What's cooking? Why is the crowd in the street? ◆What's doing tonight at the club?*

what's with *or* **what's up with** *also* **what's by** *slang* What is happening to; what is wrong; how is everything; what can you tell me about. ◆*Mary looks worried. What's with her?*

what with *prep.* Because; as a result of. ◆*I couldn't visit you, what with the snowstorm and the cold I had.*

wheel and deal *v. phr., slang* To make many big plans or schemes; especially with

important people in government and business; in matters of money and influence; handle money or power for your own advantage; plan important matters in a smart or skillful way and sometimes in a tricky, or not strictly honest way. ◆*Mr. Smith made a fortune by wheeling and dealing on the stock market.*—**wheeler-dealer** *n. phr., slang* A person with power and control. ◆*The biggest wheeler-dealer in the state has many friends in high places in business and government.*

when hell freezes over *adv. phr., slang* Never. ◆*I'll believe you when hell freezes over.*

when in Rome, do as the Romans do When one is in a strange or new place, it is a good idea to imitate the customs of the natives.—A proverb. ◆*"I cannot get used to eating with chopsticks," Sam complained to his wife. "Well, you'd better learn to use them, since we are in China," Mary replied. "Remember the old saying 'When in Rome, do as the Romans do.'"*

when push comes to shove *adv. phr.* A time when a touchy situation becomes actively hostile or a quarrel turns into a fight. ◆*Can we count on the boss' goodwill, when push comes to shove?*

when the chips are down *adv. cl., informal* When the winner and loser of a bet or a game are decided; at the most important or dangerous time. ◆*When the chips were down, the two countries decided not to have war.*

where it's at *adv. phr., informal* That which is important; that which is at the forefront of on-going social, personal, or scientific undertakings. ◆*We send sophisticated machines to Mars instead of people, that's where it's at.*

where the action is *n. phr., informal* Where the prostitutes hang out in bars, where there is gambling, legal or illegal. ◆*"Show us where the action is," the tourists asked the taxi driver when they got into Reno, Nevada.*

where the shoe pinches *n. phr., informal* Where or what the discomfort or trouble is. ◆*Johnny thinks the job is easy, but he will find out where the shoe pinches when he tries it.*

while ago *adv.* At a time several minutes in the past; a few minutes ago; a short time ago.—Used with *a.* ◆*I laid my glasses on this table a while ago; and now they're gone.*

while away *v.* To make time go by pleasantly or without being bored; pass or spend. ◆*We whiled away the summer swimming and fishing.*

while back *adv.* At a time several weeks or months in the past.—Used with *a.* ◆*We had a good rain a while back, but we need more now.*

whipping boy *n. phr.* The person who gets punished for someone else's mistake. ◆*"I used to be the whipping boy during my early days at the company," he musingly remembered.*

whip up *v., informal* **1.** To make or do quickly or easily. ◆*The reporter whipped up a story about the fire for his paper.* **2.** To make active; stir to action; excite. ◆*The girls are trying to*

whip up interest for a dance Saturday night.

whispering campaign *n.* The spreading of false rumors, or saying bad things, about a person or group, especially in politics or public life. ◆*A bad man has started a whispering campaign against the mayor, saying that he isn't honest.*

whistle in the dark *v. phr., informal* To try to stay brave and forget your fear. ◆*Tom said he could fight the bully with one hand, but we knew that he was just whistling in the dark.*

white elephant *n. phr.* Unwanted property, such as real estate, that is hard to sell. ◆*That big house of theirs on the corner sure is a white elephant.*

white lie *n. phr.* An innocent social excuse. ◆*I am too busy to go to their house for dinner tonight. I will call them and tell a little white lie about having the flu.*

whitewash *n., informal* A soothing official report that attempts to tranquilize the public. ◆*Some people believe that the Warren Commission's report on the Kennedy assassination was a whitewash.*

whitewash something *v., informal* To explain a major, national scandal in soothing official terms so as to assure the public that things are under control and there is no need to panic. ◆*Many people in the United States believe that President Kennedy's assassination was whitewashed by the Warren Commission.*

whodunit *n.* A detective story; a murder story; a thriller. ◆*Agatha Christie was a true master of the whodunit.*

whole cheese *slang or informal* **whole show** *n., informal* The only important person; big boss. ♦*Joe thought he was the whole cheese in the game because he owned the ball.* ♦*You're not the whole show just because you got all A's.*

wildcat strike *n. informal* A strike not ordered by a labor union; a strike spontaneously arranged by a group of workers. ♦*The garbage collectors have gone on a wildcat strike, but the union is going to stop it.*

wild goose chase *n. phr.* An absurd and completely futile errand. ♦*I was on a wild goose chase when I was sent to find a man who never really existed.*

wild horses would not drag it from me No power on earth can make me give away the secret, or to divulge it.—A proverb. ♦*"Do you know where grandpa buried the sixteen gold bullions after the bank robbery?" Fred asked his older brother. "I do," came the answer, "but wild horses would not drag it from me."*

will a duck swim? *v. phr., rhetorical question* Of course; naturally; certainly. ♦*"Will Bush run again for president?" Jack asked. "Will a duck swim?" Peter replied.*

windbag *n.* Someone who talks too much; a boring person. ♦*Uncle Joe goes on and on; he is a boring windbag.*

windfall *n.* An unexpected gift or gain of sizeable proportion. ♦*The unexpected retroactive pay raise was a most welcome windfall.*

window dressing *n. phr.* An elaborate exterior, sometimes designed to conceal one's real motives. ♦*All those fancy invitations turned out to be nothing but window dressing.*

window-shop *v. phr.* To walk from store to store and look at the merchandise without buying it. ♦*When I have no money, I like to window-shop and plan on what I might get when I will be able to afford it.*

wind up *v.* **1.** To tighten the spring of a machine; to make it work or run. ♦*He doesn't have to wind up his watch because it is run by a battery.* **2.** To make very excited, nervous, upset. ♦*The excitement of her birthday party got Jane all wound up so she could not sleep.* **3.** *informal* To bring or come to an end; finish; stop. ♦*Before Jim knew it, he had spent all his money and he wound up broke.* **4.** To put (your business or personal affairs) in order; arrange; settle. ♦*Fred wound up his business and personal affairs before joining the Navy.*

win hands down *v. phr.* To win conclusively and without external help. ♦*The opposition was so weak that Dan won the election hands down.*

winning streak *n.* A series of several wins one after the other. ♦*The team extended their winning streak to ten.*

wipeout *n.* (stress on *wipe*) A total failure. ♦*The guy is so bad at his job that he is a total wipeout.*

wipe out *v.* (stress on *out*) **1.** To remove or erase by wiping or rubbing. ♦*The teacher wiped out with an eraser what she had written on the board.* **2.** *informal* To remove, kill, or destroy completely. ♦*Doctors are searching for a cure that will wipe out cancer.*

wisecrack n. A joke or witty remark usually made at someone else's expense. ♦*The comedians kept up a steady stream of wisecracks.*

wise guy n. phr., informal A person who acts as if he were smarter than other people; a person who jokes or shows off too much ♦*Bill is a wise guy and displeases others by what he says.*

wise up to v. phr., slang To finally understand what is really going on after a period of ignorance. ♦*Joe immediately quit his job when he wised up to what was really going on.*

wish on v. 1. To use as a lucky charm while making a wish. ♦*Mary wished on a star that she could go to the dance.*

witch-hunt n. phr. A hysterical movement during which people are persecuted for having views (political or religious) considered different or unpopular. ♦*During the McCarthy era many innocent Americans were accused of being Communists, as Republican patriotism deteriorated into a witch-hunt.*

with child adv. phr., literary Going to have a baby; pregnant. ♦*The angel told Mary she was with child.*

with flying colors adv. phr. With great or total success; victoriously. ♦*Tom finished the race with flying colors.*

within an ace of informal or **within an inch of** adv. phr. Almost but not quite; very close to; nearly. ♦*Tim came within an ace of losing the election.*

♦*John was within an inch of drowning before he was pulled out of the water.*

within an inch of one's life adv. phr. Until you are almost dead; near to dying. ♦*The bear clawed the hunter within an inch of his life.*

without fail adv. phr. Without failing to do it or failing in the doing of it; certainly, surely. ♦*Be here at 8 o'clock sharp, without fail.*

with the best or **with the best of them** adv. phr. As well as anyone. ♦*John can bowl with the best of them.*

wolf down v. phr. To eat or drink in a great hurry, mostly standing up in the kitchen. ♦*Ted was so hungry and had so little time, that he grabbed two cold frankfurters out of his refrigerator and just wolfed them down.*

wolf in sheep's clothing n. phr. A person who pretends to be good but really is bad. ♦*Mrs. Martin trusted the lawyer until she realized that he was a wolf in sheep's clothing.*

word for word adv. phr. In exactly the same words. ♦*Mary copied Sally's composition word for word.*

word of mouth n. phr. Communication by oral rather than written means. ♦*The merchant told us that the best customers he had were recommended to him by word of mouth.*

words of one syllable n. phr. Language that makes the meaning very clear; simple, or frank language. ♦*Mary explained the job to Ann in words of one syllable so that she would be sure to understand.*

worked up *adj.* Feeling strongly; excited; angry; worried. ♦*Mary was all worked up about the exam.*

work in *v.* **1.** To rub in. ♦*The nurse told Mary to put some cream on her skin and to work it in gently with her fingers.* **2.** To slip in; mix in; put in; ♦*When Mary was planning the show, she worked a part in for her friend Susan.*

working girl *n.,* slang **1.** (*vulgar, avoid!*) A prostitute. ♦*I didn't know Roxanne was a working girl.* **2.** A girl, usually single, who supports herself by working in an honest job, such as in an office, etc. ♦*The average working girl can't afford such a fancy car.*

work into *v.* **1.** Force into little by little. ♦*John worked his foot into the boot by pushing and pulling.* **2.** Put into; mix into. ♦*Mary worked some blue into the rug she was weaving.*

work off *v.* To make (something) go away, especially by working. ♦*John worked off the fat around his waist by doing exercise every morning.*

work on *also* **work upon** *v.* **1.** Have an effect on; influence. ♦*Some pills work on the nerves and make people feel more relaxed.* **2.** To try to influence or convince. ♦*Senator Smith worked on the other committee members to vote for the bill.*

work one's fingers to the bone *v. phr.* To work very hard. ♦*"I have to work my fingers to the bone for a measly pittance of a salary," Fred complained.*

workout *n.* (stress on *work*) A physical exercise session. ♦*My morning workout consists of sit-ups and push-ups.*

work out *v. phr.* (stress on *out*) **1.** To find an answer to. ♦*John worked out his math problems all by himself.* **2.** To plan; develop. ♦*Mary worked out a beautiful design for a sweater.* **3.** To accomplish; arrange. ♦*The engineers worked out a system for getting electricity to the factory.* **4.** To be efficient; get results. ♦*If the traffic plan works out, it will be used in other cities too.* **5.** To exercise. ♦*John works out in the gym two hours every day.*

work over *v. phr.,* slang To beat someone up very roughly in order to intimidate him or extort payment, etc. ♦*Matthew was worked over by the hoodlums in the park right after midnight.*

work up *v.* **1.** To stir up; arouse; excite. ♦*I can't work up any interest in this book.* ♦*He worked up a sweat weeding the garden.* **2.** To develop; originate. ♦*He worked up an interesting plot for a play.*

world is one's oyster Everything is possible for you; the world belongs to you; you can get anything you want. ♦*When John won the scholarship, he felt as though the world was his oyster.*

world without end *adv. phr.,* literary Endlessly; forever; eternally. ♦*Each human being has to die, but mankind goes on world without end.*

worse for wear *adj. phr.* Not as good as new; worn out; damaged by use.—Used with *the.* ♦*Her favorite tablecloth was beginning to look the worse for wear.*—Often used with *none* to mean: as good as new. ♦*The doll was Mary's favorite toy but it was none the worse for wear.*

worth a cent *adj. phr.* Worth anything; of any value.—Used in negative, interrogative, and conditional sentences. ♦*The book was old and it was not worth a cent.*

worth one's salt *adj. phr.* Being a good worker, or a productive person; worth what you cost. ♦*Mr. Brown showed that he was worth his salt as a salesman when he got the highest sales record for the year.*—Used with *not* or *hardly.* ♦*When the basketball team did so poorly, people felt that the coach was hardly worth his salt.*

wrapped up in *adj. phr.* Thinking only of; interested only in. ♦*John has no time for sports because he is all wrapped up in his work.*

wrap up *or* **bundle up** *v. phr.* **1.** To put on warm clothes; dress warmly. ♦*Mother told Mary to wrap up before going out into the cold.* **2.** *informal* To finish (a job). ♦*Let's wrap up the job and go home.* **3.** *informal* To win a game. ♦*The Mets wrapped up the baseball game in the seventh inning.*

wreak havoc with *v. phr.* To cause damage; ruin something. ♦*His rebellious attitude is bound to wreak havoc at the company.*

wringing wet *adj.* Wet through and through; soaked; dripping. ♦*He was wringing wet because he was caught in the rain without an umbrella.*

write home about *v. phr.* To become especially enthusiastic or excited about; boast about. ♦*Joe did a good enough job of painting but it was nothing to write home about.*

write off *v. phr.* (stress on *off*) **1.** To remove (an amount) from a business record; cancel (a debt); accept as a loss. ♦*If a customer dies when he owes the store money, the store must often write it off.* **2.** To accept (a loss or trouble) and not worry anymore about it; forget. ♦*Jim's mistake cost him time and money, but he wrote it off to experience.* To say that (something) will fail or not be good; believe worthless. ♦*Just because the boys on the team are young, don't write the team off.*

write-off *n.* (stress on *write*) A loss. ♦*This last unfortunate business venture of ours is an obvious write-off.*

write-up *n.* (stress on *write*) A report or story in a newspaper or magazine. ♦*I read an interesting write-up about the President in a new magazine.*

write up *v.* (stress on *up*) **1.** To write the story of; describe in writing; give a full account of. ♦*Reporters from many newspapers are here to write up the game.* ♦*The magazine is writing up the life of the President.* **2.** To put something thought or talked about into writing; finish writing (something). ♦*The author had an idea for a story when he saw the old house, and he wrote it up later.*

writing *or* **handwriting on the wall** *n. phr., literary* A warning; a message of some urgency. ♦ *"This nuclear plant is about to explode, I think," the chief engineer said. "We'd better get out of here in a hurry, the handwriting is on the wall."*

x-double minus *adj., slang, informal* Extremely poorly done, bad, inferior (said mostly about theatrical or musical performances). ◆*Patsy gave an x-double minus performance at the audition and lost her chance for the lead role.*

x-ing something out *v. phr.* To delete words or entire sentences from a manuscript by typing the letter xxxxxxxx many times. ◆*I can't make out the rest of this letter; all the words have been x-ed out from the last paragraph.*

X marks the spot. An indication made on maps or documents of importance to call attention to a place or a feature of some importance. ◆*The treasure hunter said to his companion, "Here it is; X marks the spot."*

Xmas *n. abbreviation for Christmas.* ◆*"Merry Xmas to you"* John scribbled on a card in haste.

x-rated *adj., slang informal* Pertaining to movies, magazines, and literature judged pornographic and therefore off limits for minors. ◆*My son celebrated his 21st birthday by going to an x-rated movie.*

x-raying machine *n., slang, citizen's band radio jargon* Speed detection device by radar used by the police. ◆*The smokies are using the x-raying machine under the bridge!*

x. y. or X. Y. *n. phr.* An unnamed person. ◆*I got a letter from an unknown person, who signed the letter as "x. y." The person said that he or she wanted to make a donation to our church, but wishes to remain nameless.*

yak-yak or **yakety-yak** or **yakib-yak** n., slang Much talk about little things; talking all the time about unimportant things. ◆Tom sat behind two girls on the bus and he got tired of their silly yak-yak.

year-round or **year-around** adj. Usable, effective, or operating all the year. ◆Colorado is a year-round resort; there is fishing in the summer and skiing in the winter.

yellow-bellied adj., slang Extremely timid, cowardly. ◆Joe Bennett is a yellow-bellied guy, don't send him on such a tough assignment!

yellow journalism n. phr. Cheap and sensational newspaper writing; inflammatory language designed to stir up popular sentiment against another country. ◆Yellow journalism is hardly ever truly informative.

yellow-livered adj. Cowardly. ◆The young boy greatly resented being called yellow-livered and started to fight right away.

yeoman service n. phr. Help in time of need; serviceable and good assistance. ◆Sam was pressed into yeoman service in organizing our annual fundraiser for cerebral palsy victims.

yes-man n., informal A person who tries to be liked by agreeing with everything said; especially, someone who always agrees with a boss or the one in charge. ◆John tries to get ahead on his job by being a yes-man.

yoo-hoo interj.—Used as an informal call or shout to a person to attract his attention. ◆Louise opened the door and called "Yoo-hoo, Mother—are you home?"

you bet or **you bet your boots** or **you bet your life** informal Most certainly; yes, indeed; without any doubt.—Used to declare with emphasis that a thing is really so. ◆Do I like to ski? You bet your life I do. ◆You bet I will be at the party. ◆You can bet your boots that Johnny will come home when his money is gone.

you can say that again See YOU SAID IT.

you can't make a silk purse out of a sow's ear One cannot make something delicate out of something coarse or inferior.—A proverb. ◆Alan was asked to edit Frank's poetry, but no matter how hard he tried, the material remained unpublishable. When his wife saw his struggle, she said: "Why bother, honey? You can't make a silk purse out of a sow's ear."

you can take (lead) a horse to water, but you can't make him drink One can do one's best to arrange a meeting, a conference, or bring one or several individuals to a common ground, but there is no guarantee that they will use the opportunity so afforded.—A proverb. ◆The president of the United States invited the two leaders of the neighboring countries at war to the White House hoping that they would sign the proposed peace agreement. When they refused to do so, the secretary of state wryly commented, "This goes to show that you can take a horse to water, but you can't make him drink."

you can't teach an old dog new tricks It is very hard or almost impossible to train an older person to acquire some new skill.—A proverb. ◆*You'll never teach your grandfather how to do his income tax on a personal computer. You can't teach an old dog new tricks.*

you don't say *or* **well, I never** *adj. phr., informal* Said in surprise or in astonishment, or disbelief; you're kidding; this sounds nonsensical. ◆*"I almost beat Steffi Graff in tennis," John's daughter declared, after a visit to Germany, where she had a chance to play the famous champion for ten minutes. "You don't say!" her father replied, laughing.* ◆*"I am a shoo-in for the Pulitzer Prize," Ted's son, a senior in high school said, when his first poem was published in the school paper. The father laughed and replied, "Well, I never…"*

you're on *v. phr., informal* An acceptance to an offer or an invitation. ◆*"So you are willing to take both of us to dinner and to the opera?" John asked his friend, Ted. "Yes, of course. I said so, didn't I? "All right, my friend, you're on!" John replied.*

you're telling me *interj., informal*—Used to show that a thing is so clear that it need not be said, or just to show strong agreement. ◆*"You're late." "You're telling me!"*

your guess is as good as mine We are both just guessing; neither one of us is really sure what the truth is.—A proverb. ◆*"Who will be the next president of the United States? George W. Bush, or a Democrat?" "I know whom I would prefer, but your guess is as good as mine."*

yours truly *adv. phr.* **1.** Signing off at the end of letters. ◆*Yours truly, Tom Smith.* **2.** I, the first person singular pronoun, frequently abbreviated as t.y. ◆*As t.y. has often pointed out…T.y. is not really interested in the offer.*

you said it *or* **you can say that again** *interj., slang*—Used to show strong agreement with what another person has said. ◆*"That sure was a good show." "You said it!"* ◆*"It sure is hot!" "You can say that again!"*

you scratch my back, and I'll scratch yours When two people do reciprocal favors for one another, this saying is often used, meaning, "If you do me the favor I ask of you, I will do you the favor you ask of me."—A proverb. ◆*"You scratch my back, and I'll scratch yours," Professor Jones said to his colleague Professor Smith, when they agreed to write letters of recommendation for one another.*

you tell 'em *interj., slang*—Used to agree with or encourage someone in what he is saying. ◆*The drunk was arguing with the bartenders and a man cried, "You tell 'em!"*

yum-yum *interj., informal*—Used usually by or to children, to express great delight, especially in the taste of food. ◆*"Yum-Yum! That pie is good!"*

zero hour *n.* **1.** The exact time when an attack or other military action is supposed to start. ◆*Zero hour for the bombers to take off was midnight.* **2.** The time when an important decision or change is supposed to come; the time for a dangerous action. ◆*It was zero hour and the doctor began the operation on the man.*

zero in on *v.* **1.** To adjust a gun so that it will exactly hit (a target); aim at. ◆*Big guns were zeroed in on the enemy fort.* ◆*American missiles have been zeroed in on certain targets, to be fired if necessary.* **2.** *slang* To give your full attention to. ◆*The Senate zeroed in on the Latin-American problems.* ◆*Let's zero in on grammar tonight.*

zero time flat *n. phr.* An extremely short duration; fractions of a second; often said as an exaggeration. ◆*"How soon can you get that letter typed up, Suzie?" Dean Doolittle asked his secretary. "I'll do it in zero time flat just for you," Suzie answered flirtatiously.*

zone defense *n.* A defense in a sport (as basketball or football) in which each player has to defend a certain area. ◆*The coach taught his team a zone defense because he thought his players weren't fast enough to defend against individual opponents.*

zonk out *v. phr., slang* **1.** To fall asleep very quickly. ◆*Can I talk to Joe?—Call back tomorrow, he zonked out.* **2.** To pass out from fatigue, or alcohol. ◆*You won't get a coherent word out of Joe, he has zonked out.*

zoom in *v. phr.* **1.** To rapidly close in on (said of airplanes and birds of prey). ◆*The fighter planes zoomed in on the enemy target.* **2.** To make a closeup of someone or something with a camera. ◆*The photographer zoomed in on the tiny bee as it hovered over a lovely tropical flower.*